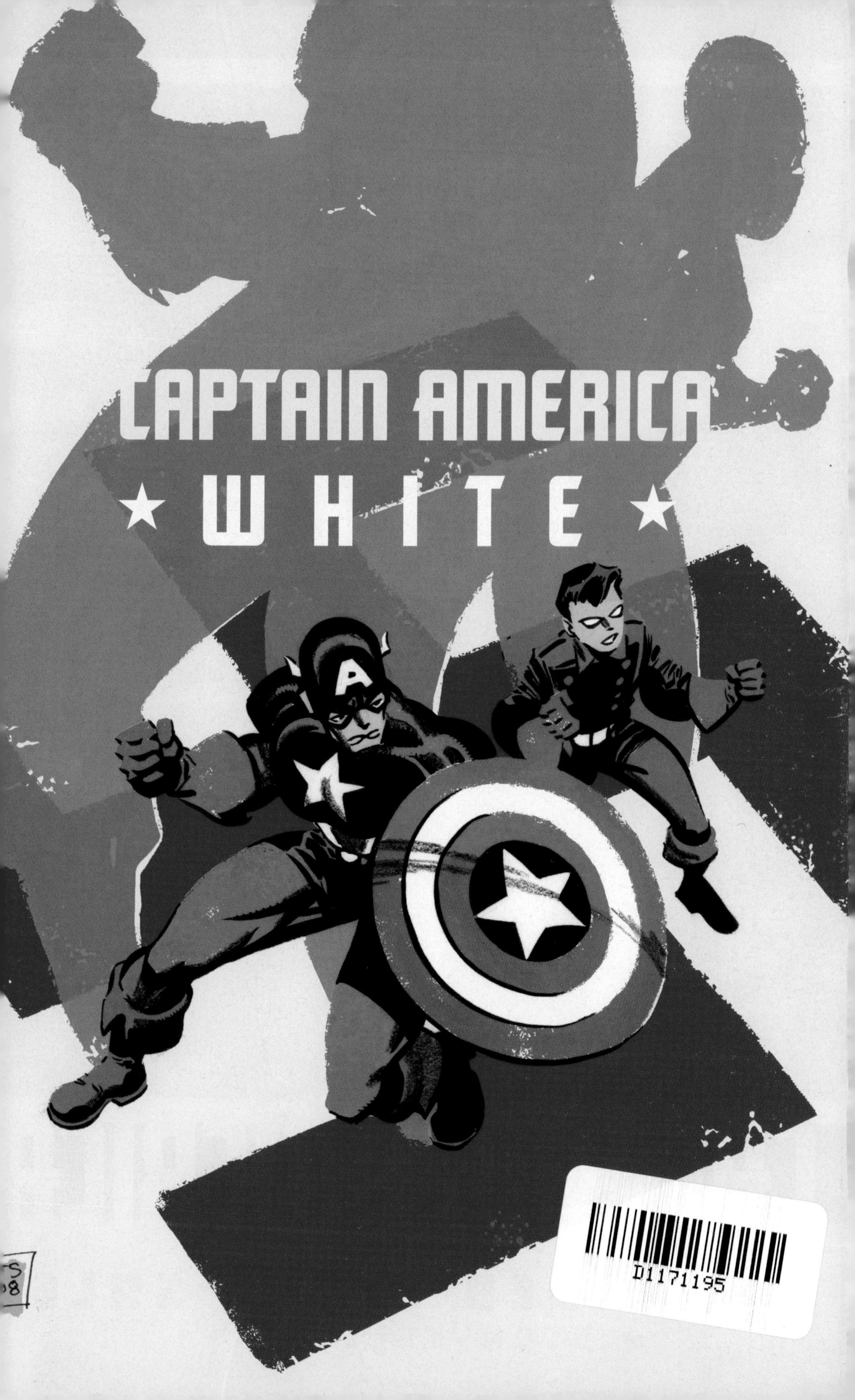
CAPTAIN AMERICA
WHITE

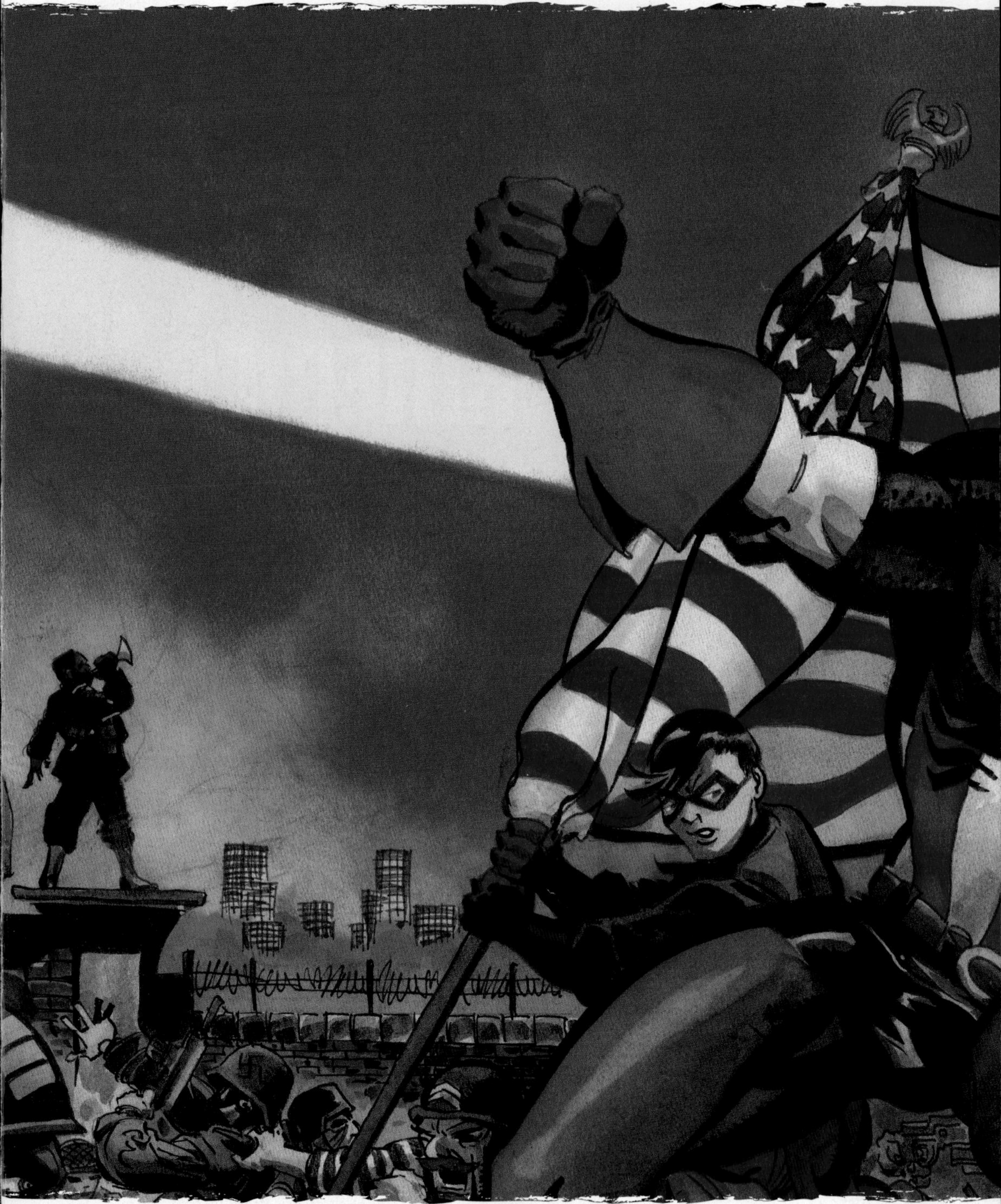

CAPTAIN AMERICA

JEPH LOEB & TIM SALE

★ STORYTELLERS ★

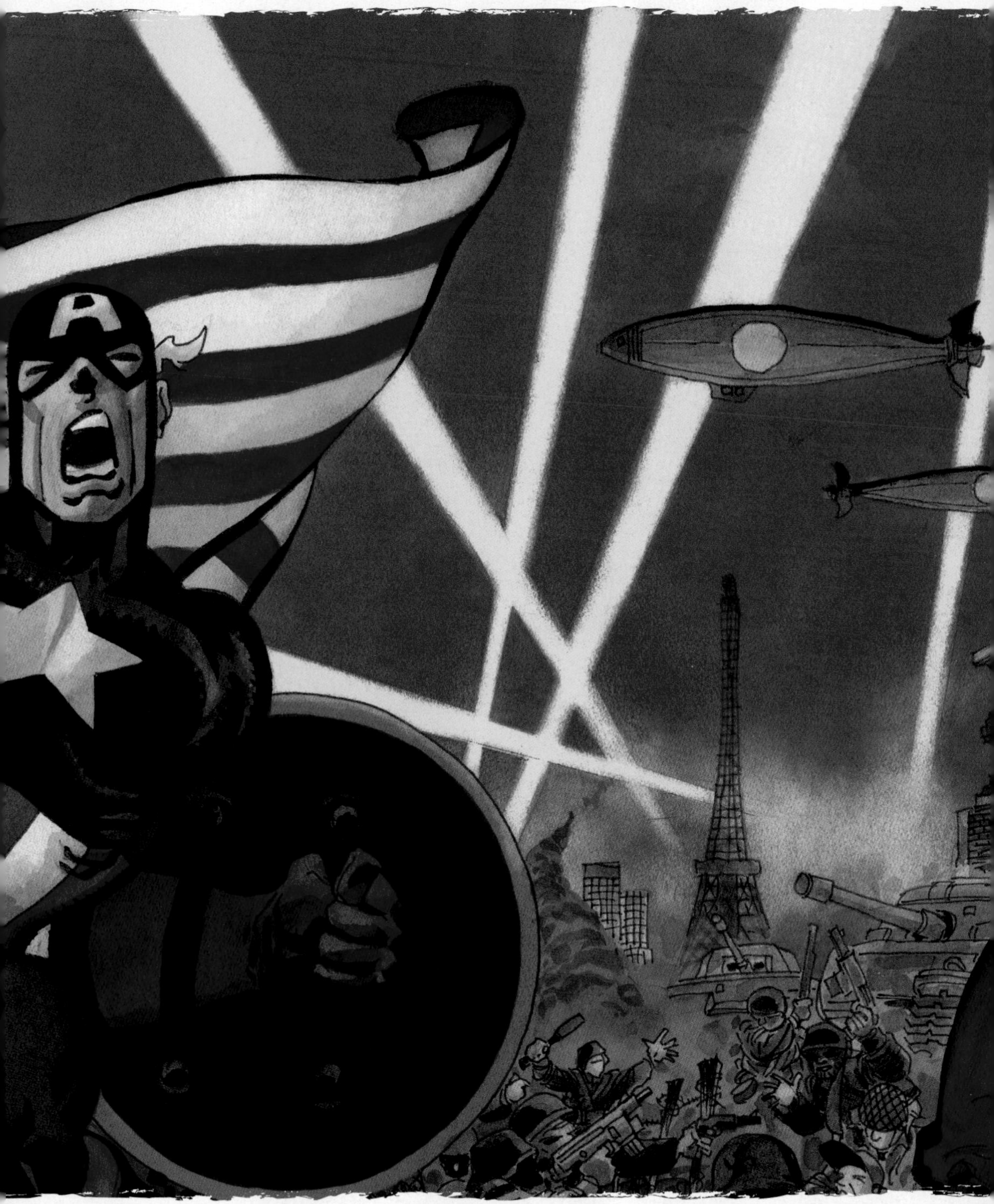

★ WHITE ★

DAVE STEWART
★ COLORS ★

RICHARD STARKINGS *of* COMICRAFT
★ LETTERING ★

CONSULTING EDITOR
RICHARD STARKINGS

ASSISTANT EDITOR
JON MOISAN

EDITOR
MARK PANICCIA

COLLECTION EDITOR
JENNIFER GRÜNWALD

ASSOCIATE
MANAGING EDITOR
KATERI WOODY

ASSOCIATE EDITOR
SARAH BRUNSTAD

EDITOR, SPECIAL PROJECTS
MARK D. BEAZLEY

VP PRODUCTION &
SPECIAL PROJECTS
JEFF YOUNGQUIST

SVP PRINT, SALES &
MARKETING
DAVID GABRIEL

BOOK DESIGN
JOHN ROSHELL OF COMICRAFT

A

★ CAPTAIN AMERICA CREATED BY ★
JOE SIMON & JACK KIRBY

CAPTAIN AMERICA: WHITE. Contains material originally published in magazine form as CAPTAIN AMERICA: WHITE #0-5. First printing 2016. ISBN# 978-0-7851-3376-6. Published by MARVEL WORLDWIDE, INC., a subsidiary of MARVEL ENTERTAINMENT, LLC. OFFICE OF PUBLICATION: 135 West 50th Street, New York, NY 10020. Copyright © 2016 MARVEL No similarity between any of the names, characters, persons, and/or institutions in this magazine with those of any living or dead person or institution is intended, and any such similarity which may exist is purely coincidental. **Printed in the U.S.A.** ALAN FINE, President, Marvel Entertainment; DAN BUCKLEY, President, TV, Publishing & Brand Management; JOE QUESADA, Chief Creative Officer; TOM BREVOORT, SVP of Publishing; DAVID BOGART, SVP of Business Affairs & Operations, Publishing & Partnership; C.B. CEBULSKI, VP of Brand Management & Development, Asia; DAVID GABRIEL, SVP of Sales & Marketing, Publishing; JEFF YOUNGQUIST, VP of Production & Special Projects; DAN CARR, Executive Director of Publishing Technology; ALEX MORALES, Director of Publishing Operations; SUSAN CRESPI, Production Manager; STAN LEE, Chairman Emeritus. For information regarding advertising in Marvel Comics or on Marvel.com, please contact Vit DeBellis, Integrated Sales Manager, at vdebellis@ marvel.com. For Marvel subscription inquiries, please call 888-511-5480. Manufactured between 9/2/2016 and 10/10/2016 by LSC COMMUNICATIONS INC., SALEM, VA, USA.

10 9 8 7 6 5 4 3 2 1

EDITOR IN CHIEF
AXEL ALONSO

CHIEF CREATIVE OFFICER
JOE QUESADA

PUBLISHER
DAN BUCKLEY

EXECUTIVE PRODUCER
ALAN FINE

UNITED STATES ARMY
OFFICIAL DOCUMENT

DECLASSIFIED

CON[redacted]DENTIAL
[redacted] CONSULATE GENERAL
APO [redacted]4 US FORCES

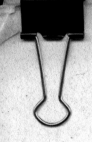

Date: DECEMBER 4, 2015

From: CHRISTOPHER MARKUS & STEPHEN MCFEELY

Subject: INTRODUCTION

"I just want to talk about a time when things almost made sense to me…or more sense than now."

That's Steve Rogers casting his mind back to World War II in the first issue of Jeph Loeb and Tim Sale's Captain America: White. It's also all of us, trying to claw some sense of innocence and clarity out of the past as we wade through the muck of our present-day lives. But the past was never as simple as it seems to us now. After all, it used to be the present. Still, time and again, writers and artists have gone back to explore Cap's early days of high adventure. We certainly did, in Marvel's Captain America: The First Avenger. The temptation to punch Hitler in the face is just too great to resist. That, and the fact that it really is the only crucible out of which Captain America can spring. Pick virtually any other time, and a man who chooses to run around in a flag costume putting his underage "pal" in danger of being killed seems less like a hero and more like a fascist with questionable decision-making skills. World War II makes it seem like the obvious thing to do.

Jeph and Tim know all of this down to their pirate boots. Their Cap and Bucky are most in their element behind enemy lines, slugging Nazis with no small amount of relish. But that relish isn't found just in the crunch of fist on jaw, but in the opportunity for an orphan and a former 90-pound weakling to show the world what they're really made of: pure American steel. It's in those personal thoughts and motivations in the middle of the broader military conflict where these books really shine. Bucky's resentments, Steve's virginity — these stories probe the vulnerable humanity beneath the bullet-riddled red, white, and blue. "Was it a simpler time?" asks Steve, torn as always by his memories. The answer is, it was and it wasn't. The threat was immediate, the enemy undeniably evil. But the morals a person could live by in the confines of a Brooklyn movie theater didn't always hold their water in the battlefields of France. It's all well and good for the American super hero to spare the lives of his captured enemies. It's quite another for a French Resistance fighter who has seen her village burned and her people

exterminated. Justice is not always an international language, and the recognition of that uncomfortable fact underlies the action throughout this story.

Of course, this is still a rollicking adventure tale, and no adventure is complete without a love story. And, yes, these books have one – the longest, most tortured one in Marvel history, in fact. We're talking about Steve and Bucky, without smirking or innuendo or raised eyebrows. Platonic though the relationship may be, from the meet cute to the tragic separation, their bond has all the elements of a classic romance. These two men love each other – as any pair of friends who faced exclusion, combat, inhumanity, and death would. Their bond stretches across half of the twentieth century. The loss of it gnaws at Steve throughout modern day, and it slices his heart in half when the Winter Soldier rears his tormented, homicidal head. Just as Jeph and Tim's earlier Daredevil: Yellow, Spider-Man: Blue, and Hulk: Gray all dealt with the major love interests in the heroes' lives, so too does Captain America: White. Steve and Bucky are each other's soulmate, if you will, because no one on Earth understands what either of them has been through as well as the other does. These books deal deftly with the strengths and weaknesses that relationship engenders. As the Red Skull himself says to Bucky, "The Captain has a...'soft spot' for you. A spot I intend to put a bullet into this very evening." Soldiers fight for their country. They fight for themselves. They fight for each other. And sometimes they die for these things, too. The ones who don't carry the memory of the ones who did for the rest of their days. Steve Rogers is no different.

That weight, the noble yet humble shouldering of his own and the world's burdens, is one of the things that makes Steve Rogers a great character. You can put him through hell – and we have – and yet he just keeps going, keeps doing his job, keeps putting the shoulder of what he feels is right against the barrier of what he knows in his heart to be wrong. It's not effortless. It's hard, it's painful, and it costs more than most people would be willing to pay. But Steve goes on doing it – not for glory or statues or free drinks at the officer's club, but because somebody somewhere needs help. And he can help. And so he does.

The world isn't black and white. It never was. But if you break it down into small enough pieces, we all still have the same choice Steve has. We can hurt, or we can help. With Captain America: White, Jeph Loeb and Tim Sale are helping.

REGRADED CONFIDENTIAL
ON
BY CDR USAINSCOM FOIP
Para 1-603 DoD5200. 1 R

CO[redacted]IDENTIAL

037

DECLASSIFIED

CHRISTOPHER MARKUS AND STEPHEN MCFEELY ARE THE SCREENWRITERS OF MARVEL'S *CAPTAIN AMERICA: THE FIRST AVENGER*, *CAPTAIN AMERICA: THE WINTER SOLDIER* AND *CAPTAIN AMERICA: CIVIL WAR*, AS WELL AS CREATORS AND EXECUTIVE PRODUCERS OF THE ABC-TV SERIES *MARVEL'S AGENT CARTER*.

ONE

IT HAPPENED

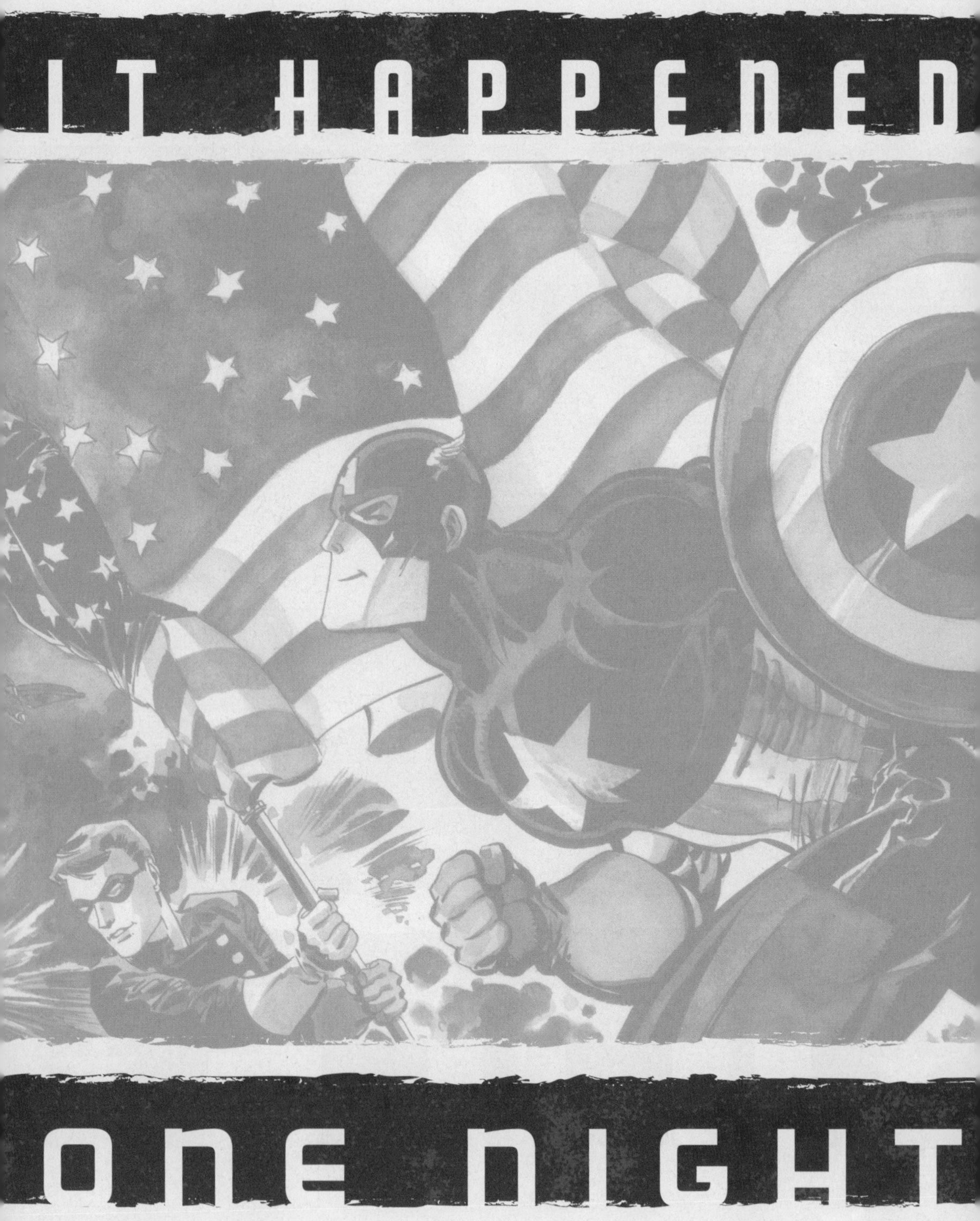

ONE NIGHT

DEDICATED TO:
JOE SIMON &
JACK KIRBY
SUPER-SOLDIERS ALL!
You were just a kid.
I mean, I wasn't that much older -- six, seven years -- but it was enough that *that's* how I saw you.
THEATER
PLAZA
ABBOTT & COSTELLO IN
BUCK PRIVATES
ALSO MOVIETONE NEWS & CARTOONS
TWO, PLEASE.
TS 08

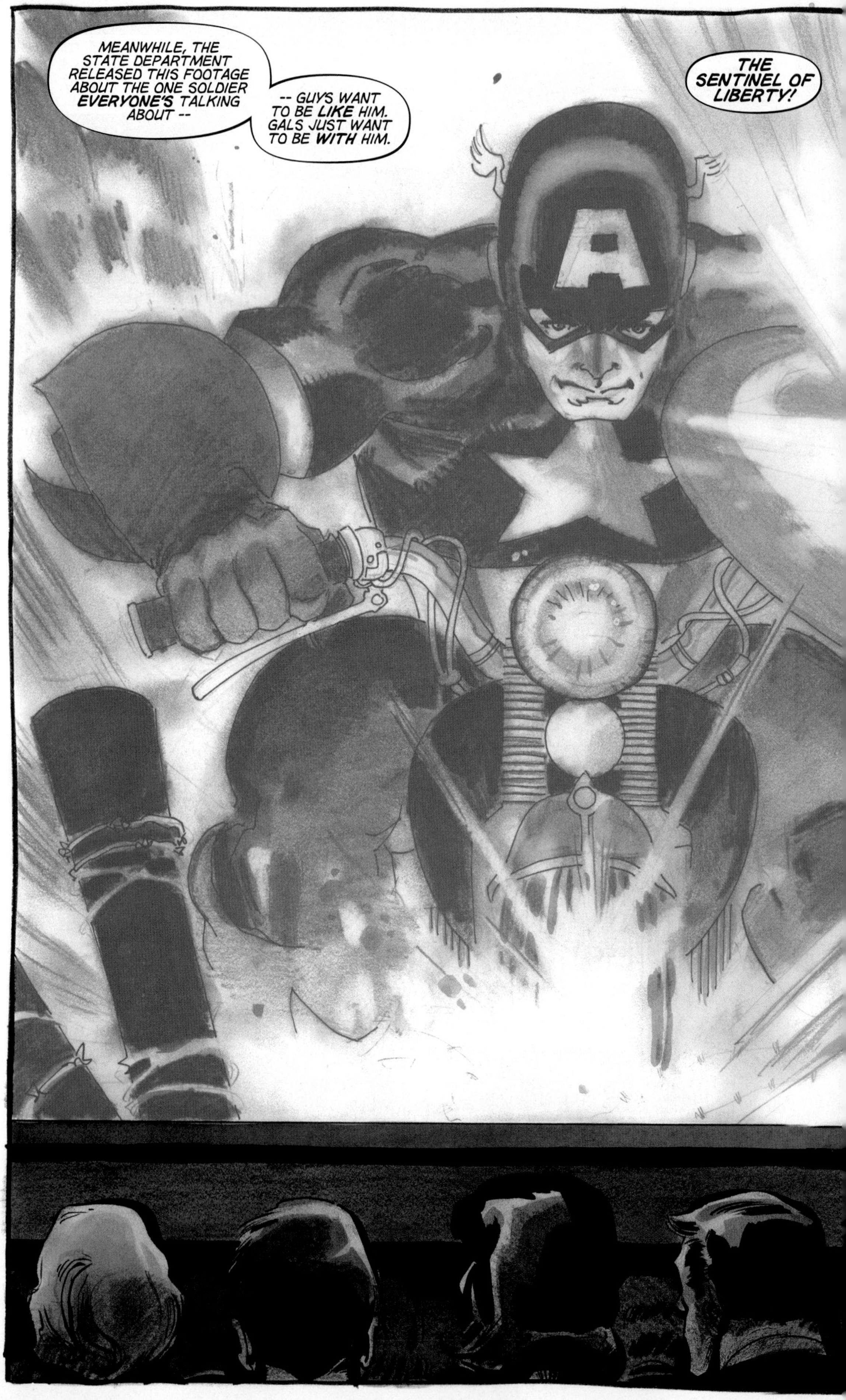
MEANWHILE, THE STATE DEPARTMENT RELEASED THIS FOOTAGE ABOUT THE ONE SOLDIER EVERYONE'S TALKING ABOUT --
-- GUYS WANT TO BE LIKE HIM. GALS JUST WANT TO BE WITH HIM.
THE SENTINEL OF LIBERTY!

THE MAN WHO IS GOING TO KICK HITLER RIGHT IN THE JAPANTZ!
CAPTAIN AMERICA!
I'M TELLIN' YA, STEVE. THIS GUY CAP IS THE REAL DEAL.
WHEN WE GO IN, HE'S GONNA WIN THE WAR FOR US!
I'M SURE HE WON'T DO IT ALONE, JAMES.
YOU TWO WANNA PIPE DOWN?
AH, BUTTON IT, PAL.

We were in basic. Fort Lehigh, Virginia. Every one of us waiting to get overseas.

Some more than others...

WHAT AM I GONNA DO WHEN *EVERYBODY ELSE SHIPS OUT?* STUCK IN THIS HICKSVILLE.

LOOK, JAMES, WAR'S NOT LIKE YOU SEE IN THE MOVIES --

-- YEAH, I HEARD IT ALL BEFORE. LISSEN, I KINDA HATE WHEN YOU CALL ME *"JAMES."*

YOU SOUND LIKE SOMEBODY'S DAD.

OKAY. WHAT DO YOU *WANT* TO BE CALLED?

ROGERS!

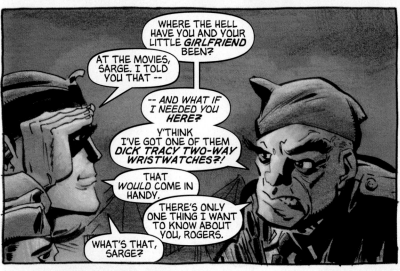

WHERE THE HELL HAVE YOU AND YOUR LITTLE *GIRLFRIEND* BEEN?

AT THE MOVIES, SARGE. I TOLD YOU THAT --

-- AND WHAT IF I NEEDED *YOU* HERE?

Y'THINK I'VE GOT ONE OF THEM *DICK TRACY TWO-WAY WRISTWATCHES?!*

THAT *WOULD* COME IN HANDY.

THERE'S ONLY ONE THING I WANT TO KNOW ABOUT YOU, ROGERS.

WHAT'S THAT, SARGE?

HOW MUCH ARE THE GERMANS *PAYING* YOU TO STAY ON *OUR* SIDE?

NOW, GET OUTTA HERE.

VRRROOM

YOUCH!

HA! I CAN'T BELIEVE YOU RAN OVER HIS FOOT!

IT WASN'T *THAT* FUNNY.

IT WAS TO *ME.* THAT GUY'S A *JERK* AND *EVERYBODY* KNOWS IT --

-- LOOK, THE SARGE IS JUST DOING HIS JOB.

NO BETTER OR WORSE THAN ANY OF US.

G'NIGHT, JAMES.

YEAH...

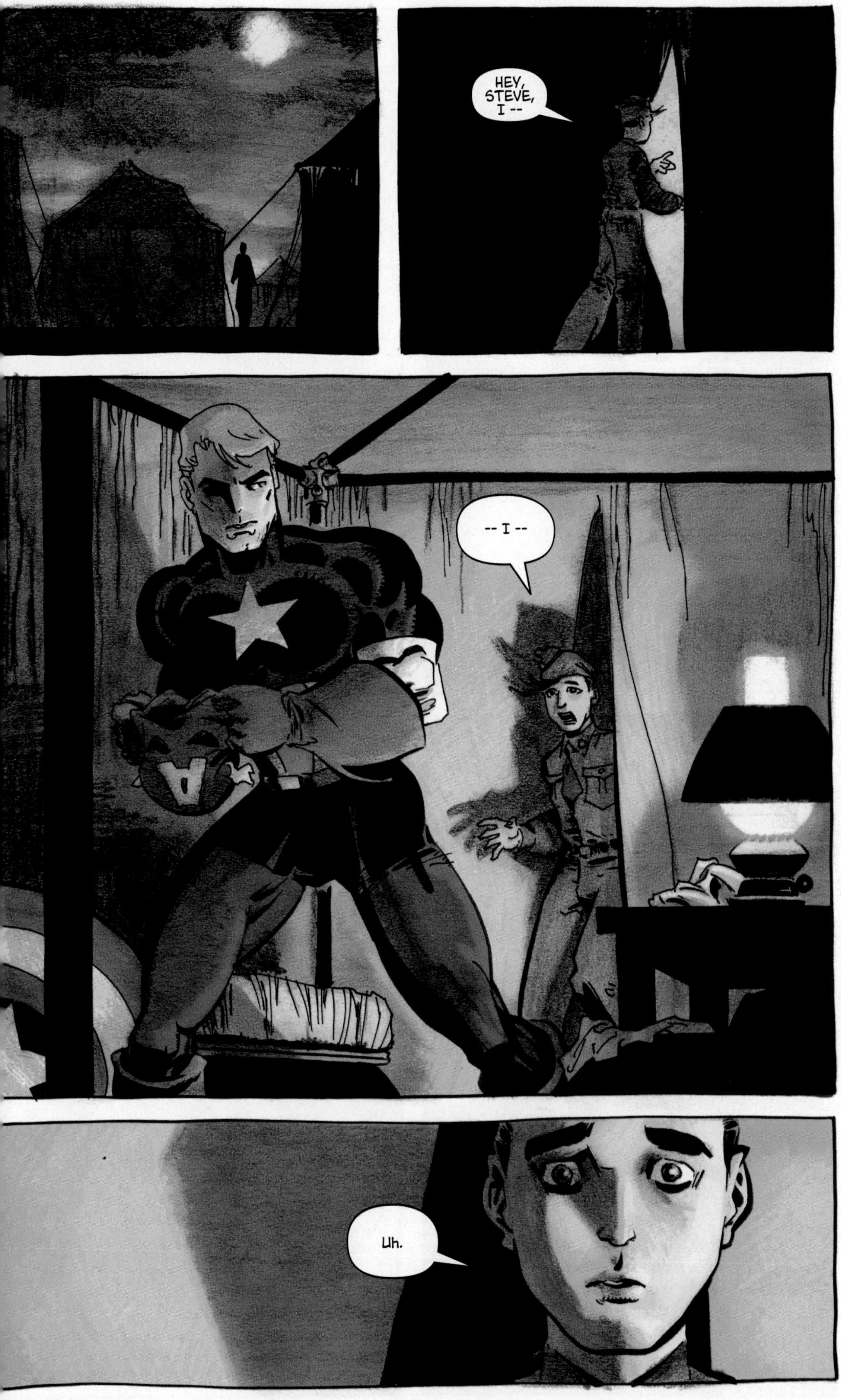
HEY, STEVE, I --
-- I --
Uh.

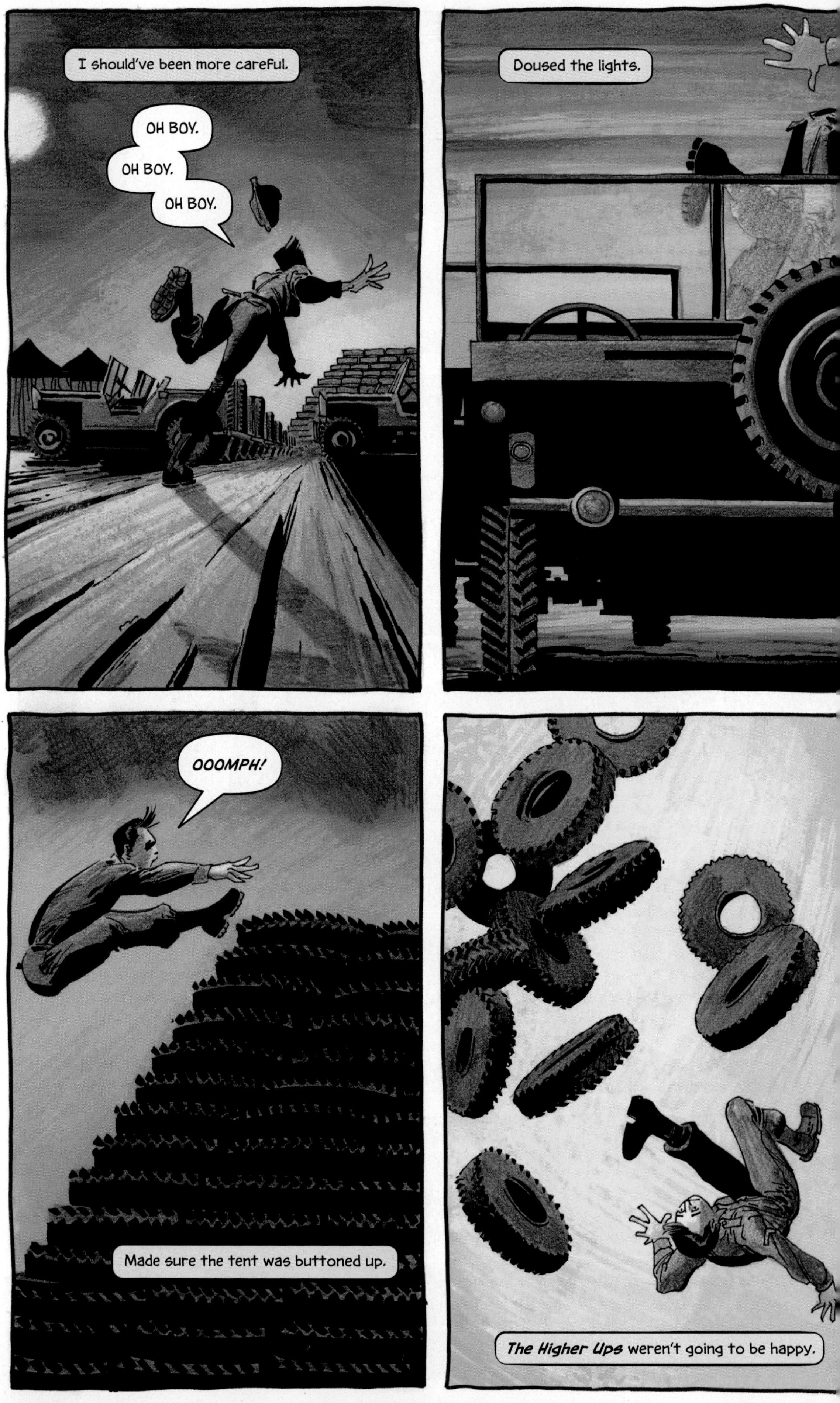
I should've been more careful.
OH BOY.
OH BOY.
OH BOY.
Doused the lights.
OOOMPH!
Made sure the tent was buttoned up.
The Higher Ups weren't going to be happy.

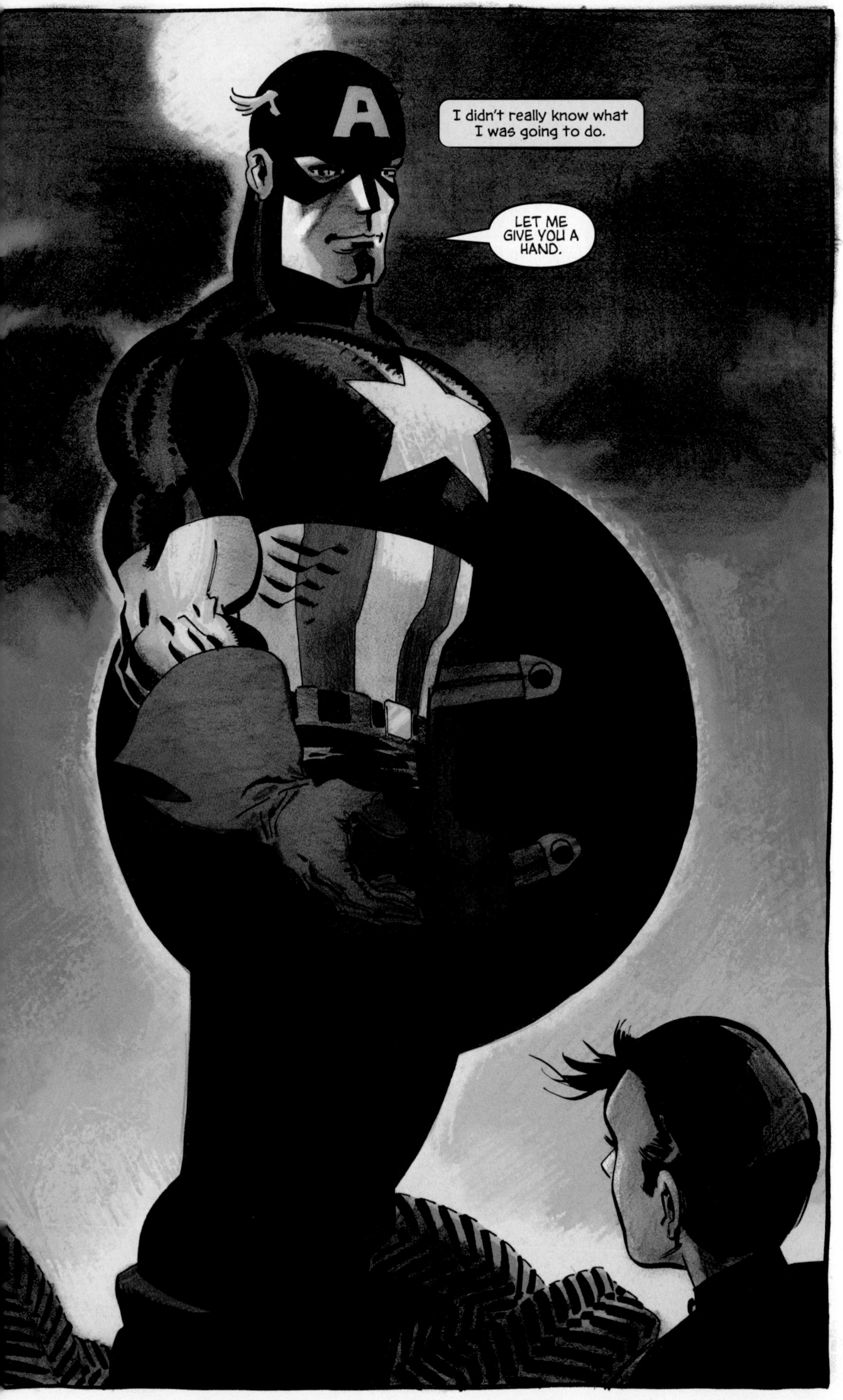
I didn't really know what I was going to do.
LET ME GIVE YOU A HAND.

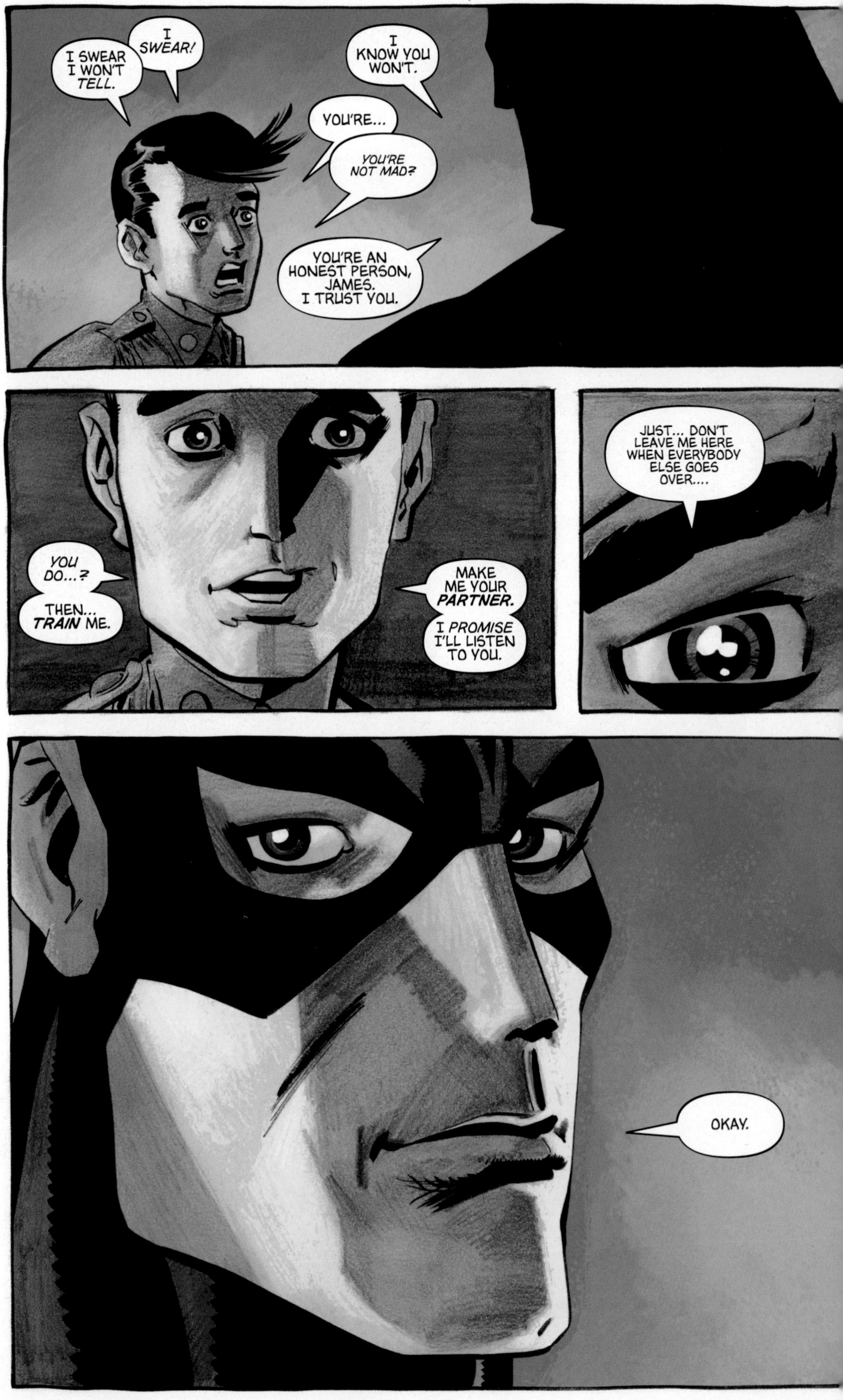
I SWEAR I WON'T *TELL.*
I *SWEAR!*
I KNOW YOU WON'T.
YOU'RE...
YOU'RE NOT MAD?
YOU'RE AN HONEST PERSON, JAMES. I TRUST YOU.
YOU DO...?
THEN... ***TRAIN*** ME.
MAKE ME YOUR ***PARTNER.***
I *PROMISE* I'LL LISTEN TO YOU.
JUST... DON'T LEAVE ME HERE WHEN EVERYBODY ELSE GOES OVER....
OKAY.

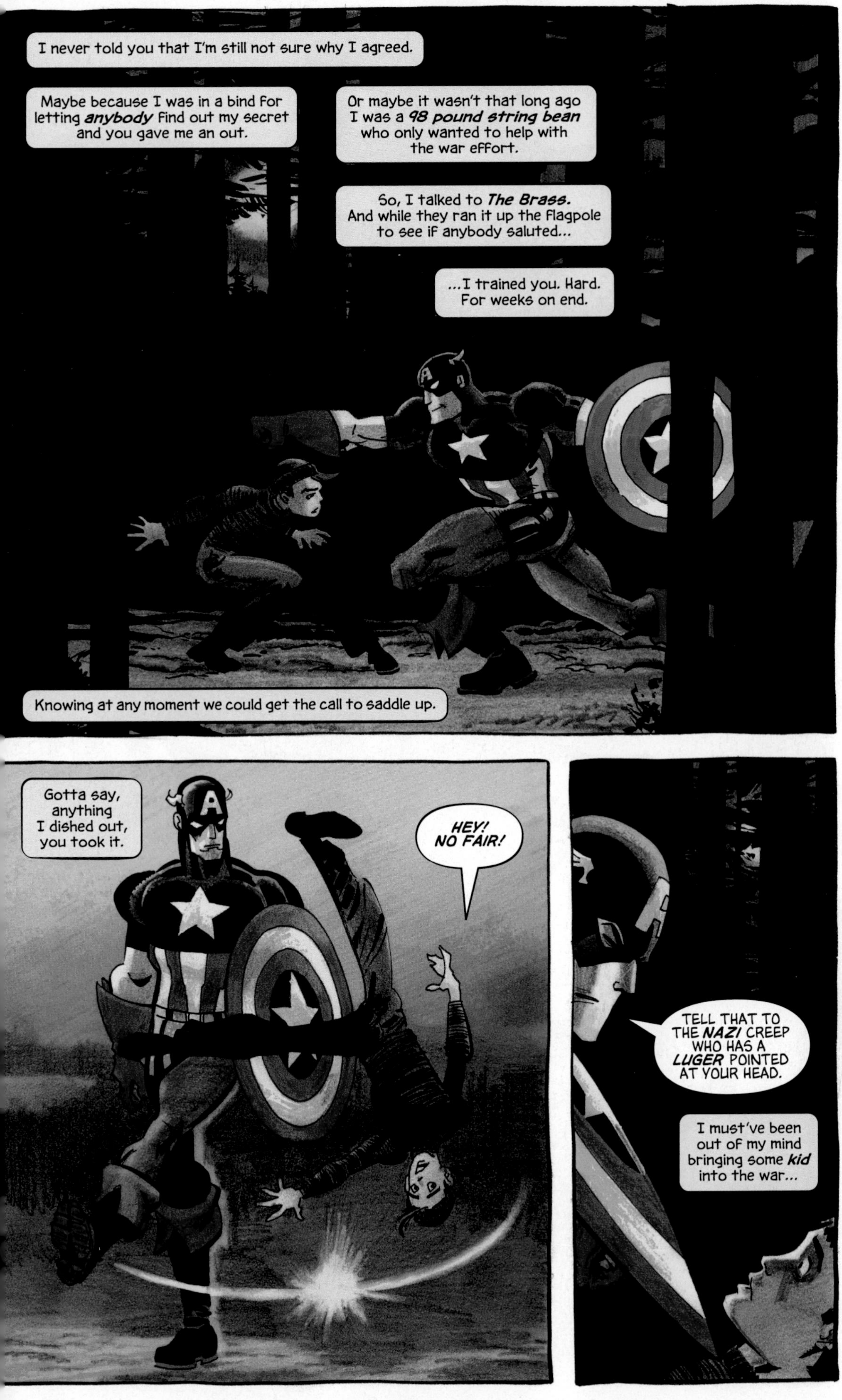
I never told you that I'm still not sure why I agreed.
Maybe because I was in a bind for letting *anybody* find out my secret and you gave me an out.
Or maybe it wasn't that long ago I was a *98 pound string bean* who only wanted to help with the war effort.
So, I talked to *The Brass.* And while they ran it up the flagpole to see if anybody saluted...
...I trained you. Hard. For weeks on end.
Knowing at any moment we could get the call to saddle up.
Gotta say, anything I dished out, you took it.
HEY! NO FAIR!
TELL THAT TO THE *NAZI* CREEP WHO HAS A *LUGER* POINTED AT YOUR HEAD.
I must've been out of my mind bringing some *kid* into the war...

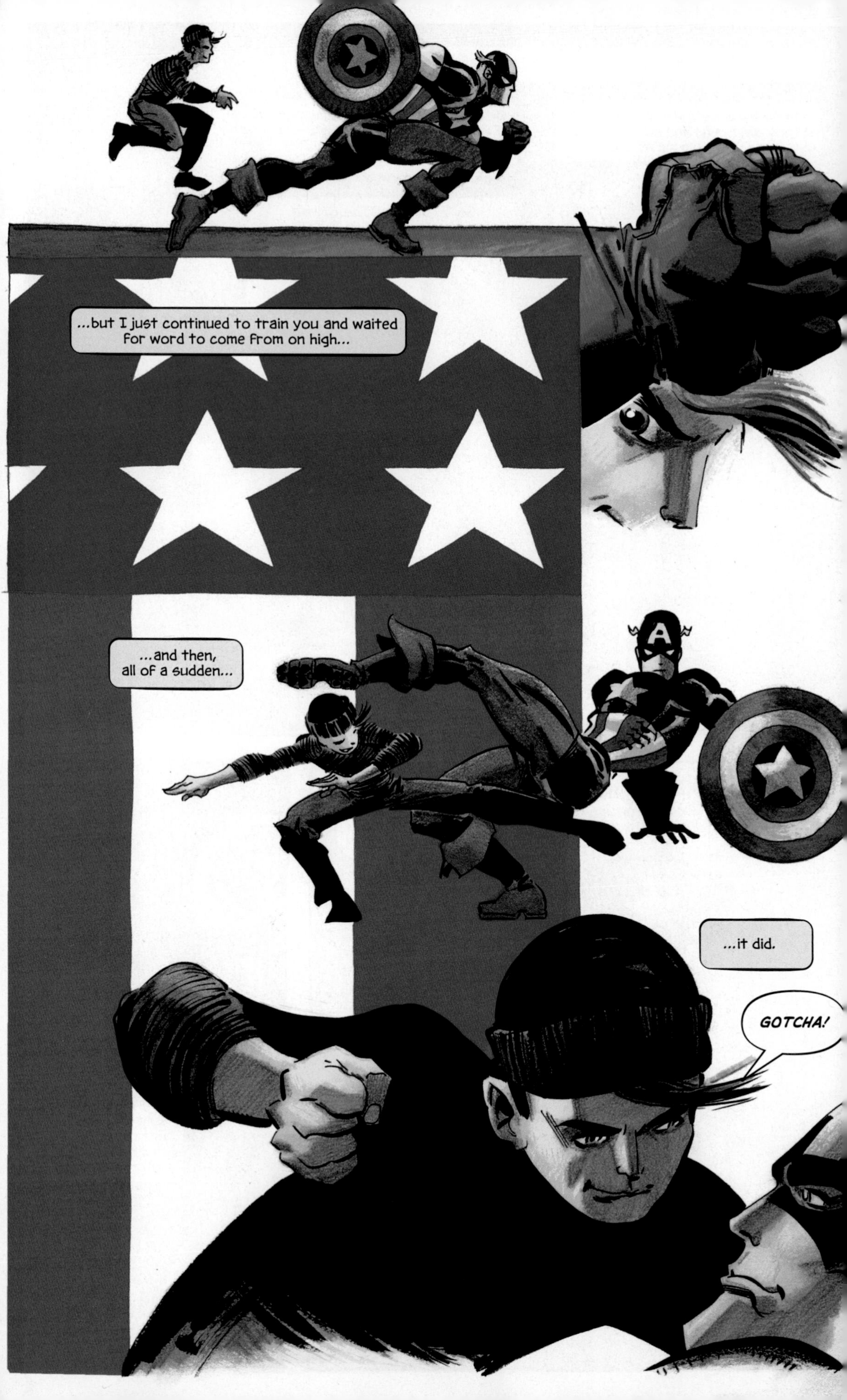
...but I just continued to train you and waited for word to come from on high...
...and then, all of a sudden...
...it did.
GOTCHA!

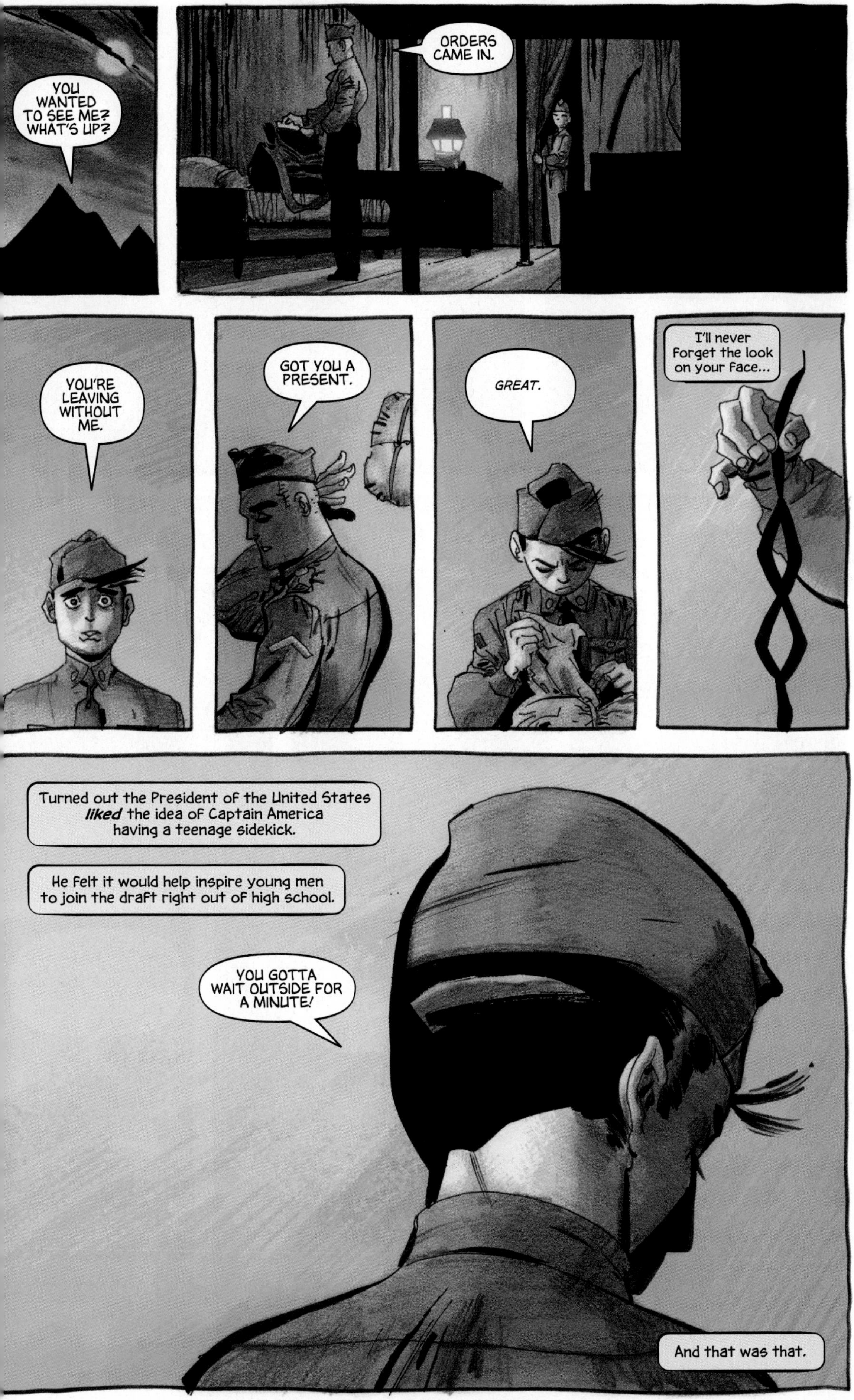
YOU WANTED TO SEE ME? WHAT'S UP?
ORDERS CAME IN.
YOU'RE LEAVING WITHOUT ME.
GOT YOU A PRESENT.
GREAT.
I'll never forget the look on your face...
Turned out the President of the United States *liked* the idea of Captain America having a teenage sidekick.
He felt it would help inspire young men to join the draft right out of high school.
YOU GOTTA WAIT OUTSIDE FOR A MINUTE!
And that was that.

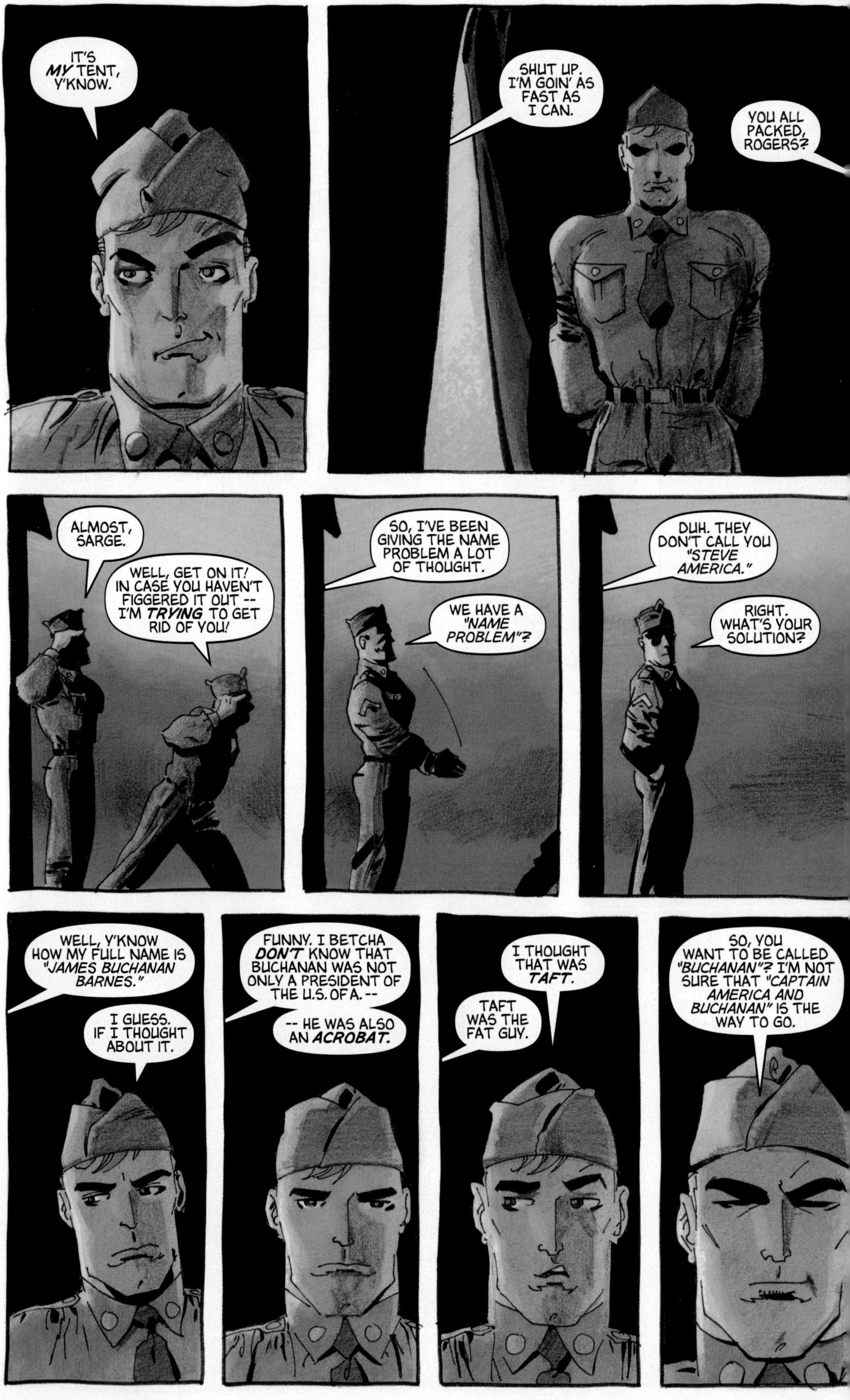
IT'S *MY* TENT, Y'KNOW.
SHUT UP. I'M GOIN' AS FAST AS I CAN.
YOU ALL PACKED, ROGERS?
ALMOST, SARGE.
WELL, GET ON IT! IN CASE YOU HAVEN'T FIGGERED IT OUT -- I'M *TRYING* TO GET RID OF YOU!
SO, I'VE BEEN GIVING THE NAME PROBLEM A LOT OF THOUGHT.
WE HAVE A *"NAME PROBLEM"*?
DUH. THEY DON'T CALL YOU *"STEVE AMERICA."*
RIGHT. WHAT'S YOUR SOLUTION?
WELL, Y'KNOW HOW MY FULL NAME IS *"JAMES BUCHANAN BARNES."*
I GUESS. IF I THOUGHT ABOUT IT.
FUNNY. I BETCHA *DON'T* KNOW THAT BUCHANAN WAS NOT ONLY A PRESIDENT OF THE U.S. OF A. --
-- HE WAS ALSO AN *ACROBAT.*
I THOUGHT THAT WAS *TAFT.*
TAFT WAS THE FAT GUY.
SO, YOU WANT TO BE CALLED *"BUCHANAN"*? I'M NOT SURE THAT *"CAPTAIN AMERICA AND BUCHANAN"* IS THE WAY TO GO.

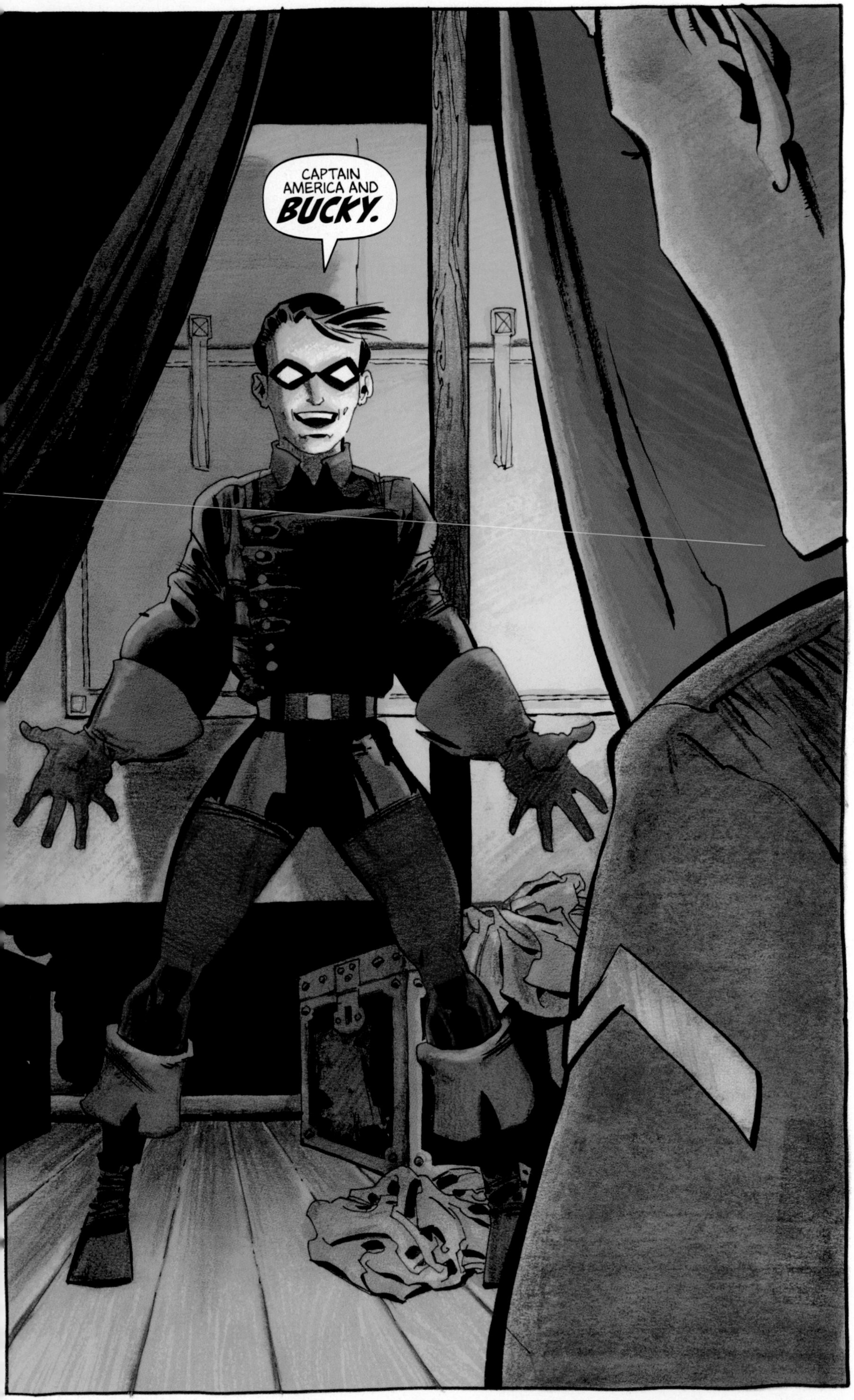
CAPTAIN AMERICA AND BUCKY.

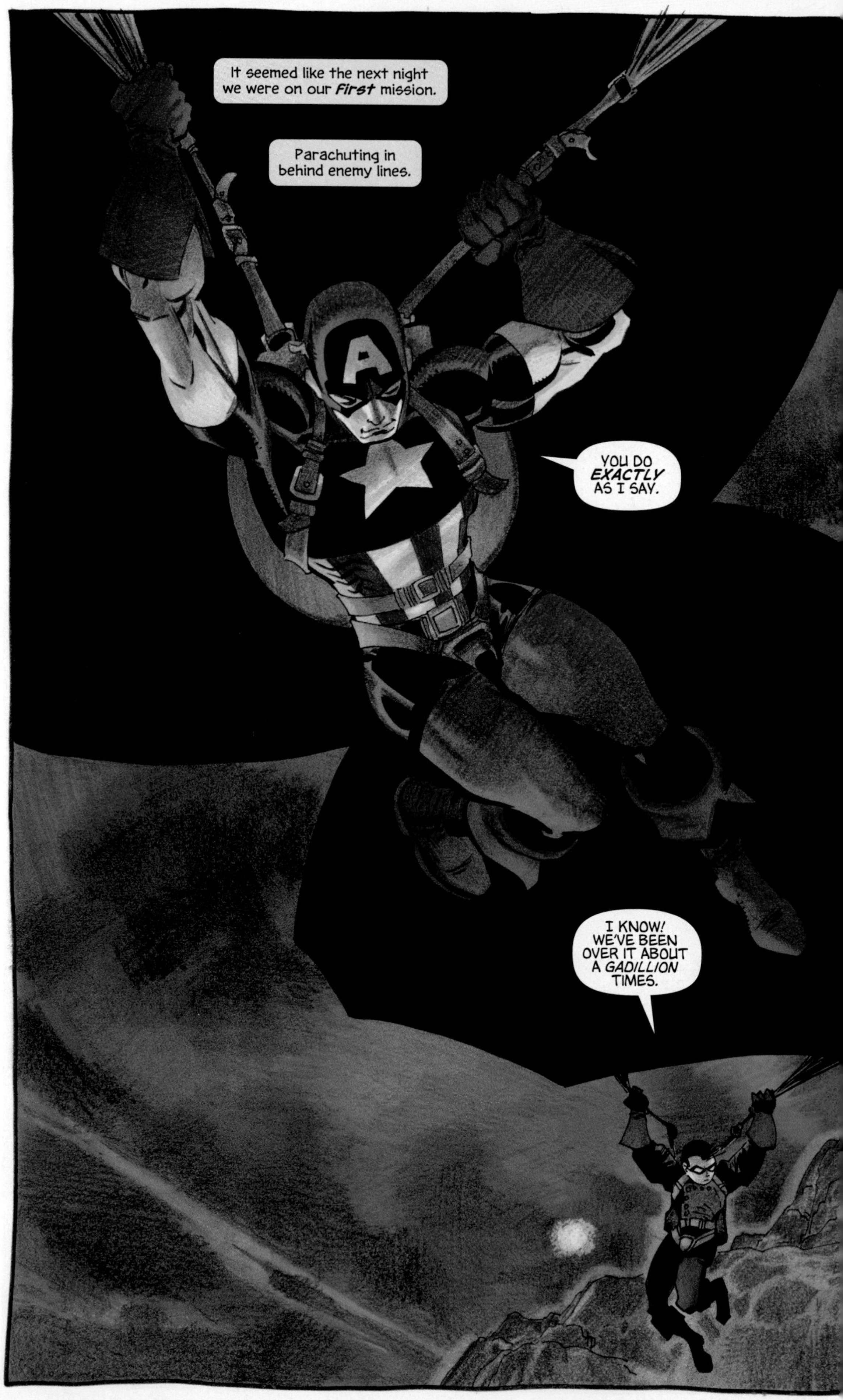
It seemed like the next night we were on our *First* mission.
Parachuting in behind enemy lines.
YOU DO *EXACTLY* AS I SAY.
I KNOW! WE'VE BEEN OVER IT ABOUT A *GADILLION* TIMES.

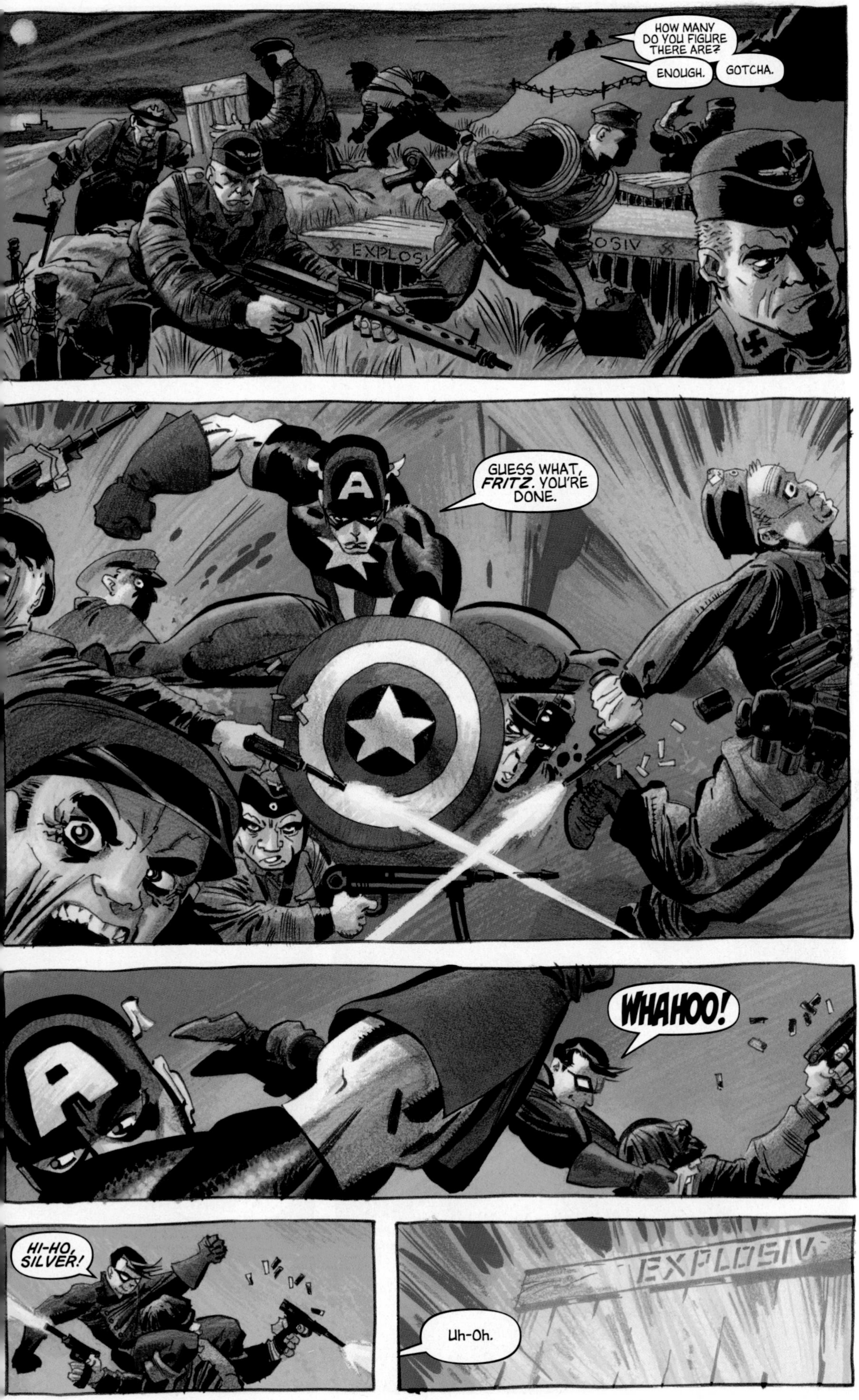
HOW MANY DO YOU FIGURE THERE ARE?
ENOUGH.
GOTCHA.
EXPLOSI
OSIV
GUESS WHAT, FRITZ. YOU'RE DONE.
WHAHOO!
HI-HO, SILVER!
EXPLOSIV
Uh-Oh.

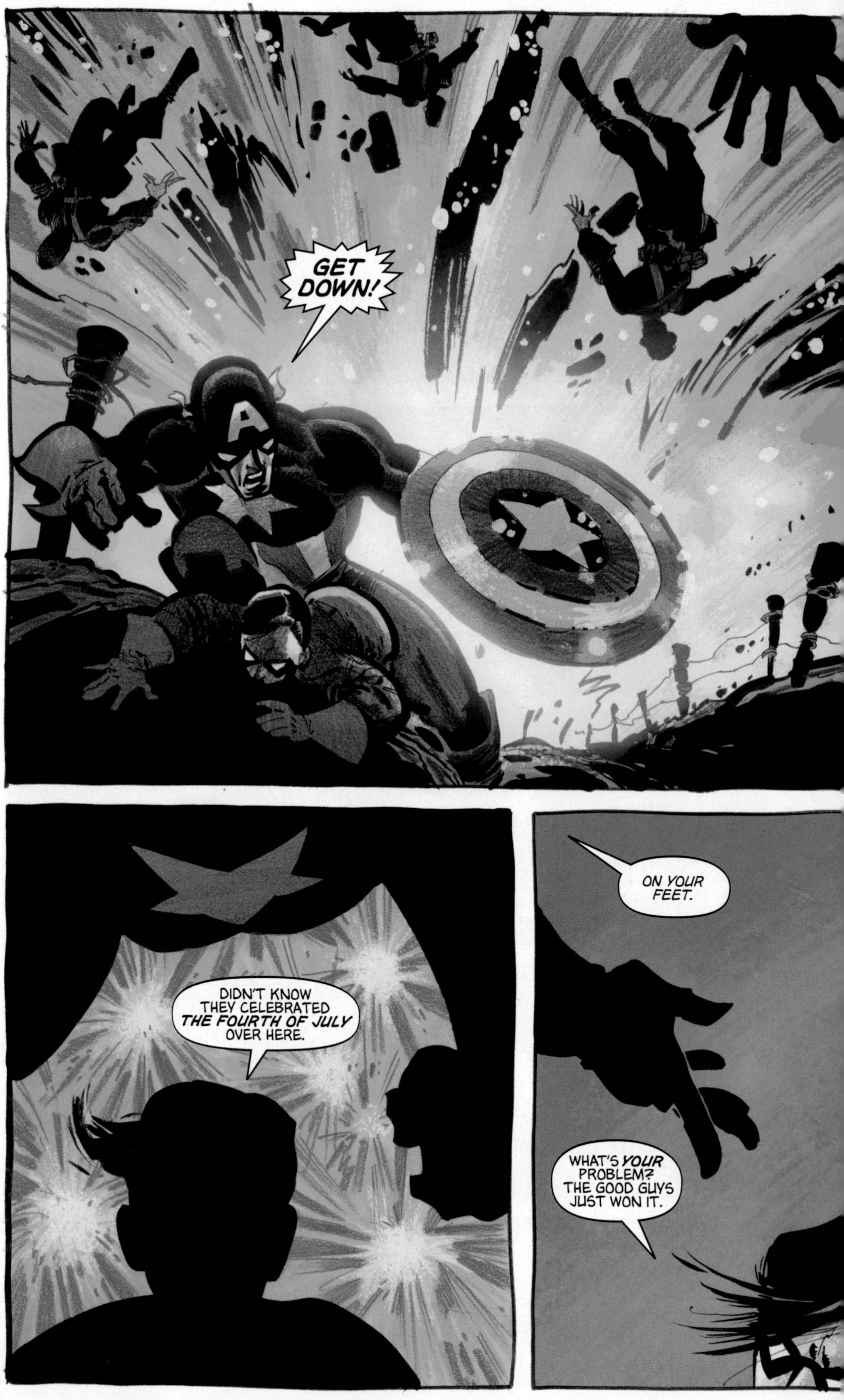
GET DOWN!
DIDN'T KNOW THEY CELEBRATED *THE FOURTH OF JULY* OVER HERE.
ON YOUR FEET.
WHAT'S *YOUR* PROBLEM? THE GOOD GUYS JUST WON IT.

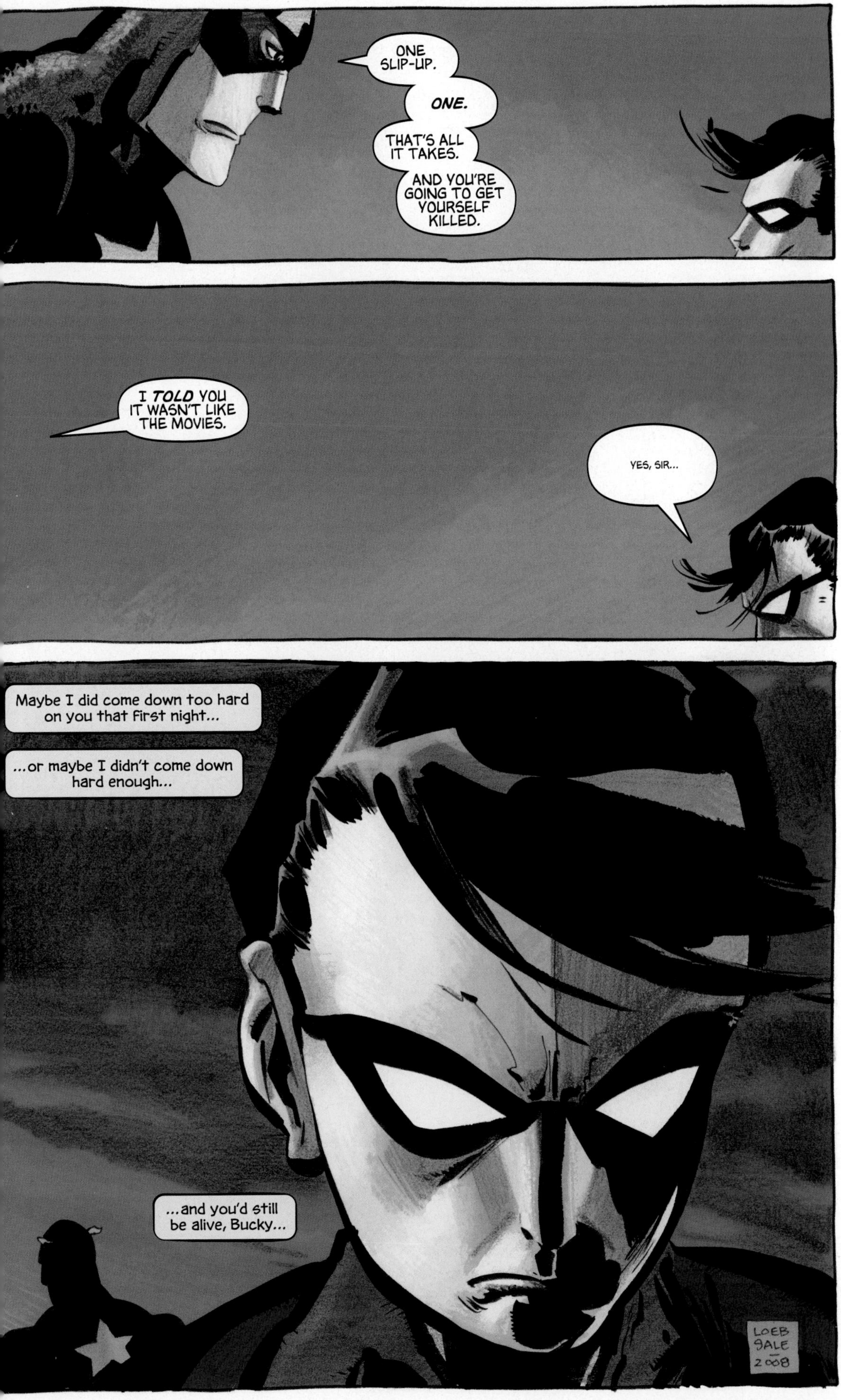
ONE SLIP-UP.
ONE.
THAT'S ALL IT TAKES.
AND YOU'RE GOING TO GET YOURSELF KILLED.
I TOLD YOU IT WASN'T LIKE THE MOVIES.
YES, SIR...
Maybe I did come down too hard on you that first night...
...or maybe I didn't come down hard enough...
...and you'd still be alive, Bucky...
LOEB GALE 2008

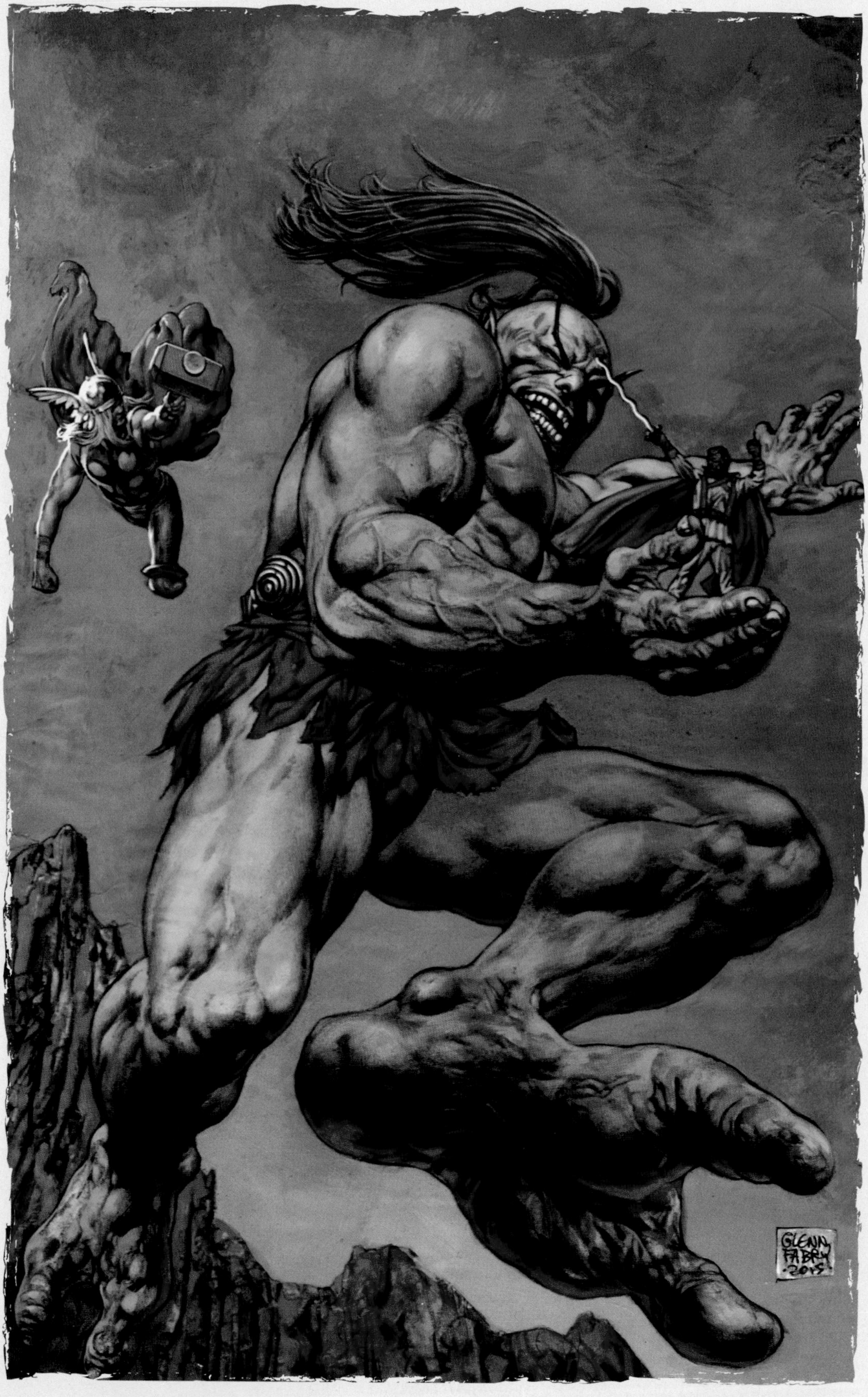
GLENN FABRY 2015

★ VARIANT COVER *by* GLENN FABRY ★

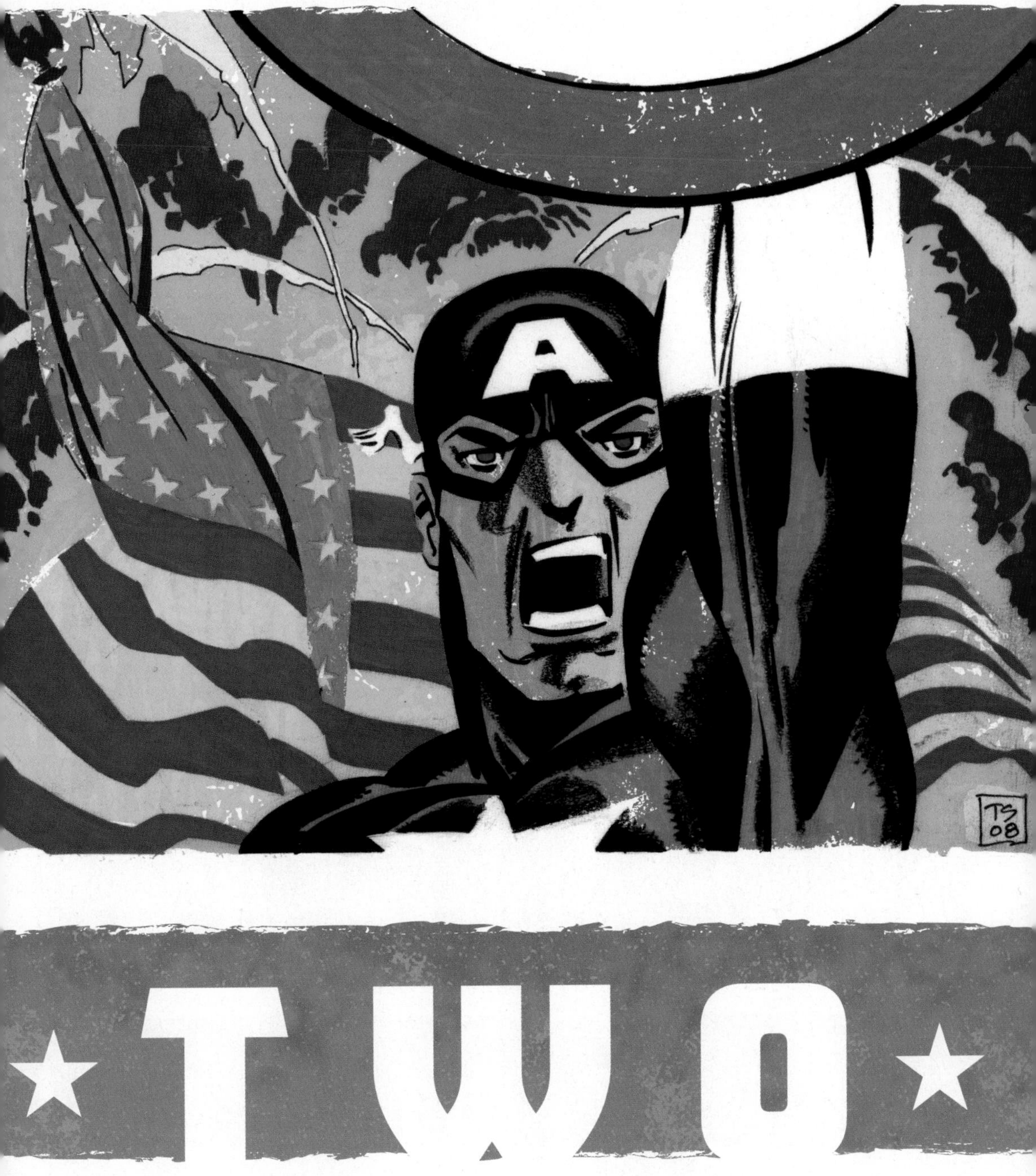
TS
08

★ TWO ★

YOU CAN'T

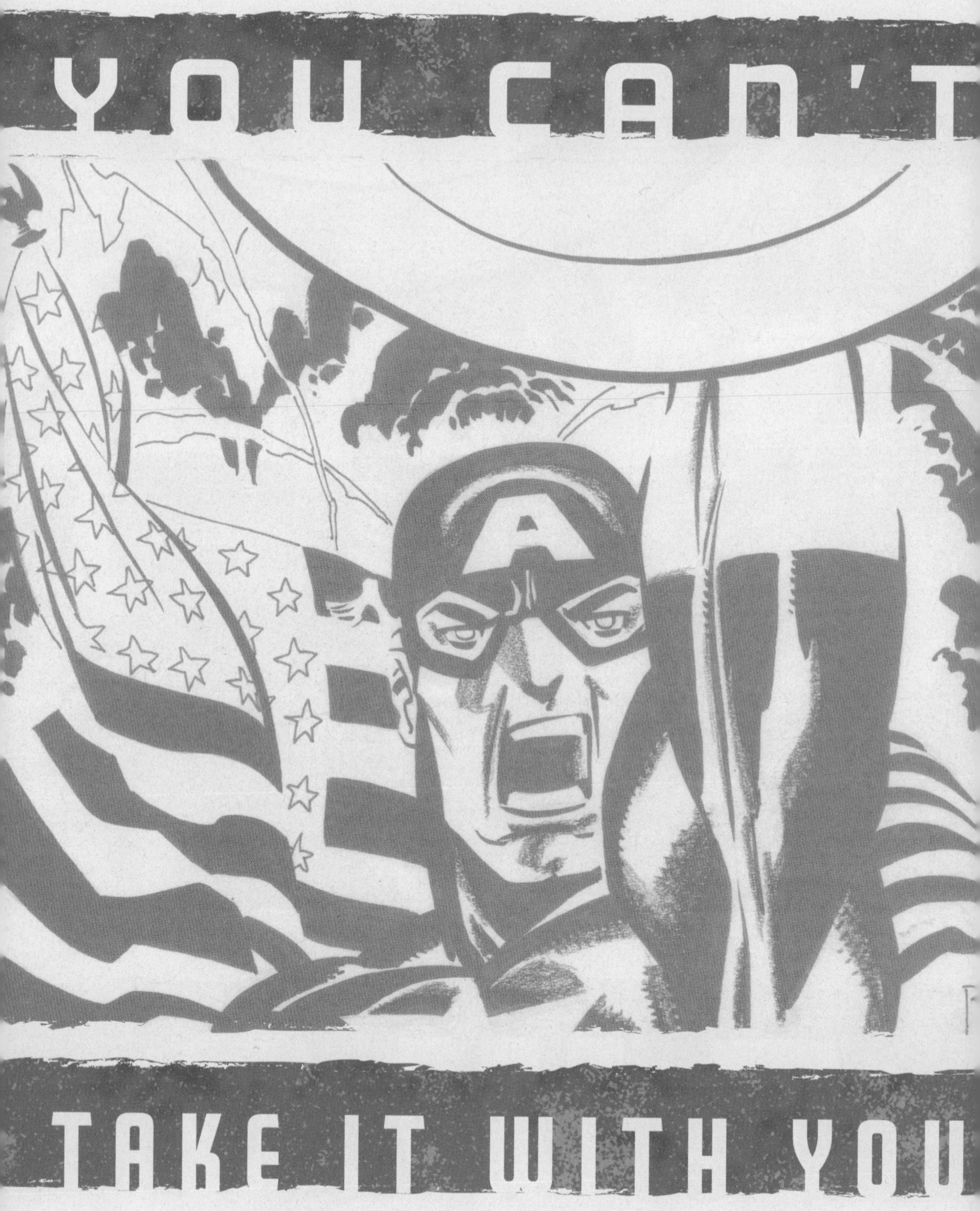

TAKE IT WITH YOU

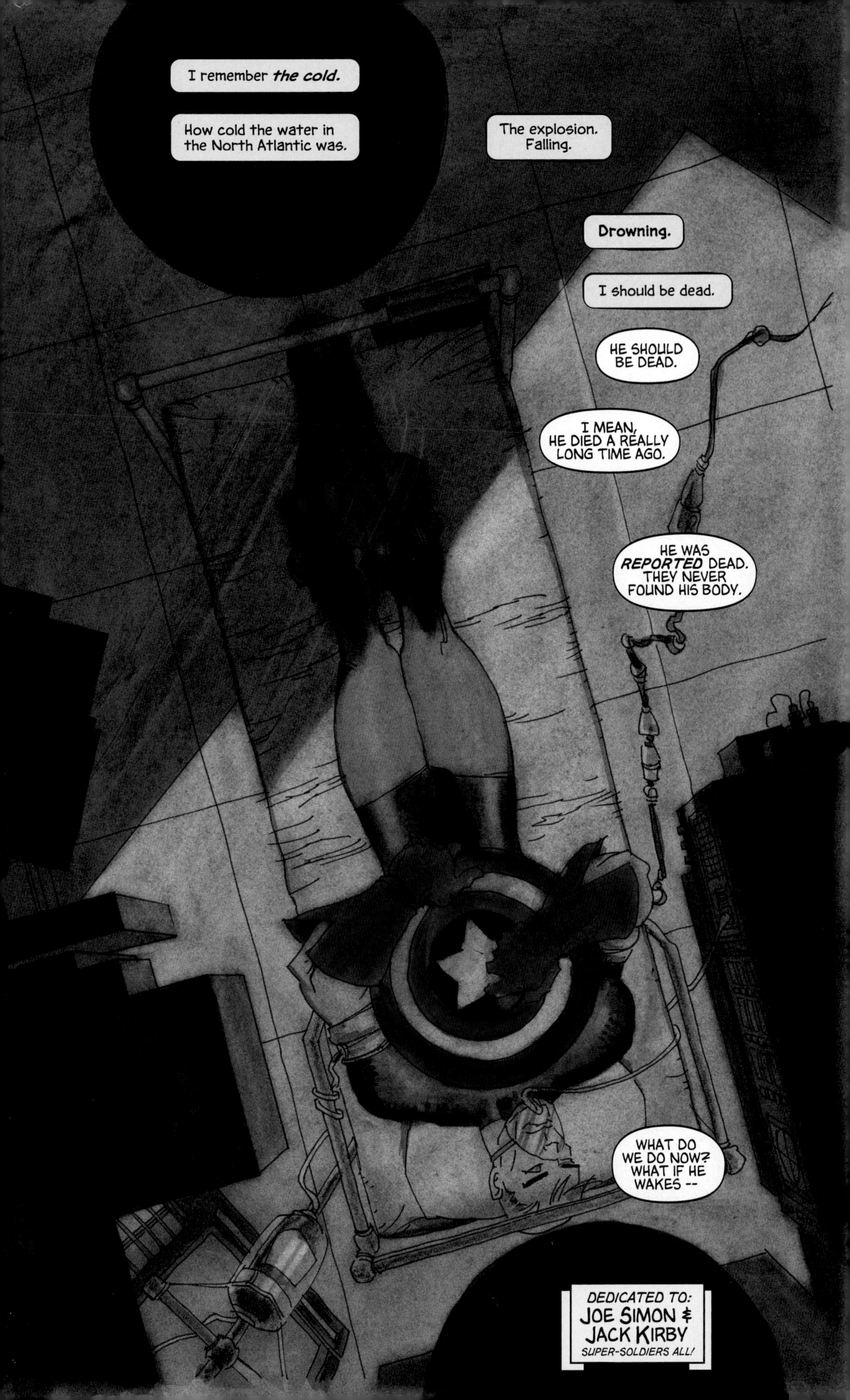
I remember *the cold.*
How cold the water in the North Atlantic was.
The explosion. Falling.
Drowning.
I should be dead.
HE SHOULD BE DEAD.
I MEAN, HE DIED A REALLY LONG TIME AGO.
HE WAS *REPORTED* DEAD. THEY NEVER FOUND HIS BODY.
WHAT DO WE DO NOW? WHAT IF HE WAKES --
DEDICATED TO: JOE SIMON & JACK KIRBY *SUPER-SOLDIERS ALL!*

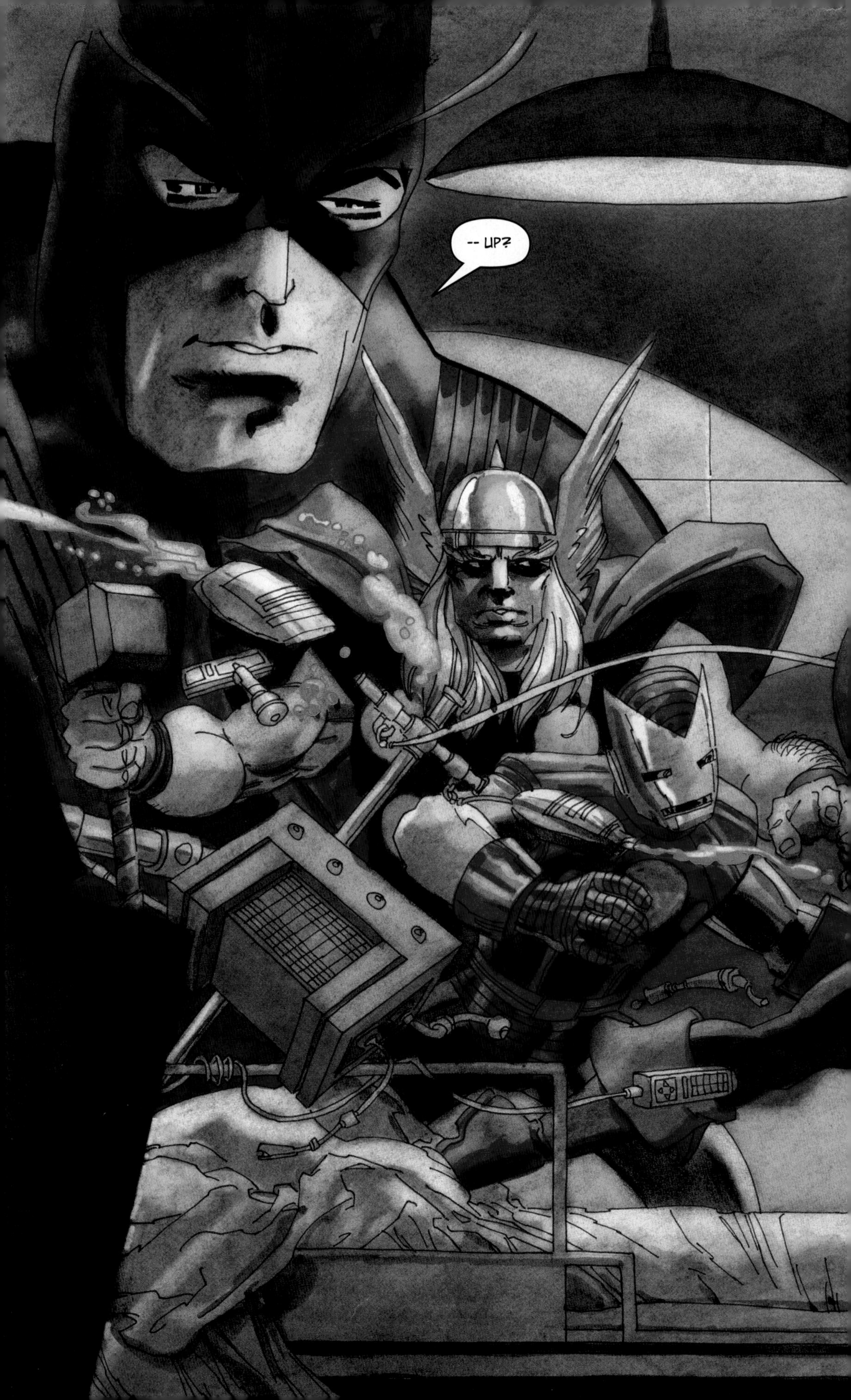
-- UP?

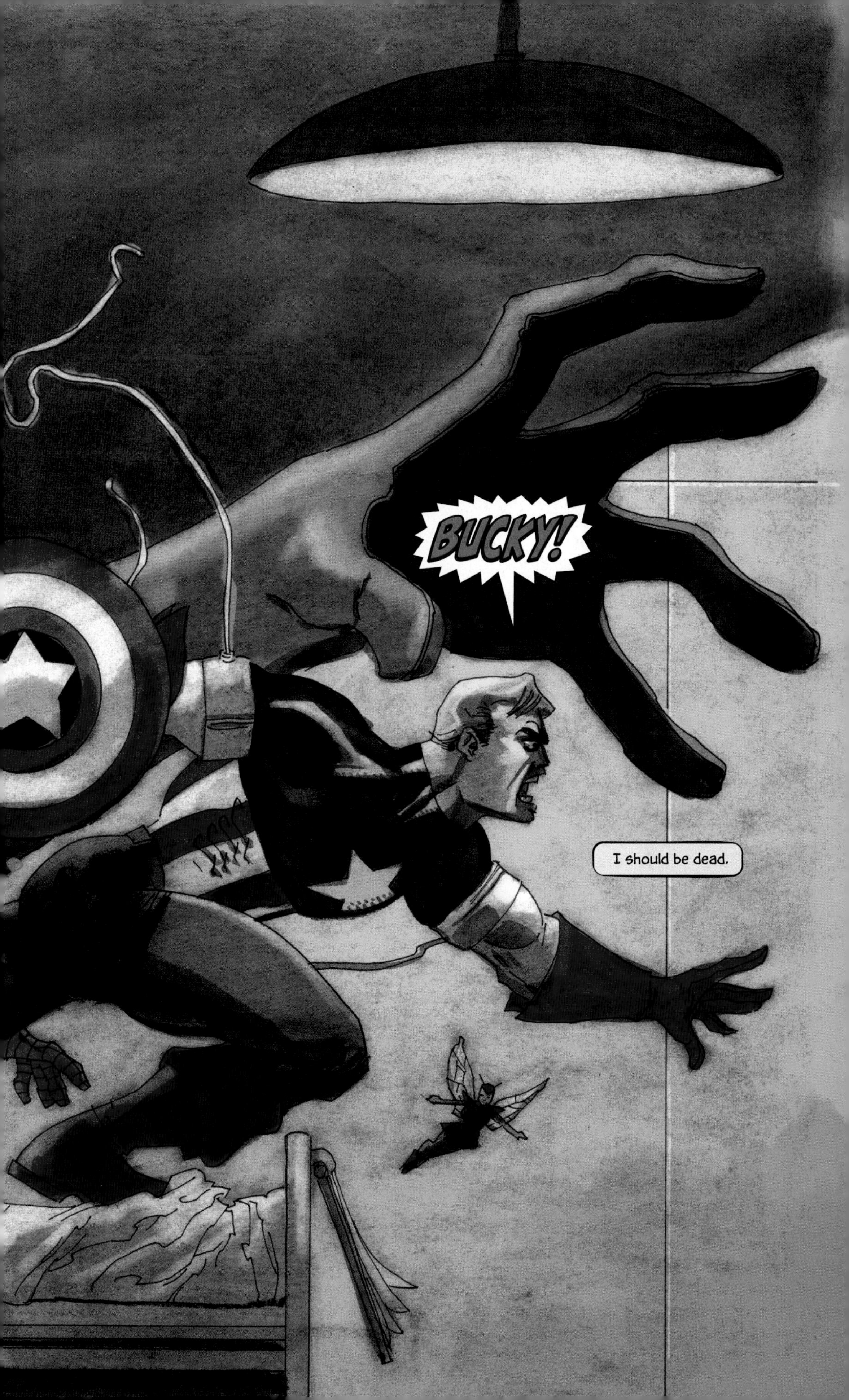
BUCKY!
I should be dead.

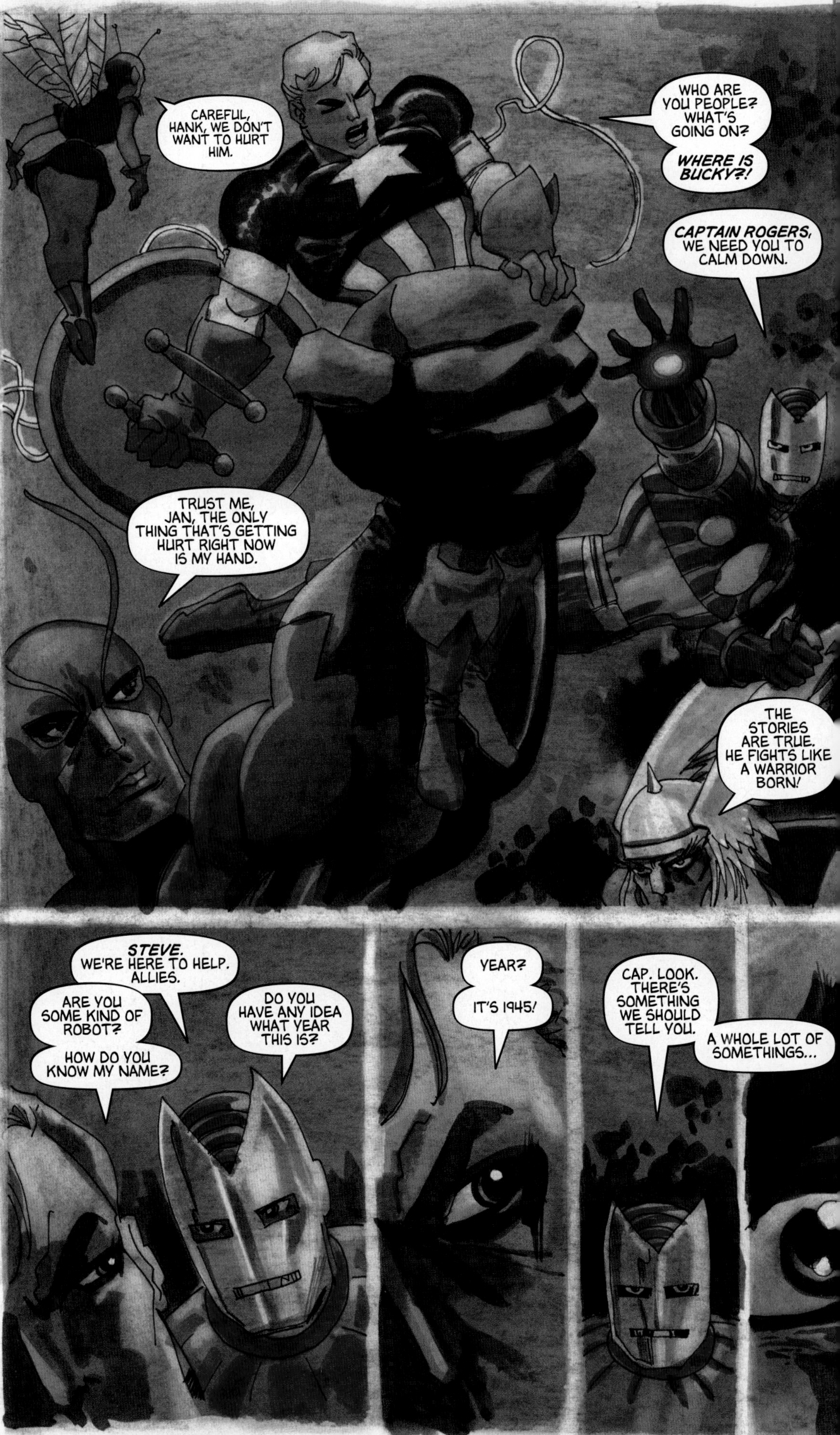
CAREFUL, HANK, WE DON'T WANT TO HURT HIM.
WHO ARE YOU PEOPLE? WHAT'S GOING ON?
WHERE IS BUCKY?!
CAPTAIN ROGERS, WE NEED YOU TO CALM DOWN.
TRUST ME, JAN, THE ONLY THING THAT'S GETTING HURT RIGHT NOW IS MY HAND.
THE STORIES ARE TRUE. HE FIGHTS LIKE A WARRIOR BORN!
STEVE. WE'RE HERE TO HELP. ALLIES.
ARE YOU SOME KIND OF ROBOT?
HOW DO YOU KNOW MY NAME?
DO YOU HAVE ANY IDEA WHAT YEAR THIS IS?
YEAR?
IT'S 1945!
CAP. LOOK. THERE'S SOMETHING WE SHOULD TELL YOU.
A WHOLE LOT OF SOMETHINGS...

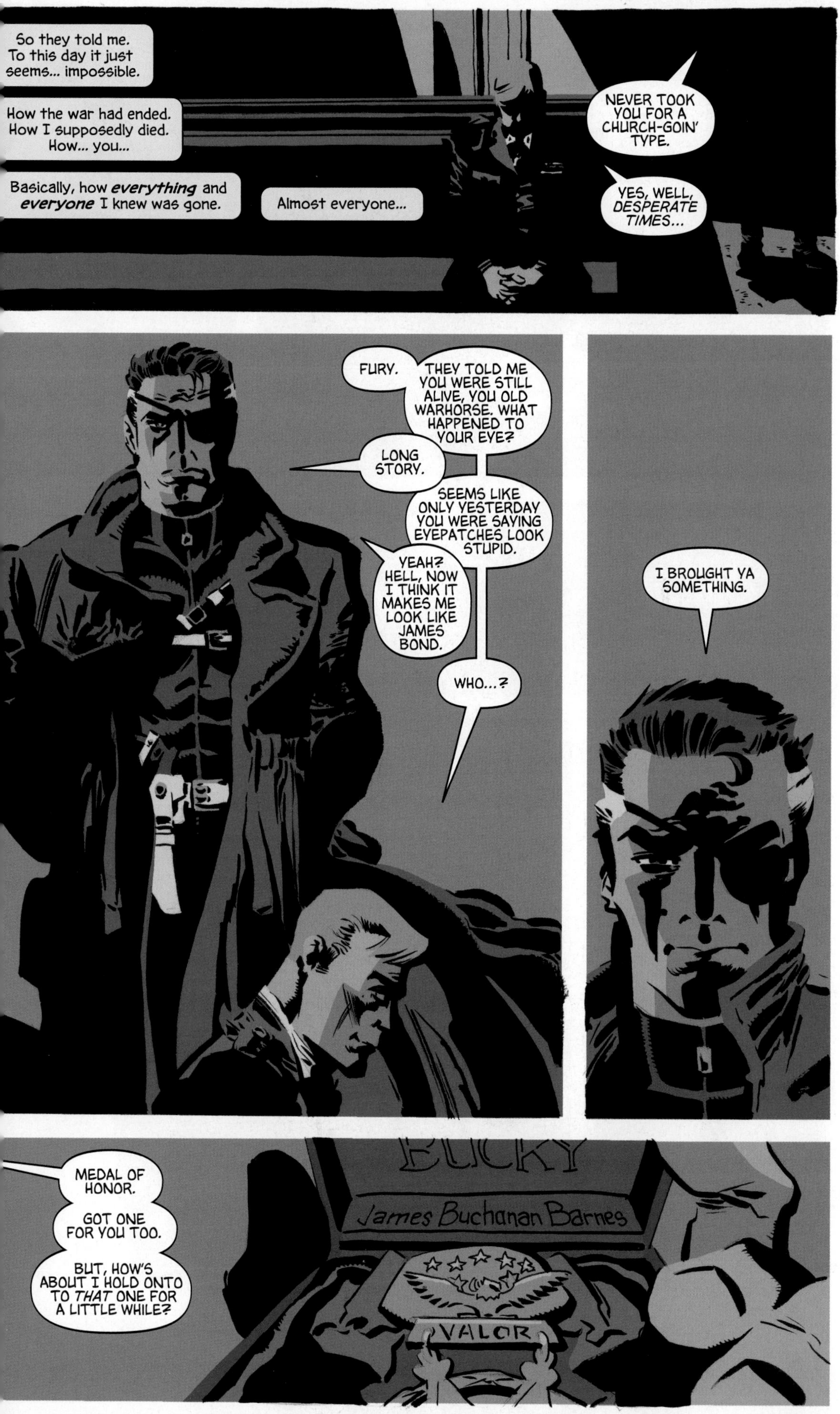

So they told me. To this day it just seems... impossible.
How the war had ended. How I supposedly died. How... you...
Basically, how *everything* and *everyone* I knew was gone.
Almost everyone...
NEVER TOOK YOU FOR A CHURCH-GOIN' TYPE.
YES, WELL, *DESPERATE TIMES*...
FURY.
THEY TOLD ME YOU WERE STILL ALIVE, YOU OLD WARHORSE. WHAT HAPPENED TO YOUR EYE?
LONG STORY.
SEEMS LIKE ONLY YESTERDAY YOU WERE SAYING EYEPATCHES LOOK STUPID.
YEAH? HELL, NOW I THINK IT MAKES ME LOOK LIKE JAMES BOND.
WHO...?
I BROUGHT YA SOMETHING.
MEDAL OF HONOR.
GOT ONE FOR YOU TOO.
BUT, HOW'S ABOUT I HOLD ONTO TO *THAT* ONE FOR A LITTLE WHILE?
BUCKY
James Buchanan Barnes
VALOR

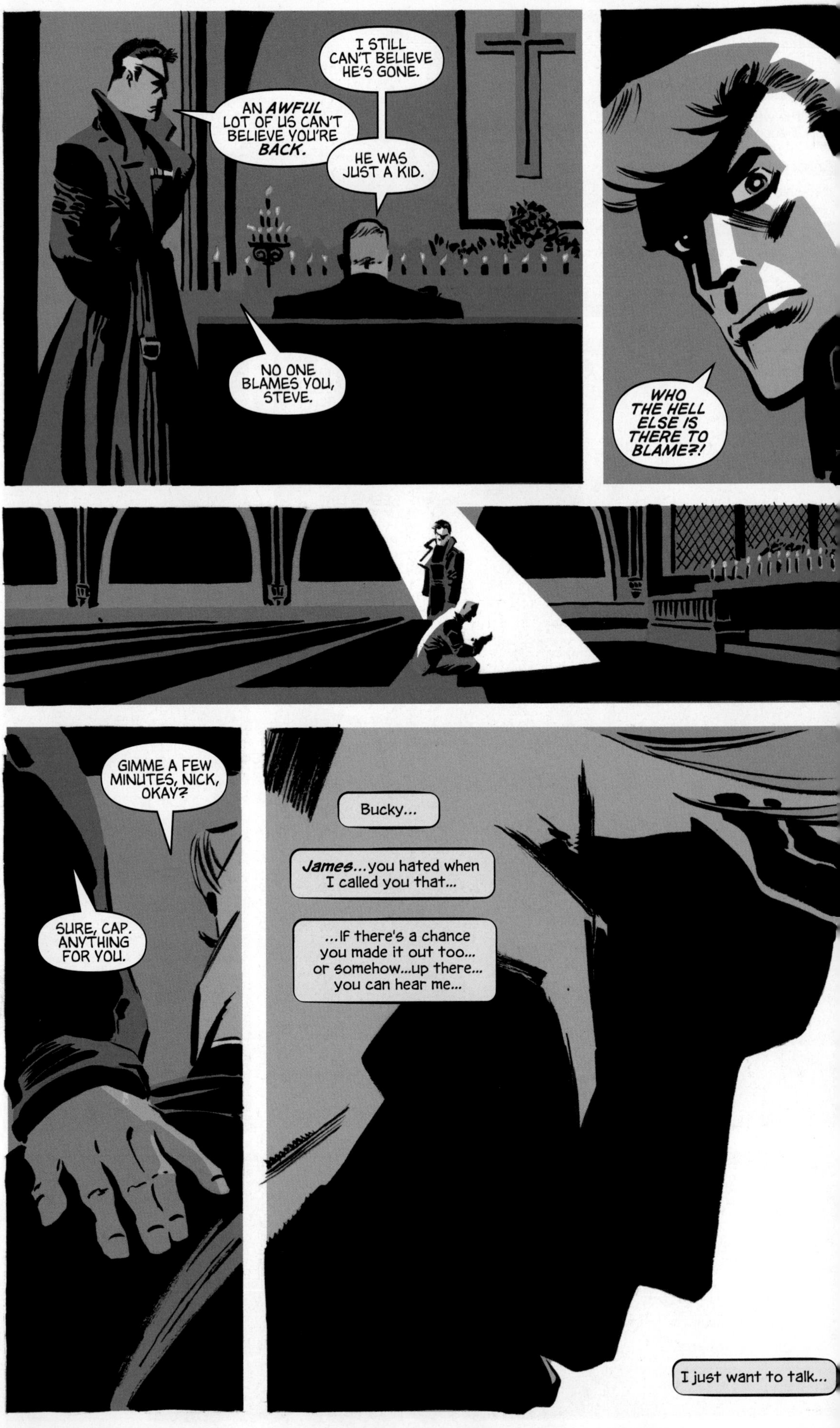
I STILL CAN'T BELIEVE HE'S GONE.
AN AWFUL LOT OF US CAN'T BELIEVE YOU'RE BACK.
HE WAS JUST A KID.
NO ONE BLAMES YOU, STEVE.
WHO THE HELL ELSE IS THERE TO BLAME?!
GIMME A FEW MINUTES, NICK, OKAY?
SURE, CAP. ANYTHING FOR YOU.
Bucky...
James...you hated when I called you that...
...If there's a chance you made it out too... or somehow...up there... you can hear me...
I just want to talk...

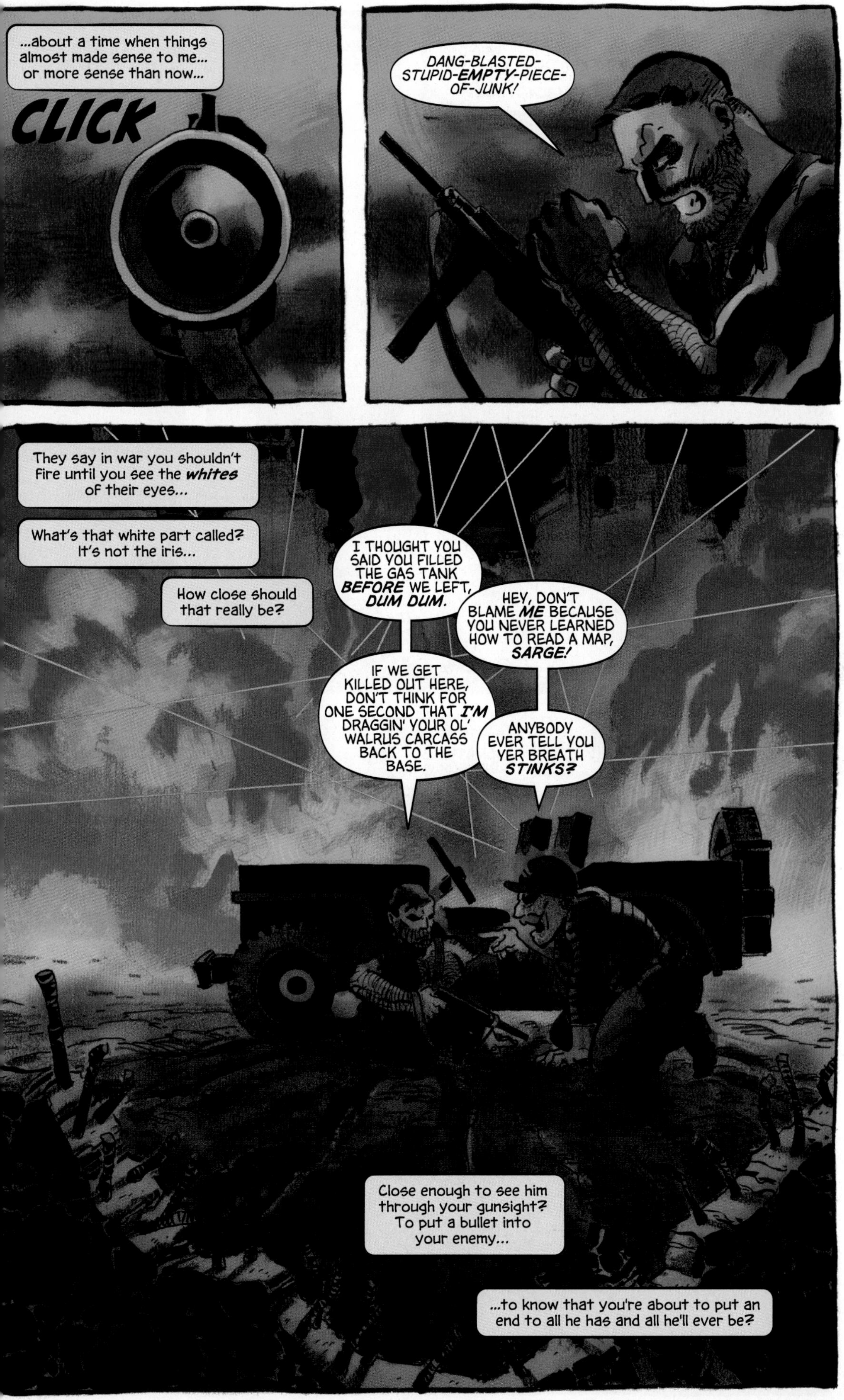
...about a time when things almost made sense to me... or more sense than now...
CLICK
DANG-BLASTED-STUPID-EMPTY-PIECE-OF-JUNK!
They say in war you shouldn't fire until you see the whites of their eyes...
What's that white part called? It's not the iris...
How close should that really be?
I THOUGHT YOU SAID YOU FILLED THE GAS TANK BEFORE WE LEFT, DUM DUM.
HEY, DON'T BLAME ME BECAUSE YOU NEVER LEARNED HOW TO READ A MAP, SARGE!
IF WE GET KILLED OUT HERE, DON'T THINK FOR ONE SECOND THAT I'M DRAGGIN' YOUR OL' WALRUS CARCASS BACK TO THE BASE.
ANYBODY EVER TELL YOU YER BREATH STINKS?
Close enough to see him through your gunsight? To put a bullet into your enemy...
...to know that you're about to put an end to all he has and all he'll ever be?

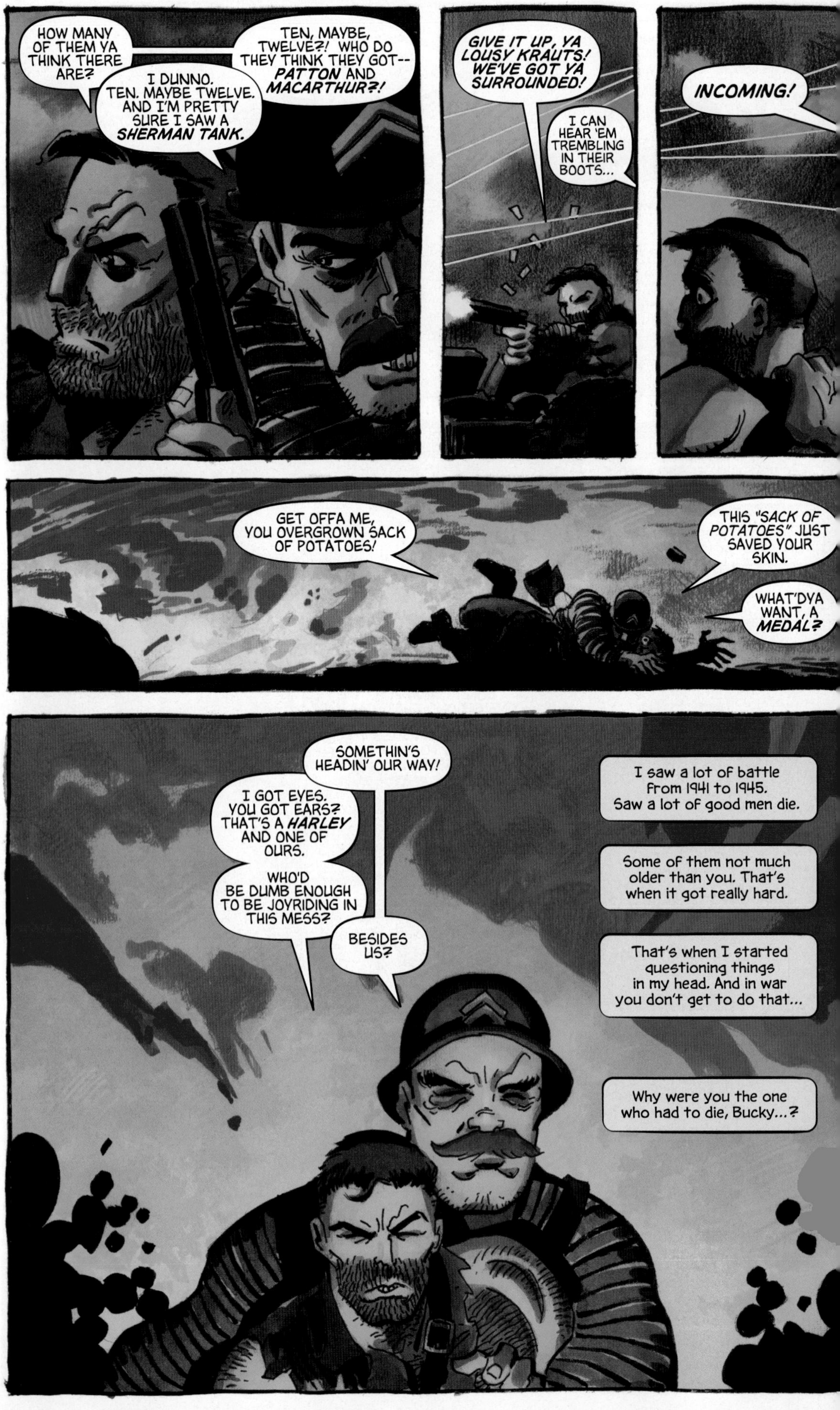
HOW MANY OF THEM YA THINK THERE ARE?
I DUNNO. TEN. MAYBE TWELVE. AND I'M PRETTY SURE I SAW A SHERMAN TANK.
TEN, MAYBE, TWELVE?! WHO DO THEY THINK THEY GOT-- PATTON AND MACARTHUR?!
GIVE IT UP, YA LOUSY KRAUTS! WE'VE GOT YA SURROUNDED!
I CAN HEAR 'EM TREMBLING IN THEIR BOOTS...
INCOMING!
GET OFFA ME, YOU OVERGROWN SACK OF POTATOES!
THIS "SACK OF POTATOES" JUST SAVED YOUR SKIN.
WHAT'DYA WANT, A MEDAL?
SOMETHIN'S HEADIN' OUR WAY!
I GOT EYES. YOU GOT EARS? THAT'S A HARLEY AND ONE OF OURS.
WHO'D BE DUMB ENOUGH TO BE JOYRIDING IN THIS MESS?
BESIDES US?
I saw a lot of battle from 1941 to 1945. Saw a lot of good men die.
Some of them not much older than you. That's when it got really hard.
That's when I started questioning things in my head. And in war you don't get to do that...
Why were you the one who had to die, Bucky...?

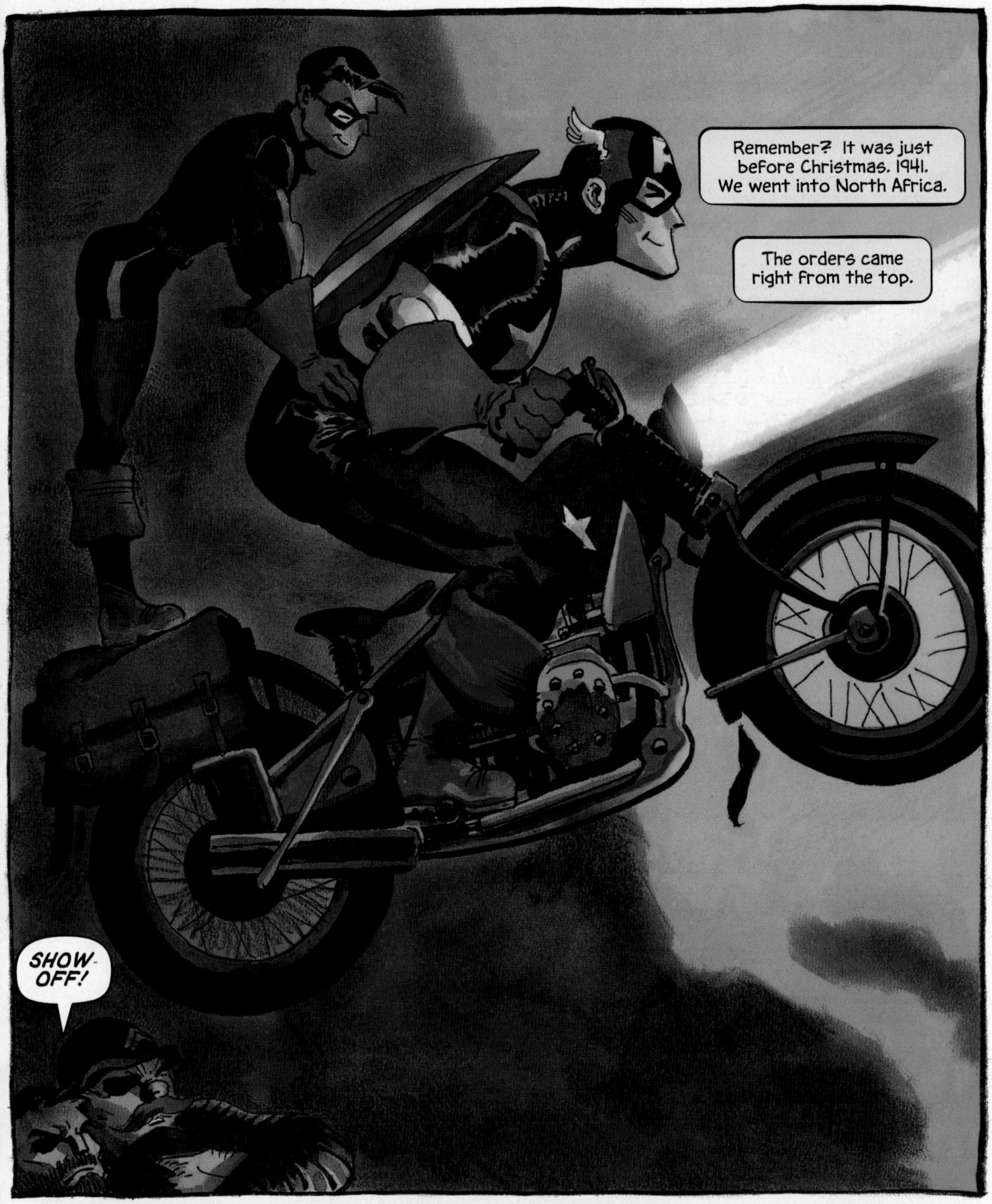
Remember? It was just before Christmas. 1941. We went into North Africa.
The orders came right from the top.
SHOW-OFF!

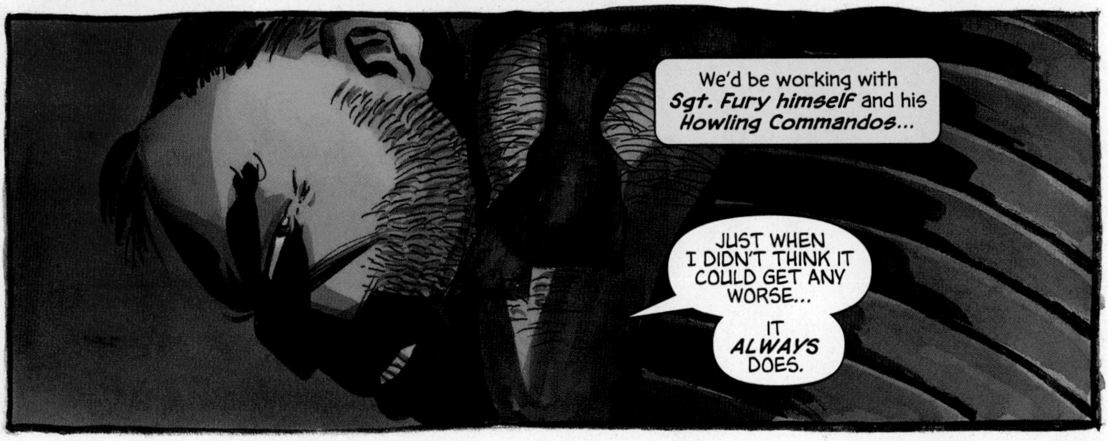
We'd be working with *Sgt. Fury himself* and his *Howling Commandos...*
JUST WHEN I DIDN'T THINK IT COULD GET ANY WORSE...
IT *ALWAYS* DOES.

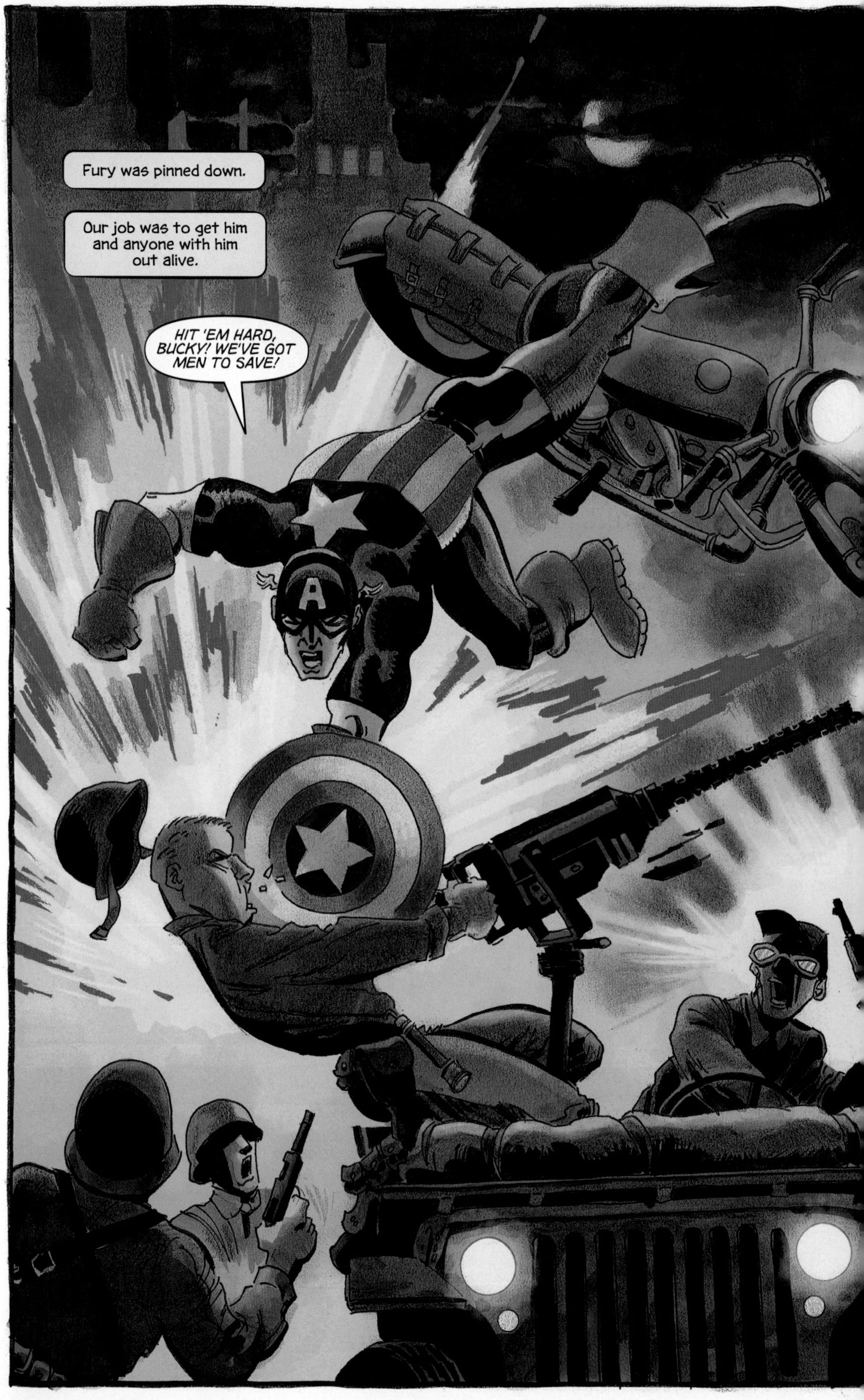
Fury was pinned down.
Our job was to get him and anyone with him out alive.
HIT 'EM HARD, BUCKY! WE'VE GOT MEN TO SAVE!

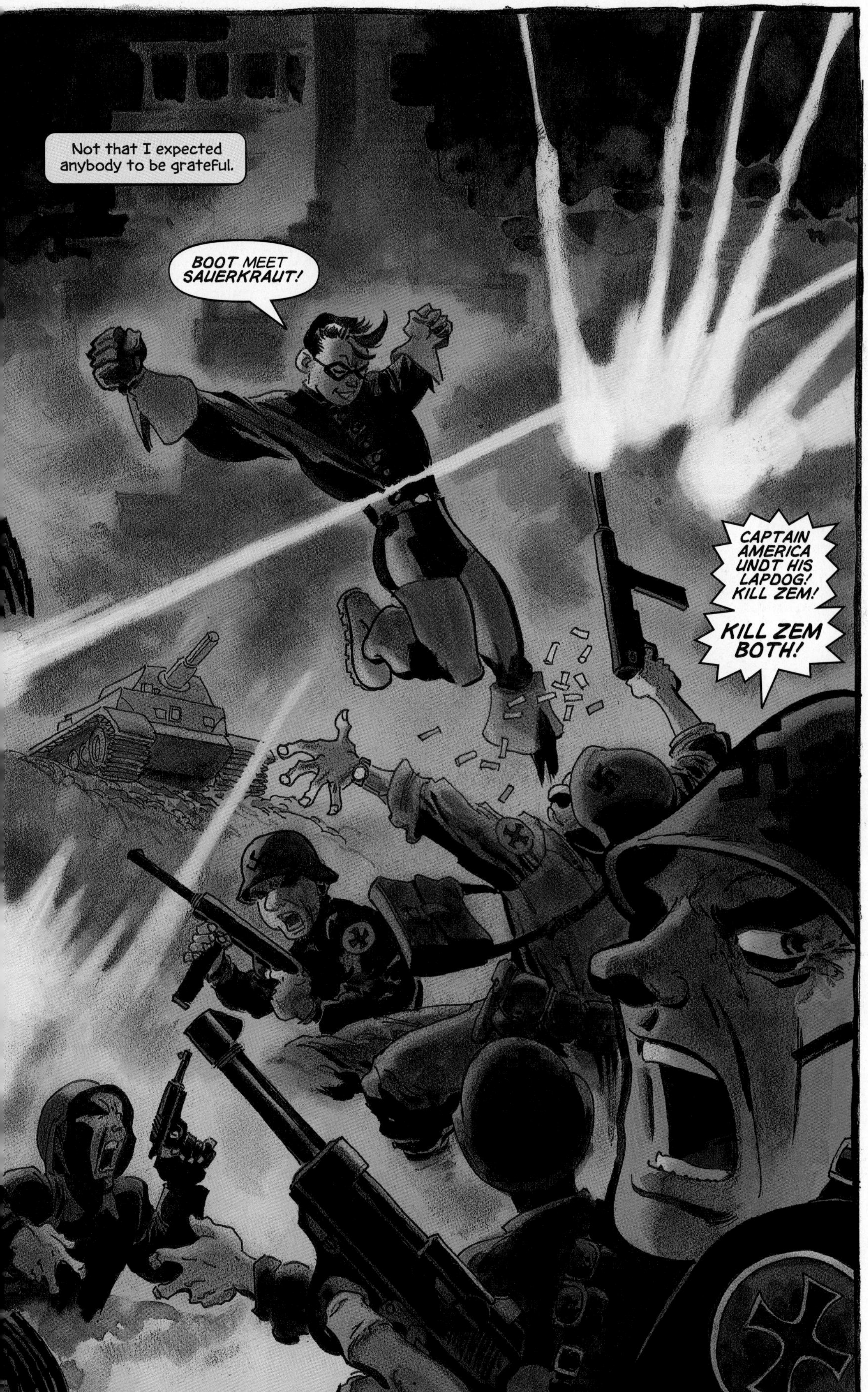
Not that I expected anybody to be grateful.
BOOT MEET SAUERKRAUT!
CAPTAIN AMERICA UNDT HIS LAPDOG! KILL ZEM!
KILL ZEM BOTH!

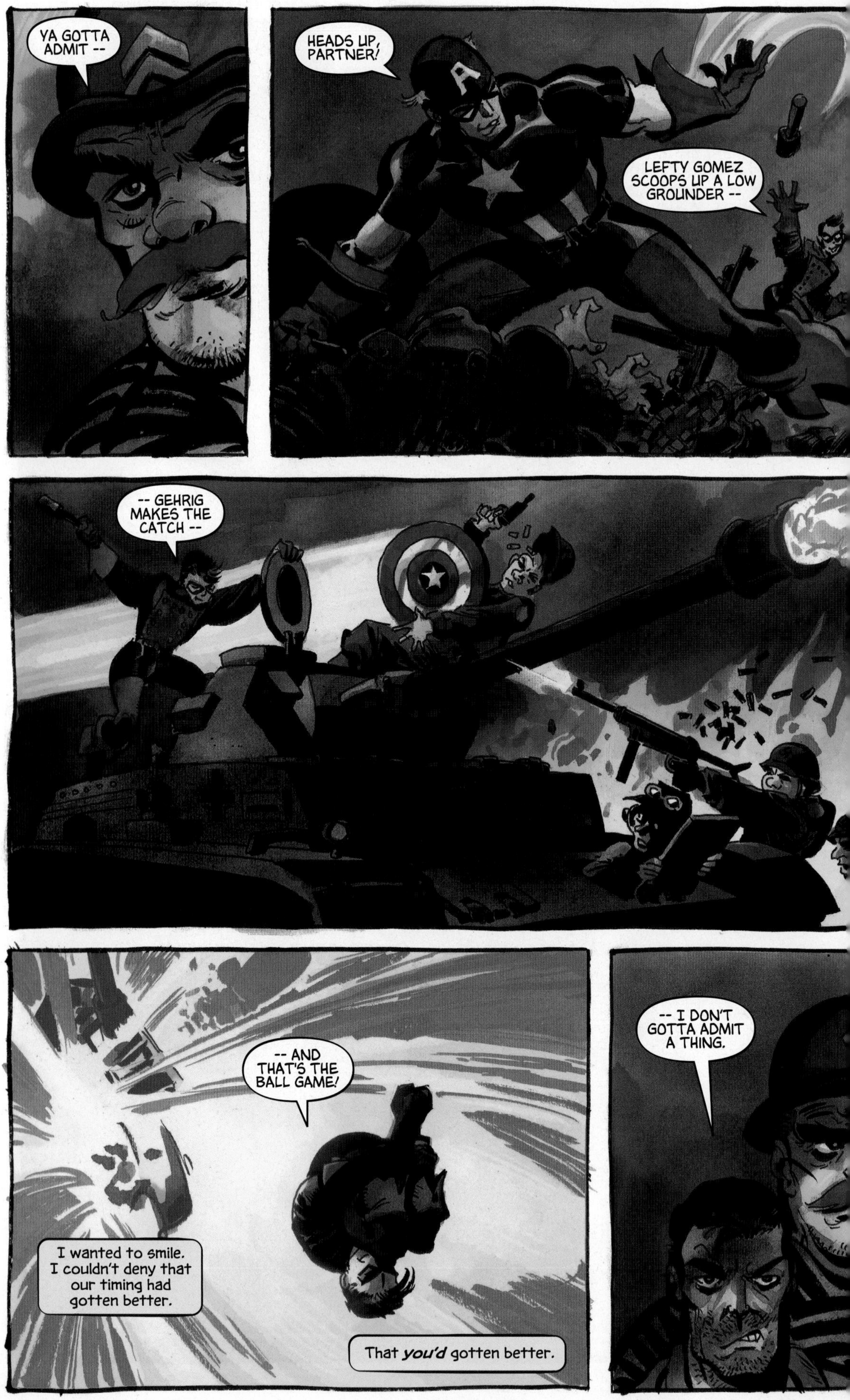
YA GOTTA ADMIT --
HEADS UP, PARTNER!
LEFTY GOMEZ SCOOPS UP A LOW GROUNDER --
-- GEHRIG MAKES THE CATCH --
-- AND THAT'S THE BALL GAME!
I wanted to smile. I couldn't deny that our timing had gotten better.
That *you'd* gotten better.
-- I DON'T GOTTA ADMIT A THING.

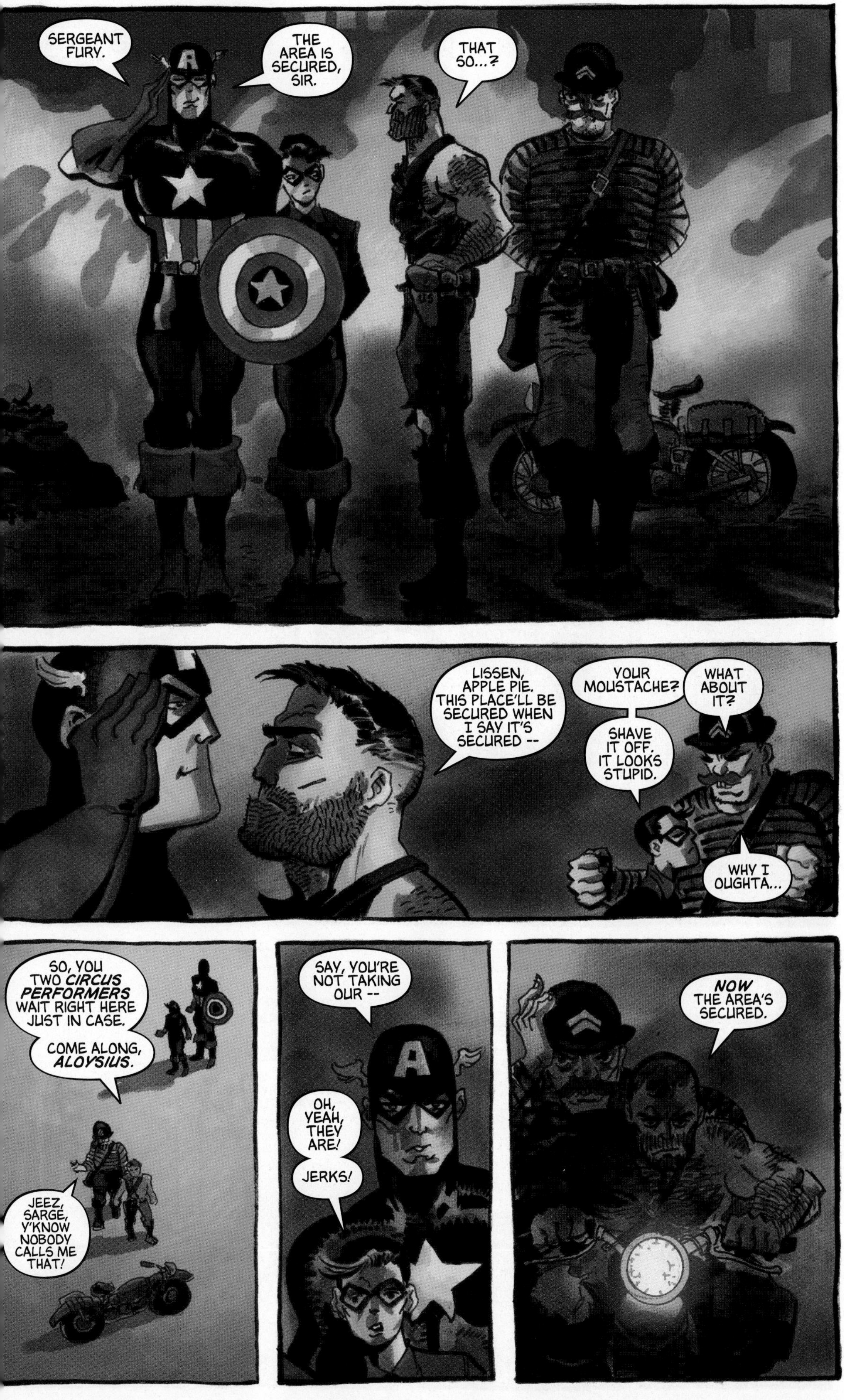
SERGEANT FURY.
THE AREA IS SECURED, SIR.
THAT SO...?
LISSEN, APPLE PIE. THIS PLACE'LL BE SECURED WHEN I SAY IT'S SECURED --
YOUR MOUSTACHE?
WHAT ABOUT IT?
SHAVE IT OFF. IT LOOKS STUPID.
WHY I OUGHTA...
SO, YOU TWO CIRCUS PERFORMERS WAIT RIGHT HERE JUST IN CASE.
COME ALONG, ALOYSIUS.
JEEZ, SARGE, Y'KNOW NOBODY CALLS ME THAT!
SAY, YOU'RE NOT TAKING OUR --
OH, YEAH, THEY ARE!
JERKS!
NOW THE AREA'S SECURED.

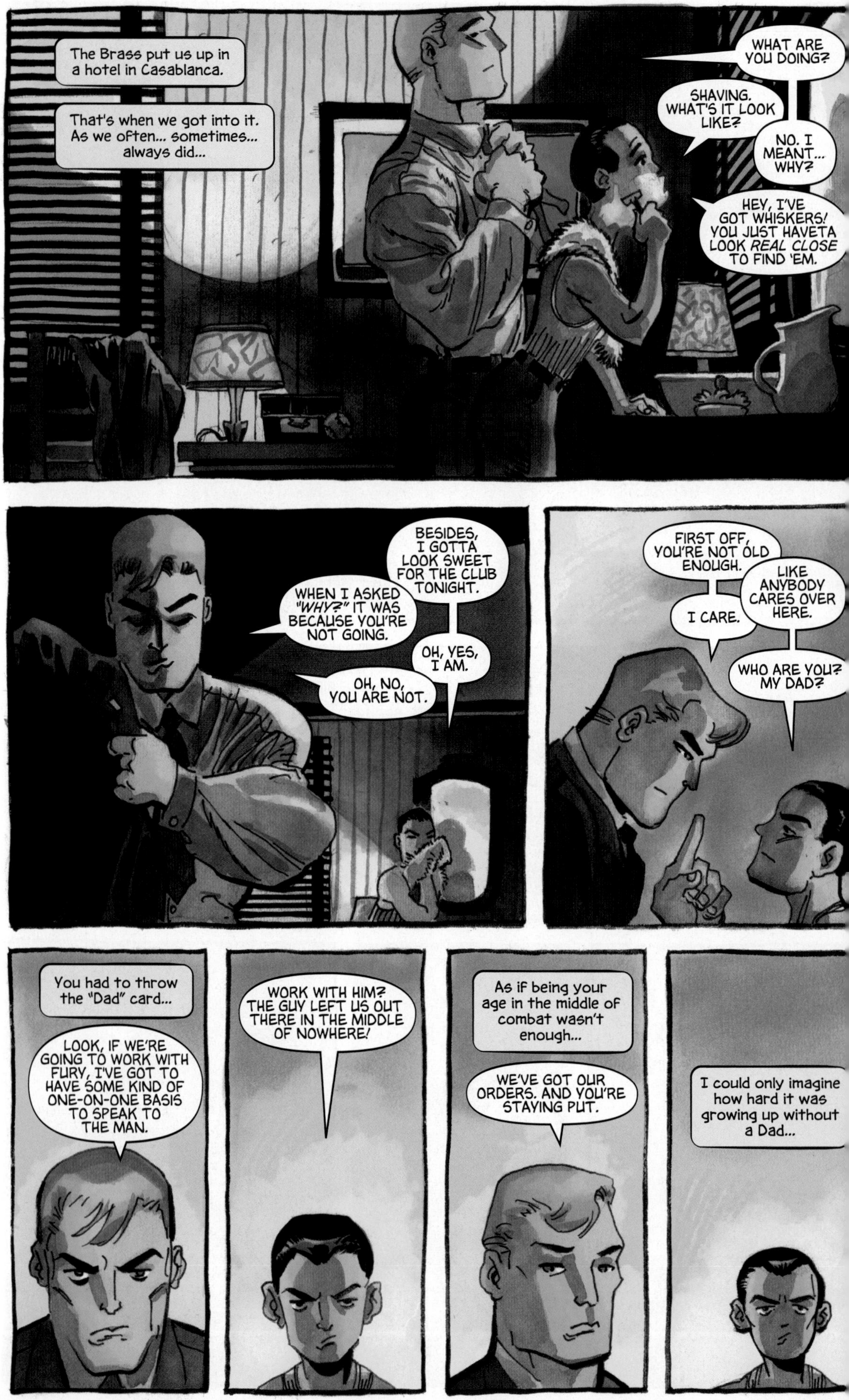

The Brass put us up in a hotel in Casablanca.
That's when we got into it. As we often... sometimes... always did...
WHAT ARE YOU DOING?
SHAVING. WHAT'S IT LOOK LIKE?
NO. I MEANT... WHY?
HEY, I'VE GOT WHISKERS! YOU JUST HAVETA LOOK *REAL CLOSE* TO FIND 'EM.
BESIDES, I GOTTA LOOK SWEET FOR THE CLUB TONIGHT.
WHEN I ASKED *"WHY?"* IT WAS BECAUSE YOU'RE NOT GOING.
OH, YES, I AM.
OH, NO, YOU ARE NOT.
FIRST OFF, YOU'RE NOT OLD ENOUGH.
LIKE ANYBODY CARES OVER HERE.
I CARE.
WHO ARE YOU? MY DAD?
You had to throw the "Dad" card...
LOOK, IF WE'RE GOING TO WORK WITH FURY, I'VE GOT TO HAVE SOME KIND OF ONE-ON-ONE BASIS TO SPEAK TO THE MAN.
WORK WITH HIM? THE GUY LEFT US OUT THERE IN THE MIDDLE OF NOWHERE!
As if being your age in the middle of combat wasn't enough...
WE'VE GOT OUR ORDERS. AND YOU'RE STAYING PUT.
I could only imagine how hard it was growing up without a Dad...

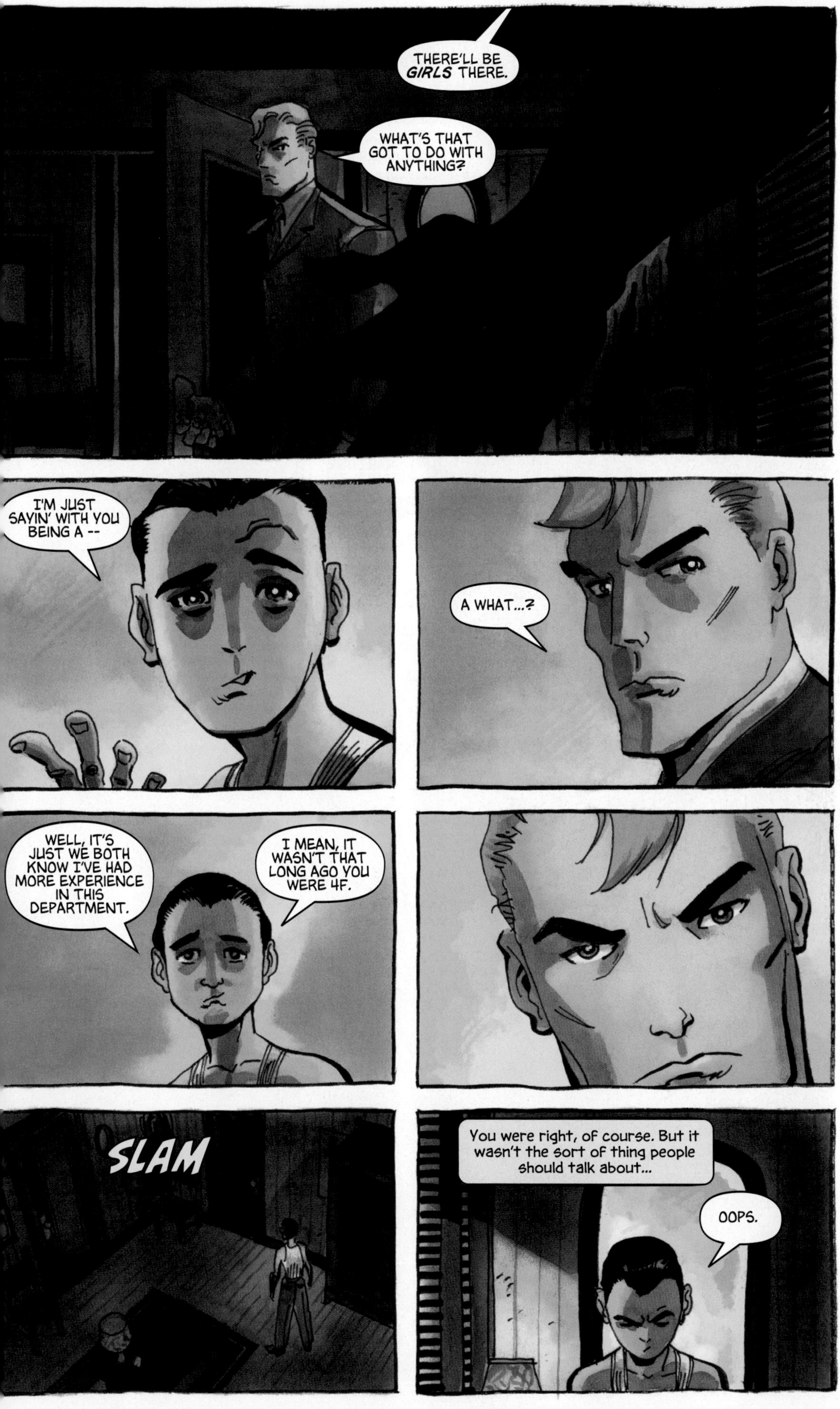
THERE'LL BE GIRLS THERE.
WHAT'S THAT GOT TO DO WITH ANYTHING?
I'M JUST SAYIN' WITH YOU BEING A --
A WHAT...?
WELL, IT'S JUST WE BOTH KNOW I'VE HAD MORE EXPERIENCE IN THIS DEPARTMENT.
I MEAN, IT WASN'T THAT LONG AGO YOU WERE 4F.
SLAM
You were right, of course. But it wasn't the sort of thing people should talk about...
OOPS.

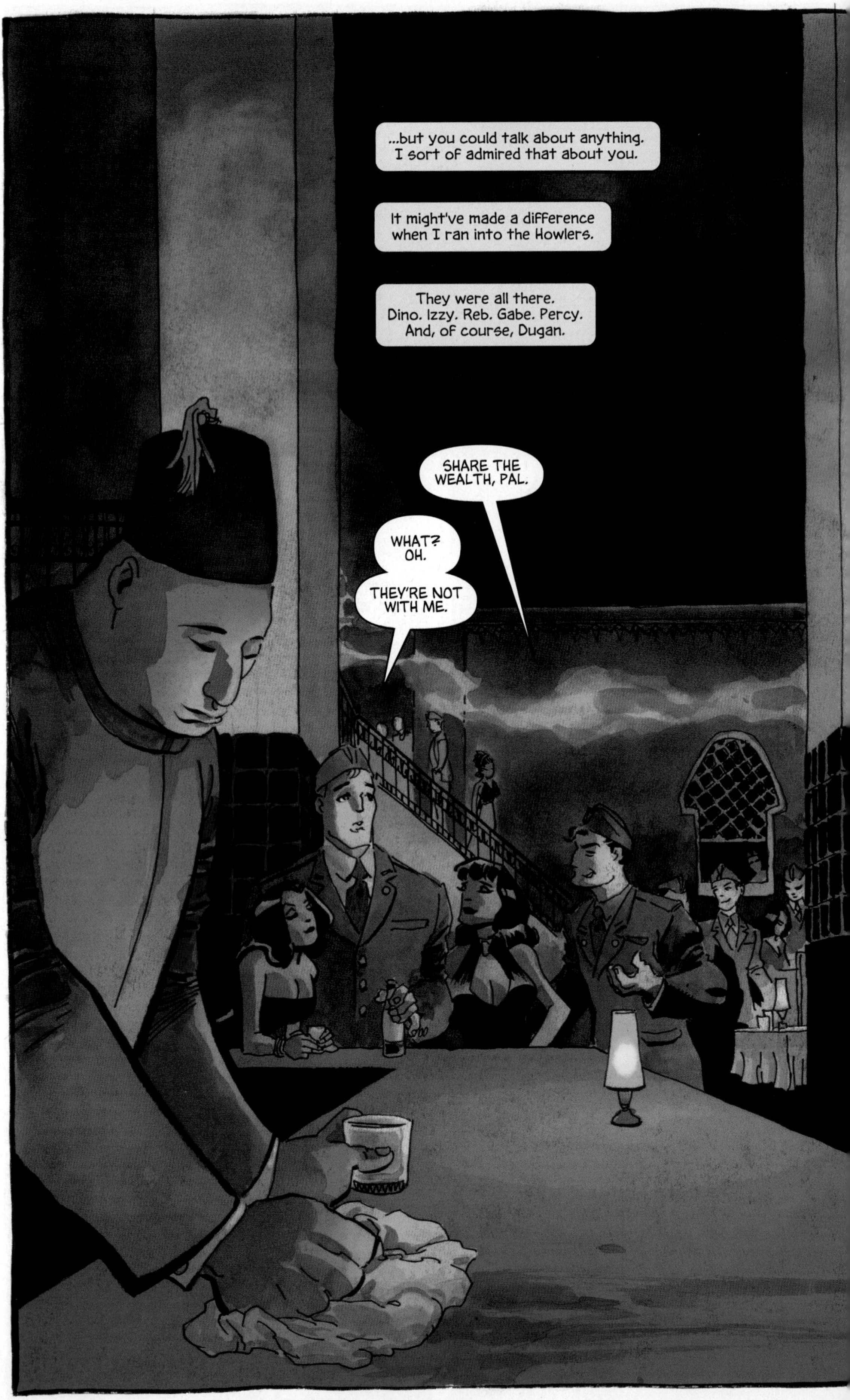
...but you could talk about anything. I sort of admired that about you.
It might've made a difference when I ran into the Howlers.
They were all there. Dino. Izzy. Reb. Gabe. Percy. And, of course, Dugan.
SHARE THE WEALTH, PAL.
WHAT? OH.
THEY'RE NOT WITH ME.

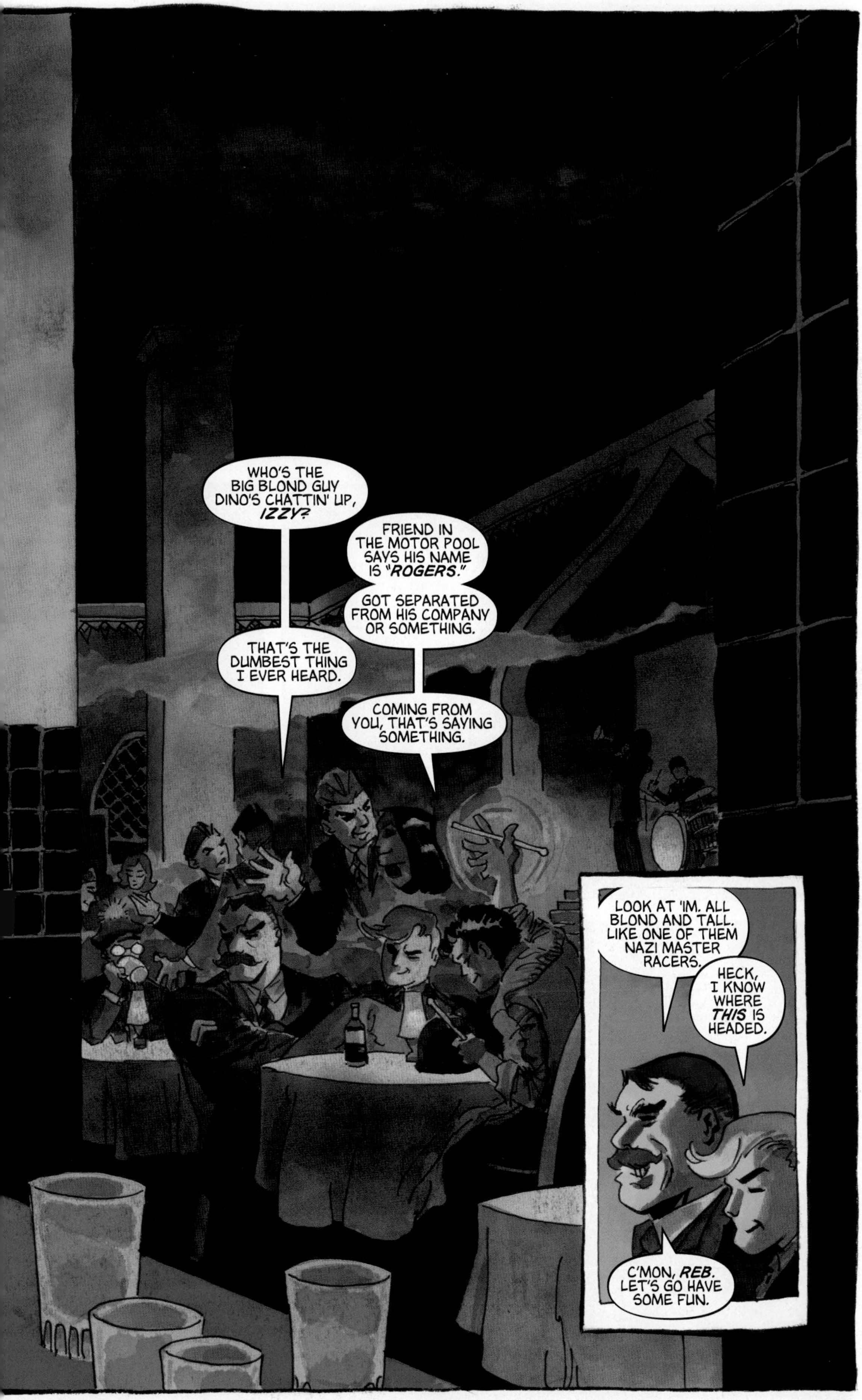
WHO'S THE BIG BLOND GUY DINO'S CHATTIN' UP, IZZY?
FRIEND IN THE MOTOR POOL SAYS HIS NAME IS "ROGERS."
GOT SEPARATED FROM HIS COMPANY OR SOMETHING.
THAT'S THE DUMBEST THING I EVER HEARD.
COMING FROM YOU, THAT'S SAYING SOMETHING.
LOOK AT 'IM. ALL BLOND AND TALL. LIKE ONE OF THEM NAZI MASTER RACERS.
HECK, I KNOW WHERE THIS IS HEADED.
C'MON, REB. LET'S GO HAVE SOME FUN.

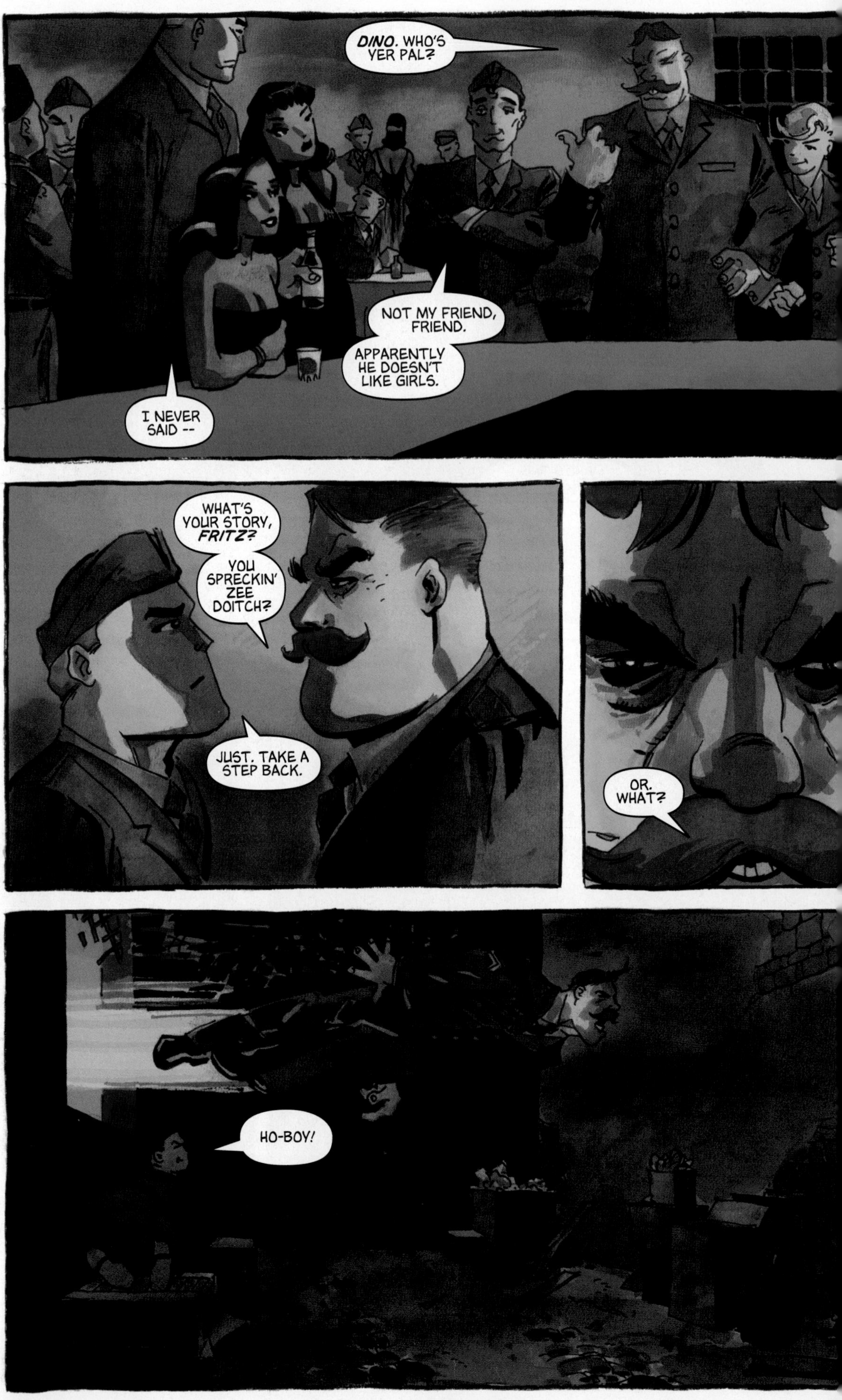
DINO. WHO'S YER PAL?
NOT MY FRIEND, FRIEND.
APPARENTLY HE DOESN'T LIKE GIRLS.
I NEVER SAID --
WHAT'S YOUR STORY, FRITZ?
YOU SPRECKIN' ZEE DOITCH?
JUST. TAKE A STEP BACK.
OR. WHAT?
HO-BOY!

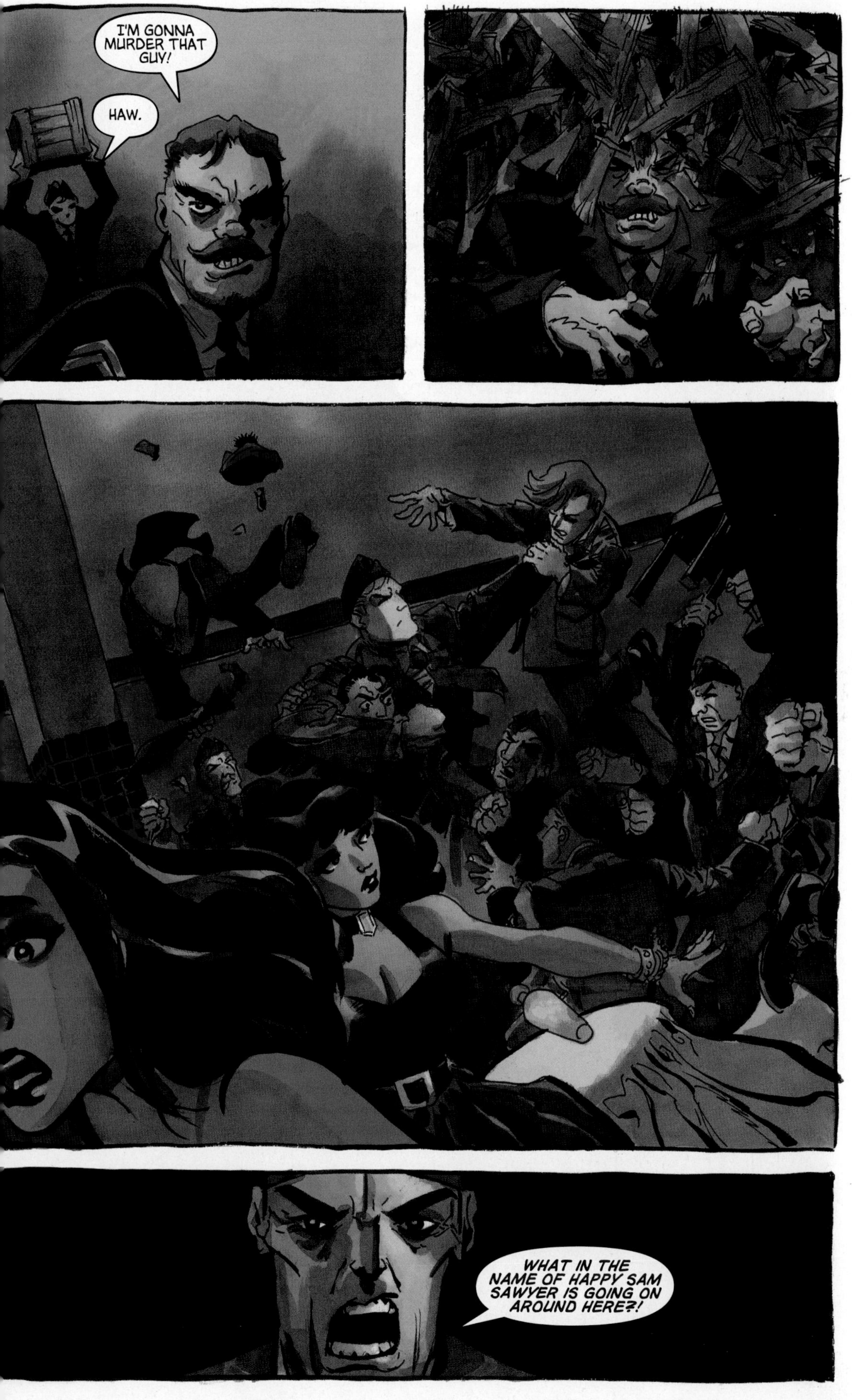

I'M GONNA MURDER THAT GUY!
HAW.
WHAT IN THE NAME OF HAPPY SAM SAWYER IS GOING ON AROUND HERE?!

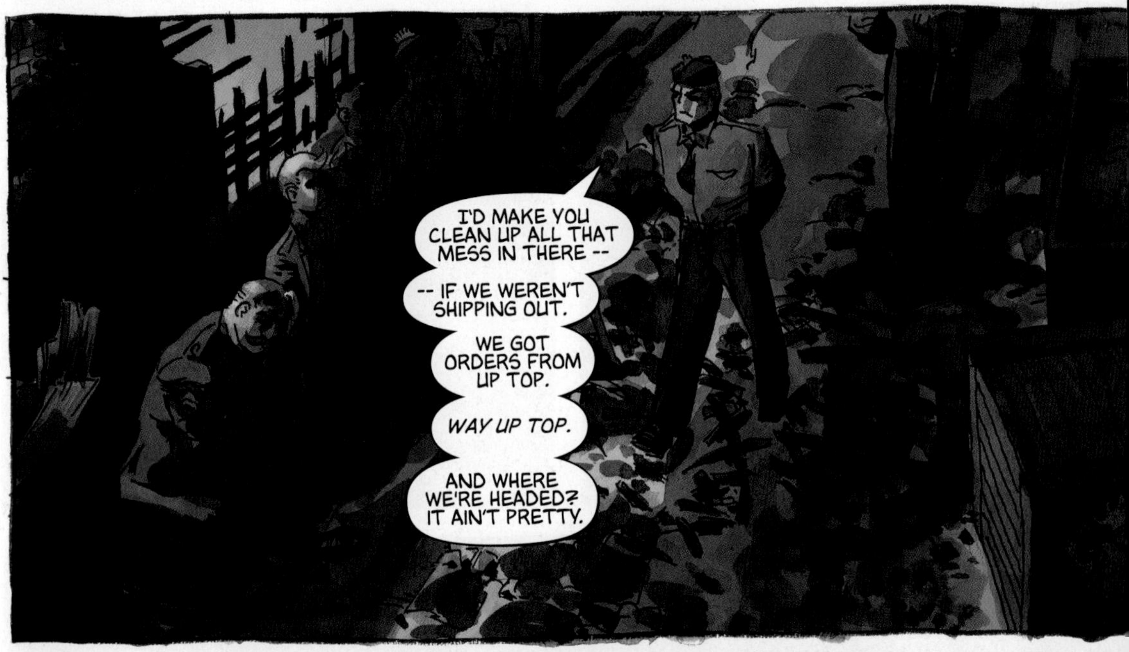
I'D MAKE YOU CLEAN UP ALL THAT MESS IN THERE --
-- IF WE WEREN'T SHIPPING OUT.
WE GOT ORDERS FROM UP TOP.
WAY UP TOP.
AND WHERE WE'RE HEADED? IT AIN'T PRETTY.

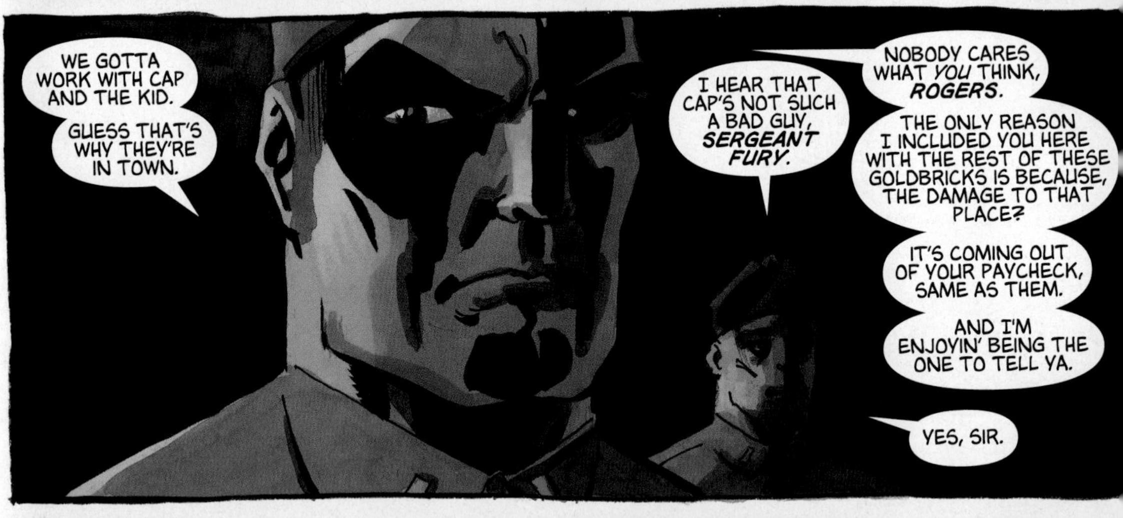
WE GOTTA WORK WITH CAP AND THE KID.
GUESS THAT'S WHY THEY'RE IN TOWN.
I HEAR THAT CAP'S NOT SUCH A BAD GUY, SERGEANT FURY.
NOBODY CARES WHAT YOU THINK, ROGERS.
THE ONLY REASON I INCLUDED YOU HERE WITH THE REST OF THESE GOLDBRICKS IS BECAUSE, THE DAMAGE TO THAT PLACE?
IT'S COMING OUT OF YOUR PAYCHECK, SAME AS THEM.
AND I'M ENJOYIN' BEING THE ONE TO TELL YA.
YES, SIR.

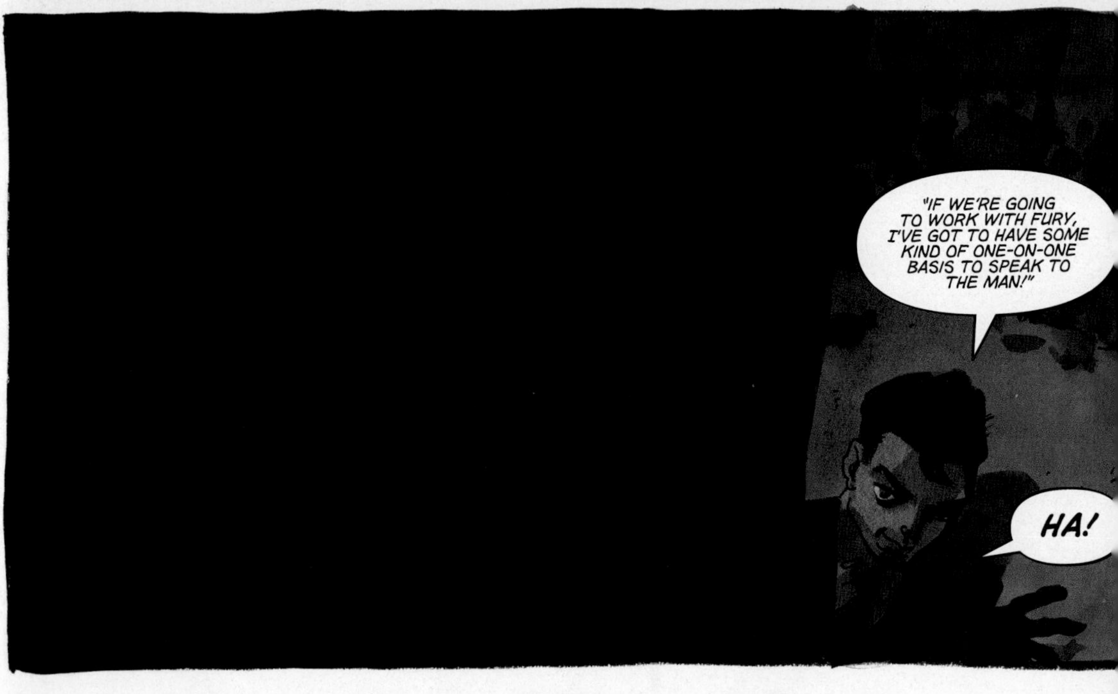
"IF WE'RE GOING TO WORK WITH FURY, I'VE GOT TO HAVE SOME KIND OF ONE-ON-ONE BASIS TO SPEAK TO THE MAN!"
HA!

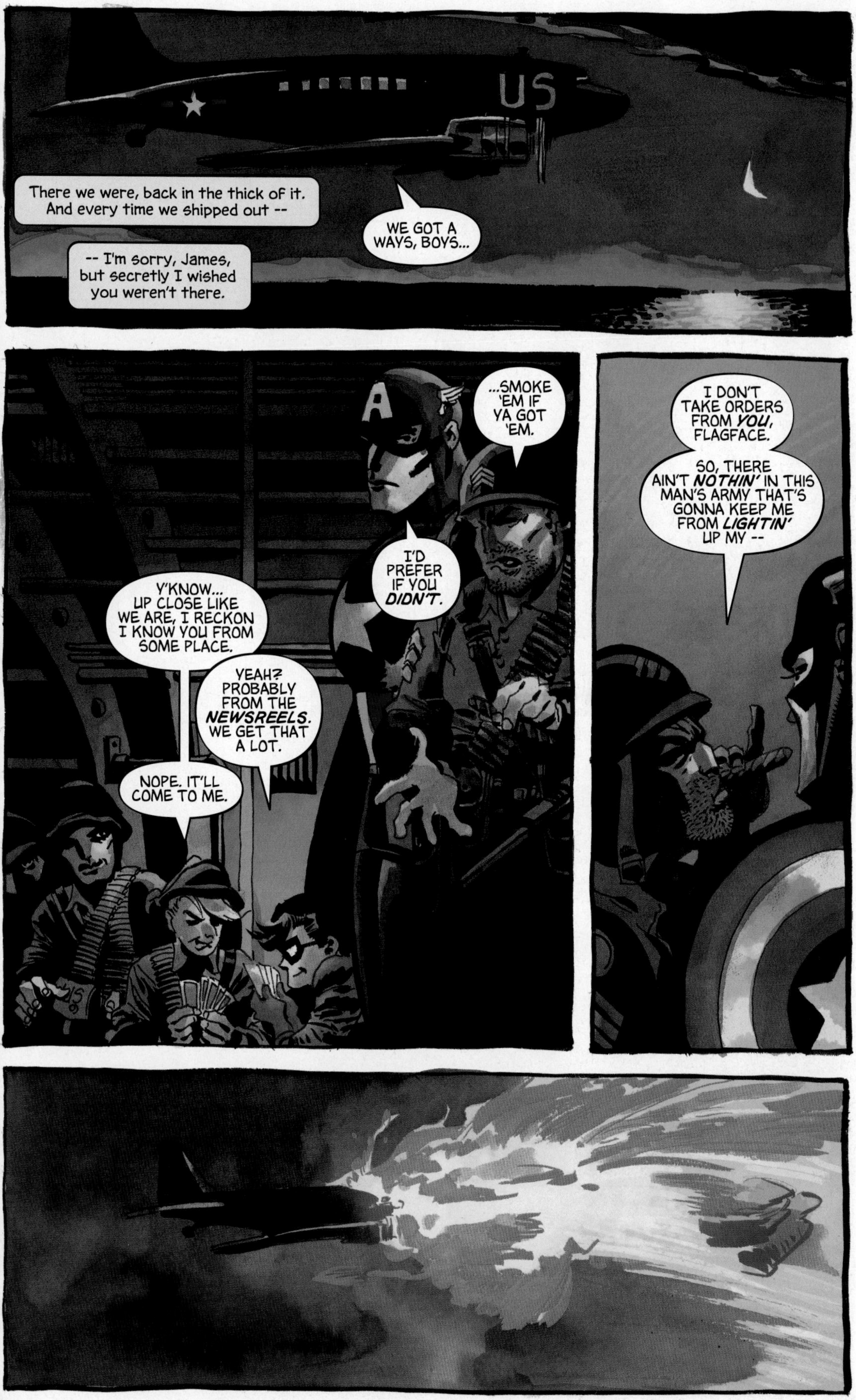
US
There we were, back in the thick of it. And every time we shipped out --
-- I'm sorry, James, but secretly I wished you weren't there.
WE GOT A WAYS, BOYS...
...SMOKE 'EM IF YA GOT 'EM.
I'D PREFER IF YOU DIDN'T.
Y'KNOW... UP CLOSE LIKE WE ARE, I RECKON I KNOW YOU FROM SOME PLACE.
YEAH? PROBABLY FROM THE NEWSREELS. WE GET THAT A LOT.
NOPE. IT'LL COME TO ME.
I DON'T TAKE ORDERS FROM YOU, FLAGFACE.
SO, THERE AIN'T NOTHIN' IN THIS MAN'S ARMY THAT'S GONNA KEEP ME FROM LIGHTIN' UP MY --

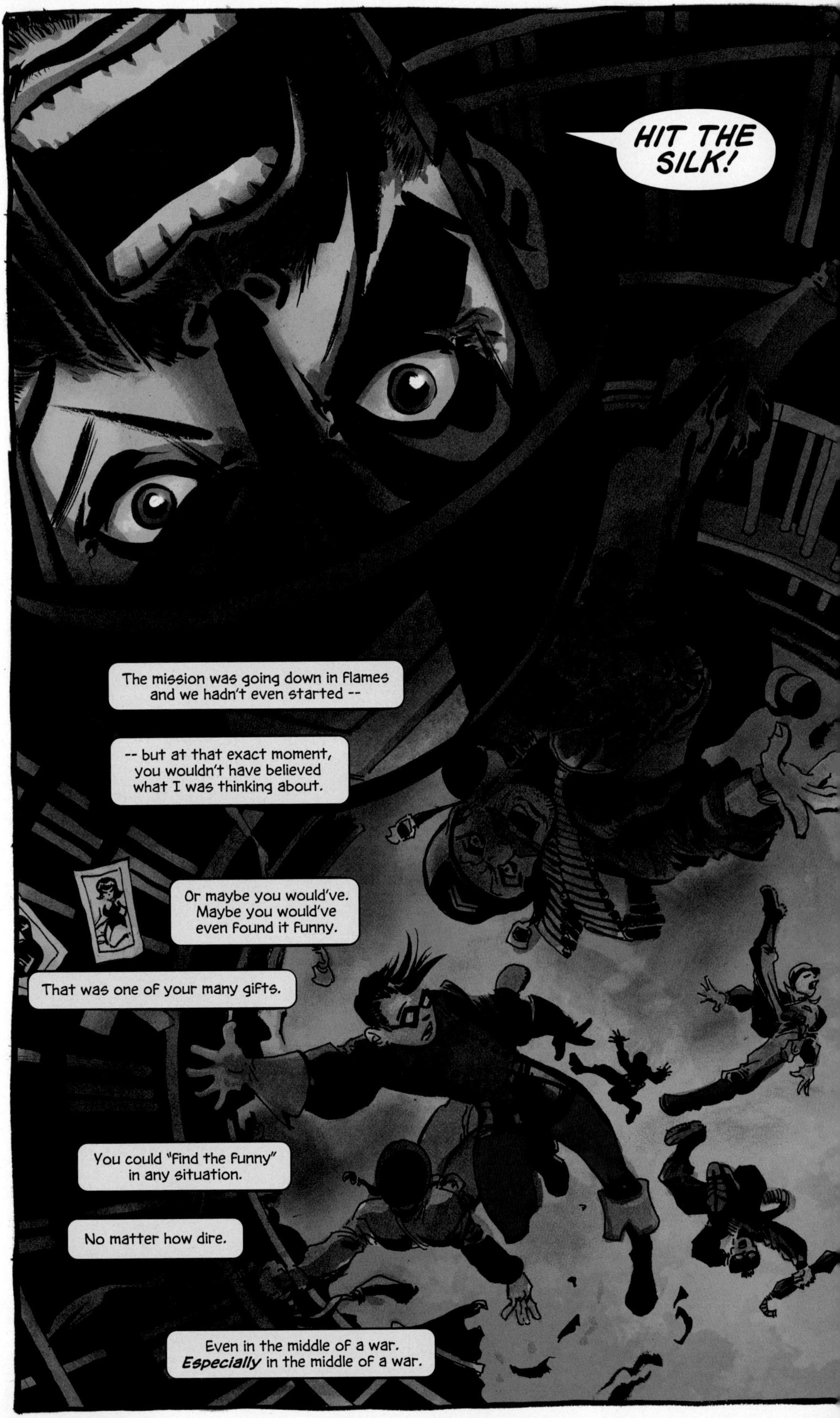
HIT THE SILK!
The mission was going down in flames and we hadn't even started --
-- but at that exact moment, you wouldn't have believed what I was thinking about.
Or maybe you would've. Maybe you would've even found it funny.
That was one of your many gifts.
You could "find the funny" in any situation.
No matter how dire.
Even in the middle of a war. *Especially* in the middle of a war.

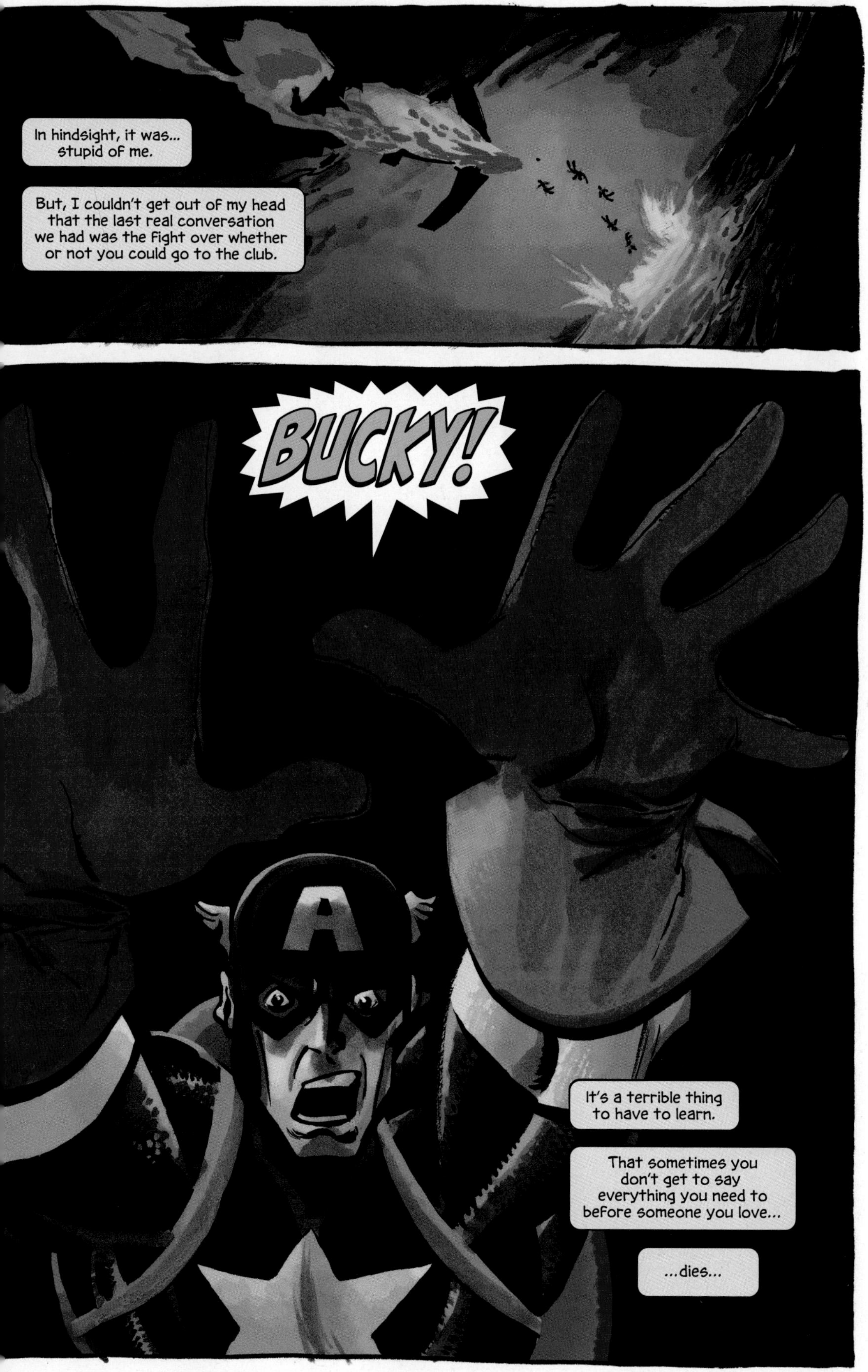
In hindsight, it was... stupid of me.
But, I couldn't get out of my head that the last real conversation we had was the fight over whether or not you could go to the club.
BUCKY!
It's a terrible thing to have to learn.
That sometimes you don't get to say everything you need to before someone you love...
...dies...

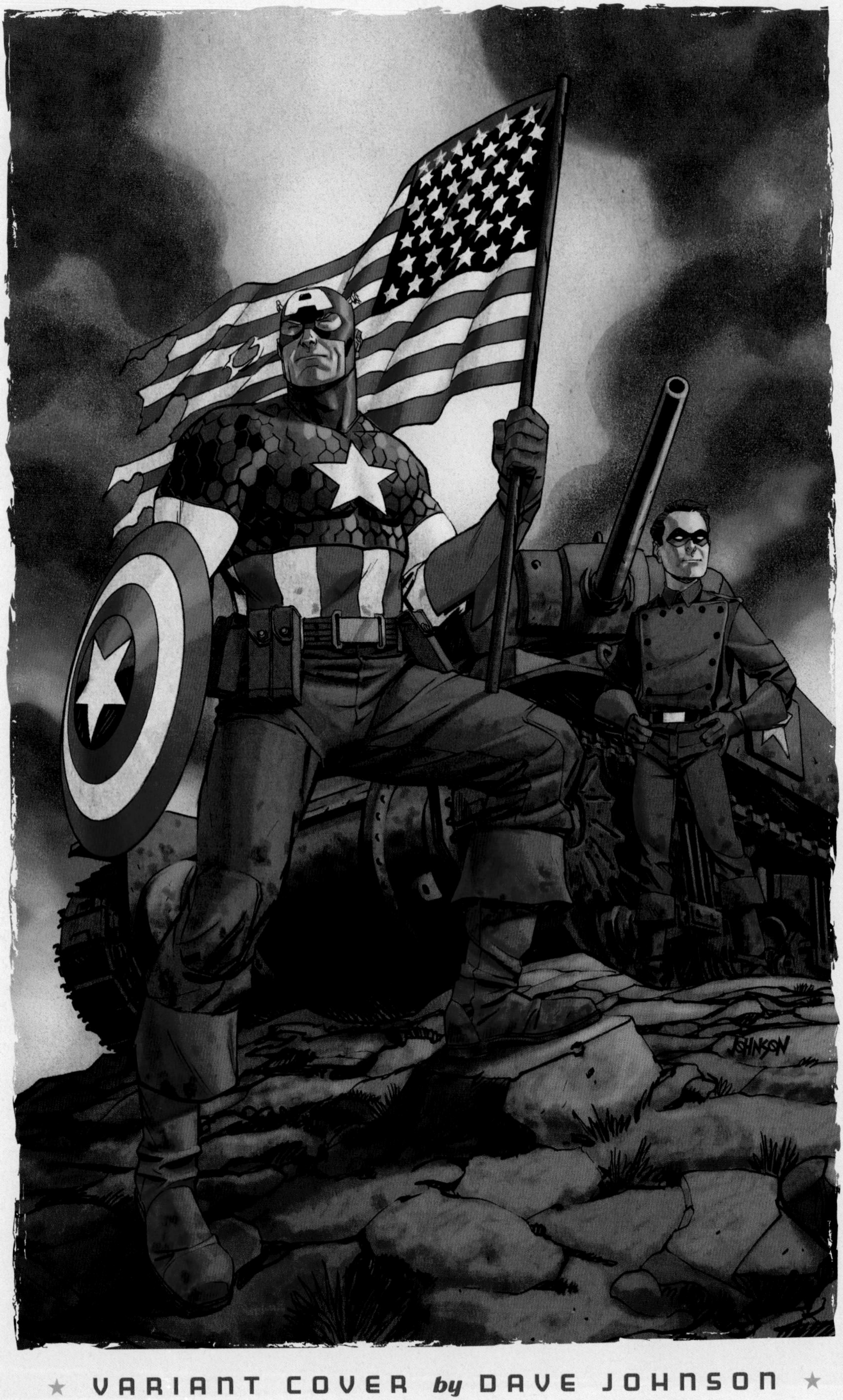

★ VARIANT COVER *by* DAVE JOHNSON ★

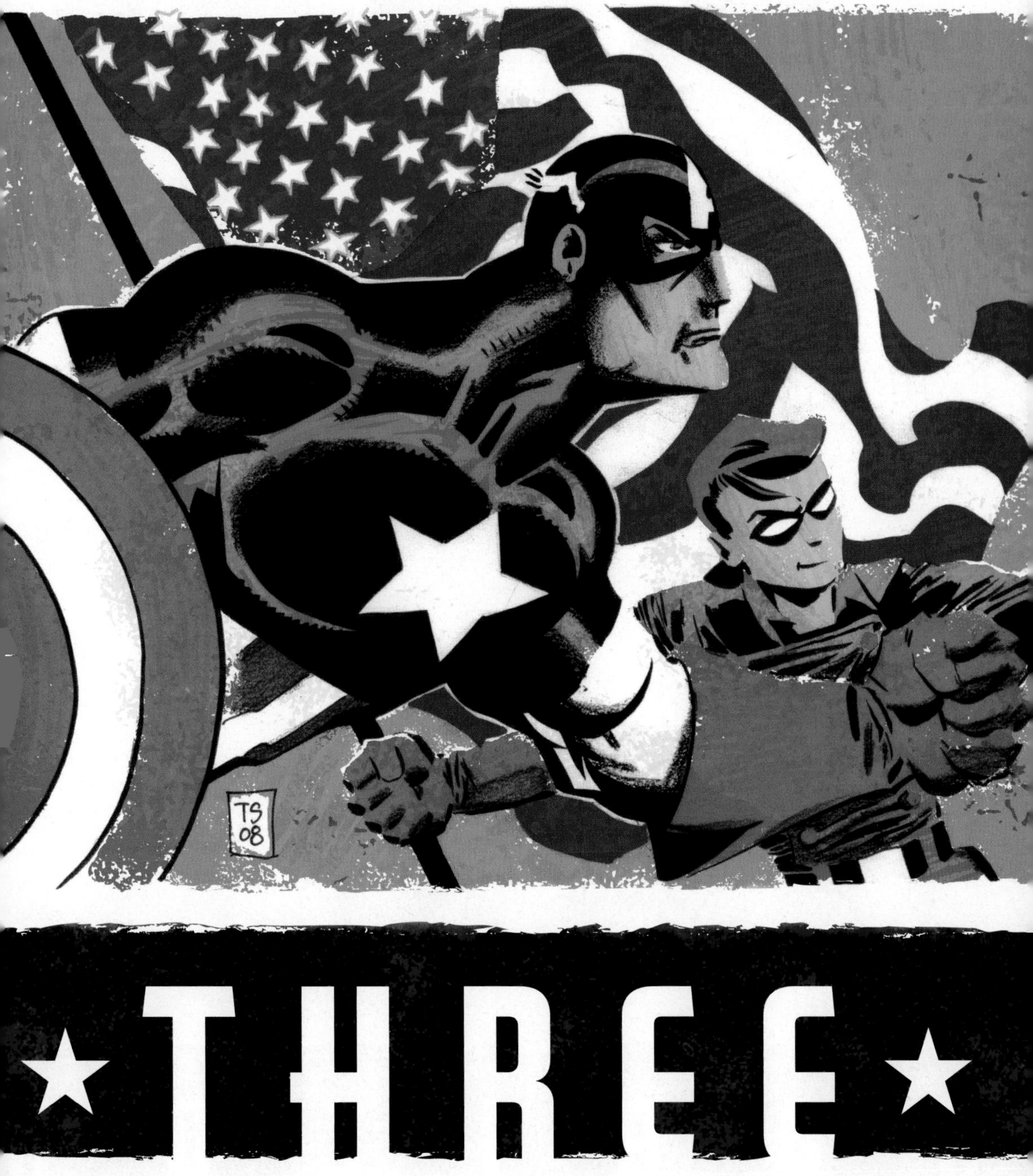
TS
08

★ THREE ★

LOST

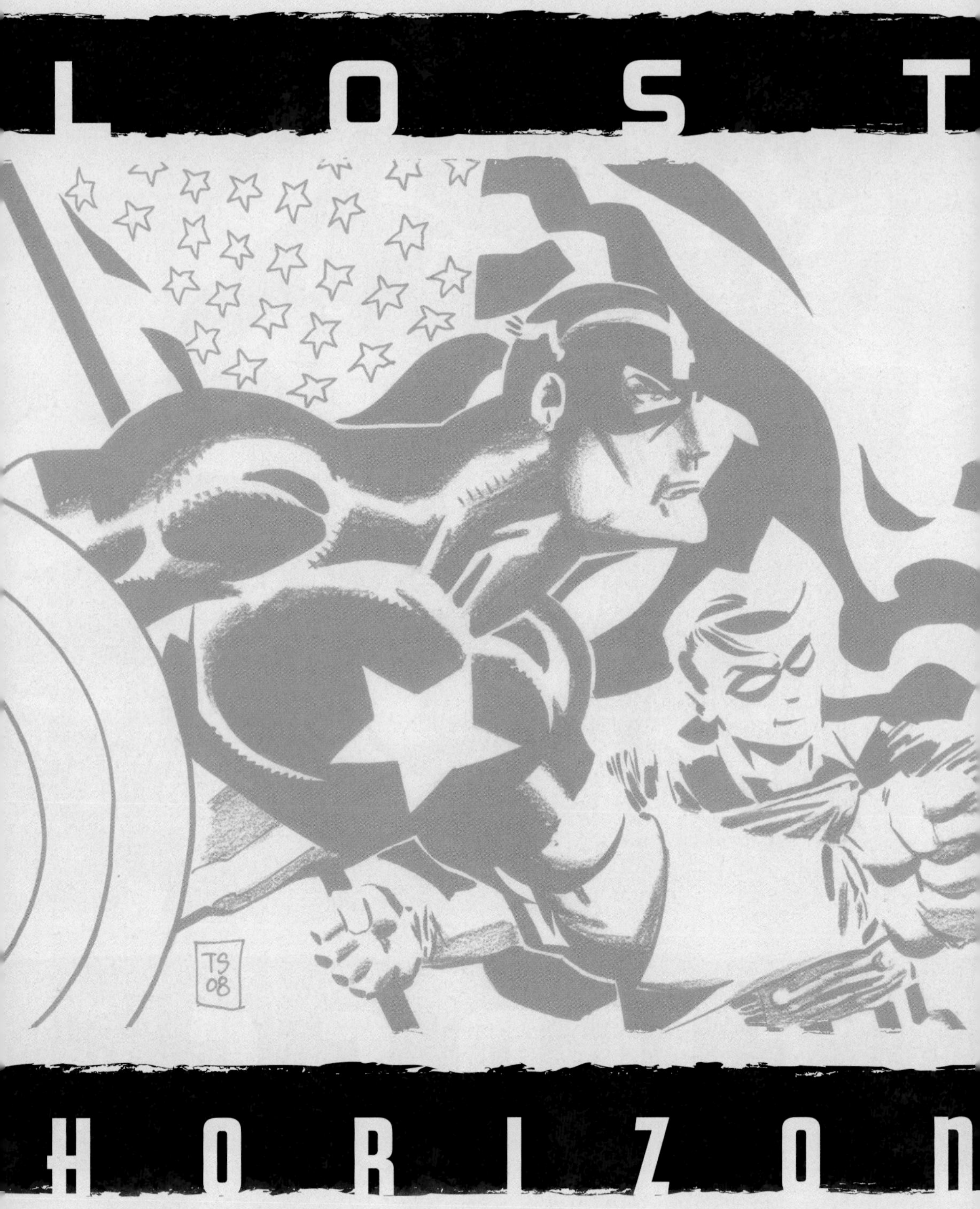

HORIZON

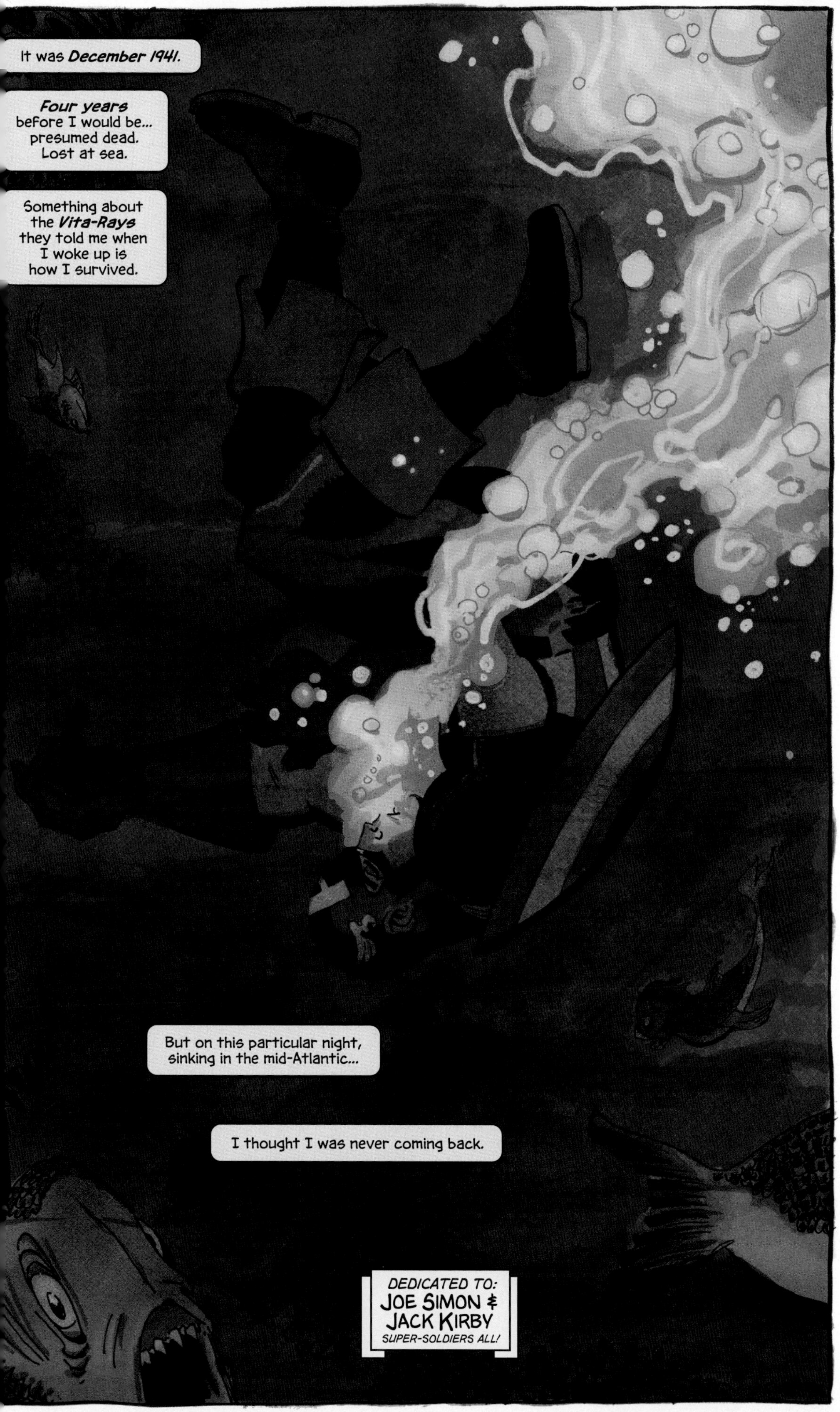
It was December 1941.
Four years before I would be... presumed dead. Lost at sea.
Something about the Vita-Rays they told me when I woke up is how I survived.
But on this particular night, sinking in the mid-Atlantic...
I thought I was never coming back.
DEDICATED TO: JOE SIMON & JACK KIRBY SUPER-SOLDIERS ALL!

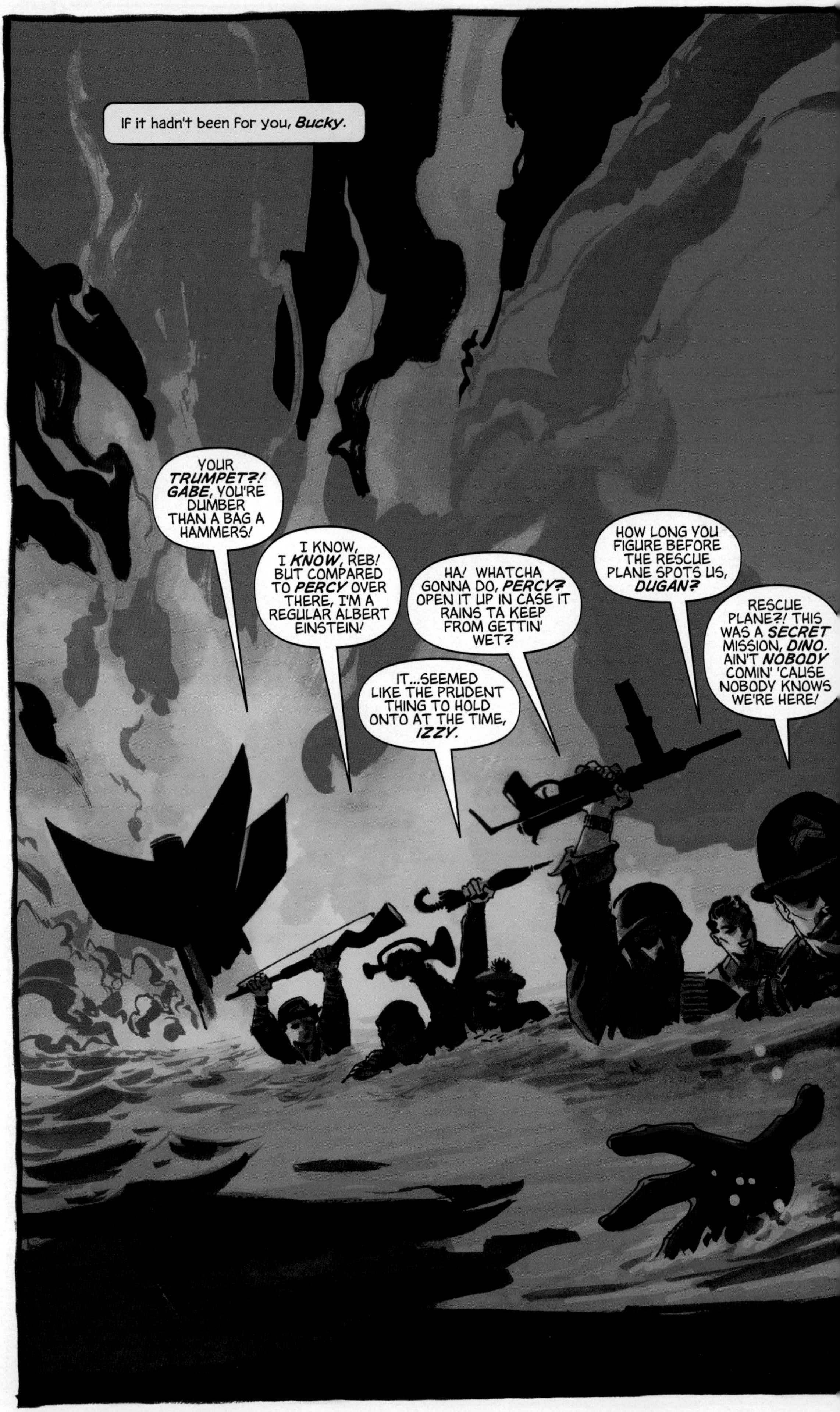
If it hadn't been for you, Bucky.
YOUR TRUMPET?! GABE, YOU'RE DUMBER THAN A BAG A HAMMERS!
I KNOW, I KNOW, REB! BUT COMPARED TO PERCY OVER THERE, I'M A REGULAR ALBERT EINSTEIN!
HA! WHATCHA GONNA DO, PERCY? OPEN IT UP IN CASE IT RAINS TA KEEP FROM GETTIN' WET?
IT...SEEMED LIKE THE PRUDENT THING TO HOLD ONTO AT THE TIME, IZZY.
HOW LONG YOU FIGURE BEFORE THE RESCUE PLANE SPOTS US, DUGAN?
RESCUE PLANE?! THIS WAS A SECRET MISSION, DINO. AIN'T NOBODY COMIN' 'CAUSE NOBODY KNOWS WE'RE HERE!

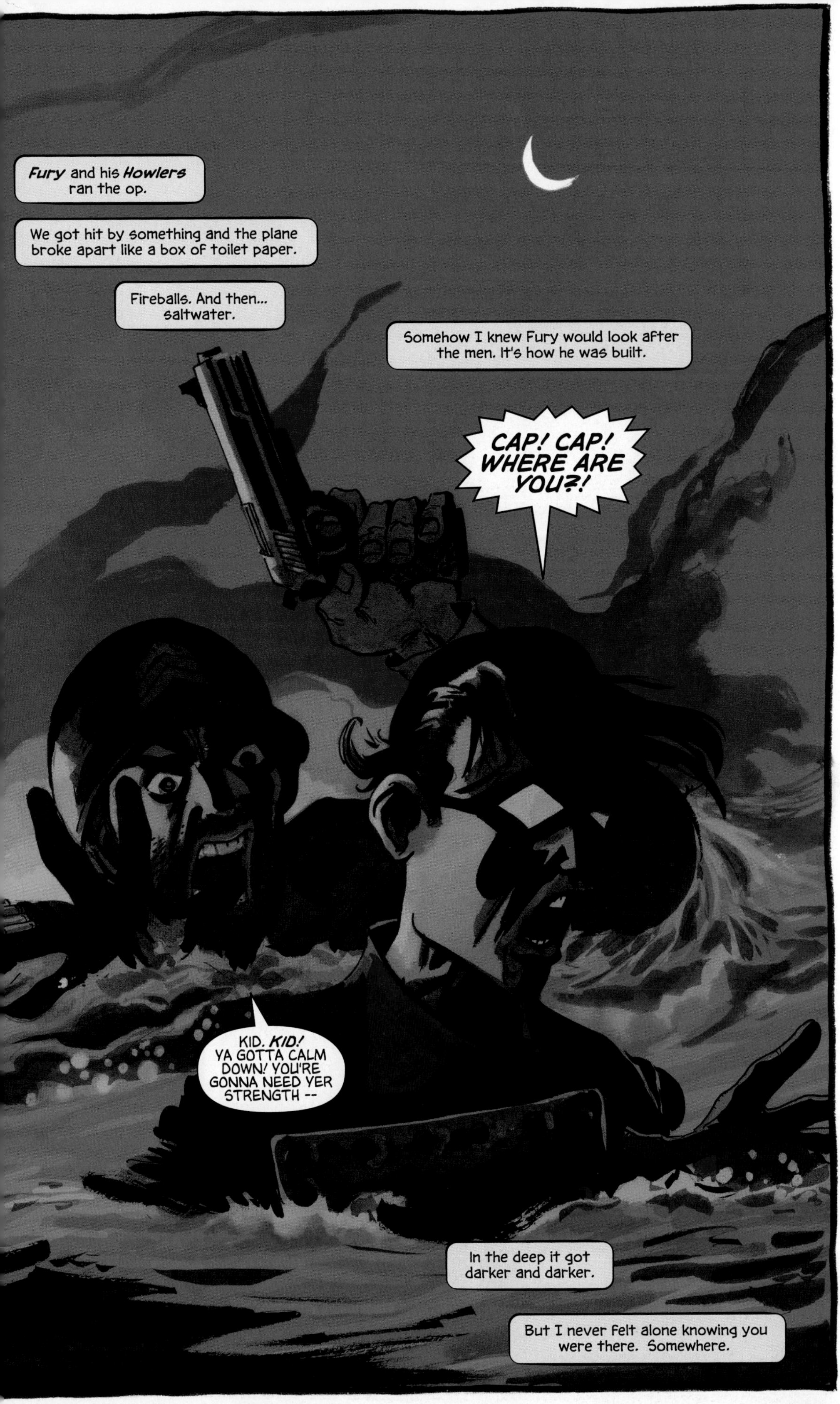
Fury and his *Howlers* ran the op.
We got hit by something and the plane broke apart like a box of toilet paper.
Fireballs. And then... saltwater.
Somehow I knew Fury would look after the men. It's how he was built.
CAP! CAP! WHERE ARE YOU?!
KID. *KID!* YA GOTTA CALM DOWN! YOU'RE GONNA NEED YER STRENGTH --
In the deep it got darker and darker.
But I never felt alone knowing you were there. Somewhere.

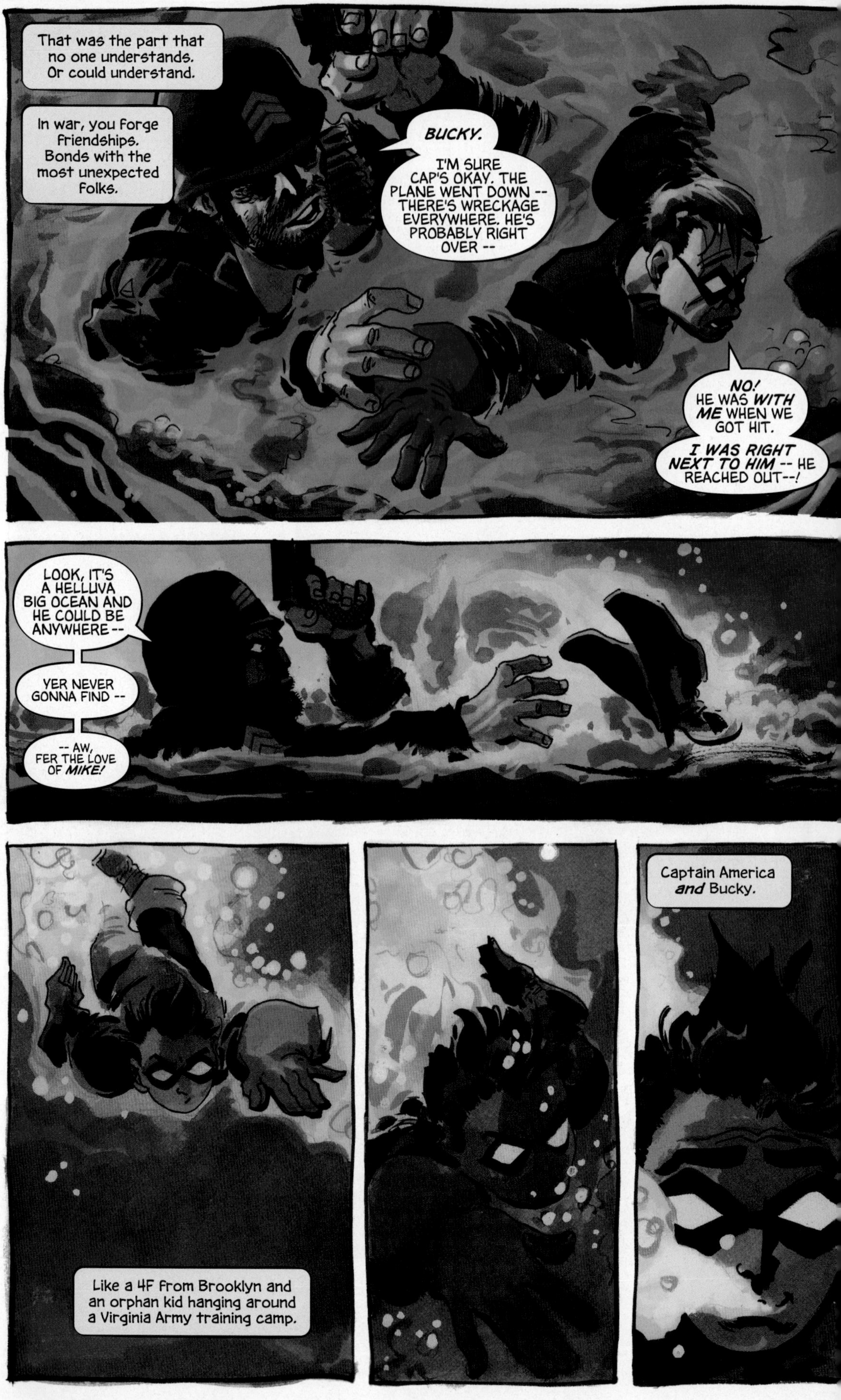
That was the part that no one understands. Or could understand.
In war, you forge friendships. Bonds with the most unexpected folks.
BUCKY.
I'M SURE CAP'S OKAY. THE PLANE WENT DOWN -- THERE'S WRECKAGE EVERYWHERE. HE'S PROBABLY RIGHT OVER --
NO! HE WAS WITH ME WHEN WE GOT HIT.
I WAS RIGHT NEXT TO HIM -- HE REACHED OUT--!
LOOK, IT'S A HELLUVA BIG OCEAN AND HE COULD BE ANYWHERE --
YER NEVER GONNA FIND --
-- AW, FER THE LOVE OF MIKE!
Like a 4F from Brooklyn and an orphan kid hanging around a Virginia Army training camp.
Captain America and Bucky.

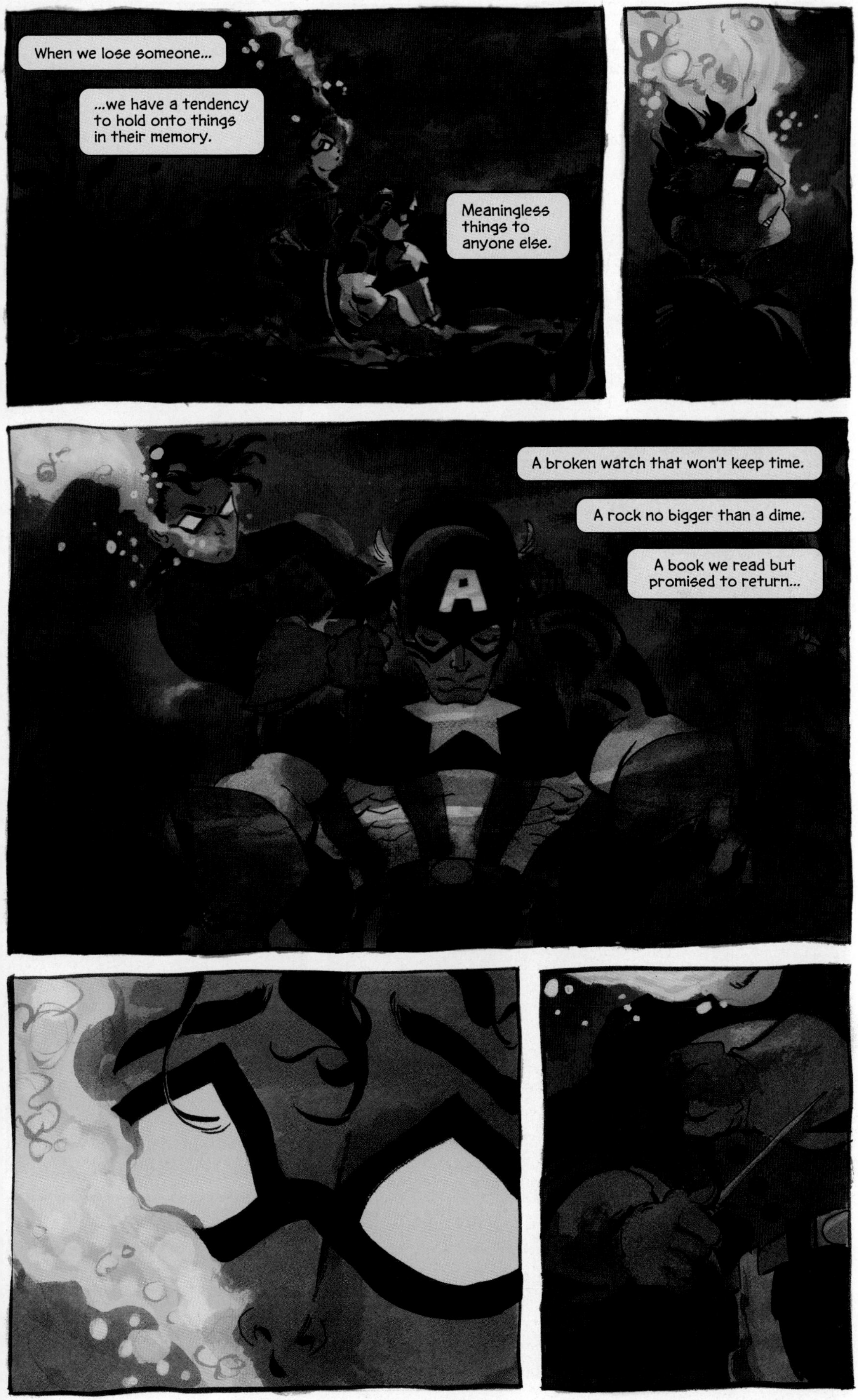
When we lose someone...
...we have a tendency to hold onto things in their memory.
Meaningless things to anyone else.
A broken watch that won't keep time.
A rock no bigger than a dime.
A book we read but promised to return...

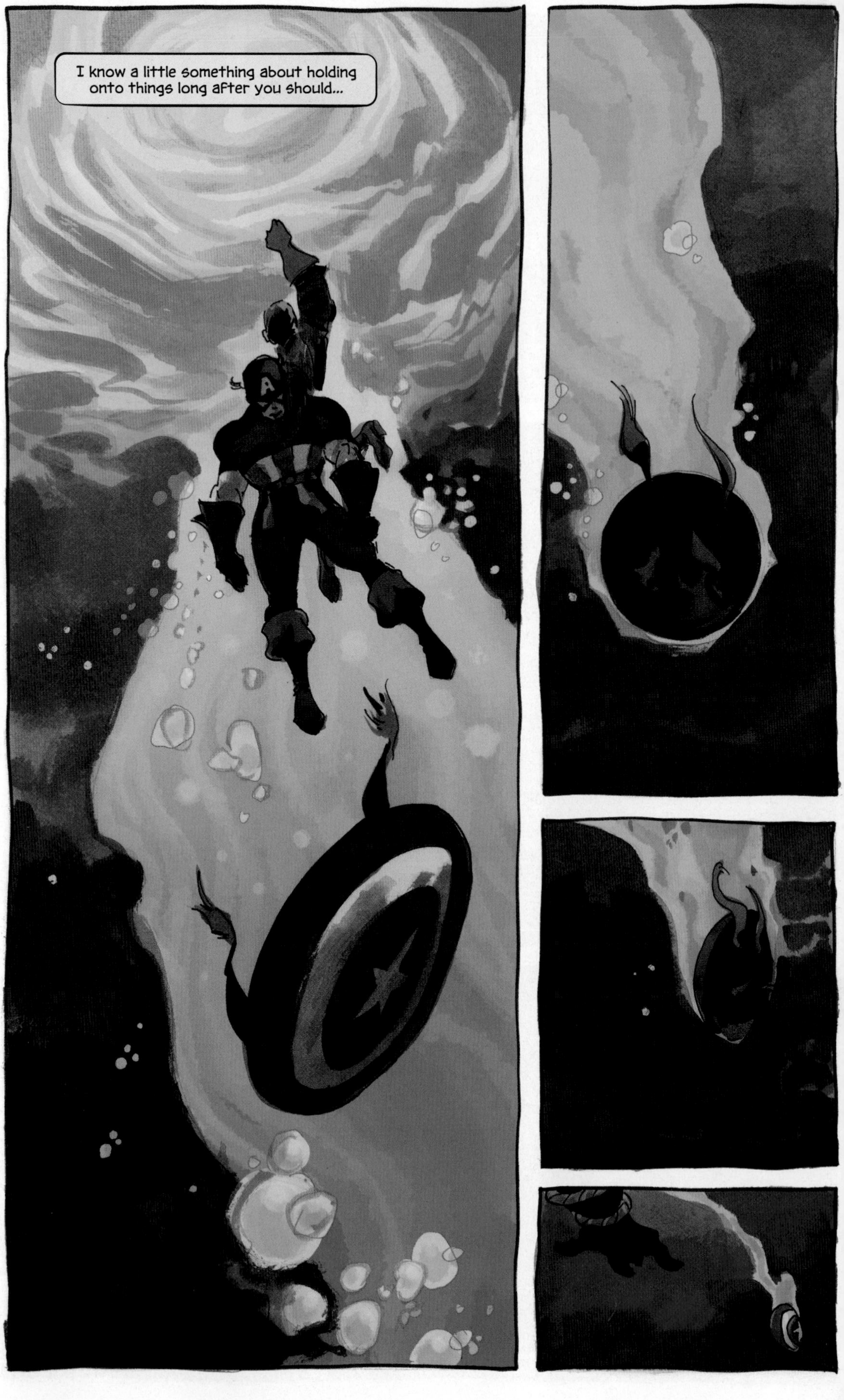
I know a little something about holding onto things long after you should...

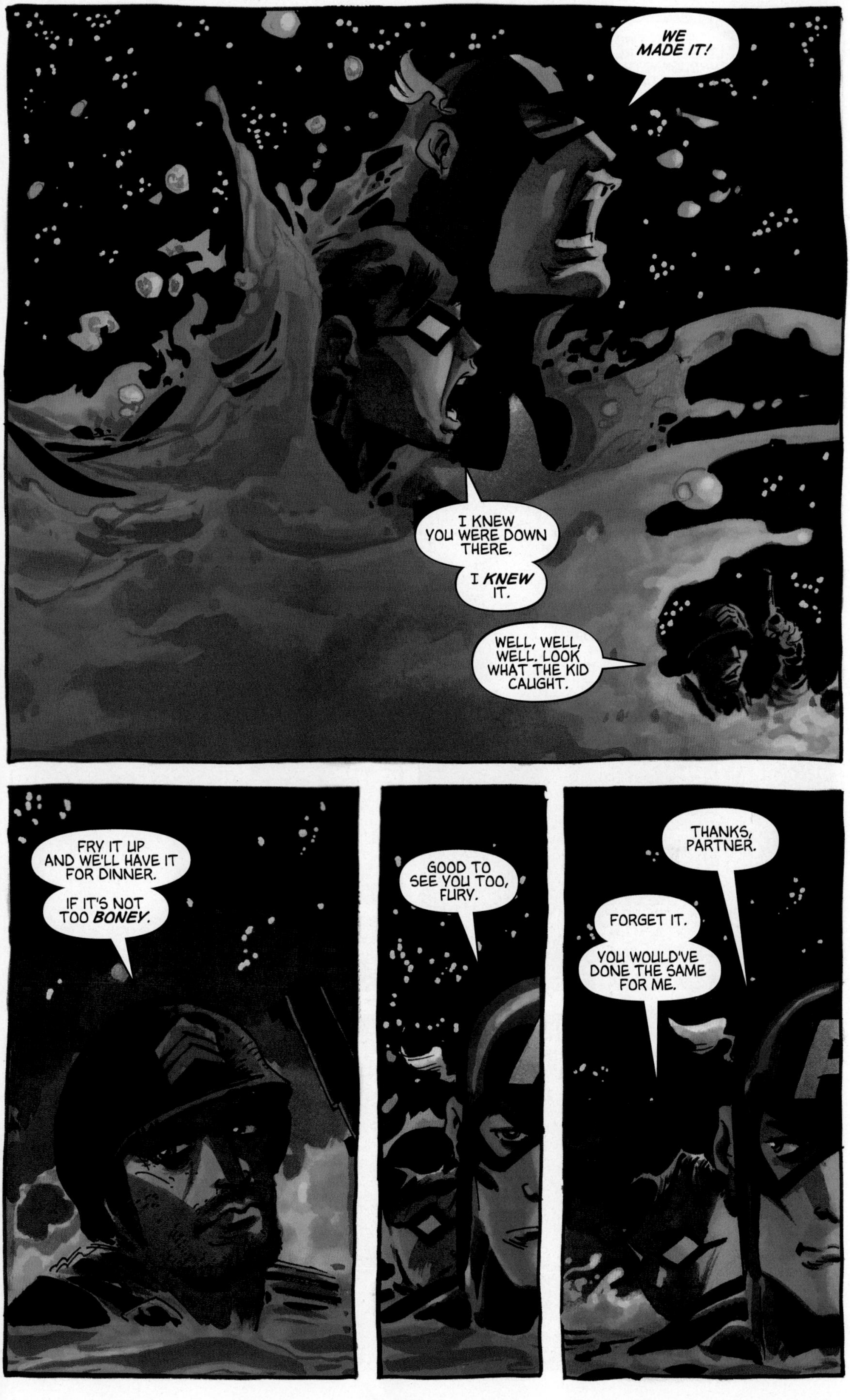
WE MADE IT!
I KNEW YOU WERE DOWN THERE.
I KNEW IT.
WELL, WELL, WELL. LOOK WHAT THE KID CAUGHT.
FRY IT UP AND WE'LL HAVE IT FOR DINNER.
IF IT'S NOT TOO BONEY.
GOOD TO SEE YOU TOO, FURY.
THANKS, PARTNER.
FORGET IT.
YOU WOULD'VE DONE THE SAME FOR ME.

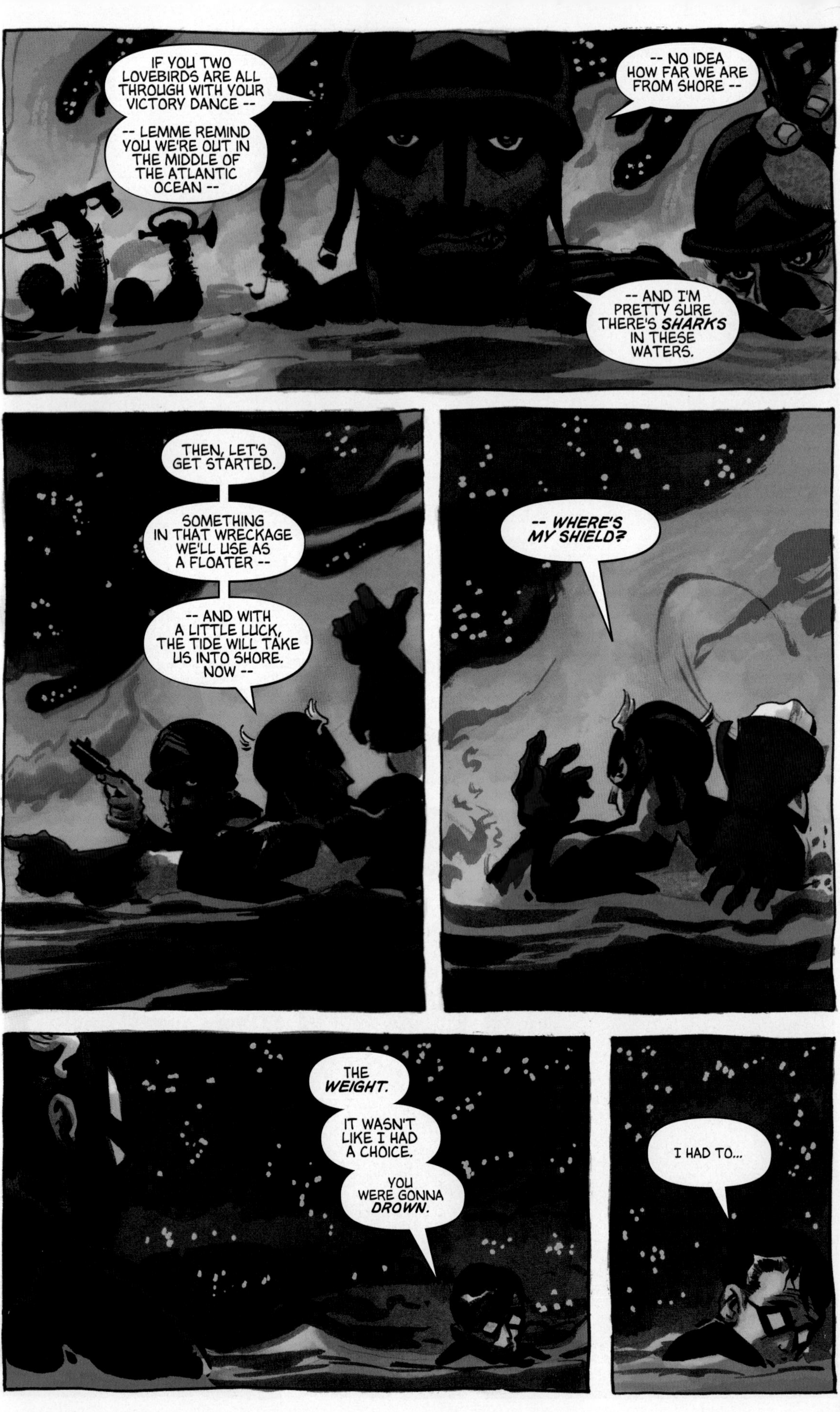
IF YOU TWO LOVEBIRDS ARE ALL THROUGH WITH YOUR VICTORY DANCE --
-- LEMME REMIND YOU WE'RE OUT IN THE MIDDLE OF THE ATLANTIC OCEAN --
-- NO IDEA HOW FAR WE ARE FROM SHORE --
-- AND I'M PRETTY SURE THERE'S *SHARKS* IN THESE WATERS.
THEN, LET'S GET STARTED.
SOMETHING IN THAT WRECKAGE WE'LL USE AS A FLOATER --
-- AND WITH A LITTLE LUCK, THE TIDE WILL TAKE US INTO SHORE. NOW --
-- WHERE'S MY SHIELD?
THE *WEIGHT.*
IT WASN'T LIKE I HAD A CHOICE.
YOU WERE GONNA *DROWN.*
I HAD TO...

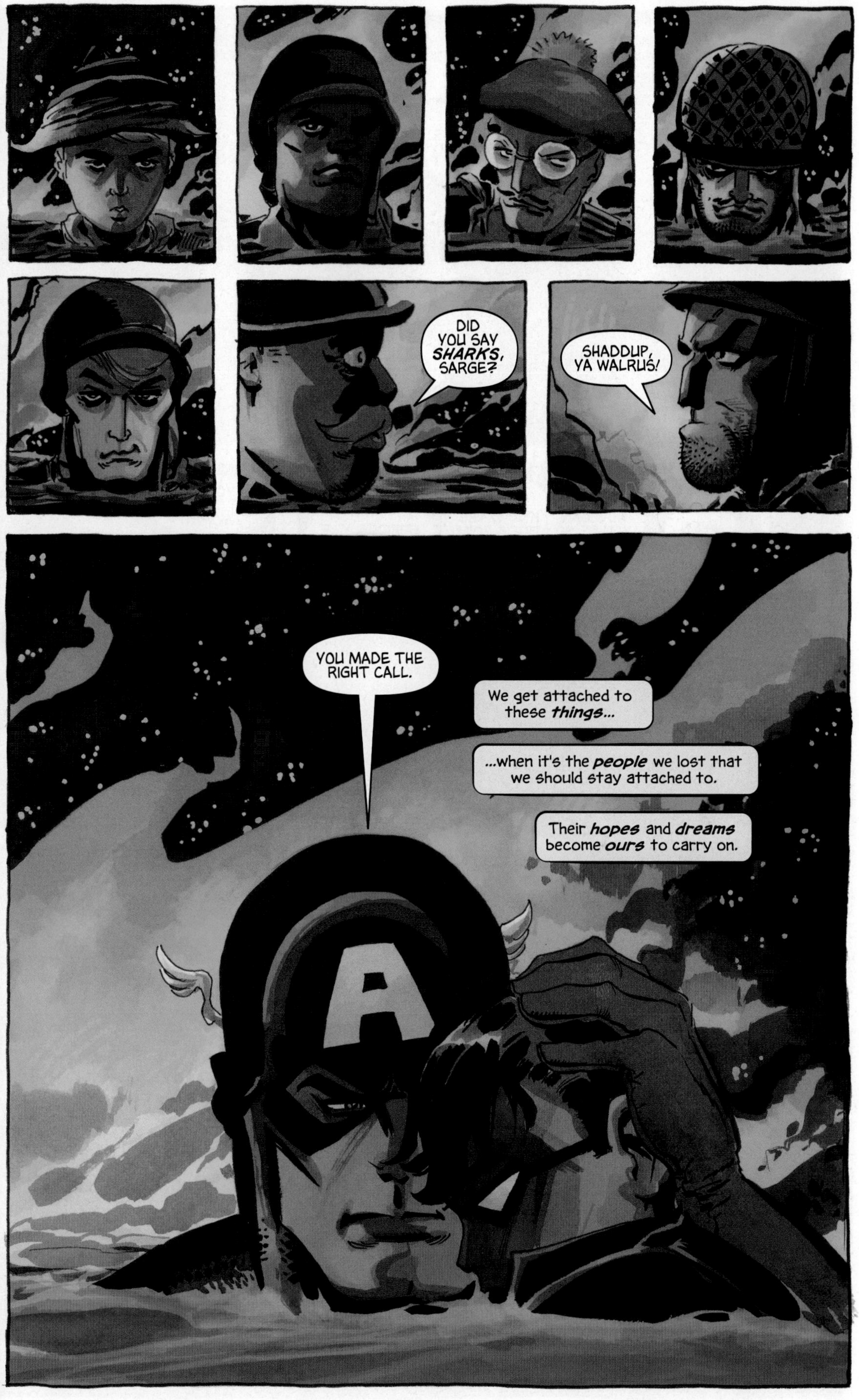
DID YOU SAY *SHARKS*, SARGE?
SHADDUP, YA WALRUS!
YOU MADE THE RIGHT CALL.
We get attached to these *things*...
...when it's the *people* we lost that we should stay attached to.
Their *hopes* and *dreams* become *ours* to carry on.

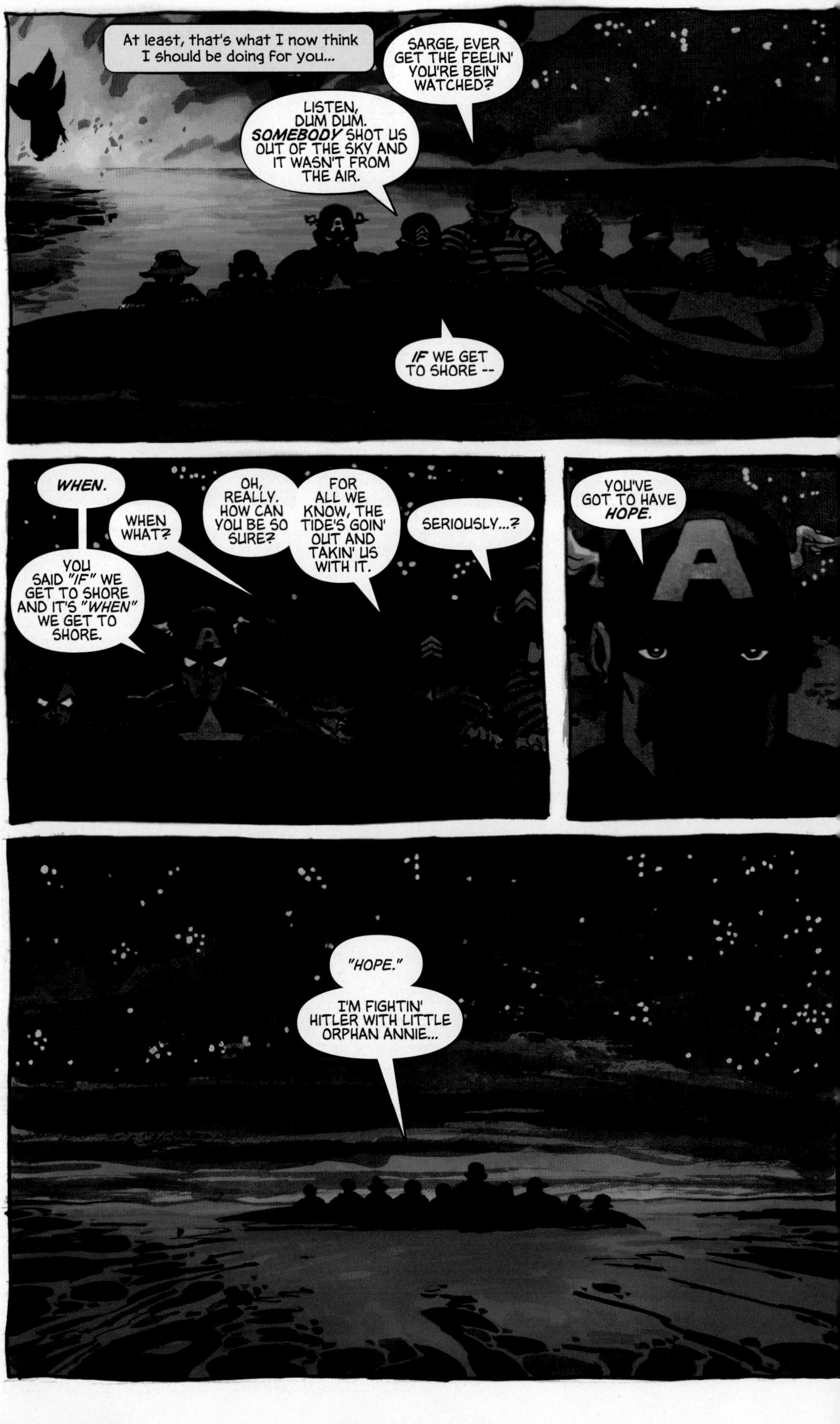
At least, that's what I now think I should be doing for you...
SARGE, EVER GET THE FEELIN' YOU'RE BEIN' WATCHED?
LISTEN, DUM DUM. SOMEBODY SHOT US OUT OF THE SKY AND IT WASN'T FROM THE AIR.
IF WE GET TO SHORE --
WHEN.
WHEN WHAT?
YOU SAID "IF" WE GET TO SHORE AND IT'S "WHEN" WE GET TO SHORE.
OH, REALLY. HOW CAN YOU BE SO SURE?
FOR ALL WE KNOW, THE TIDE'S GOIN' OUT AND TAKIN' US WITH IT.
SERIOUSLY...?
YOU'VE GOT TO HAVE HOPE.
"HOPE."
I'M FIGHTIN' HITLER WITH LITTLE ORPHAN ANNIE...

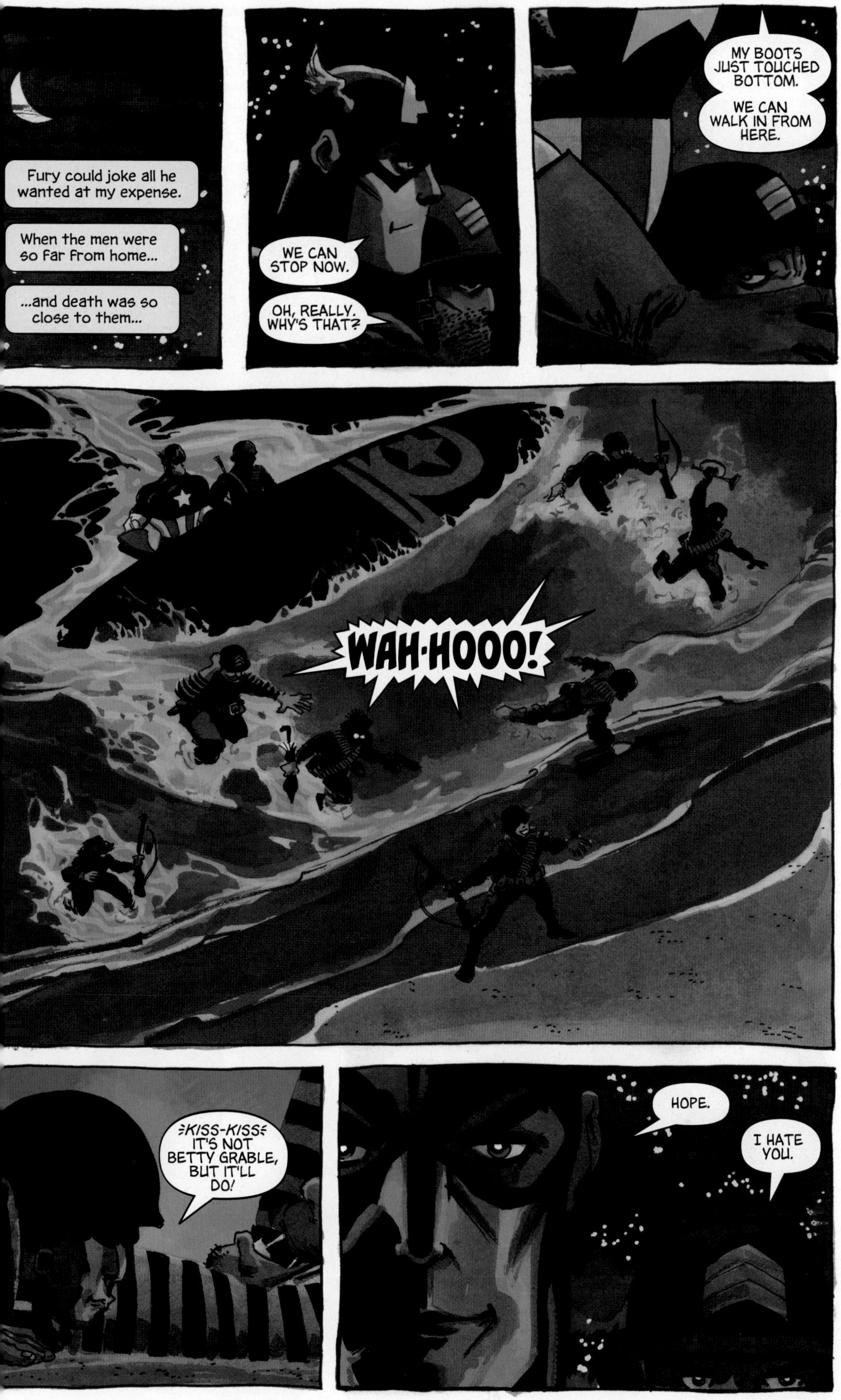
Fury could joke all he wanted at my expense.
When the men were so far from home...
...and death was so close to them...
WE CAN STOP NOW.
OH, REALLY. WHY'S THAT?
MY BOOTS JUST TOUCHED BOTTOM.
WE CAN WALK IN FROM HERE.
WAH-HOOO!
KISS-KISS IT'S NOT BETTY GRABLE, BUT IT'LL DO!
HOPE.
I HATE YOU.

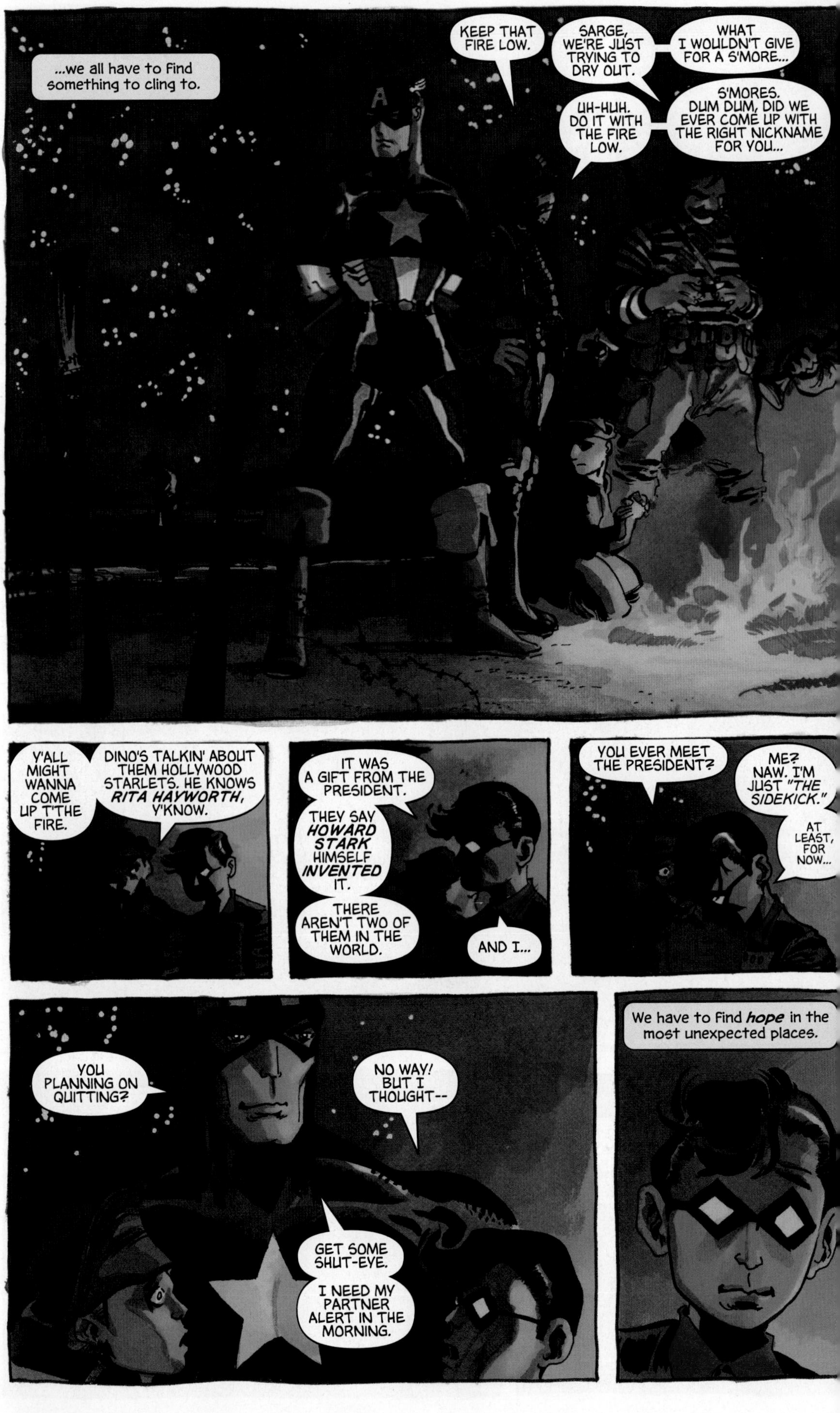
...we all have to find something to cling to.
KEEP THAT FIRE LOW.
SARGE, WE'RE JUST TRYING TO DRY OUT.
WHAT I WOULDN'T GIVE FOR A S'MORE...
UH-HUH. DO IT WITH THE FIRE LOW.
S'MORES. DUM DUM, DID WE EVER COME UP WITH THE RIGHT NICKNAME FOR YOU...
Y'ALL MIGHT WANNA COME UP T'THE FIRE.
DINO'S TALKIN' ABOUT THEM HOLLYWOOD STARLETS. HE KNOWS RITA HAYWORTH, Y'KNOW.
IT WAS A GIFT FROM THE PRESIDENT.
THEY SAY HOWARD STARK HIMSELF INVENTED IT.
THERE AREN'T TWO OF THEM IN THE WORLD.
AND I...
YOU EVER MEET THE PRESIDENT?
ME? NAW. I'M JUST "THE SIDEKICK."
AT LEAST, FOR NOW...
YOU PLANNING ON QUITTING?
NO WAY! BUT I THOUGHT--
GET SOME SHUT-EYE.
I NEED MY PARTNER ALERT IN THE MORNING.
We have to find hope in the most unexpected places.

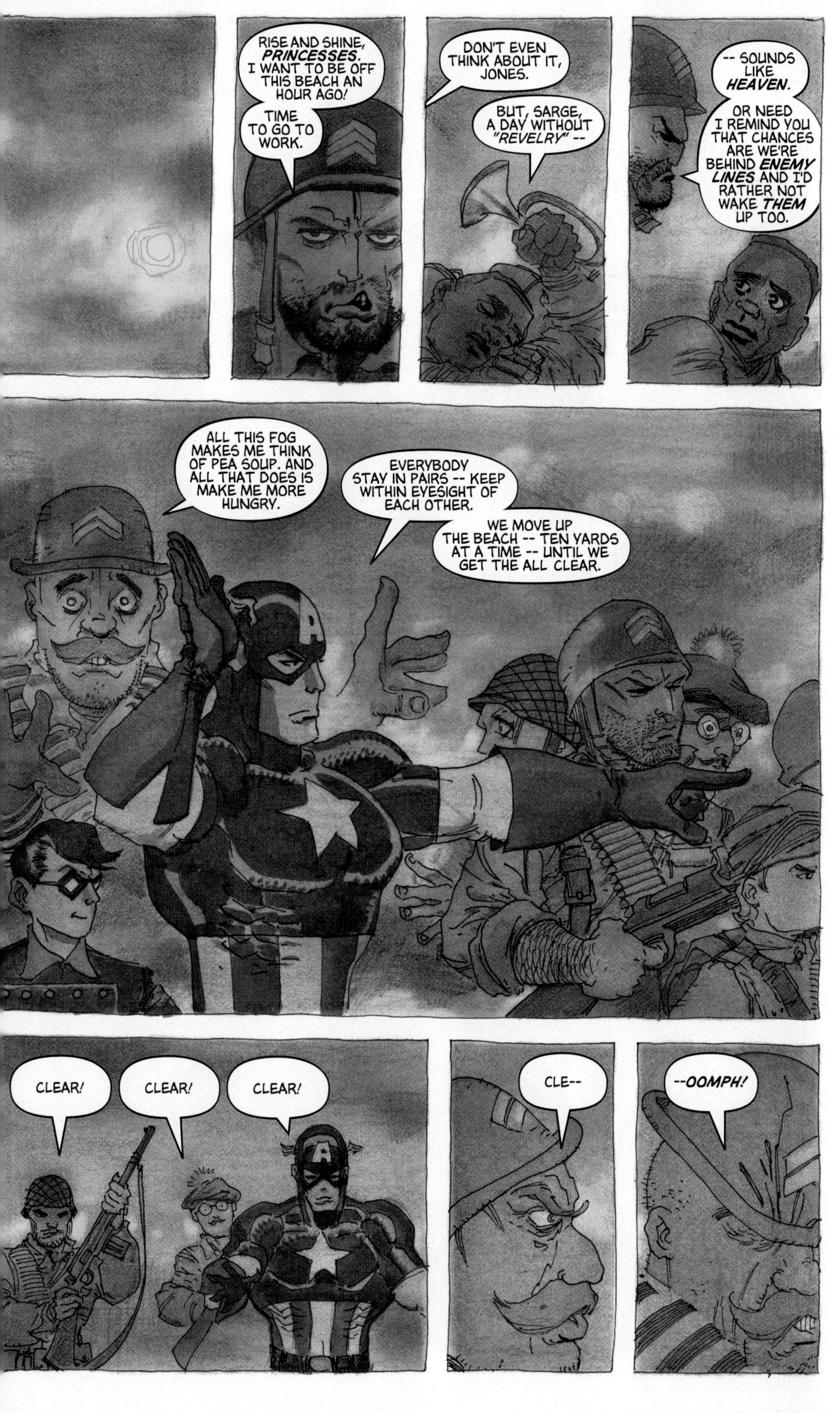
RISE AND SHINE, PRINCESSES. I WANT TO BE OFF THIS BEACH AN HOUR AGO!
TIME TO GO TO WORK.
DON'T EVEN THINK ABOUT IT, JONES.
BUT, SARGE, A DAY WITHOUT "REVELRY" --
-- SOUNDS LIKE HEAVEN.
OR NEED I REMIND YOU THAT CHANCES ARE WE'RE BEHIND ENEMY LINES AND I'D RATHER NOT WAKE THEM UP TOO.
ALL THIS FOG MAKES ME THINK OF PEA SOUP. AND ALL THAT DOES IS MAKE ME MORE HUNGRY.
EVERYBODY STAY IN PAIRS -- KEEP WITHIN EYESIGHT OF EACH OTHER.
WE MOVE UP THE BEACH -- TEN YARDS AT A TIME -- UNTIL WE GET THE ALL CLEAR.
CLEAR!
CLEAR!
CLEAR!
CLE--
--OOMPH!

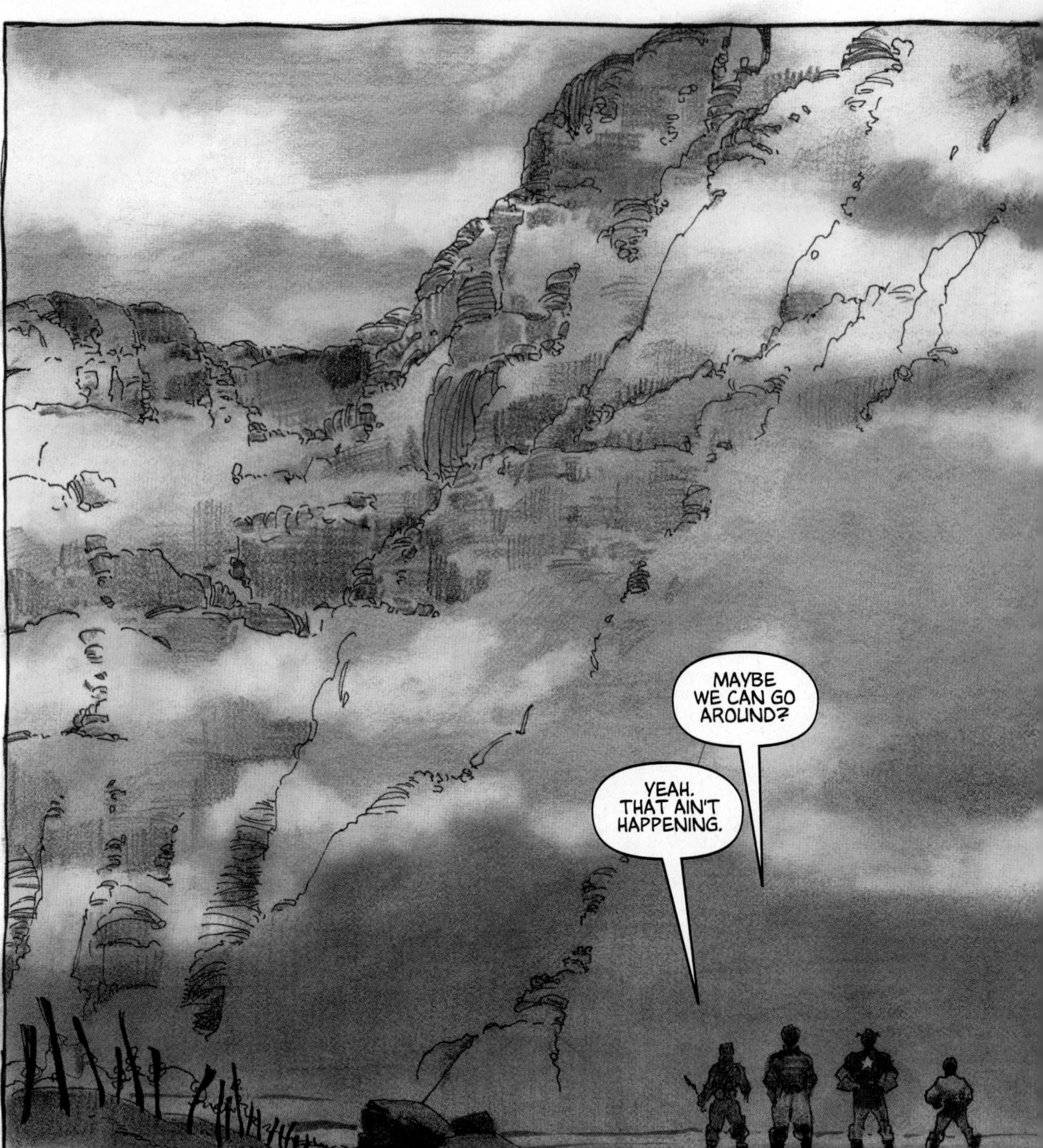
MAYBE WE CAN GO AROUND?
YEAH. THAT AIN'T HAPPENING.

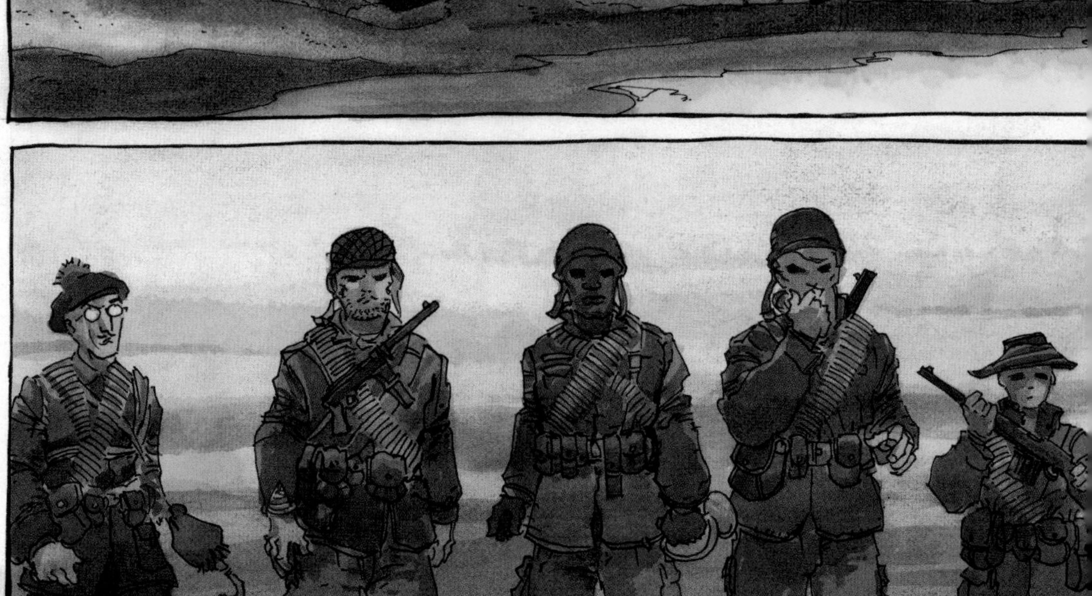

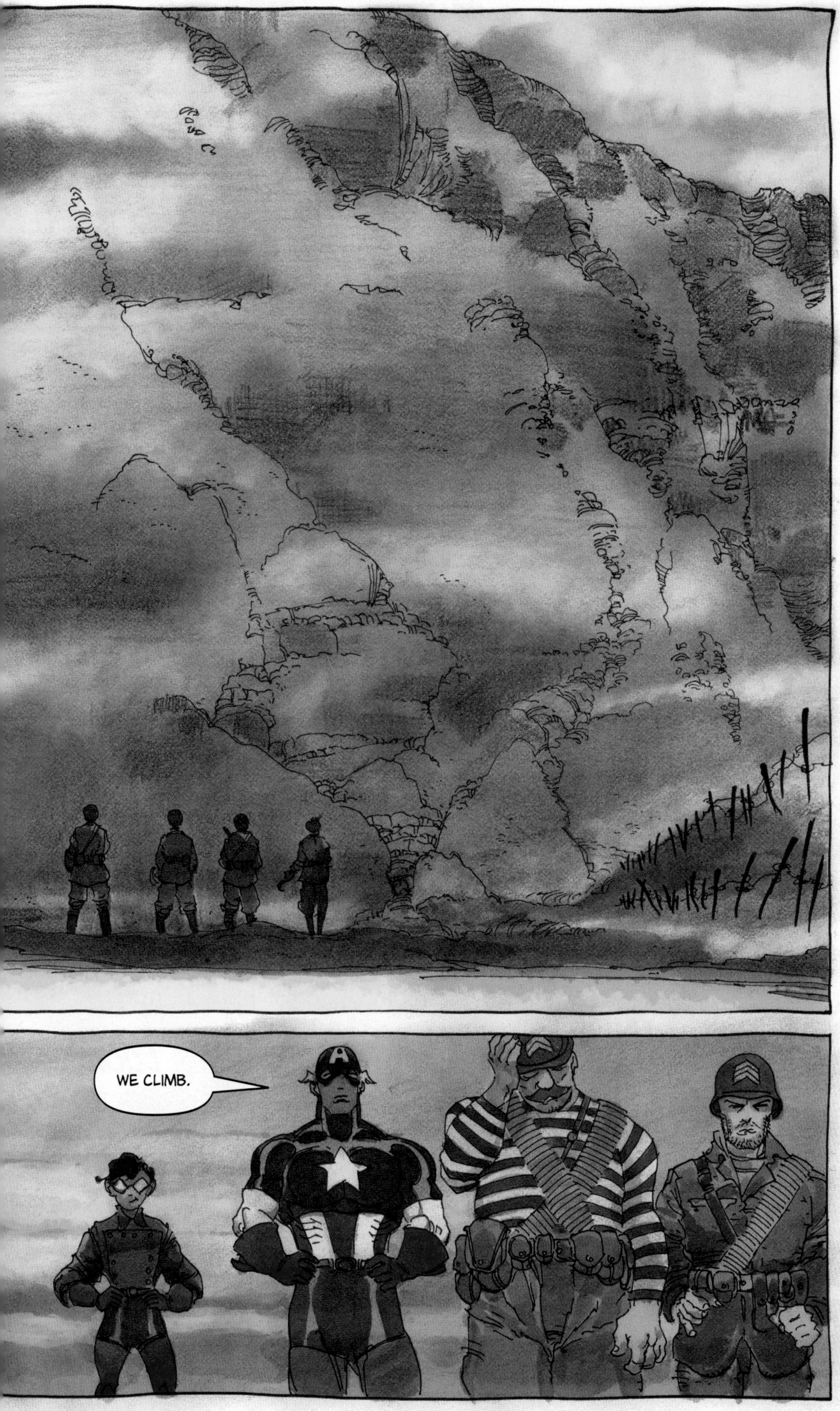
WE CLIMB.

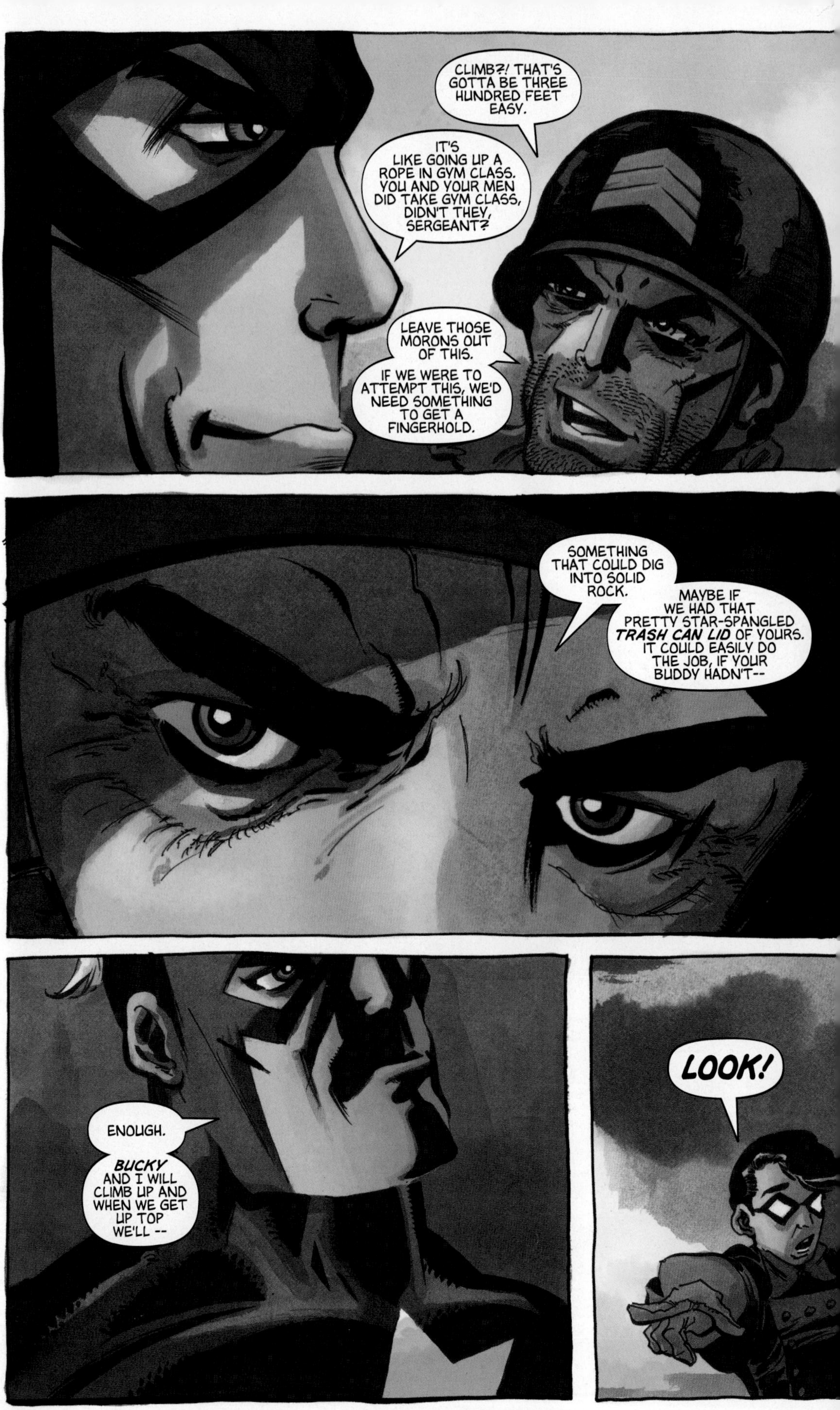
CLIMB?! THAT'S GOTTA BE THREE HUNDRED FEET EASY.
IT'S LIKE GOING UP A ROPE IN GYM CLASS. YOU AND YOUR MEN DID TAKE GYM CLASS, DIDN'T THEY, SERGEANT?
LEAVE THOSE MORONS OUT OF THIS.
IF WE WERE TO ATTEMPT THIS, WE'D NEED SOMETHING TO GET A FINGERHOLD.
SOMETHING THAT COULD DIG INTO SOLID ROCK.
MAYBE IF WE HAD THAT PRETTY STAR-SPANGLED *TRASH CAN LID* OF YOURS. IT COULD EASILY DO THE JOB, IF YOUR BUDDY HADN'T--
ENOUGH.
BUCKY AND I WILL CLIMB UP AND WHEN WE GET UP TOP WE'LL --
LOOK!

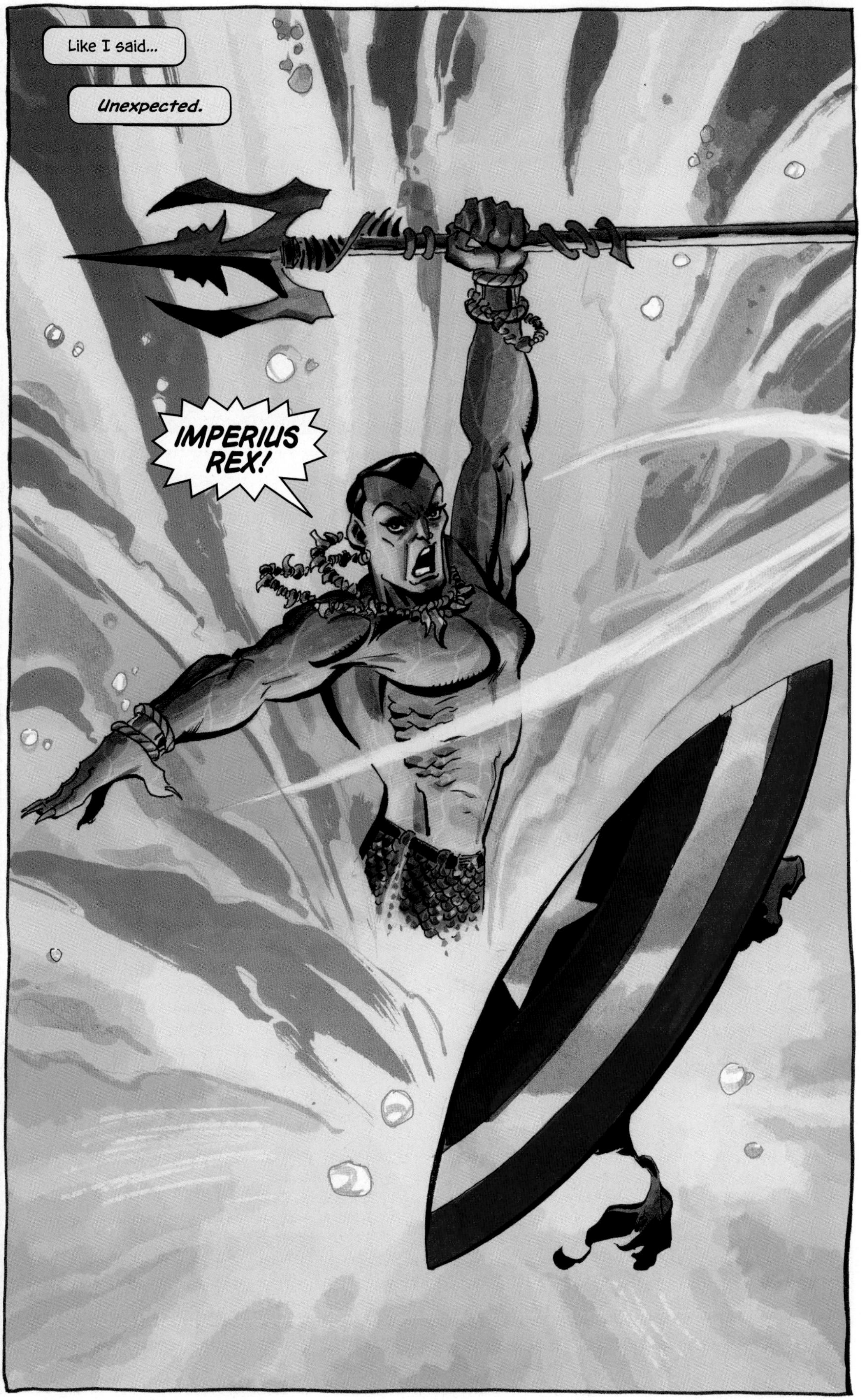
Like I said...
Unexpected.
IMPERIUS REX!

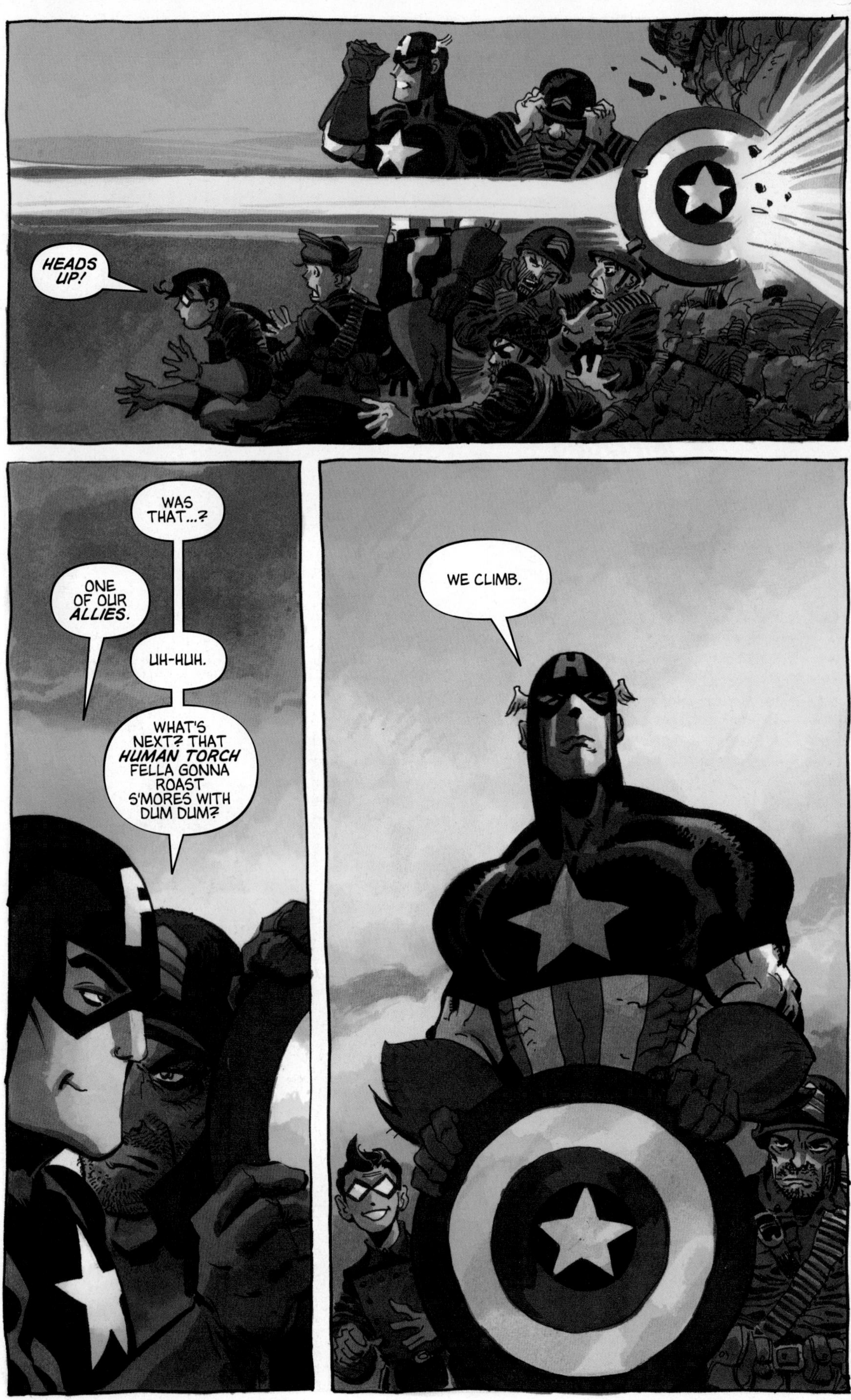
HEADS UP!
WAS THAT...?
ONE OF OUR ALLIES.
UH-HUH.
WHAT'S NEXT? THAT HUMAN TORCH FELLA GONNA ROAST S'MORES WITH DUM DUM?
WE CLIMB.

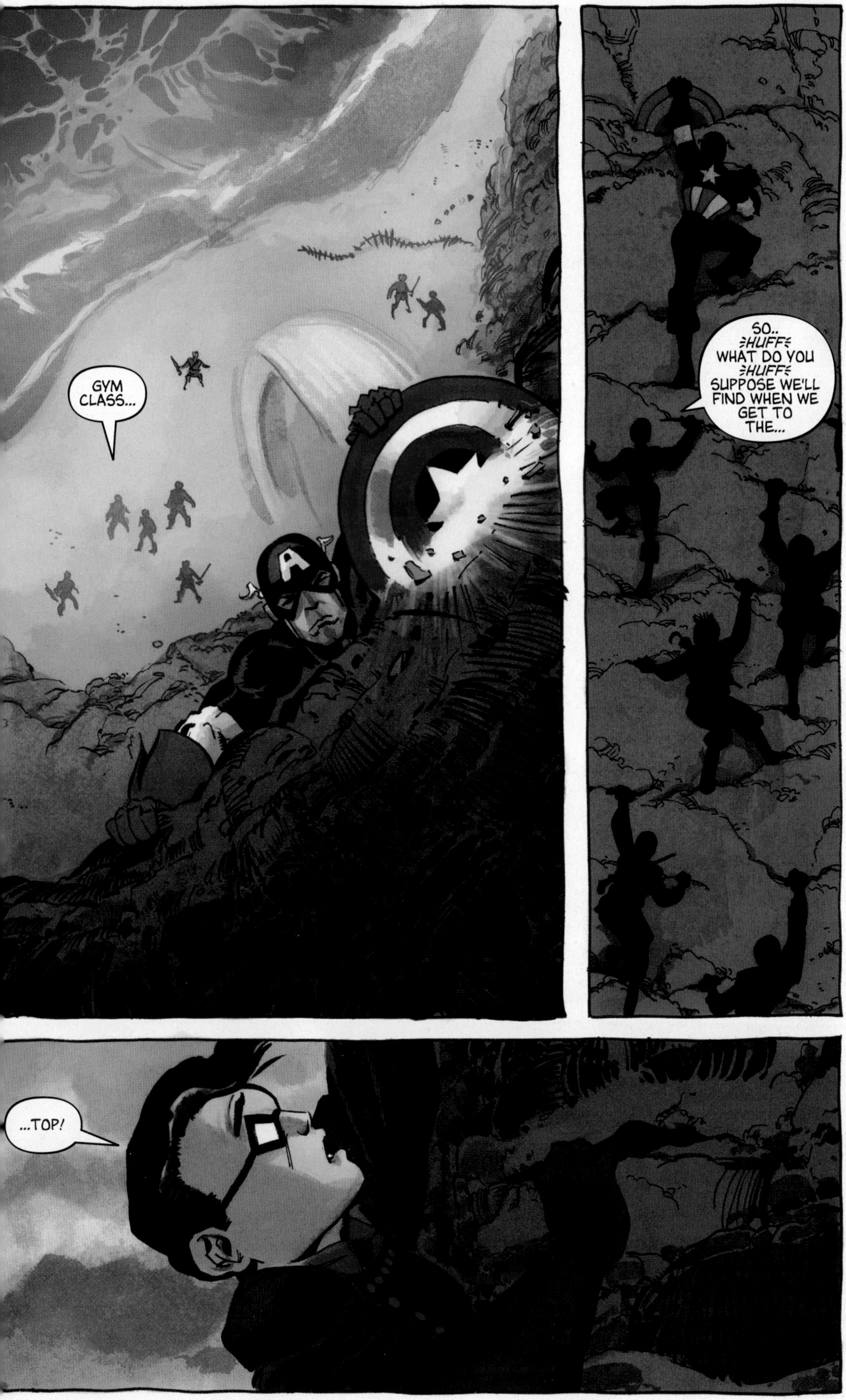
GYM CLASS...
SO.. HUFF WHAT DO YOU HUFF SUPPOSE WE'LL FIND WHEN WE GET TO THE...
...TOP!

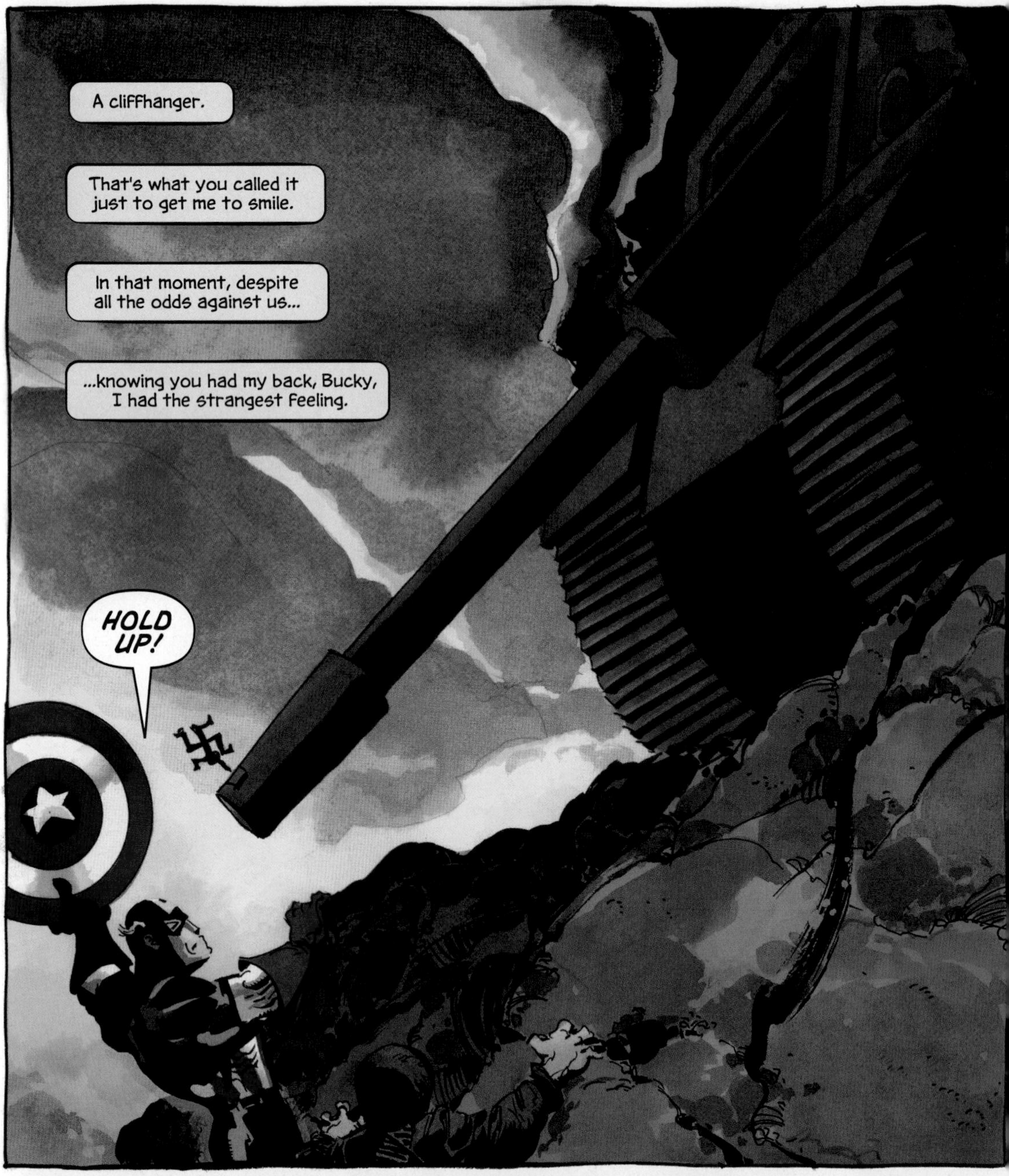
A cliffhanger.
That's what you called it just to get me to smile.
In that moment, despite all the odds against us...
...knowing you had my back, Bucky, I had the strangest feeling.
HOLD UP!

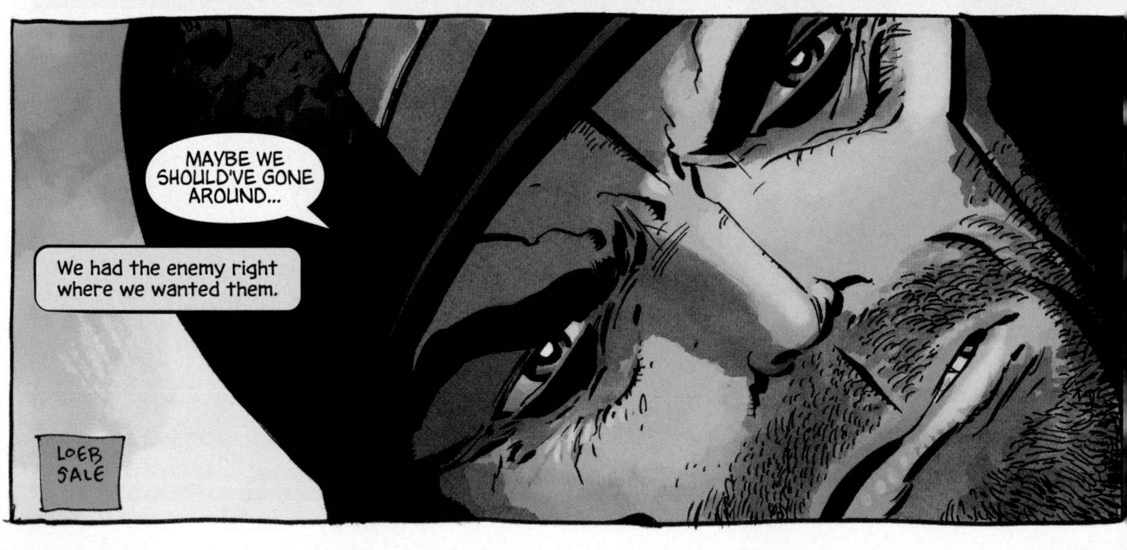
MAYBE WE SHOULD'VE GONE AROUND...
We had the enemy right where we wanted them.
LOEB SALE

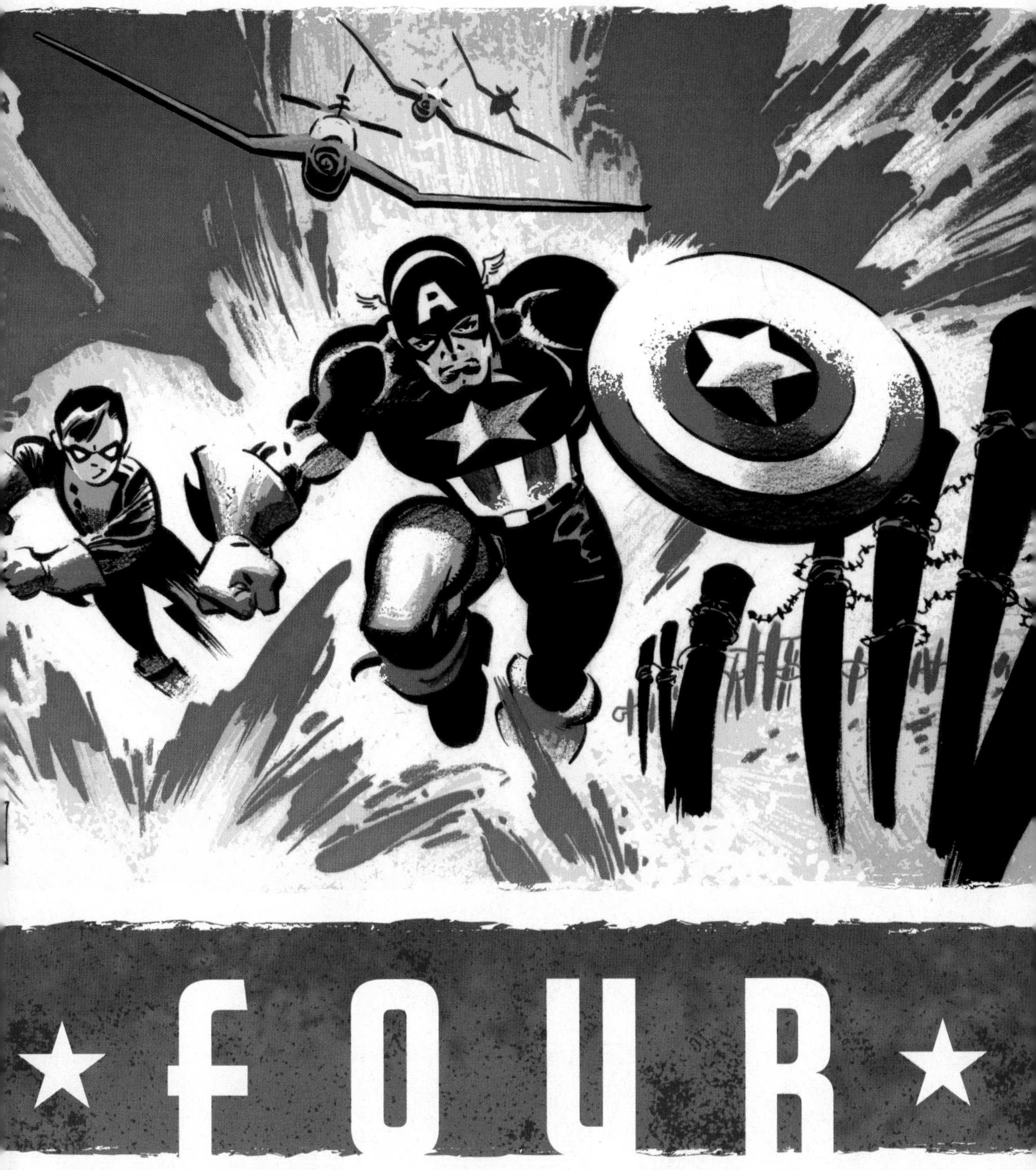

★ FOUR ★

A HOLE

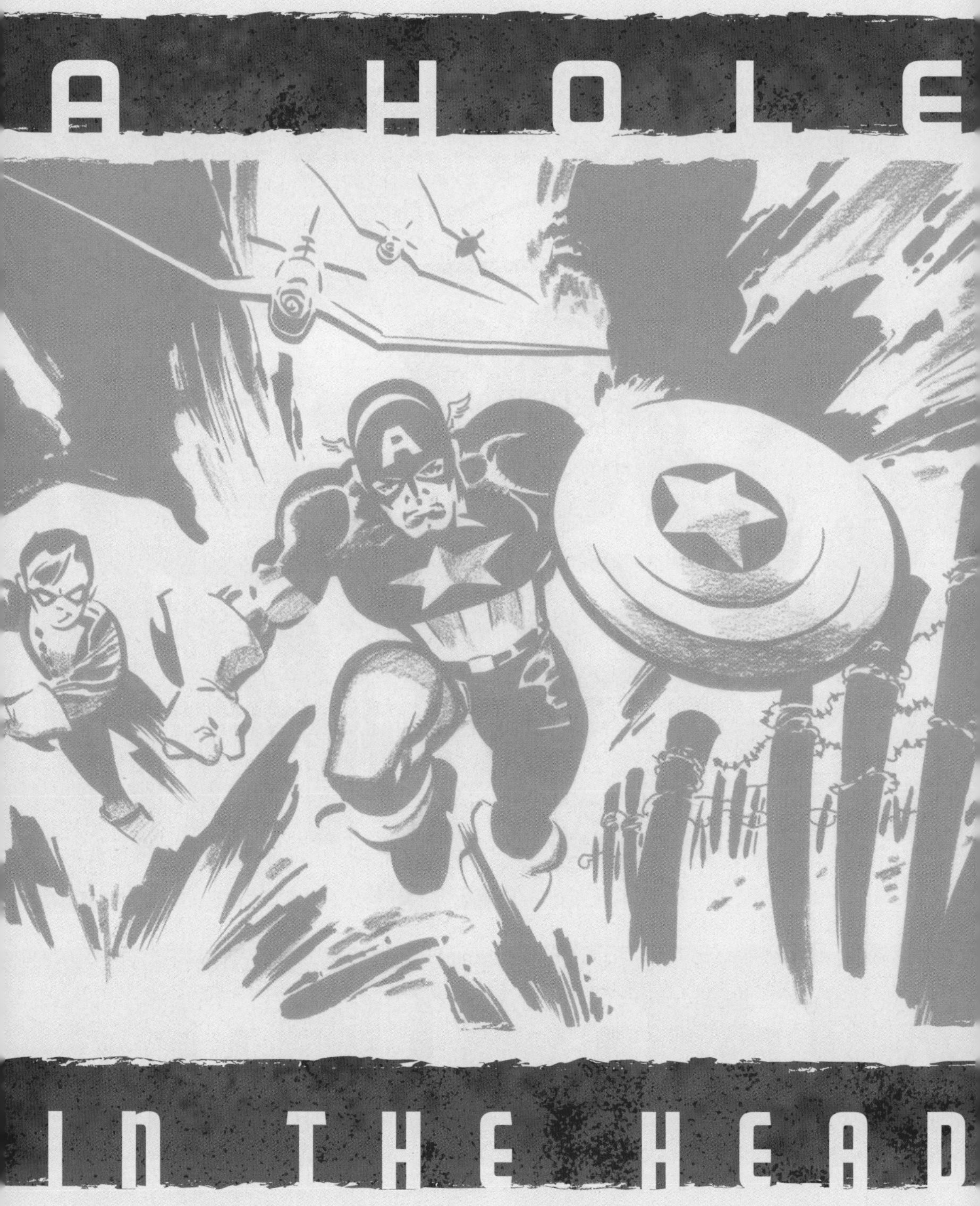

IN THE HEAD

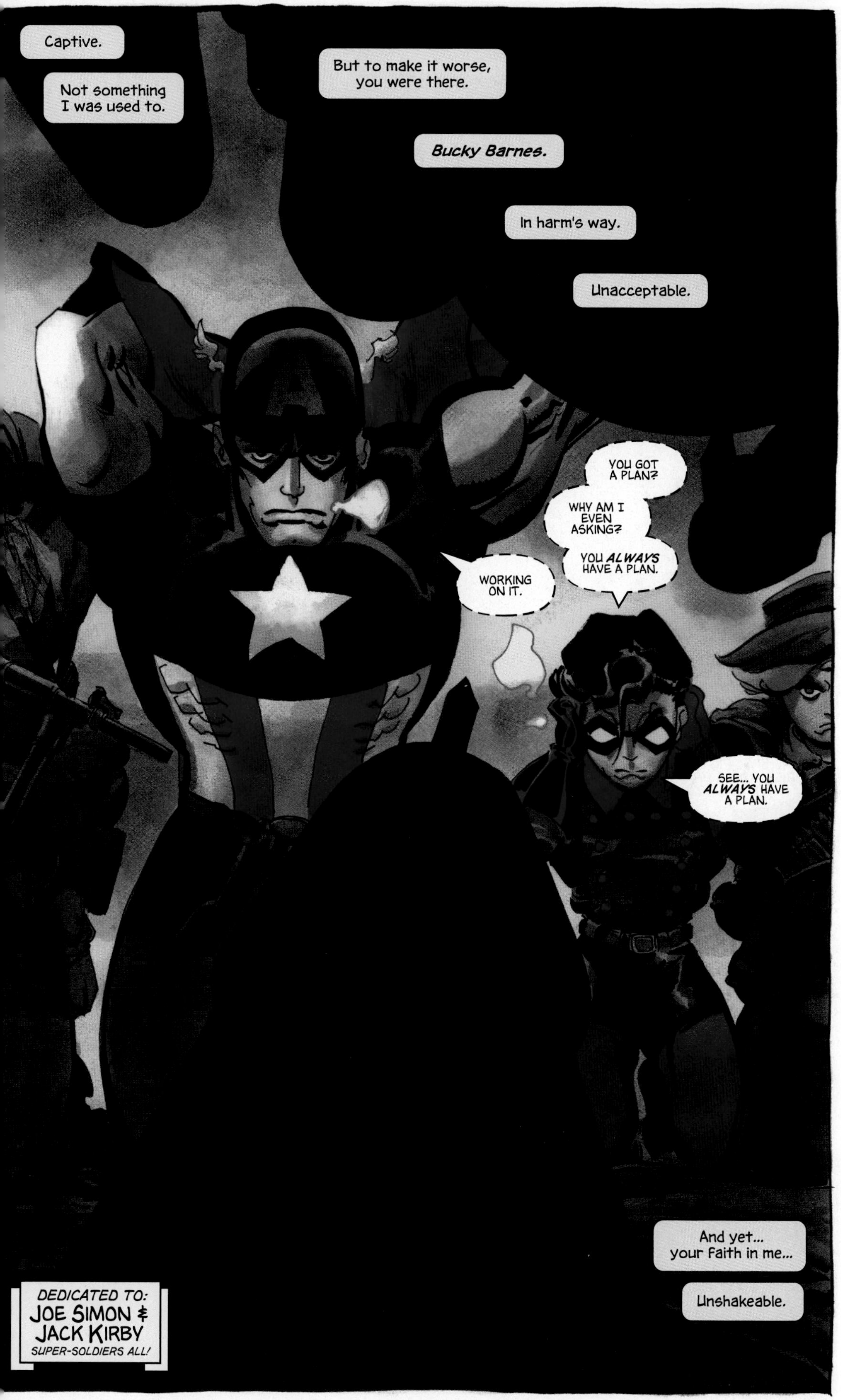

Captive.
Not something I was used to.
But to make it worse, you were there.
Bucky Barnes.
In harm's way.
Unacceptable.
YOU GOT A PLAN?
WHY AM I EVEN ASKING?
YOU ALWAYS HAVE A PLAN.
WORKING ON IT.
SEE... YOU ALWAYS HAVE A PLAN.
And yet... your faith in me...
Unshakeable.
DEDICATED TO: JOE SIMON & JACK KIRBY SUPER-SOLDIERS ALL!

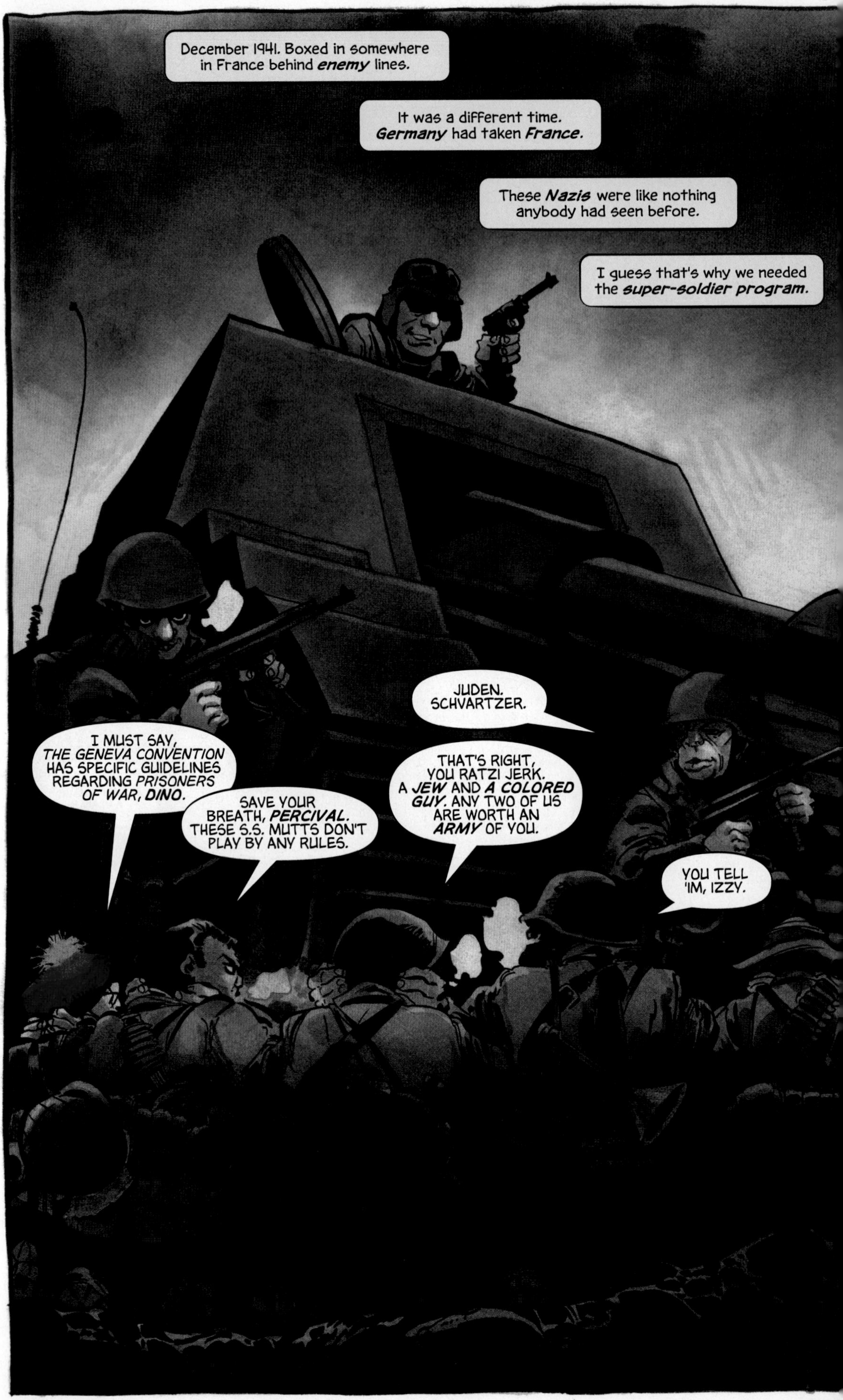

December 1941. Boxed in somewhere in France behind *enemy* lines.
It was a different time. *Germany* had taken *France*.
These *Nazis* were like nothing anybody had seen before.
I guess that's why we needed the *super-soldier program*.
JUDEN. SCHVARTZER.
I MUST SAY, *THE GENEVA CONVENTION* HAS SPECIFIC GUIDELINES REGARDING *PRISONERS OF WAR*, ***DINO***.
SAVE YOUR BREATH, ***PERCIVAL***. THESE S.S. MUTTS DON'T PLAY BY ANY RULES.
THAT'S RIGHT, YOU RATZI JERK. A ***JEW*** AND ***A COLORED GUY***. ANY TWO OF US ARE WORTH AN ***ARMY*** OF YOU.
YOU TELL 'IM, IZZY.

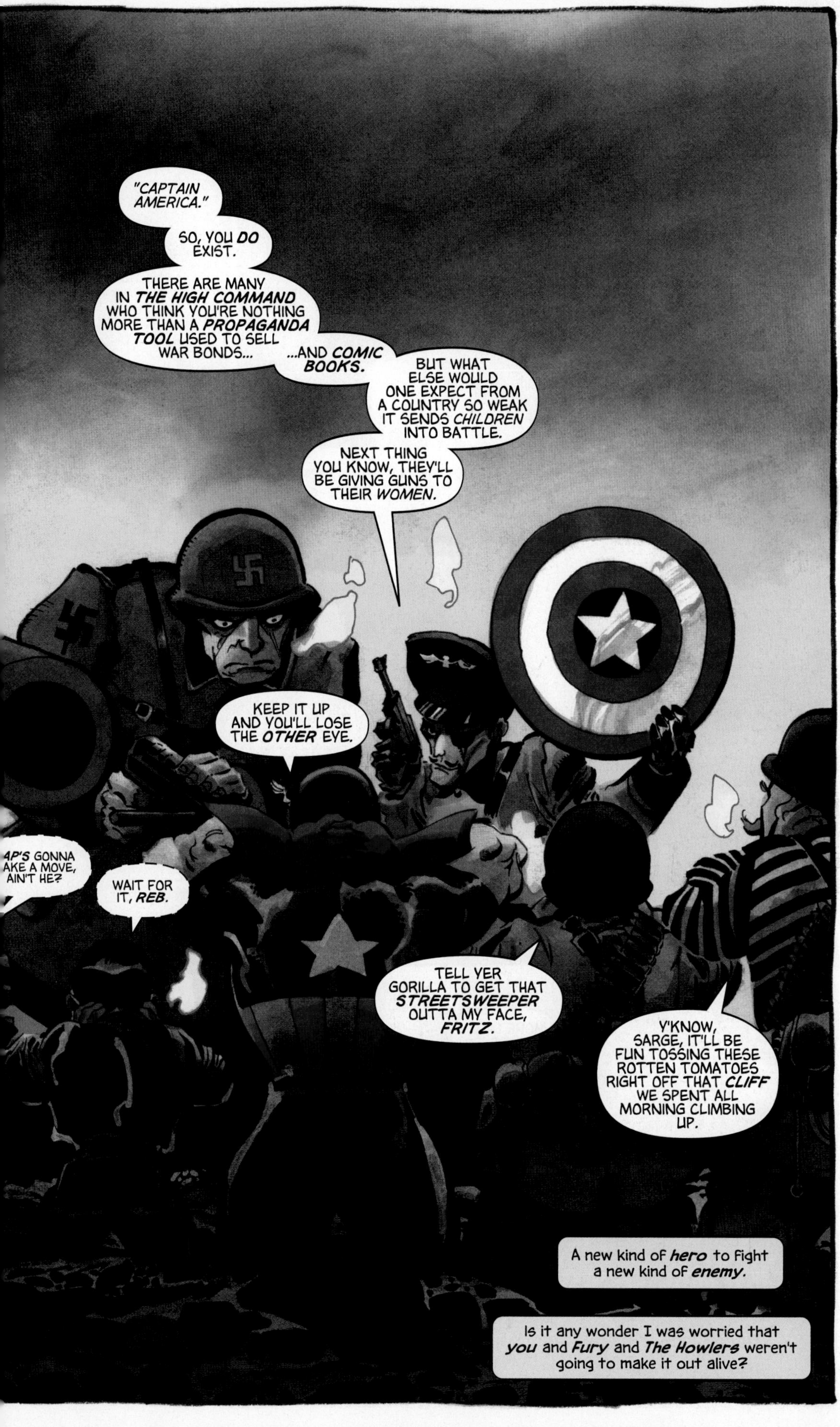
"CAPTAIN AMERICA."
SO, YOU DO EXIST.
THERE ARE MANY IN THE HIGH COMMAND WHO THINK YOU'RE NOTHING MORE THAN A PROPAGANDA TOOL USED TO SELL WAR BONDS...
...AND COMIC BOOKS.
BUT WHAT ELSE WOULD ONE EXPECT FROM A COUNTRY SO WEAK IT SENDS CHILDREN INTO BATTLE.
NEXT THING YOU KNOW, THEY'LL BE GIVING GUNS TO THEIR WOMEN.
KEEP IT UP AND YOU'LL LOSE THE OTHER EYE.
AP'S GONNA AKE A MOVE, AIN'T HE?
WAIT FOR IT, REB.
TELL YER GORILLA TO GET THAT STREETSWEEPER OUTTA MY FACE, FRITZ.
Y'KNOW, SARGE, IT'LL BE FUN TOSSING THESE ROTTEN TOMATOES RIGHT OFF THAT CLIFF WE SPENT ALL MORNING CLIMBING UP.
A new kind of hero to fight a new kind of enemy.
Is it any wonder I was worried that you and Fury and The Howlers weren't going to make it out alive?

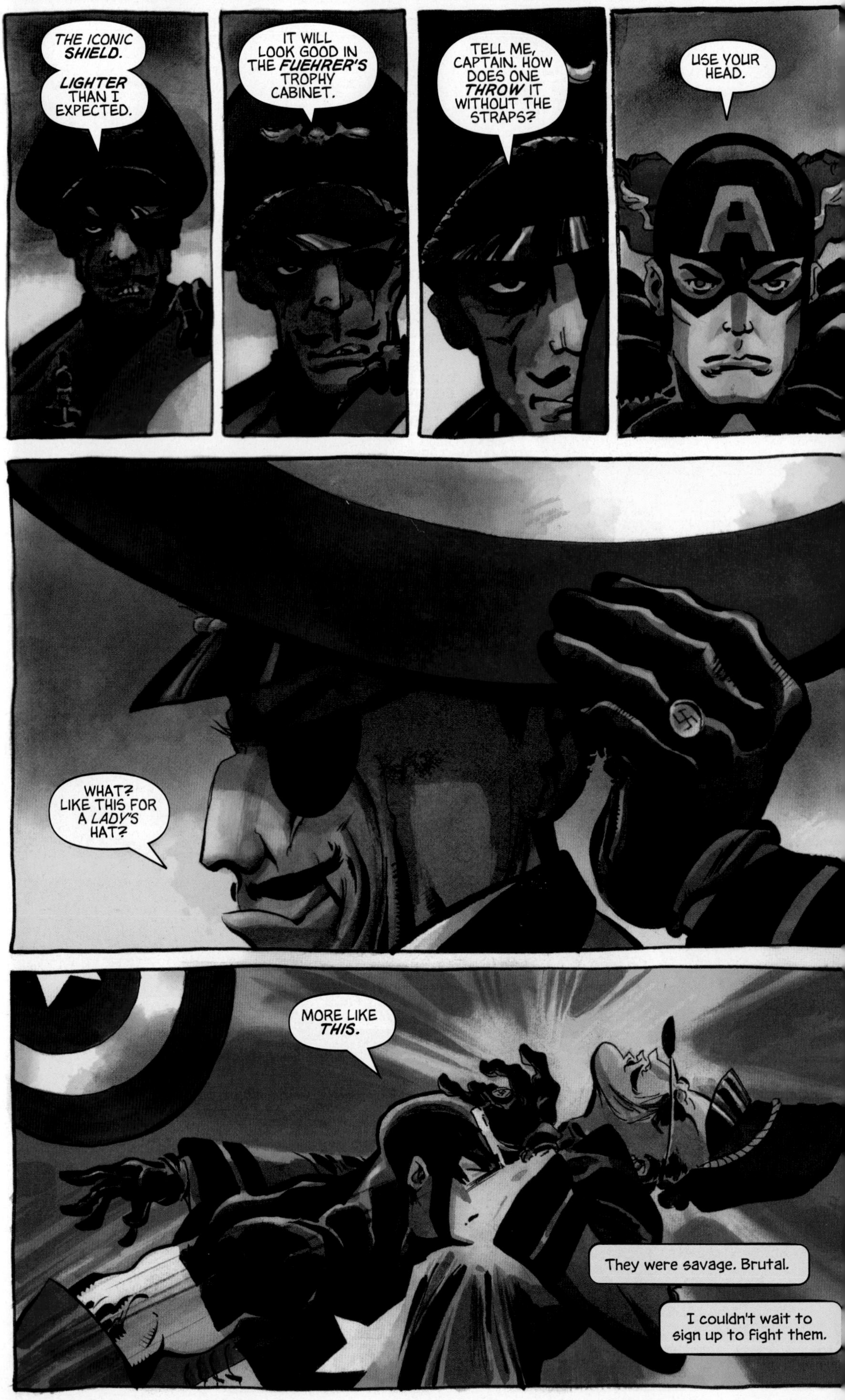
THE ICONIC SHIELD.
LIGHTER THAN I EXPECTED.
IT WILL LOOK GOOD IN THE FUEHRER'S TROPHY CABINET.
TELL ME, CAPTAIN. HOW DOES ONE THROW IT WITHOUT THE STRAPS?
USE YOUR HEAD.
WHAT? LIKE THIS FOR A LADY'S HAT?
MORE LIKE THIS.
They were savage. Brutal.
I couldn't wait to sign up to fight them.

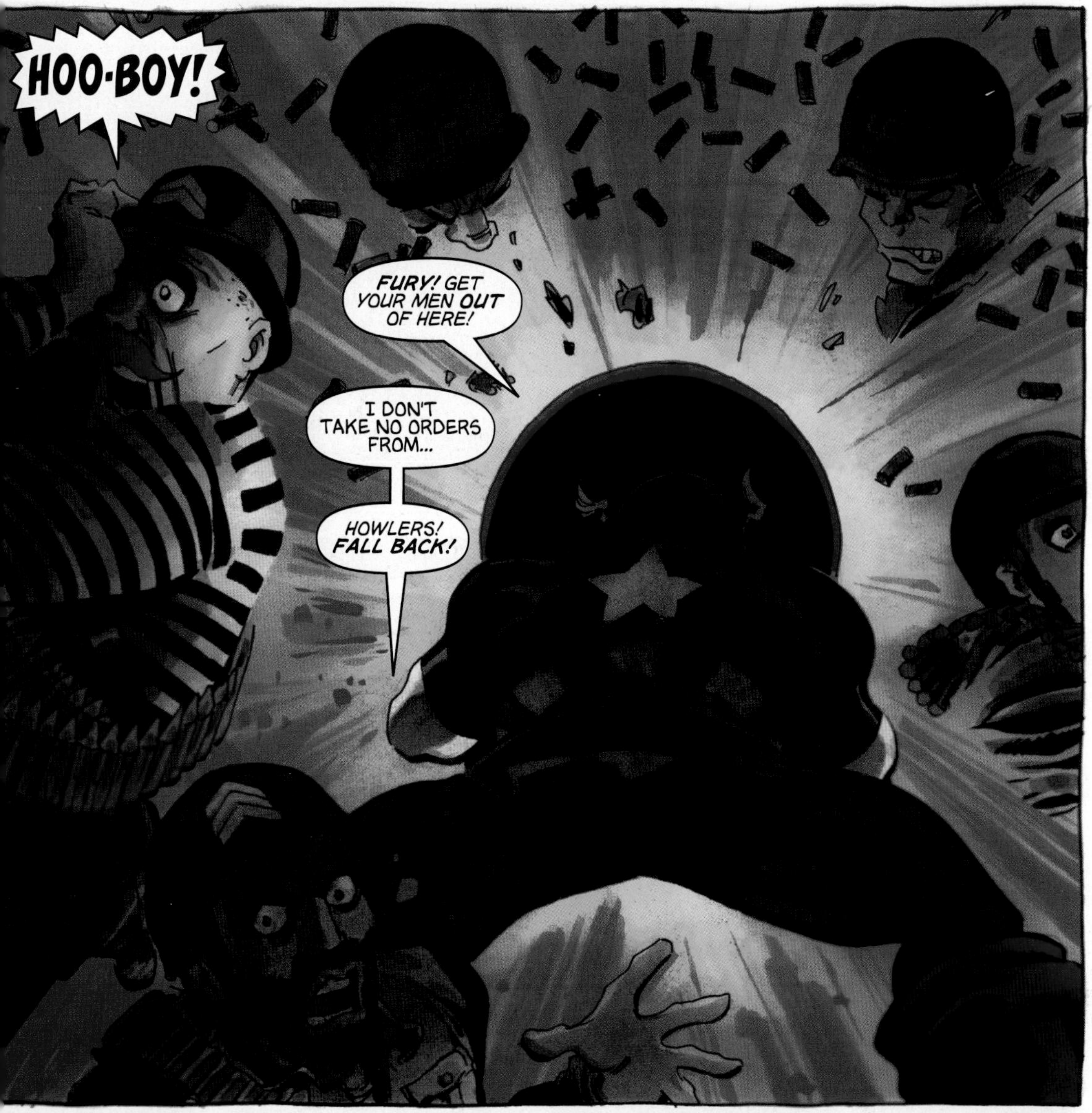
HOO-BOY!
FURY! GET YOUR MEN OUT OF HERE!
I DON'T TAKE NO ORDERS FROM...
HOWLERS! FALL BACK!

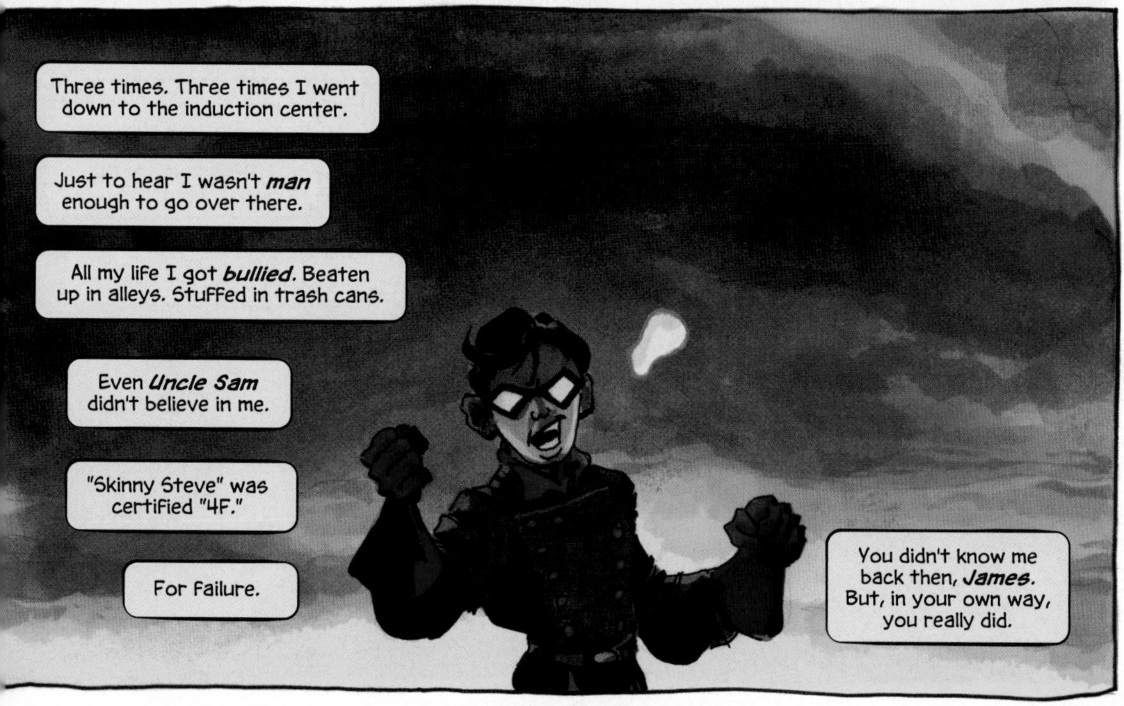
Three times. Three times I went down to the induction center.
Just to hear I wasn't man enough to go over there.
All my life I got bullied. Beaten up in alleys. Stuffed in trash cans.
Even Uncle Sam didn't believe in me.
"Skinny Steve" was certified "4F."
For failure.
You didn't know me back then, James. But, in your own way, you really did.

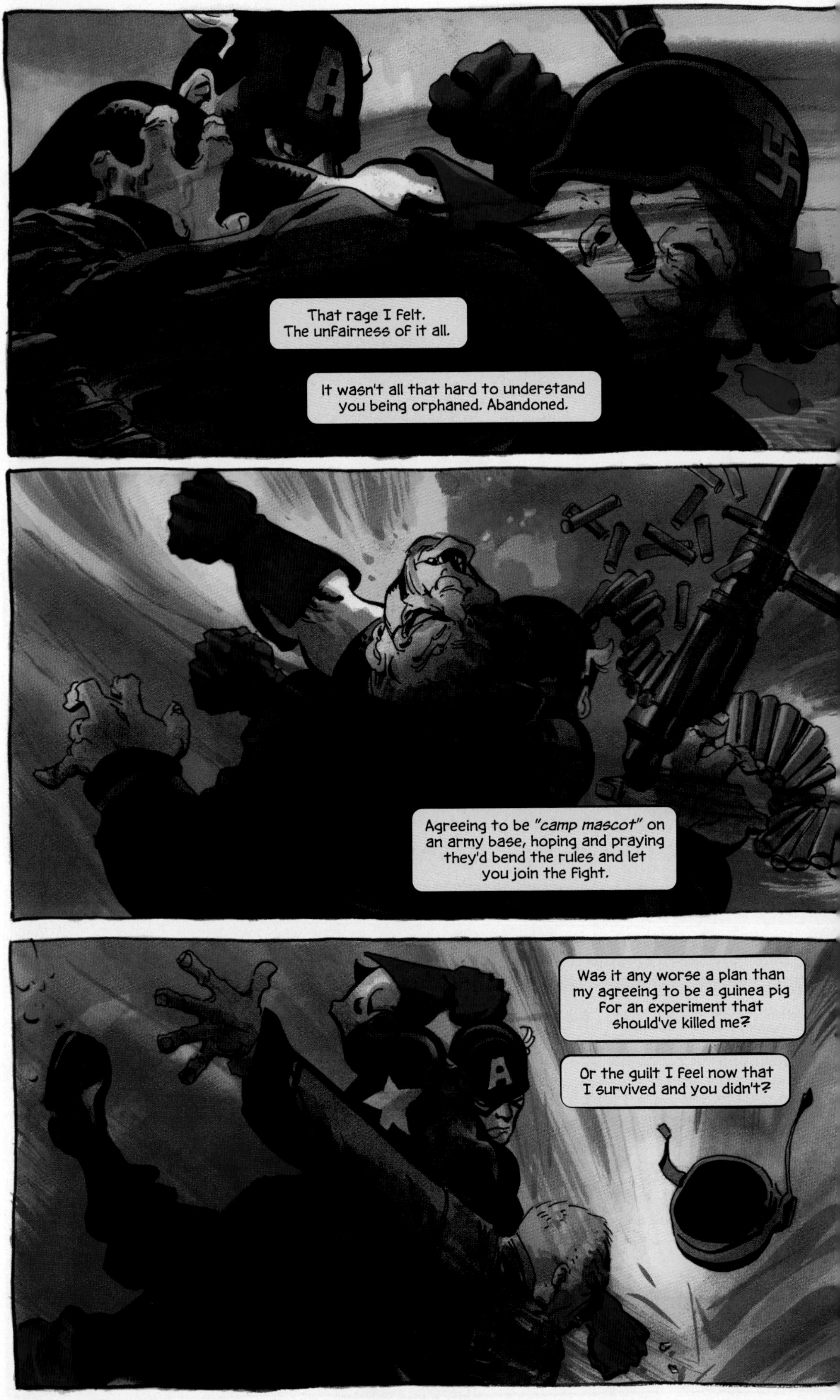
That rage I felt. The unfairness of it all.
It wasn't all that hard to understand you being orphaned. Abandoned.
Agreeing to be "camp mascot" on an army base, hoping and praying they'd bend the rules and let you join the fight.
Was it any worse a plan than my agreeing to be a guinea pig for an experiment that should've killed me?
Or the guilt I feel now that I survived and you didn't?

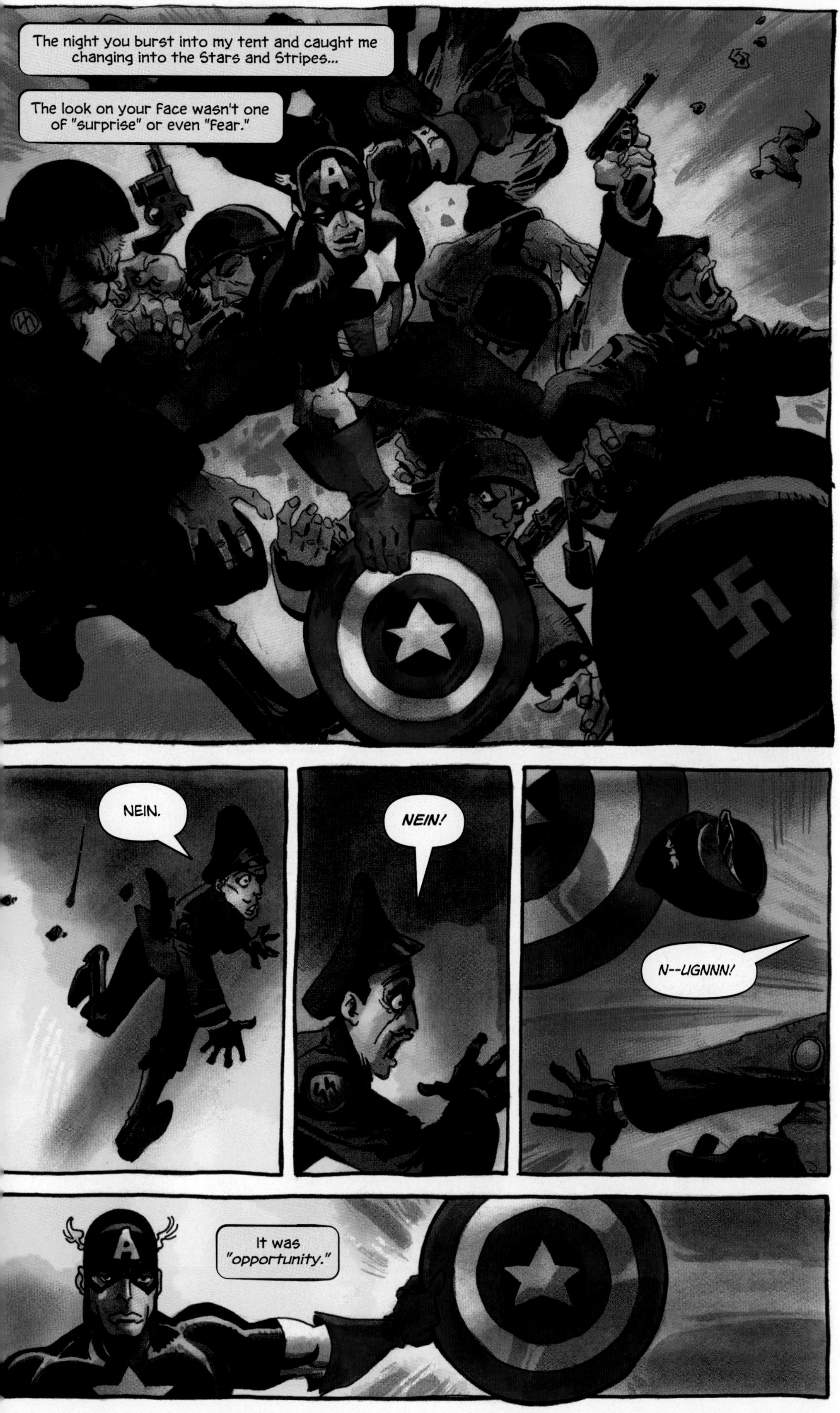
The night you burst into my tent and caught me changing into the Stars and Stripes...
The look on your face wasn't one of "surprise" or even "fear."
NEIN.
NEIN!
N--UGNNN!
It was "opportunity."

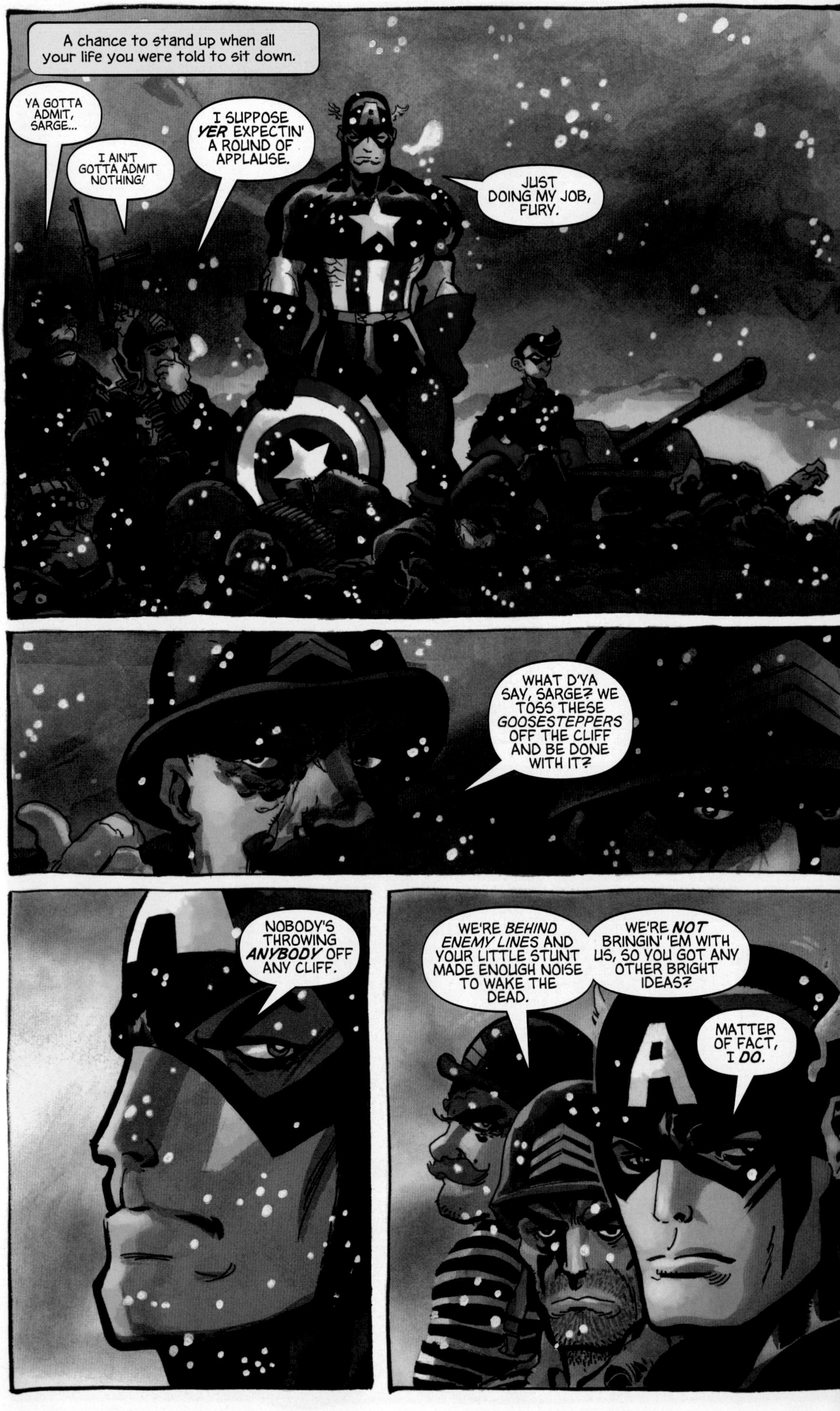
A chance to stand up when all your life you were told to sit down.
YA GOTTA ADMIT, SARGE...
I AIN'T GOTTA ADMIT NOTHING!
I SUPPOSE YER EXPECTIN' A ROUND OF APPLAUSE.
JUST DOING MY JOB, FURY.
WHAT D'YA SAY, SARGE? WE TOSS THESE GOOSESTEPPERS OFF THE CLIFF AND BE DONE WITH IT?
NOBODY'S THROWING ANYBODY OFF ANY CLIFF.
WE'RE BEHIND ENEMY LINES AND YOUR LITTLE STUNT MADE ENOUGH NOISE TO WAKE THE DEAD.
WE'RE NOT BRINGIN' 'EM WITH US, SO YOU GOT ANY OTHER BRIGHT IDEAS?
MATTER OF FACT, I DO.

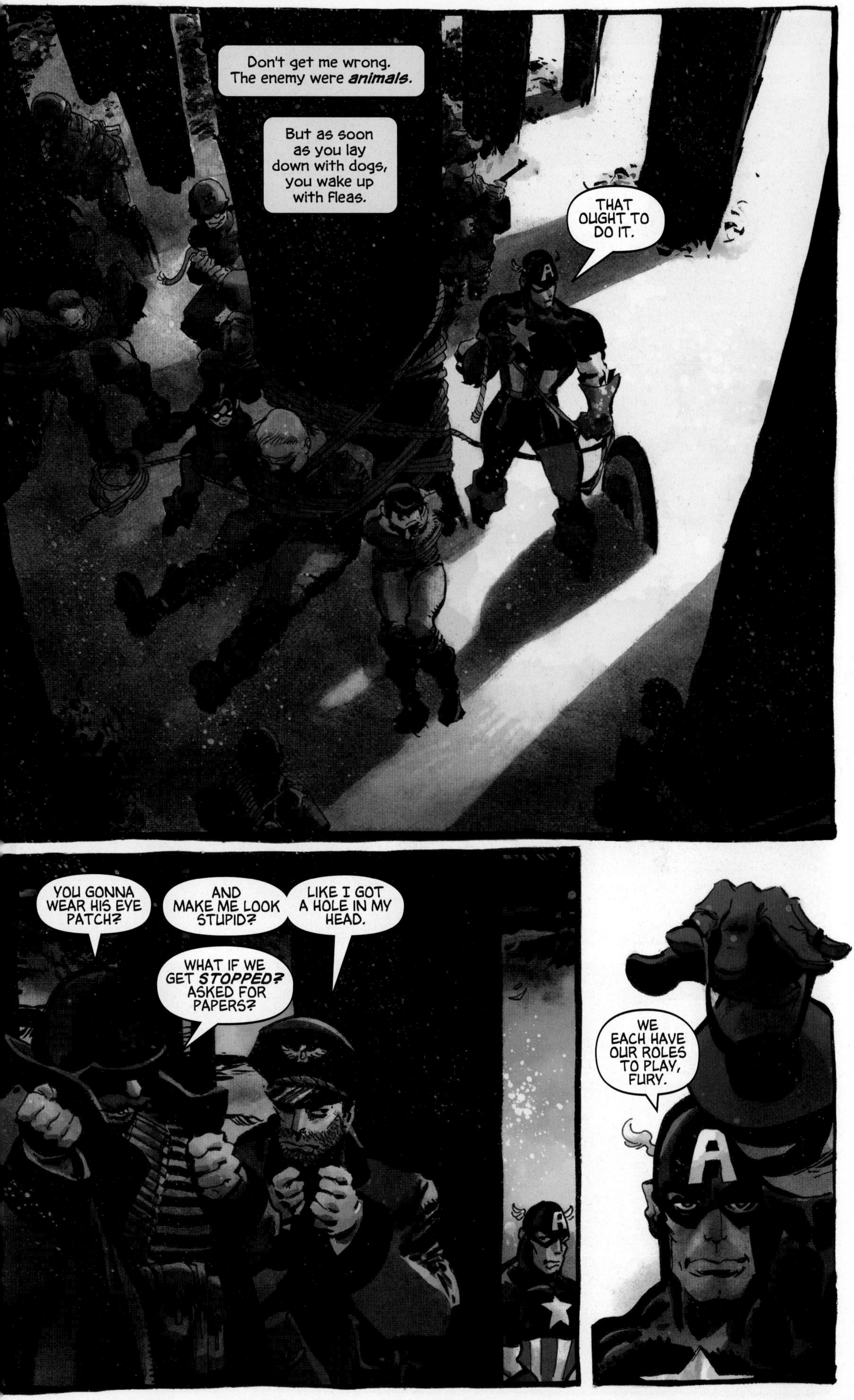

Don't get me wrong. The enemy were *animals.*
But as soon as you lay down with dogs, you wake up with fleas.
THAT OUGHT TO DO IT.
YOU GONNA WEAR HIS EYE PATCH?
AND MAKE ME LOOK STUPID?
LIKE I GOT A HOLE IN MY HEAD.
WHAT IF WE GET *STOPPED?* ASKED FOR PAPERS?
WE EACH HAVE OUR ROLES TO PLAY, FURY.

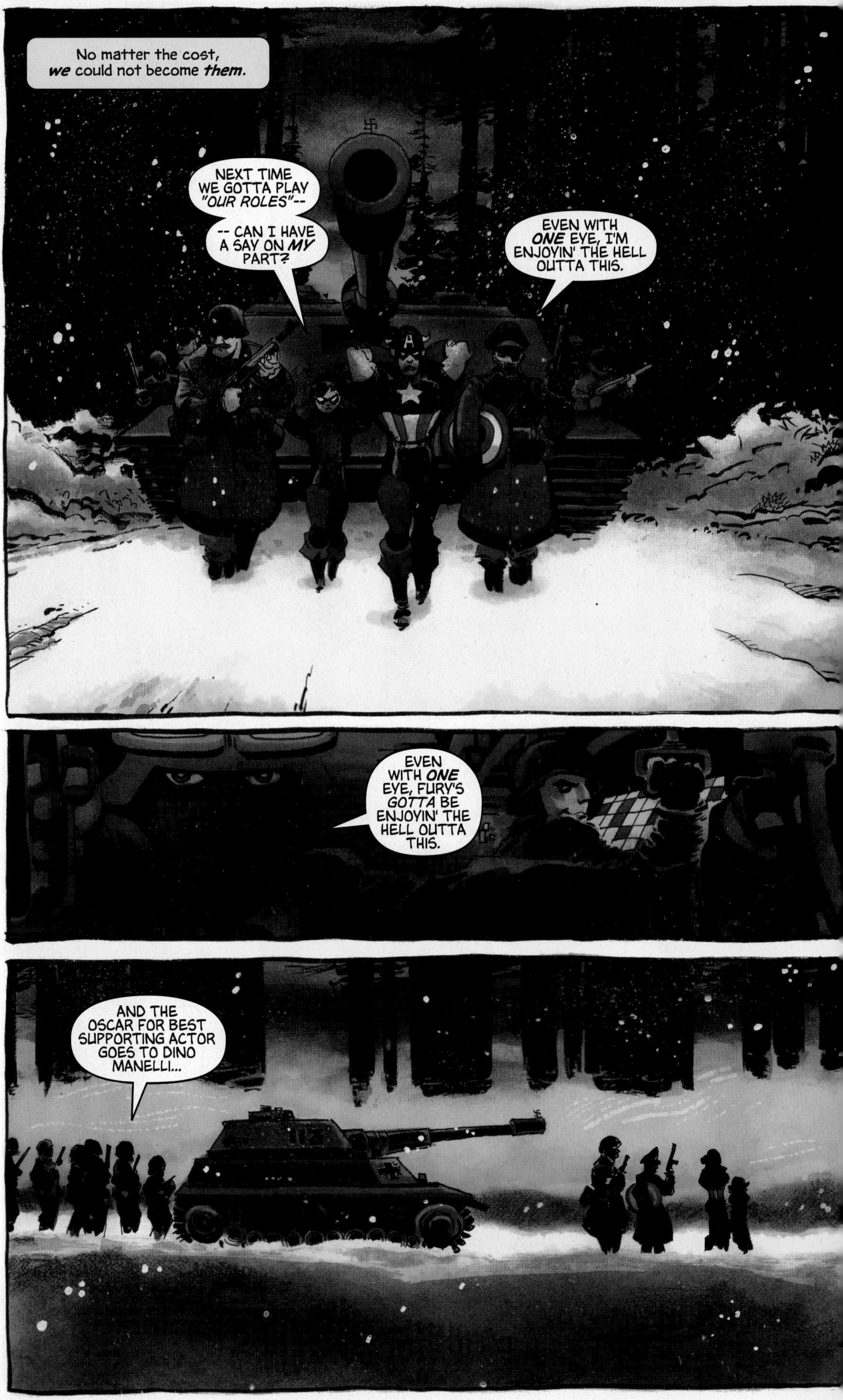
No matter the cost,
we could not become them.
NEXT TIME WE GOTTA PLAY "OUR ROLES"--
-- CAN I HAVE A SAY ON MY PART?
EVEN WITH ONE EYE, I'M ENJOYIN' THE HELL OUTTA THIS.
EVEN WITH ONE EYE, FURY'S GOTTA BE ENJOYIN' THE HELL OUTTA THIS.
AND THE OSCAR FOR BEST SUPPORTING ACTOR GOES TO DINO MANELLI...

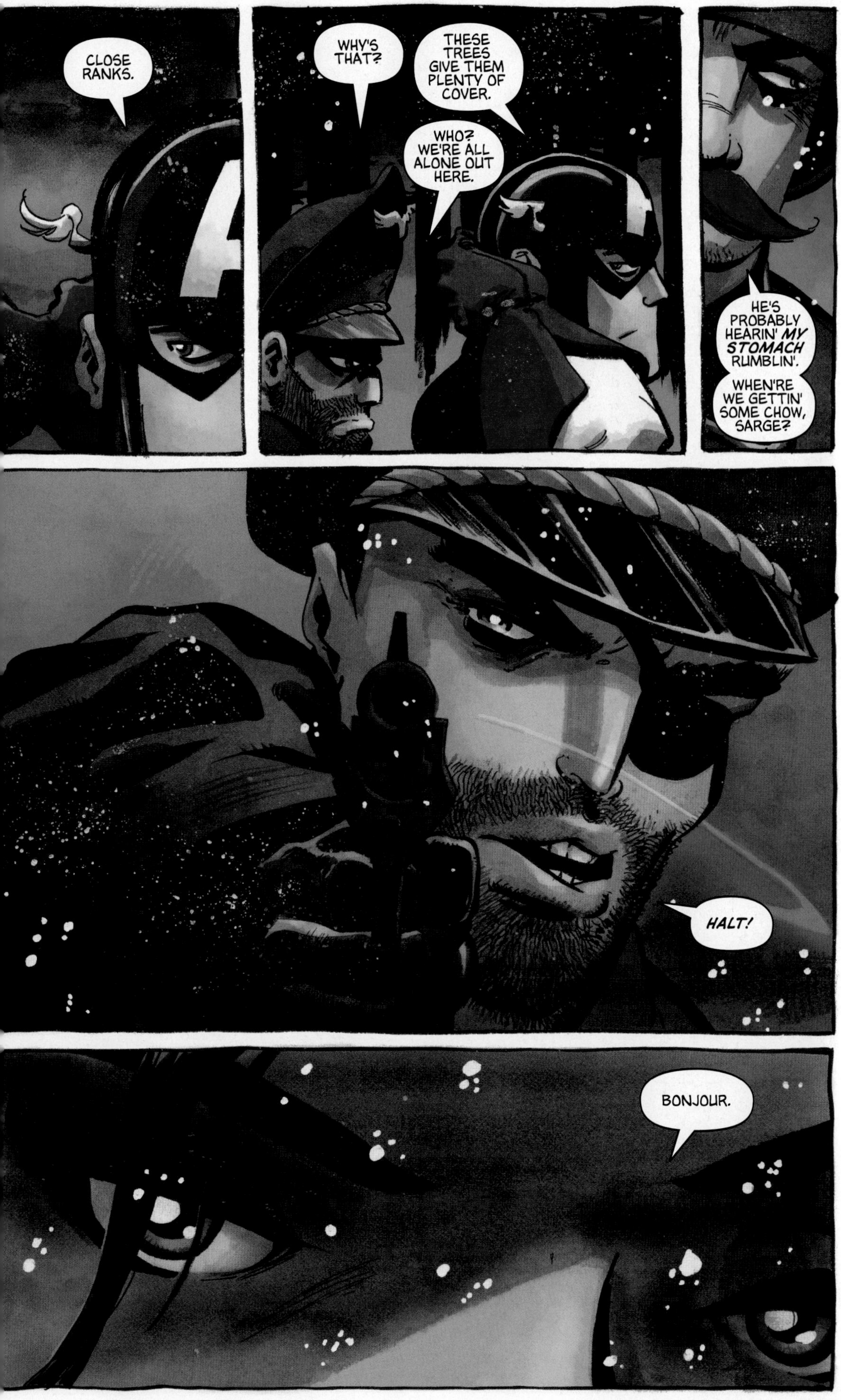
CLOSE RANKS.
WHY'S THAT?
THESE TREES GIVE THEM PLENTY OF COVER.
WHO? WE'RE ALL ALONE OUT HERE.
HE'S PROBABLY HEARIN' *MY STOMACH* RUMBLIN'.
WHEN'RE WE GETTIN' SOME CHOW, SARGE?
HALT!
BONJOUR.

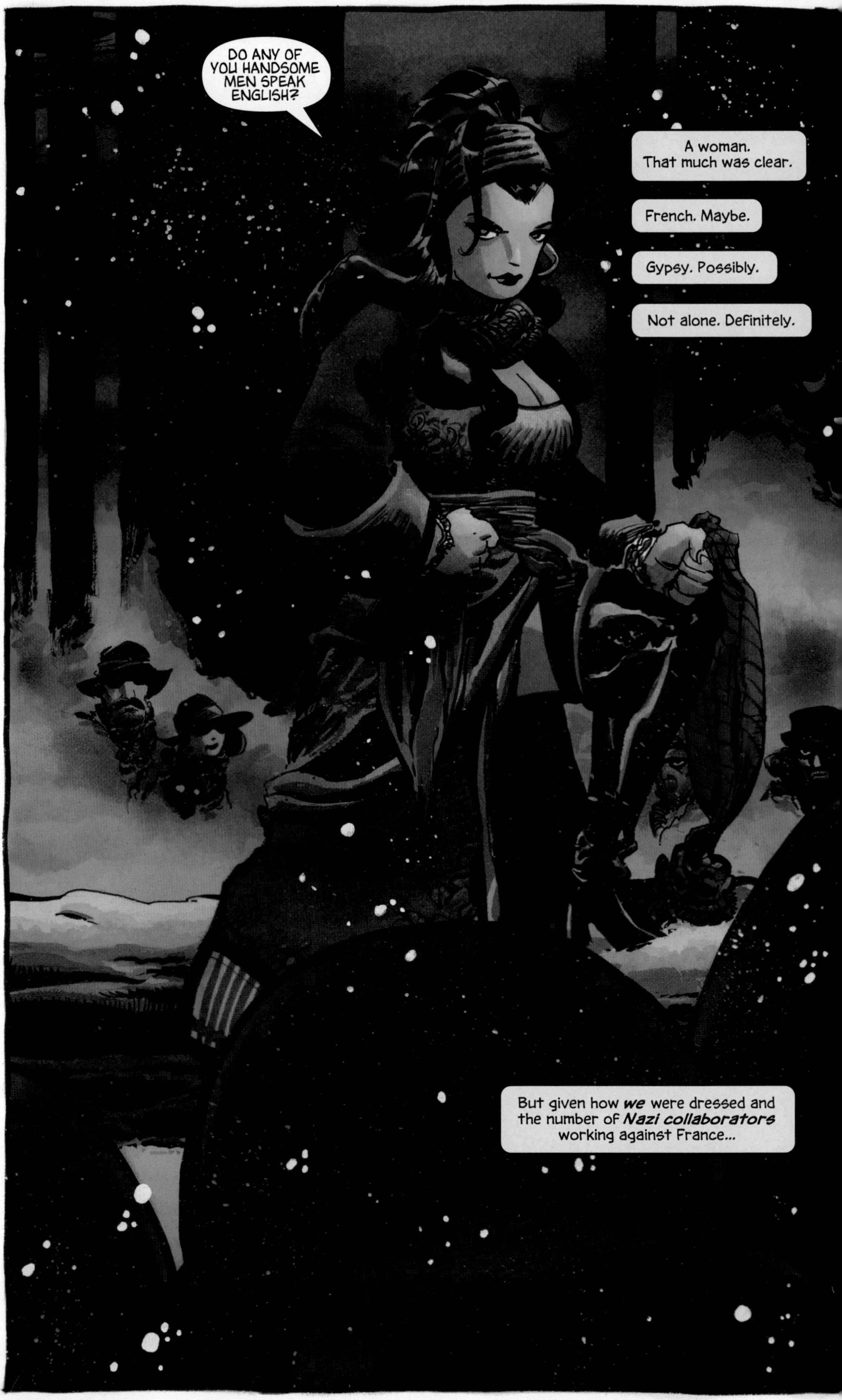
DO ANY OF YOU HANDSOME MEN SPEAK ENGLISH?
A woman. That much was clear.
French. Maybe.
Gypsy. Possibly.
Not alone. Definitely.
But given how *we* were dressed and the number of ***Nazi collaborators*** working against France...

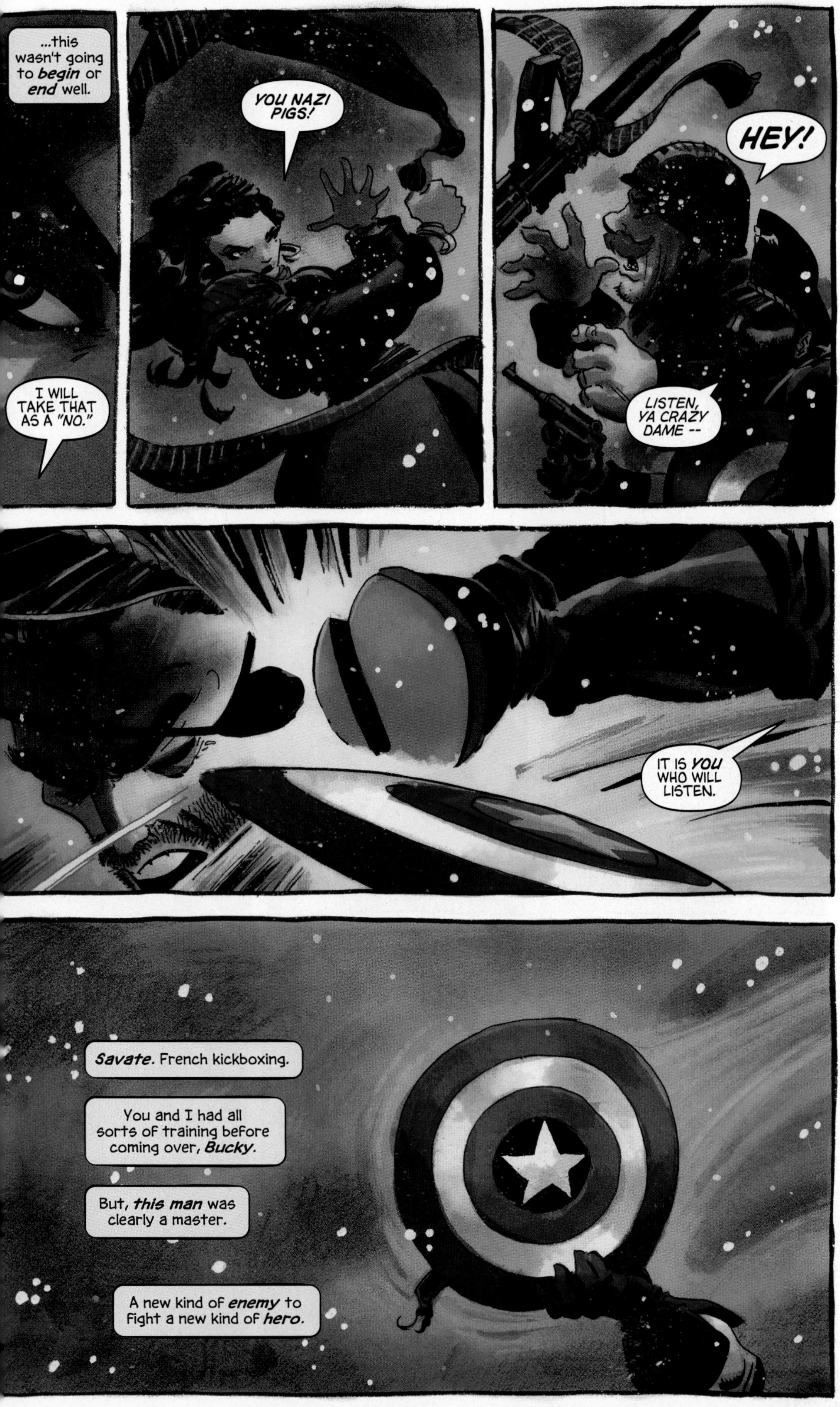
...this wasn't going to *begin* or *end* well.
I WILL TAKE THAT AS A "NO."
YOU NAZI PIGS!
HEY!
LISTEN, YA CRAZY DAME --
IT IS *YOU* WHO WILL LISTEN.
Savate. French kickboxing.
You and I had all sorts of training before coming over, *Bucky*.
But, *this man* was clearly a master.
A new kind of *enemy* to fight a new kind of *hero*.

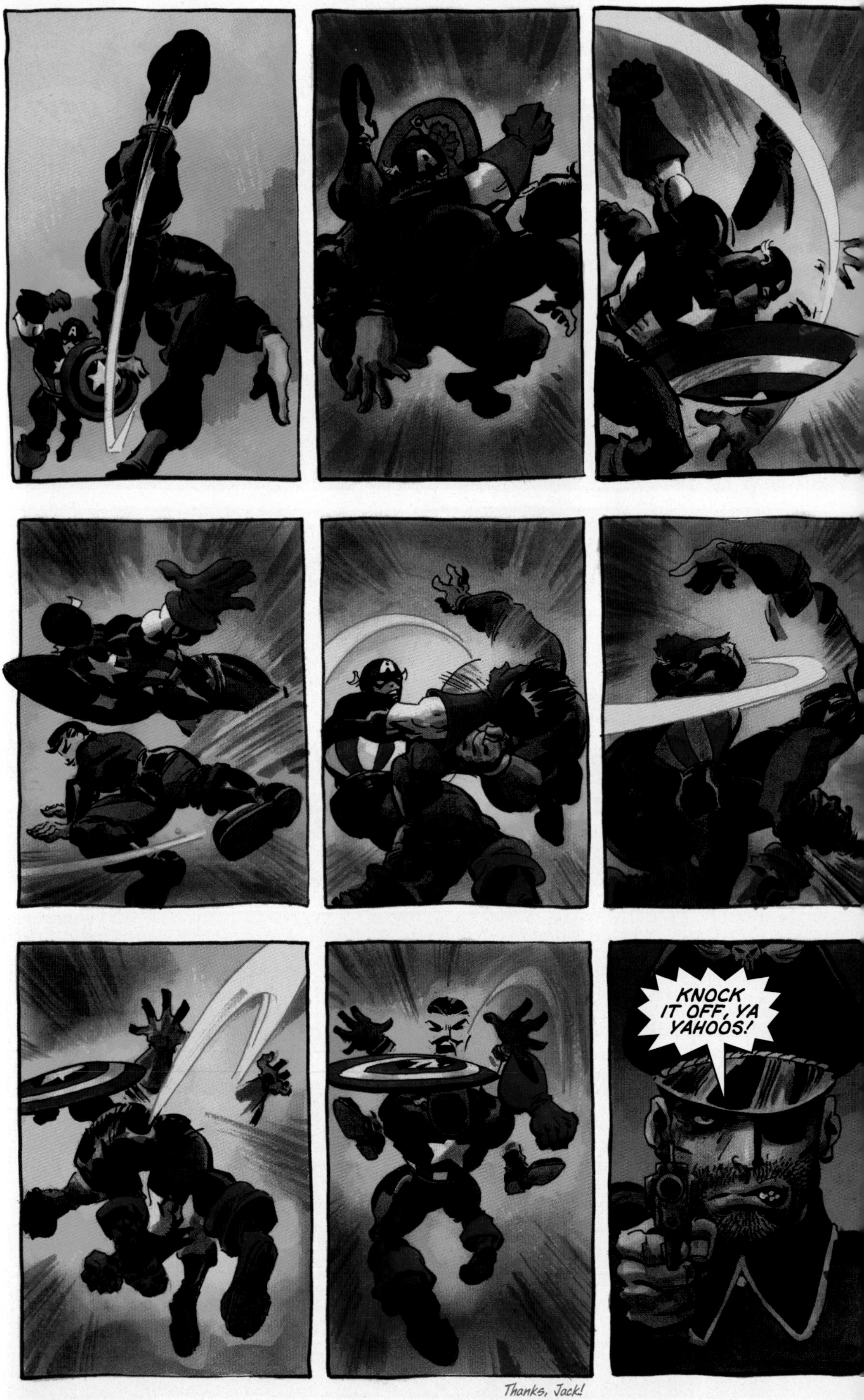
KNOCK IT OFF, YA YAHOOS!

Thanks, Jack!

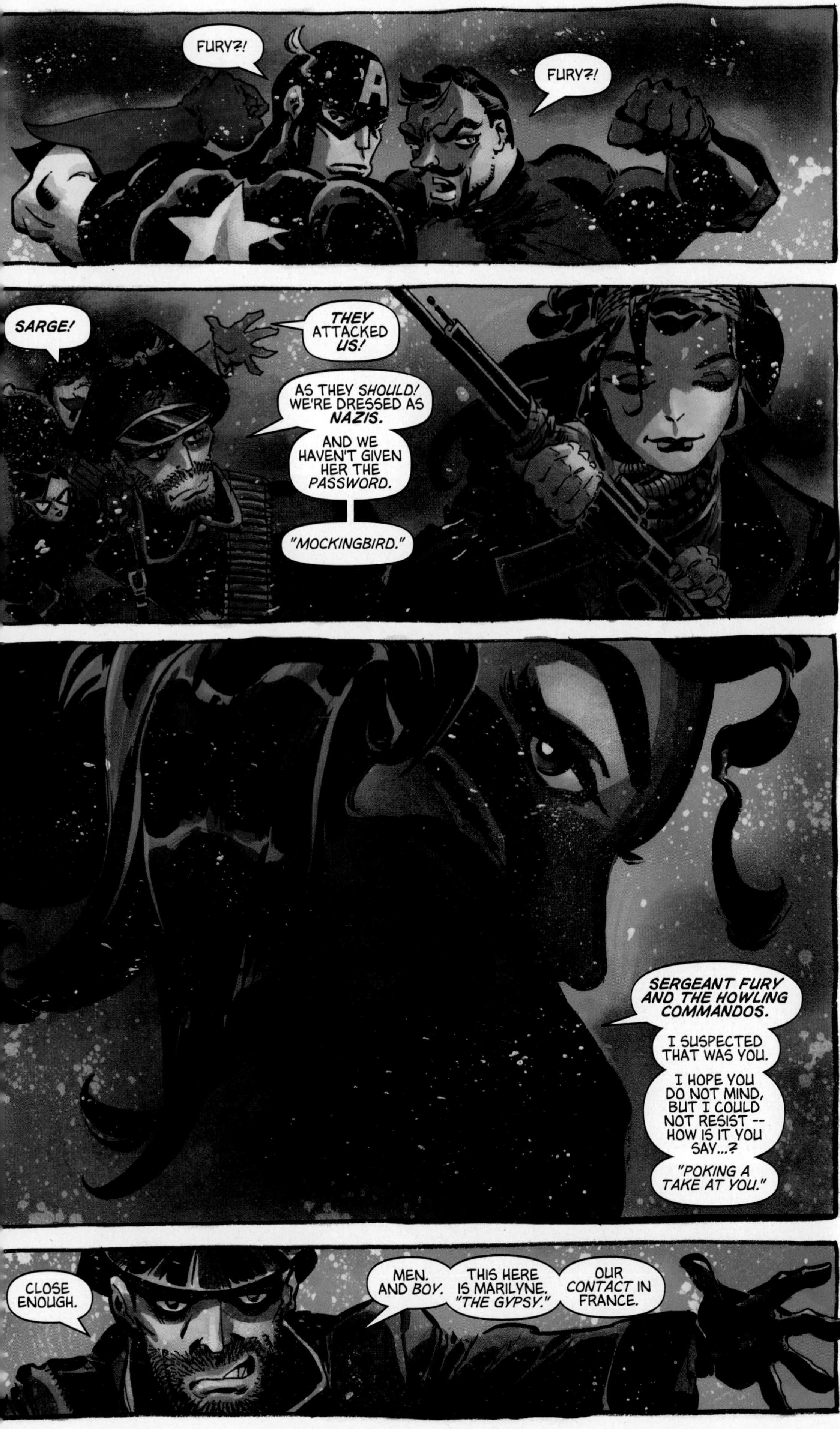

FURY?!
FURY?!
SARGE!
THEY ATTACKED US!
AS THEY SHOULD! WE'RE DRESSED AS NAZIS.
AND WE HAVEN'T GIVEN HER THE PASSWORD.
"MOCKINGBIRD."
SERGEANT FURY AND THE HOWLING COMMANDOS.
I SUSPECTED THAT WAS YOU.
I HOPE YOU DO NOT MIND, BUT I COULD NOT RESIST -- HOW IS IT YOU SAY...?
"POKING A TAKE AT YOU."
CLOSE ENOUGH.
MEN. AND BOY.
THIS HERE IS MARILYNE. "THE GYPSY."
OUR CONTACT IN FRANCE.

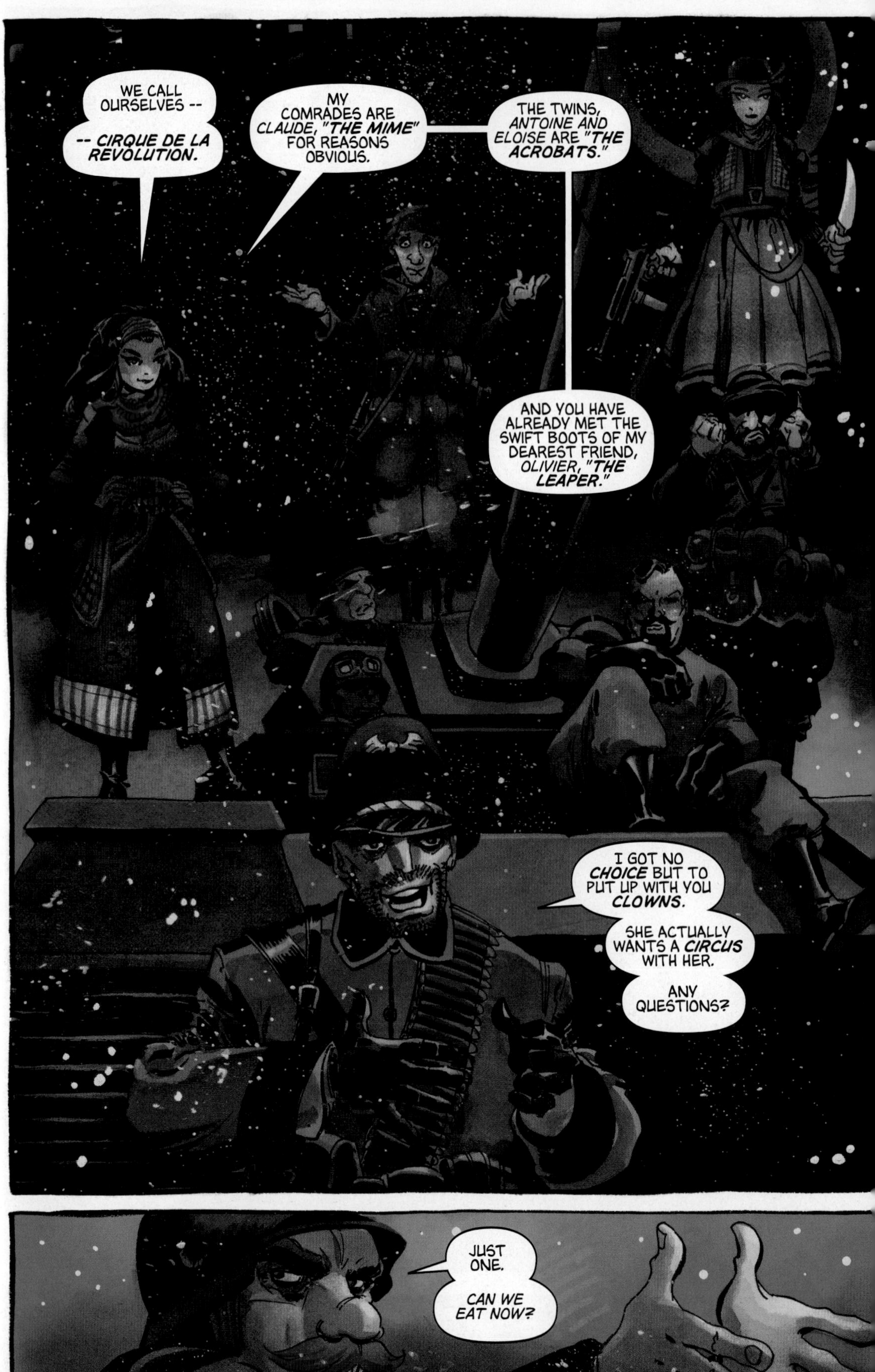
WE CALL OURSELVES --
-- CIRQUE DE LA REVOLUTION.
MY COMRADES ARE CLAUDE, "THE MIME" FOR REASONS OBVIOUS.
THE TWINS, ANTOINE AND ELOISE ARE "THE ACROBATS."
AND YOU HAVE ALREADY MET THE SWIFT BOOTS OF MY DEAREST FRIEND, OLIVIER, "THE LEAPER."
I GOT NO CHOICE BUT TO PUT UP WITH YOU CLOWNS.
SHE ACTUALLY WANTS A CIRCUS WITH HER.
ANY QUESTIONS?

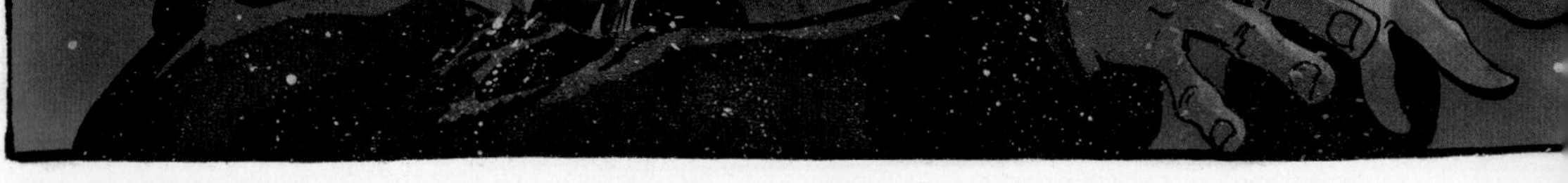
JUST ONE.
CAN WE EAT NOW?

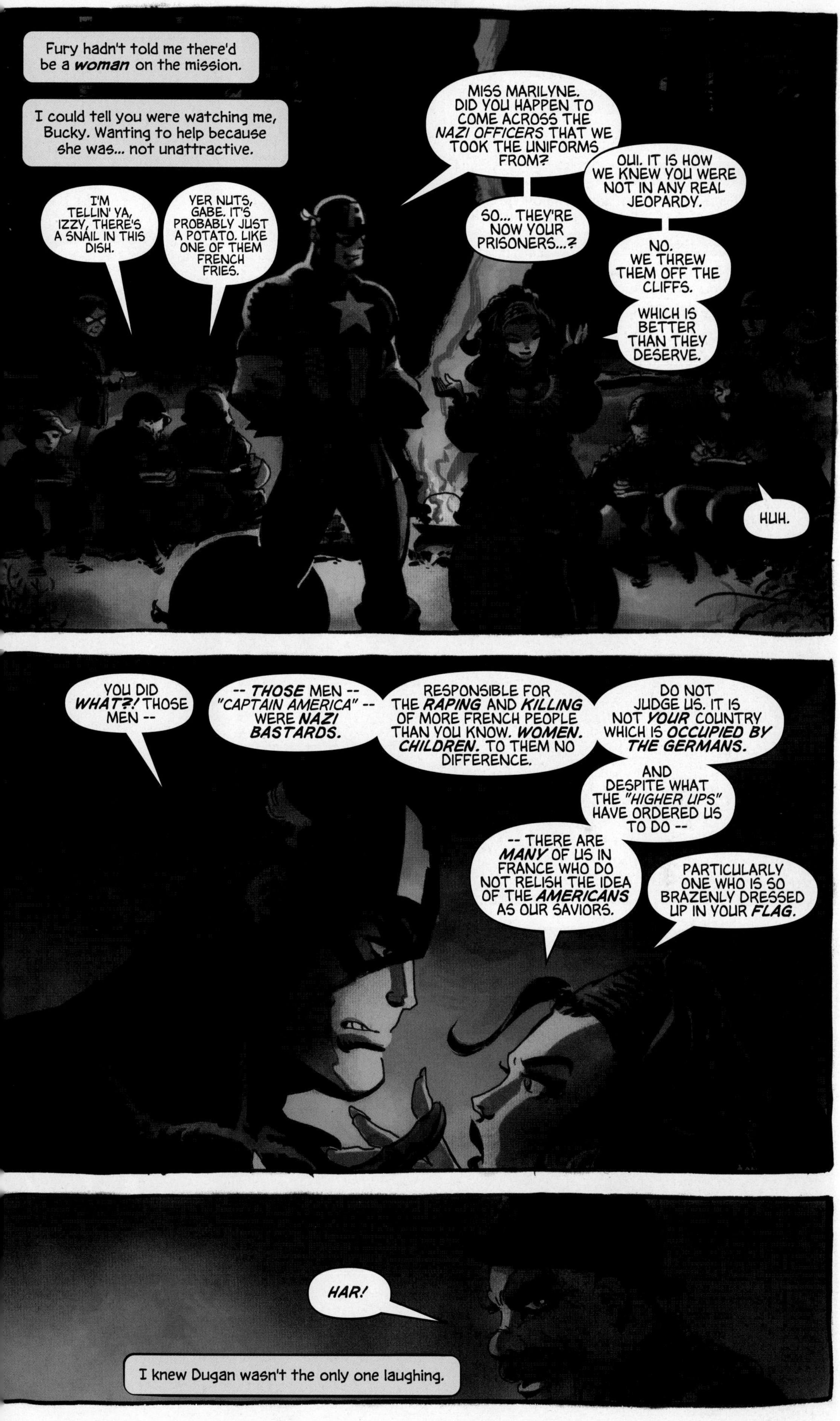

Fury hadn't told me there'd be a *woman* on the mission.
I could tell you were watching me, Bucky. Wanting to help because she was... not unattractive.
I'M TELLIN' YA, IZZY, THERE'S A SNAIL IN THIS DISH.
YER NUTS, GABE. IT'S PROBABLY JUST A POTATO. LIKE ONE OF THEM FRENCH FRIES.
MISS MARILYNE. DID YOU HAPPEN TO COME ACROSS THE *NAZI OFFICERS* THAT WE TOOK THE UNIFORMS FROM?
SO... THEY'RE NOW YOUR PRISONERS...?
OUI. IT IS HOW WE KNEW YOU WERE NOT IN ANY REAL JEOPARDY.
NO. WE THREW THEM OFF THE CLIFFS.
WHICH IS BETTER THAN THEY DESERVE.
HUH.
YOU DID *WHAT?!* THOSE MEN --
-- *THOSE* MEN -- "*CAPTAIN AMERICA*" -- WERE *NAZI BASTARDS.*
RESPONSIBLE FOR THE *RAPING* AND *KILLING* OF MORE FRENCH PEOPLE THAN YOU KNOW. *WOMEN. CHILDREN.* TO THEM NO DIFFERENCE.
DO NOT JUDGE US. IT IS NOT *YOUR* COUNTRY WHICH IS *OCCUPIED BY THE GERMANS.*
AND DESPITE WHAT THE "*HIGHER UPS*" HAVE ORDERED US TO DO --
-- THERE ARE *MANY* OF US IN FRANCE WHO DO NOT RELISH THE IDEA OF THE *AMERICANS* AS OUR SAVIORS.
PARTICULARLY ONE WHO IS SO BRAZENLY DRESSED UP IN YOUR *FLAG.*
HAR!
I knew Dugan wasn't the only one laughing.

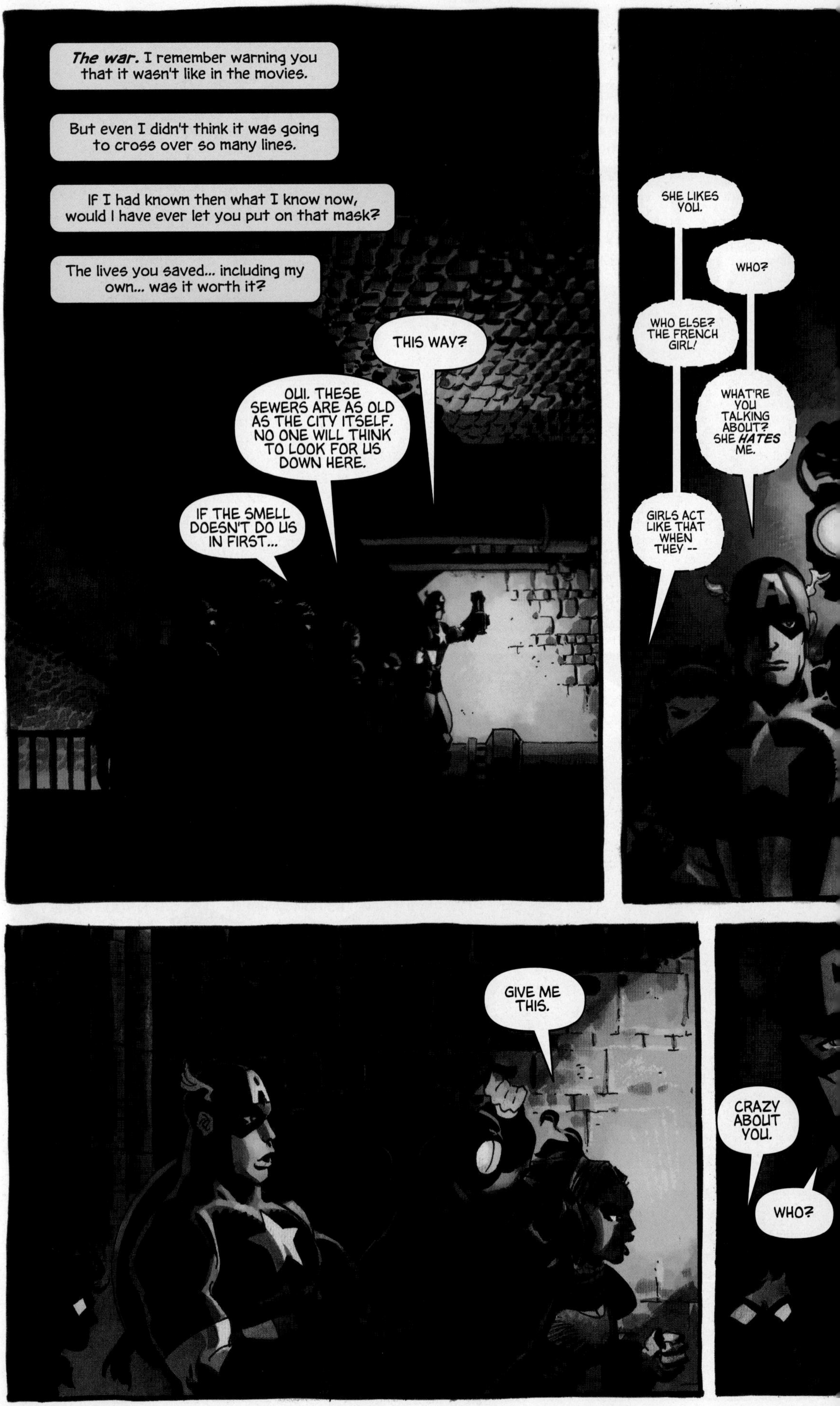
The war. I remember warning you that it wasn't like in the movies.
But even I didn't think it was going to cross over so many lines.
If I had known then what I know now, would I have ever let you put on that mask?
The lives you saved... including my own... was it worth it?
THIS WAY?
OUI. THESE SEWERS ARE AS OLD AS THE CITY ITSELF. NO ONE WILL THINK TO LOOK FOR US DOWN HERE.
IF THE SMELL DOESN'T DO US IN FIRST...
SHE LIKES YOU.
WHO?
WHO ELSE? THE FRENCH GIRL!
WHAT'RE YOU TALKING ABOUT? SHE *HATES* ME.
GIRLS ACT LIKE THAT WHEN THEY --
GIVE ME THIS.
CRAZY ABOUT YOU.
WHO?

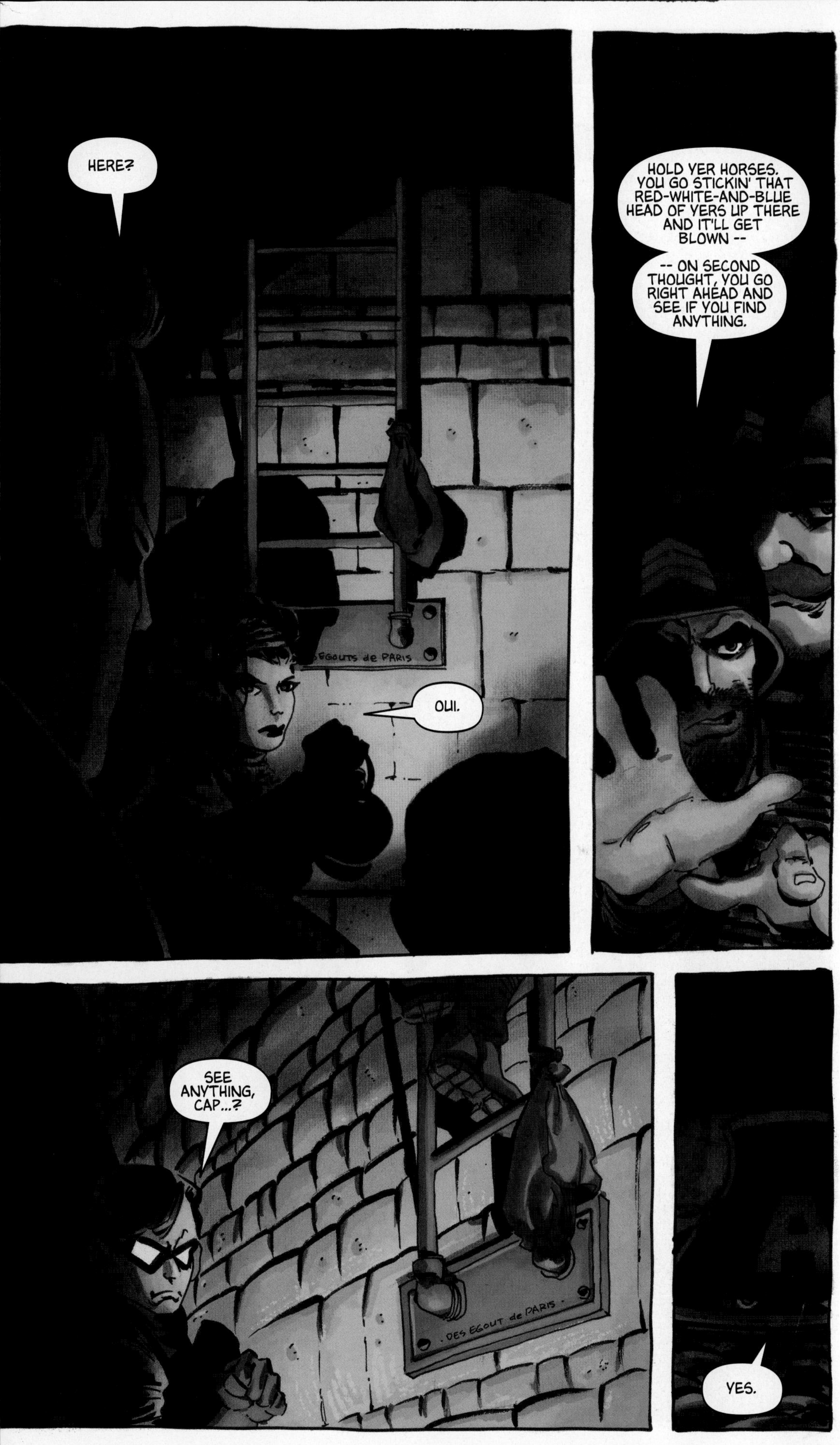
HERE?
HOLD YER HORSES. YOU GO STICKIN' THAT RED-WHITE-AND-BLUE HEAD OF YERS UP THERE AND IT'LL GET BLOWN --
-- ON SECOND THOUGHT, YOU GO RIGHT AHEAD AND SEE IF YOU FIND ANYTHING.
DES EGOUTS de PARIS
OUI.
SEE ANYTHING, CAP...?
DES EGOUT de PARIS
YES.

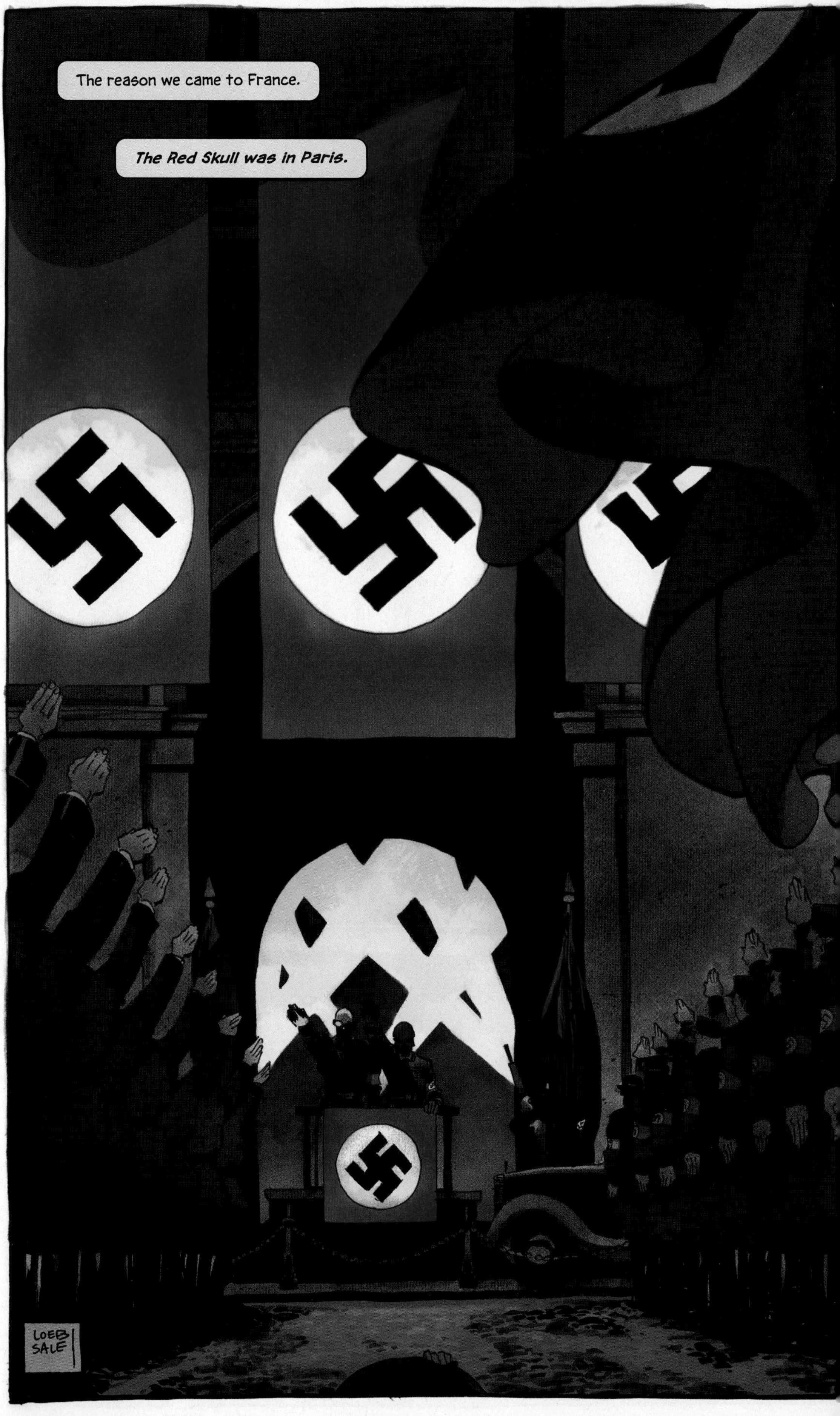
The reason we came to France.
The Red Skull was in Paris.
LOEB SALE

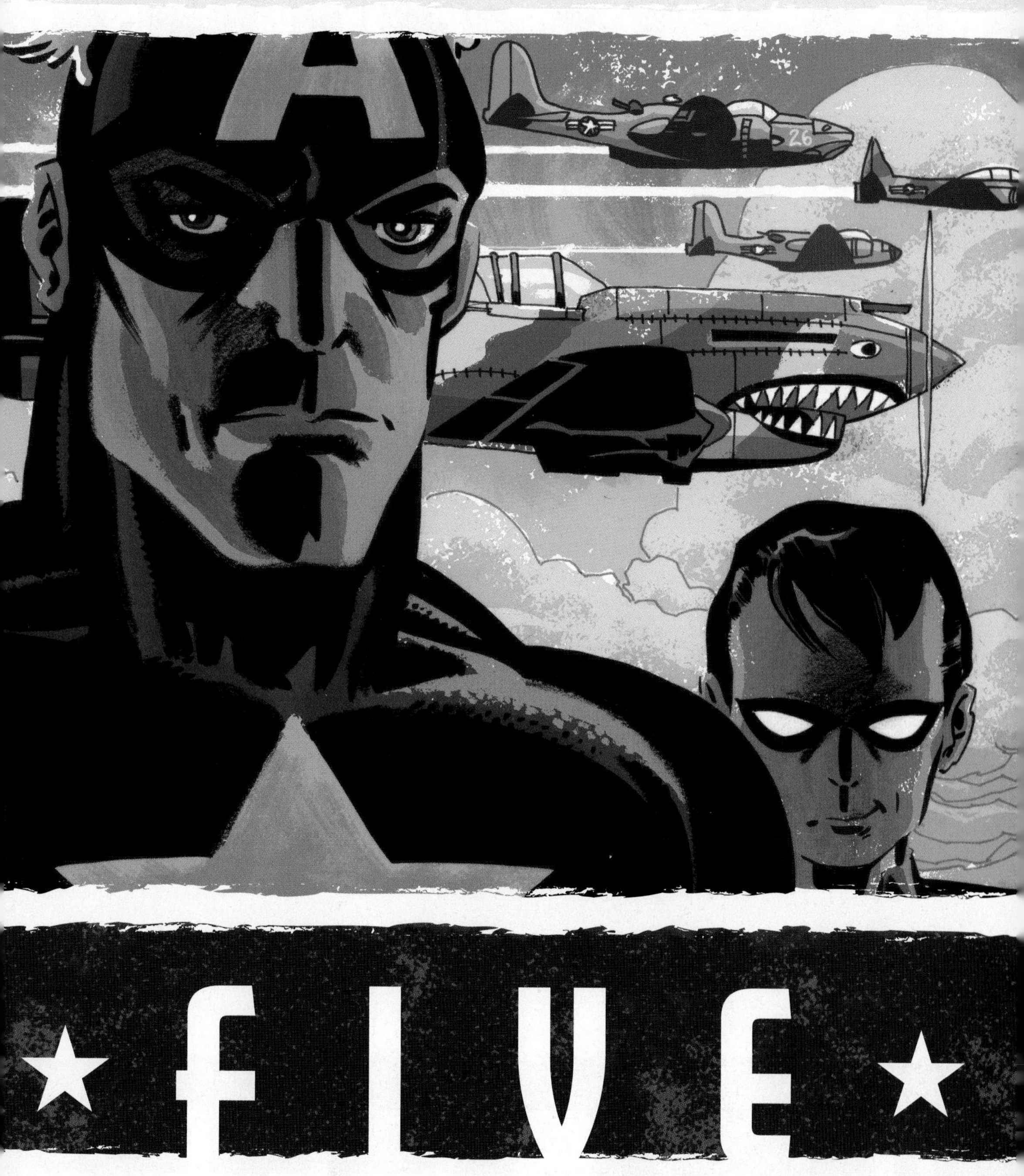
26

FIVE

POCKETFUL OF

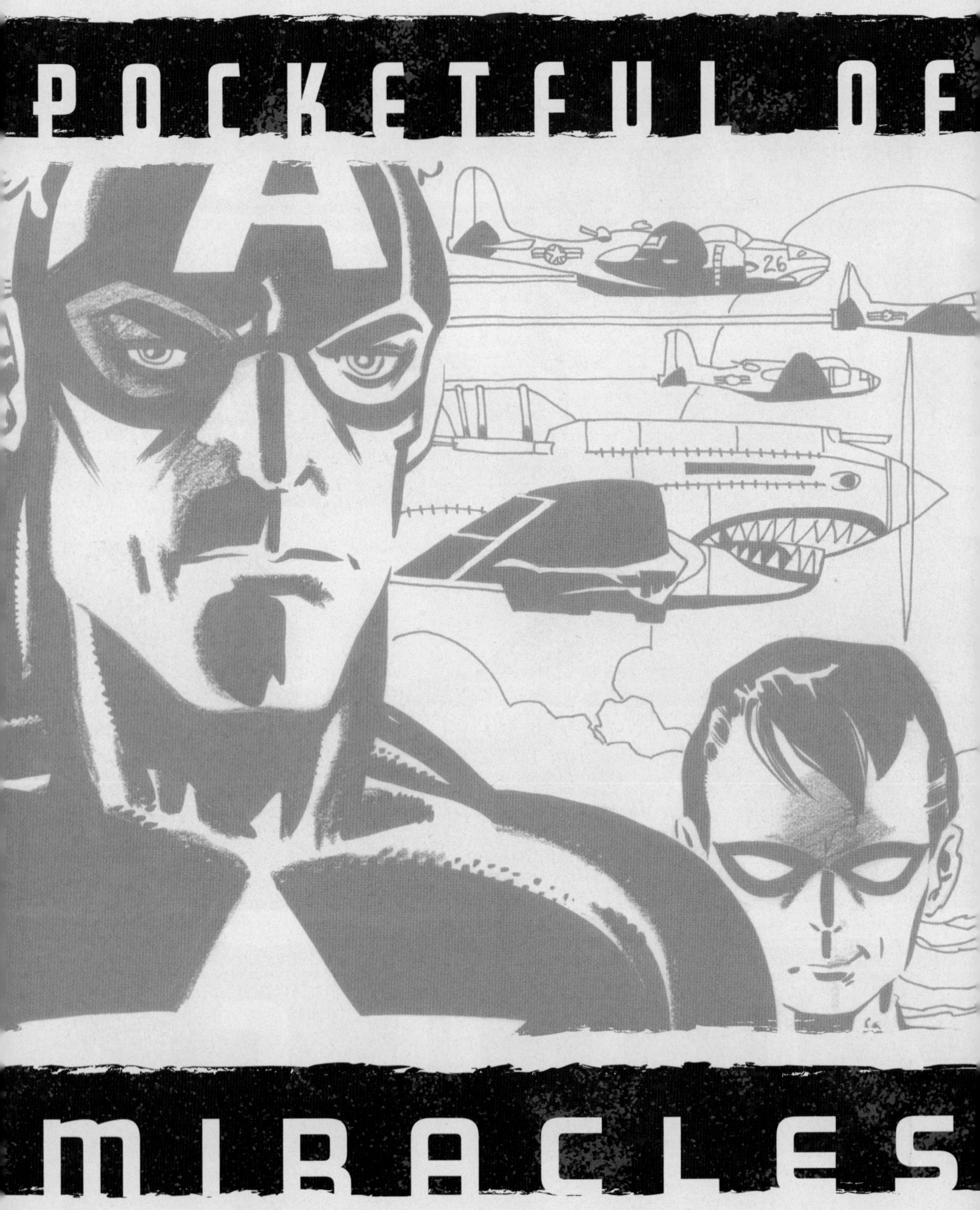
26

MIRACLES

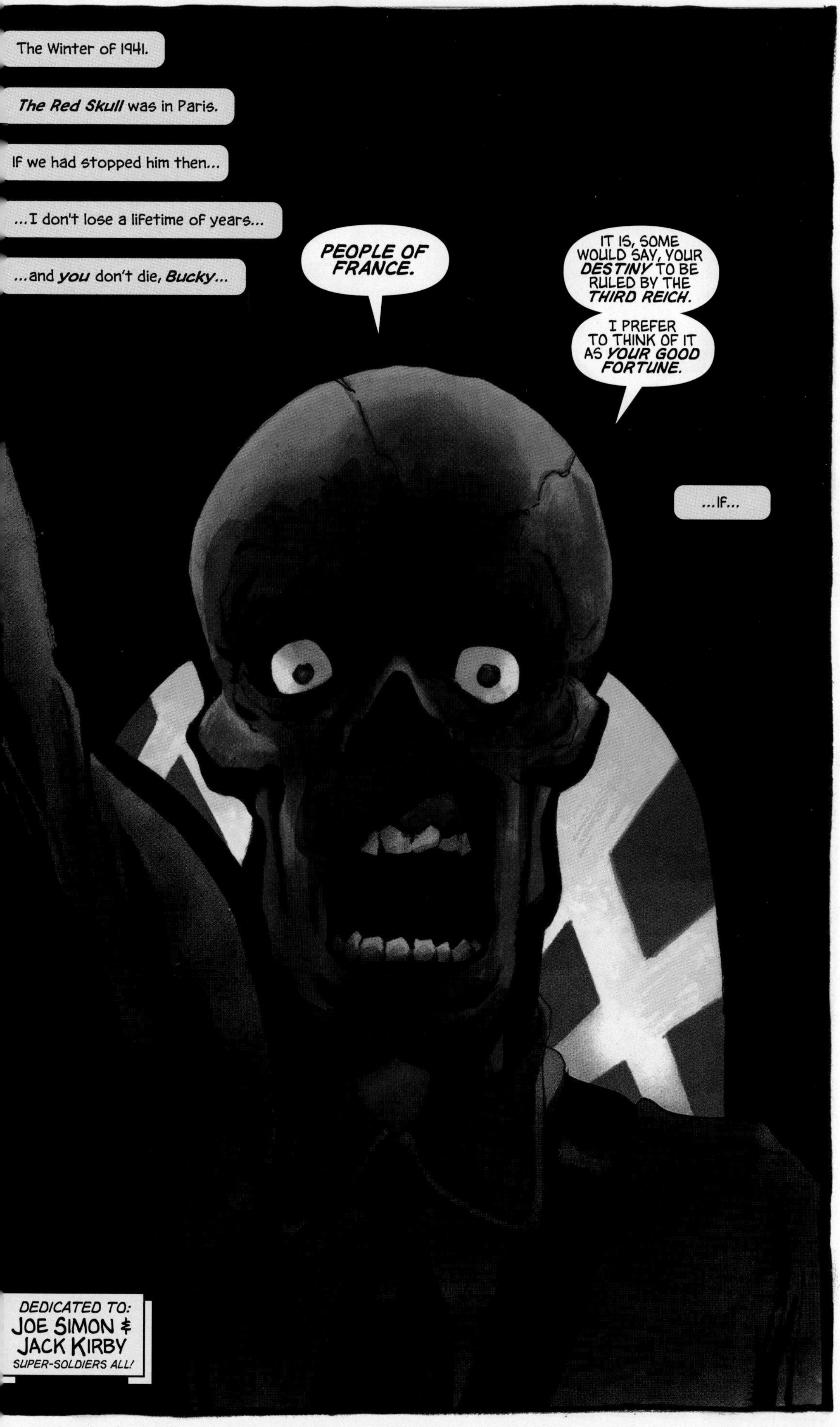
The Winter of 1941.
The Red Skull was in Paris.
If we had stopped him then...
...I don't lose a lifetime of years...
...and *you* don't die, *Bucky*...
PEOPLE OF FRANCE.
IT IS, SOME WOULD SAY, YOUR *DESTINY* TO BE RULED BY THE *THIRD REICH.*
I PREFER TO THINK OF IT AS *YOUR GOOD FORTUNE.*
...IF...
DEDICATED TO: JOE SIMON & JACK KIRBY *SUPER-SOLDIERS ALL!*

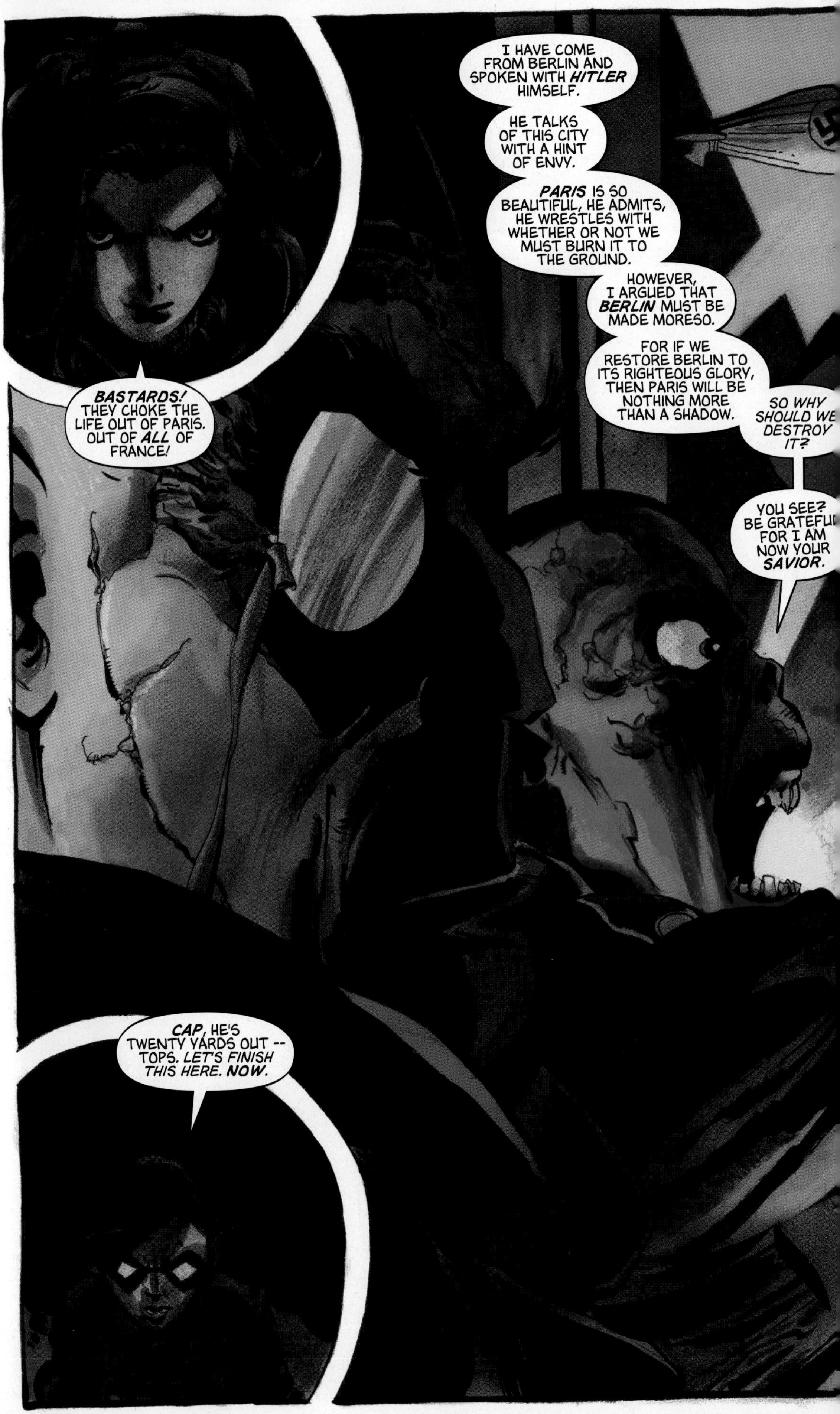
I HAVE COME FROM BERLIN AND SPOKEN WITH *HITLER* HIMSELF.
HE TALKS OF THIS CITY WITH A HINT OF ENVY.
PARIS IS SO BEAUTIFUL, HE ADMITS, HE WRESTLES WITH WHETHER OR NOT WE MUST BURN IT TO THE GROUND.
HOWEVER, I ARGUED THAT *BERLIN* MUST BE MADE MORESO.
FOR IF WE RESTORE BERLIN TO ITS RIGHTEOUS GLORY, THEN PARIS WILL BE NOTHING MORE THAN A SHADOW.
SO WHY SHOULD WE DESTROY IT?
BASTARDS! THEY CHOKE THE LIFE OUT OF PARIS. OUT OF *ALL* OF FRANCE!
YOU SEE? BE GRATEFUL FOR I AM NOW YOUR *SAVIOR*.
CAP, HE'S TWENTY YARDS OUT -- TOPS. *LET'S FINISH THIS HERE. NOW*.

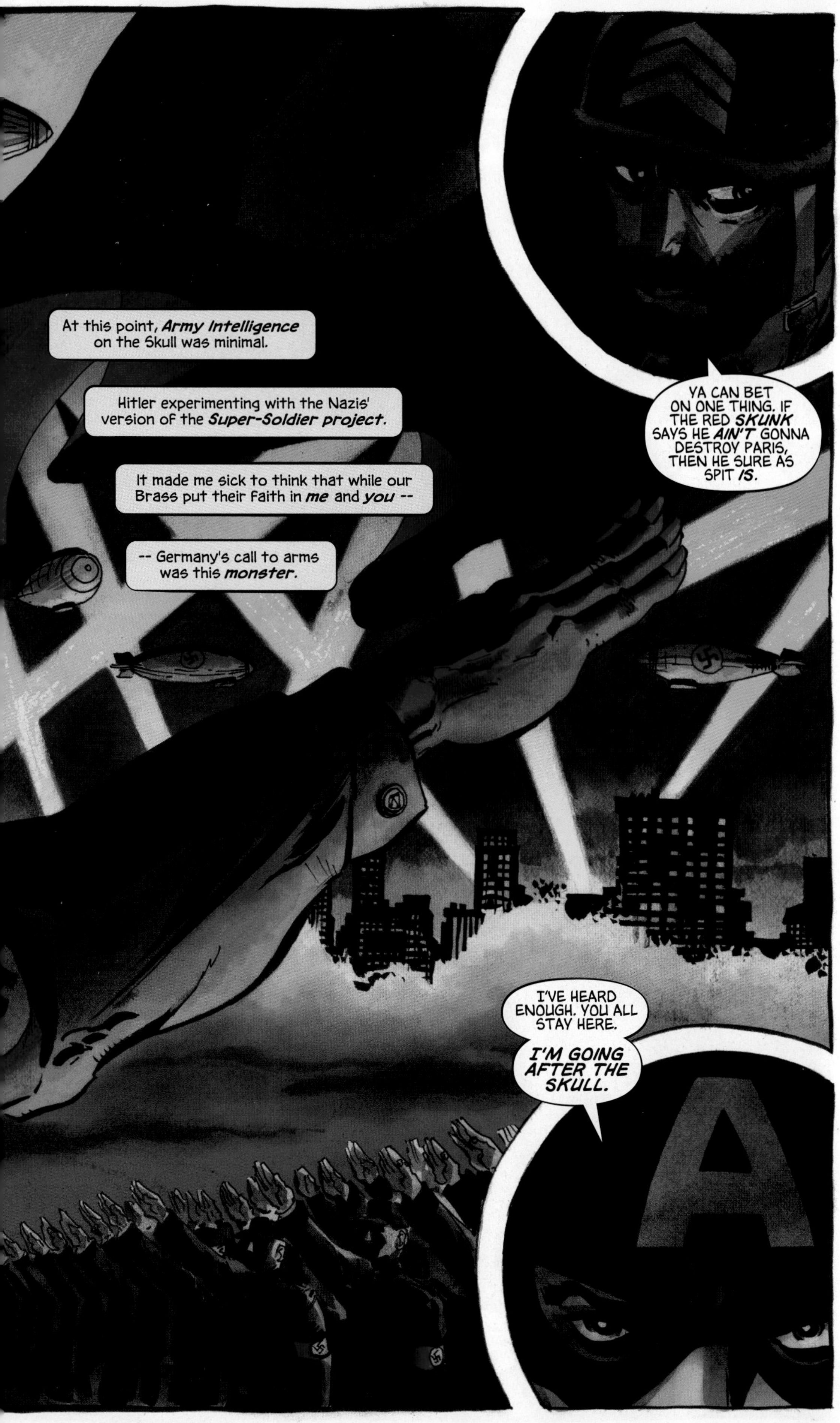
At this point, Army Intelligence on the Skull was minimal.
Hitler experimenting with the Nazis' version of the Super-Soldier project.
It made me sick to think that while our Brass put their faith in me and you --
-- Germany's call to arms was this monster.
YA CAN BET ON ONE THING. IF THE RED SKUNK SAYS HE AIN'T GONNA DESTROY PARIS, THEN HE SURE AS SPIT IS.
I'VE HEARD ENOUGH. YOU ALL STAY HERE.
I'M GOING AFTER THE SKULL.

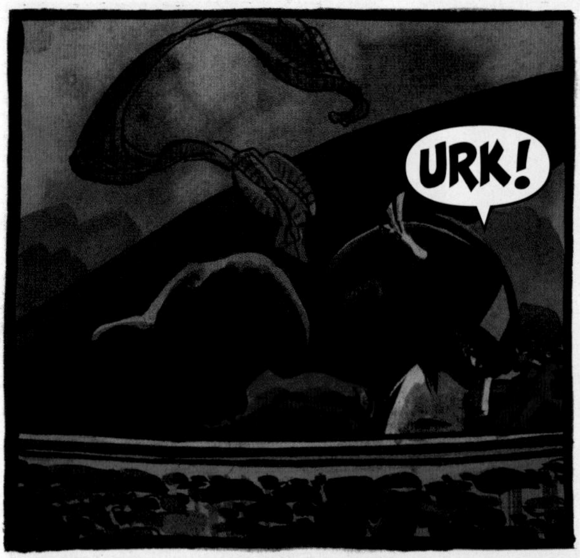
URK!

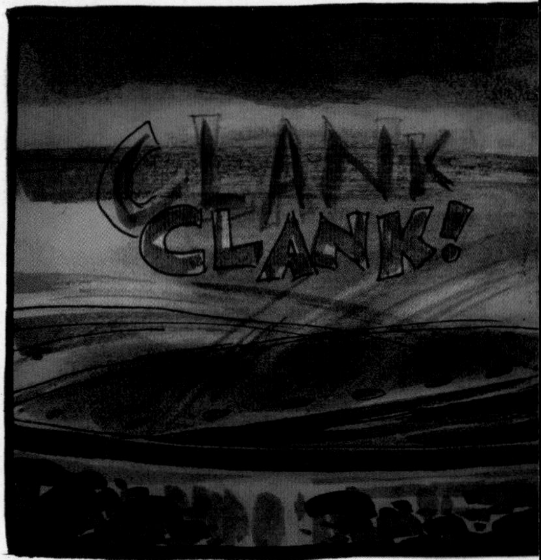
CLANK
CLANK!

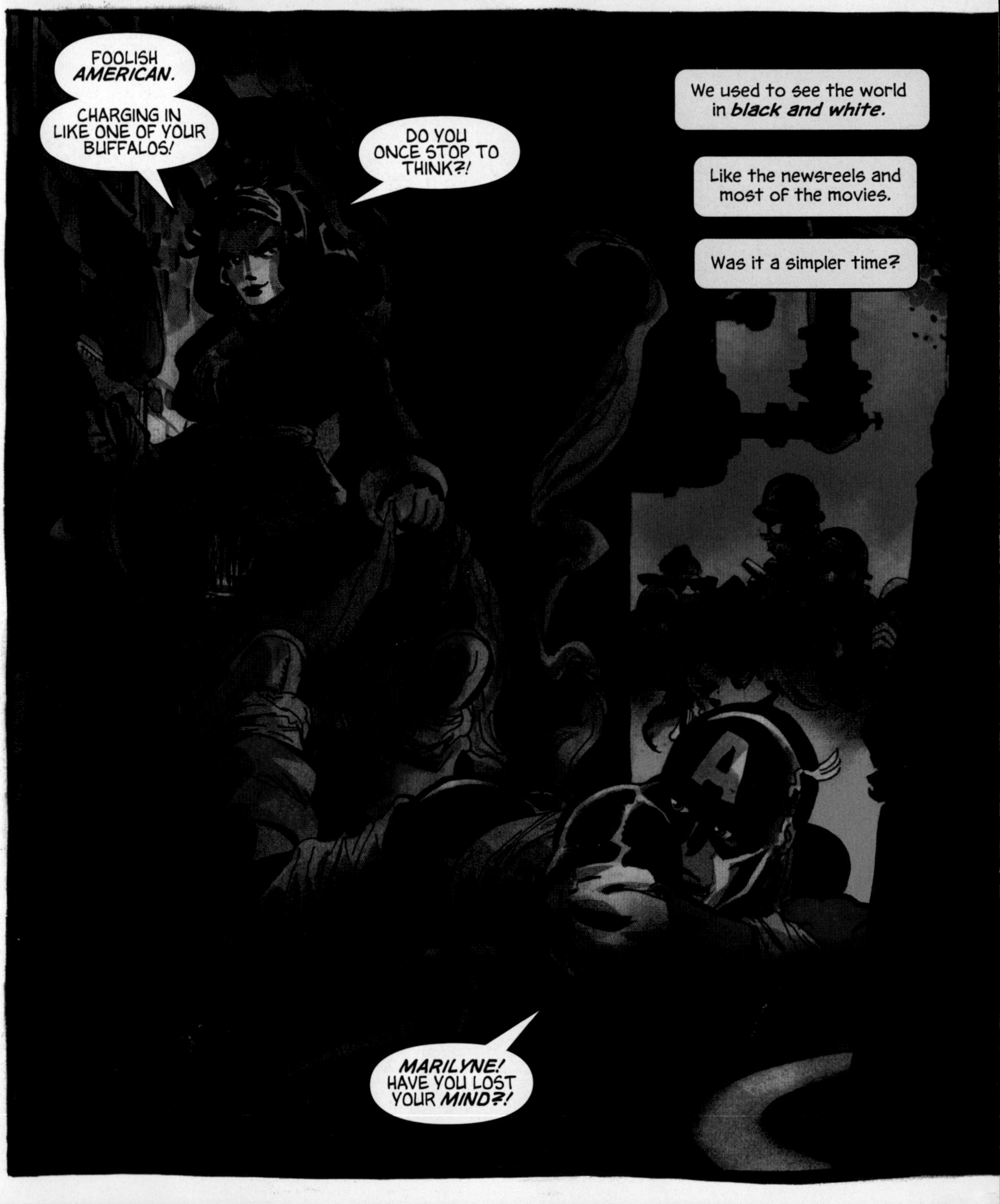
FOOLISH AMERICAN.
CHARGING IN LIKE ONE OF YOUR BUFFALOS!
DO YOU ONCE STOP TO THINK?!
We used to see the world in black and white.
Like the newsreels and most of the movies.
Was it a simpler time?
MARILYNE! HAVE YOU LOST YOUR MIND?!

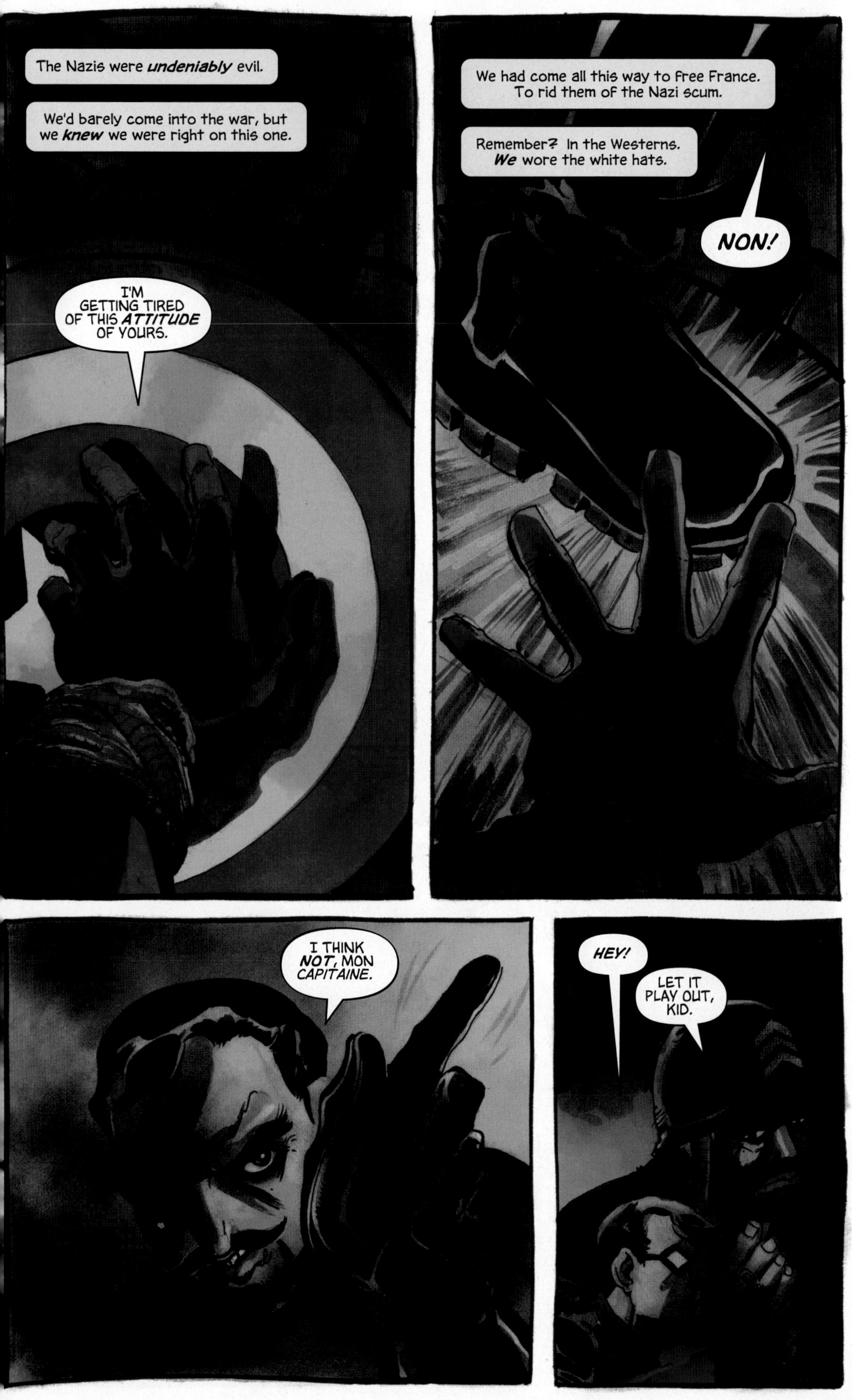
The Nazis were *undeniably* evil.
We'd barely come into the war, but we *knew* we were right on this one.
I'M GETTING TIRED OF THIS *ATTITUDE* OF YOURS.
We had come all this way to free France. To rid them of the Nazi scum.
Remember? In the Westerns. *We* wore the white hats.
NON!
I THINK *NOT*, MON CAPITAINE.
HEY!
LET IT PLAY OUT, KID.

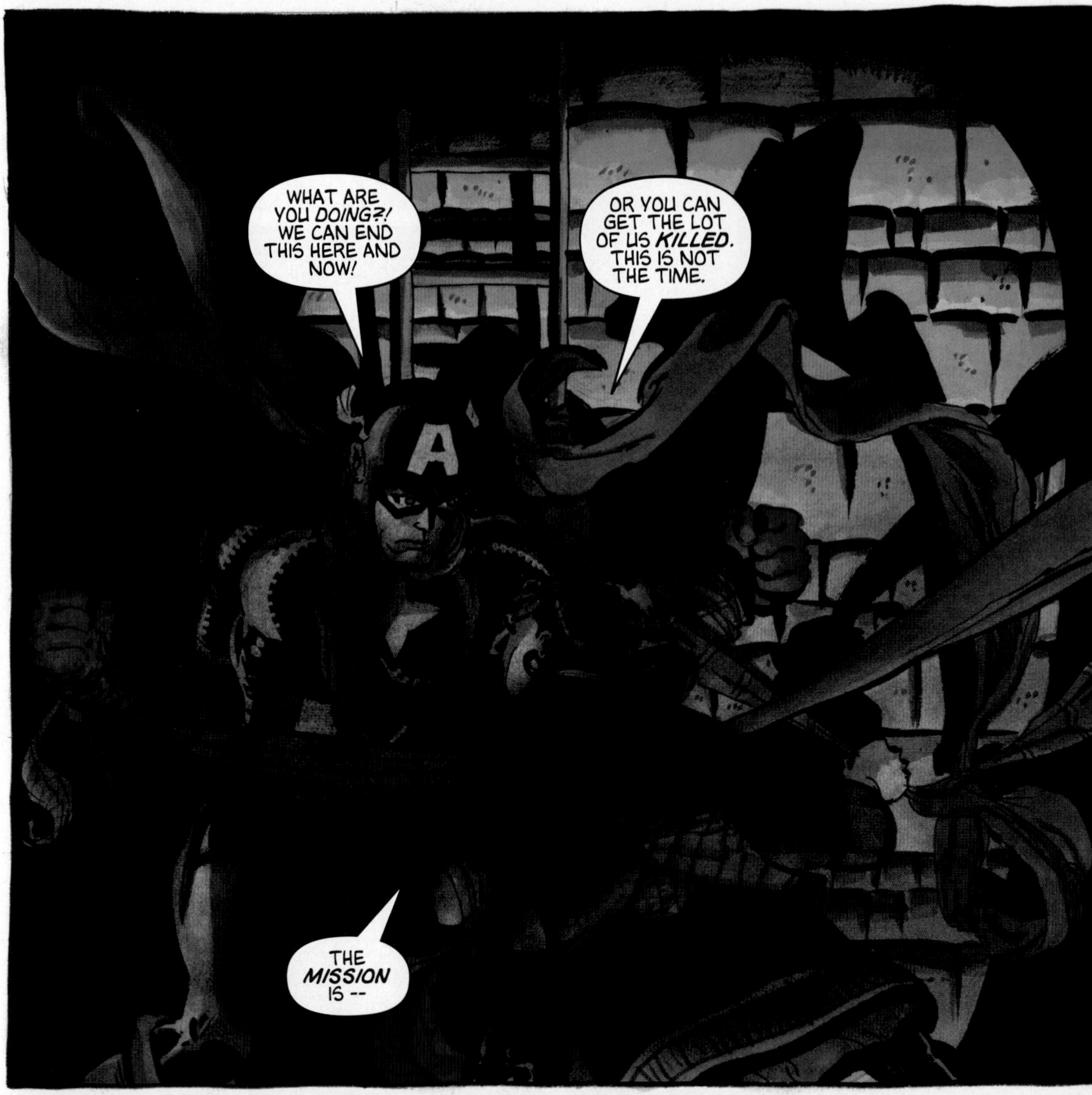
WHAT ARE YOU DOING?! WE CAN END THIS HERE AND NOW!
OR YOU CAN GET THE LOT OF US KILLED. THIS IS NOT THE TIME.
THE MISSION IS --

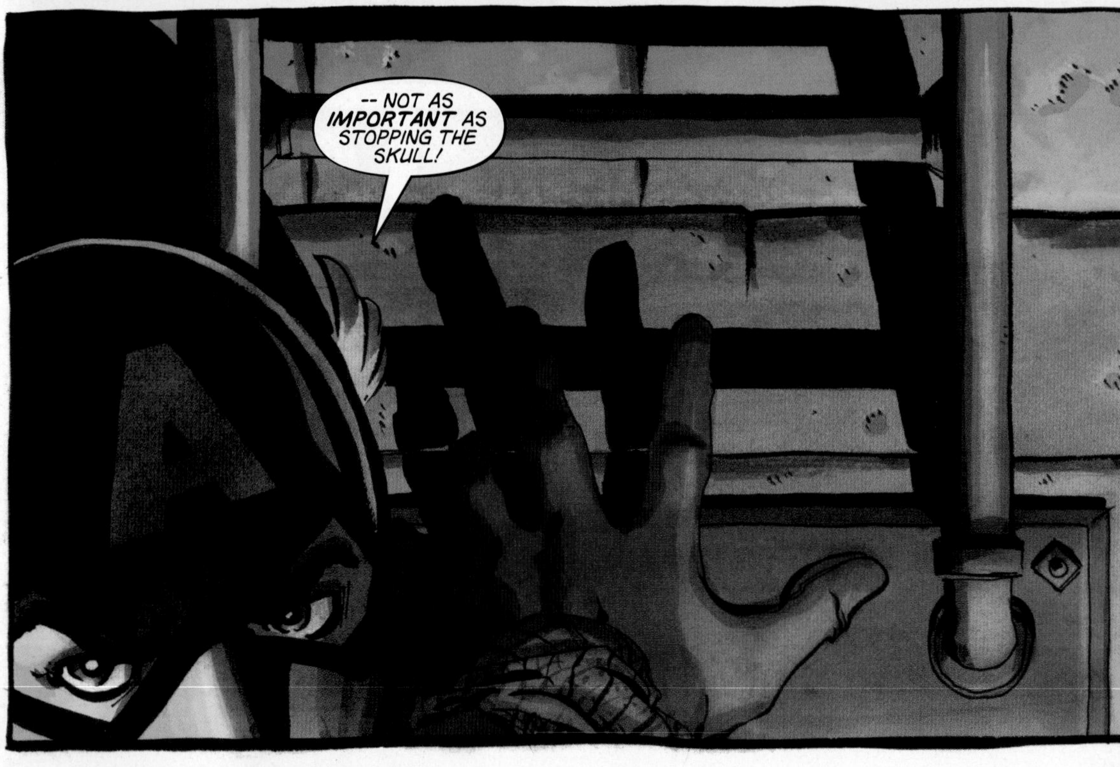
-- NOT AS IMPORTANT AS STOPPING THE SKULL!

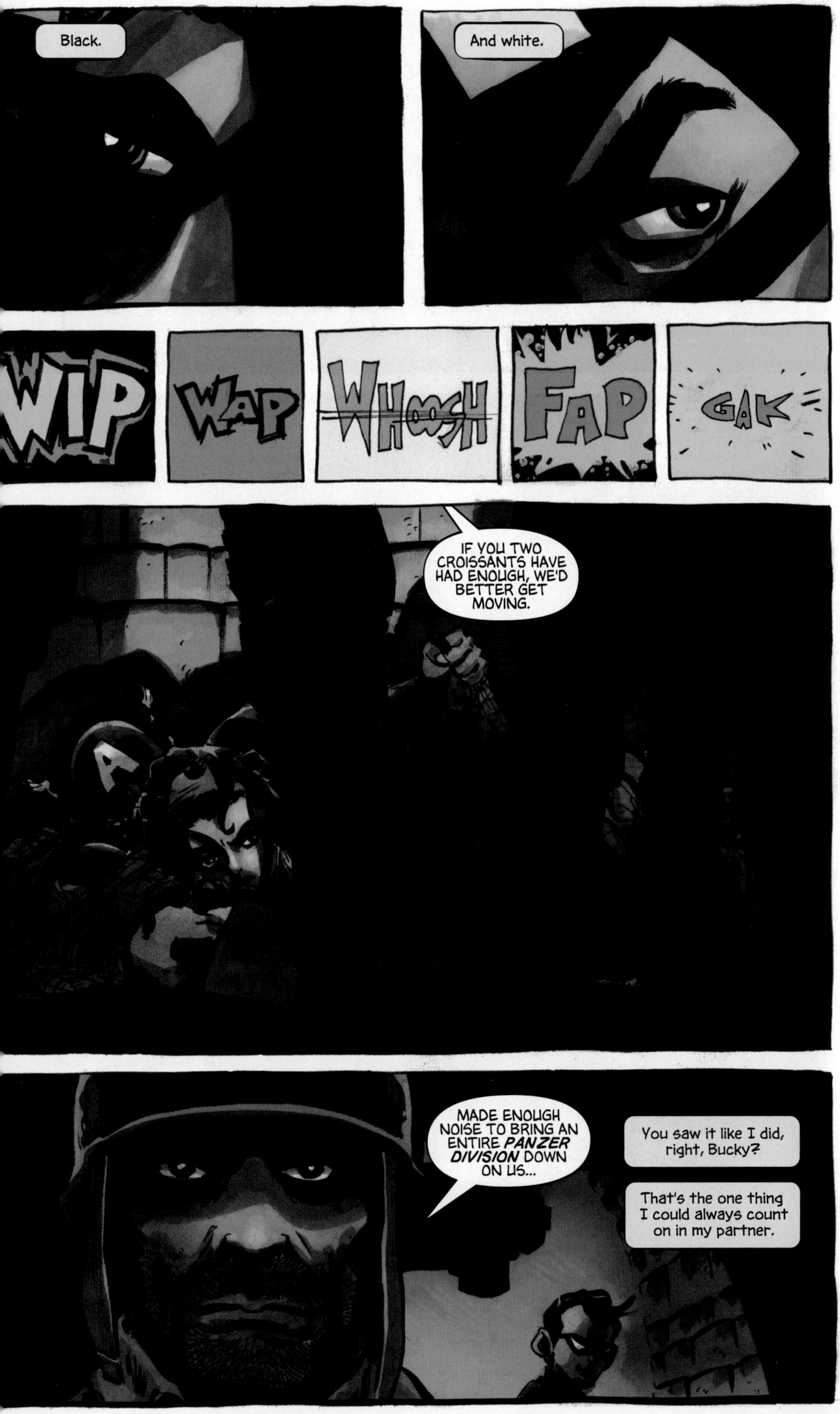

Black.
And white.
WIP
WAP
WHOOSH
FAP
GAK
IF YOU TWO CROISSANTS HAVE HAD ENOUGH, WE'D BETTER GET MOVING.
MADE ENOUGH NOISE TO BRING AN ENTIRE *PANZER DIVISION* DOWN ON US...
You saw it like I did, right, Bucky?
That's the one thing I could always count on in my partner.

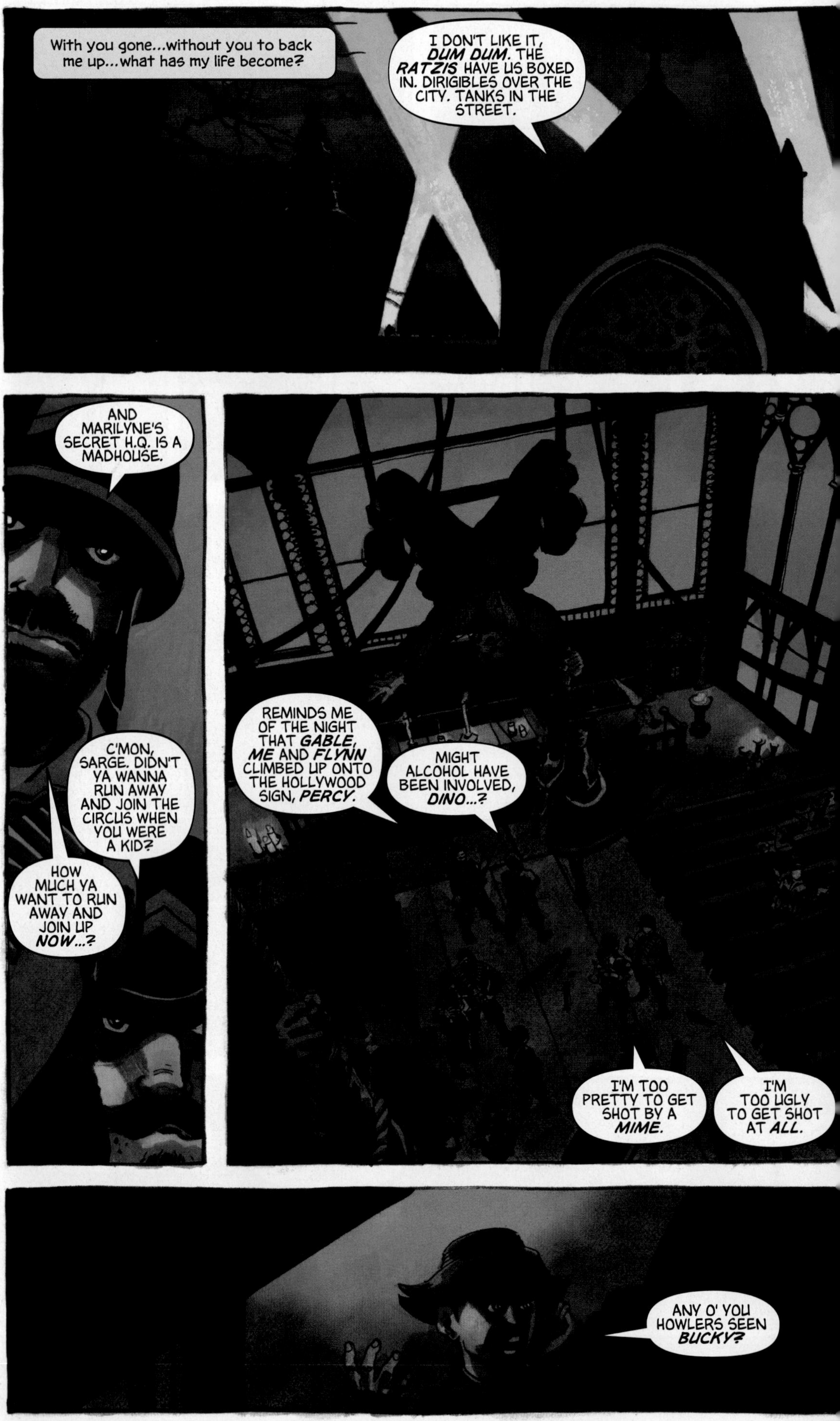
With you gone...without you to back me up...what has my life become?
I DON'T LIKE IT, DUM DUM. THE RATZIS HAVE US BOXED IN. DIRIGIBLES OVER THE CITY. TANKS IN THE STREET.
AND MARILYNE'S SECRET H.Q. IS A MADHOUSE.
C'MON, SARGE. DIDN'T YA WANNA RUN AWAY AND JOIN THE CIRCUS WHEN YOU WERE A KID?
HOW MUCH YA WANT TO RUN AWAY AND JOIN UP NOW...?
REMINDS ME OF THE NIGHT THAT GABLE, ME AND FLYNN CLIMBED UP ONTO THE HOLLYWOOD SIGN, PERCY.
MIGHT ALCOHOL HAVE BEEN INVOLVED, DINO...?
I'M TOO PRETTY TO GET SHOT BY A MIME.
I'M TOO UGLY TO GET SHOT AT ALL.
ANY O' YOU HOWLERS SEEN BUCKY?

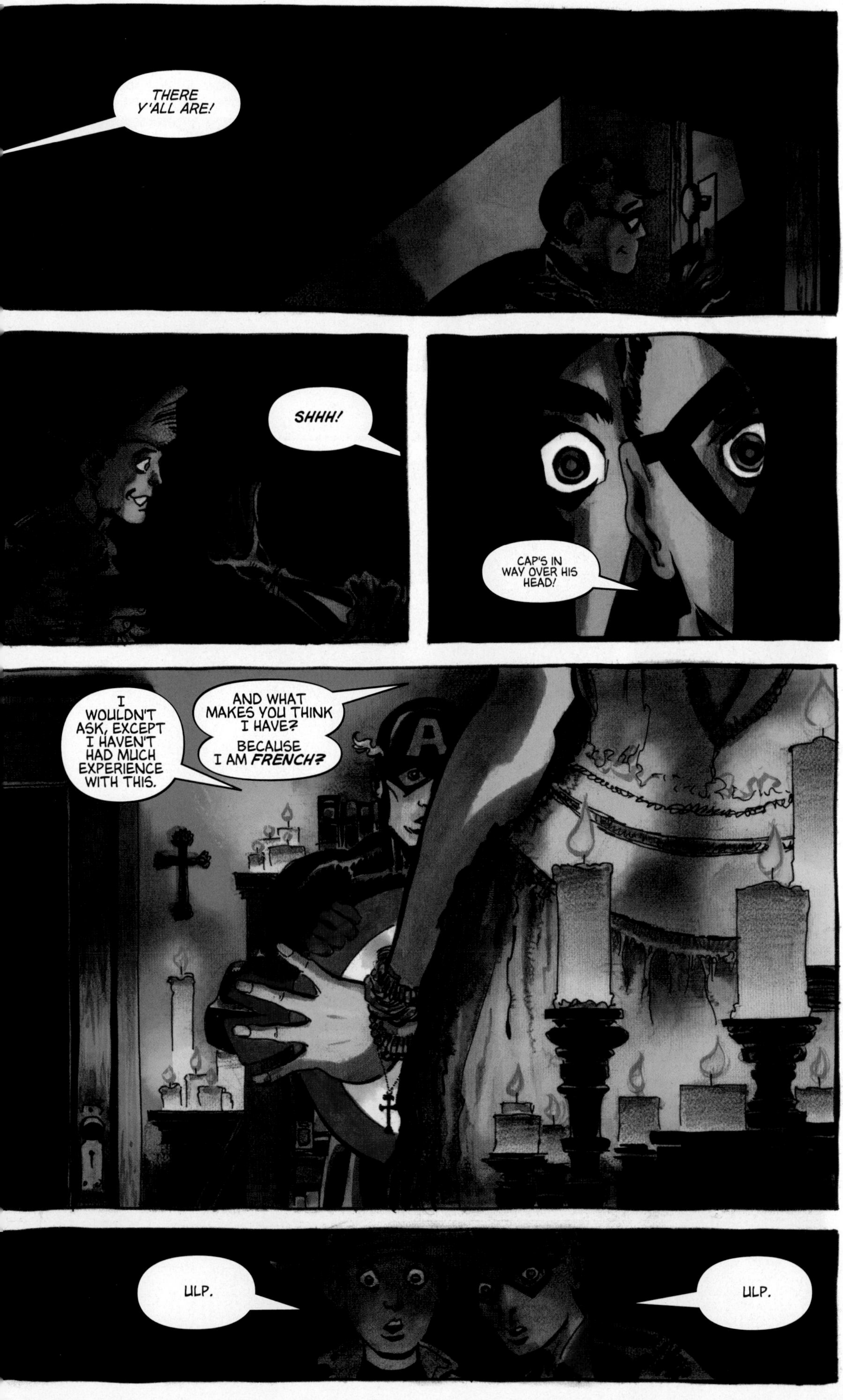
THERE Y'ALL ARE!
SHHH!
CAP'S IN WAY OVER HIS HEAD!
I WOULDN'T ASK, EXCEPT I HAVEN'T HAD MUCH EXPERIENCE WITH THIS.
AND WHAT MAKES YOU THINK I HAVE?
BECAUSE I AM FRENCH?
ULP.
ULP.

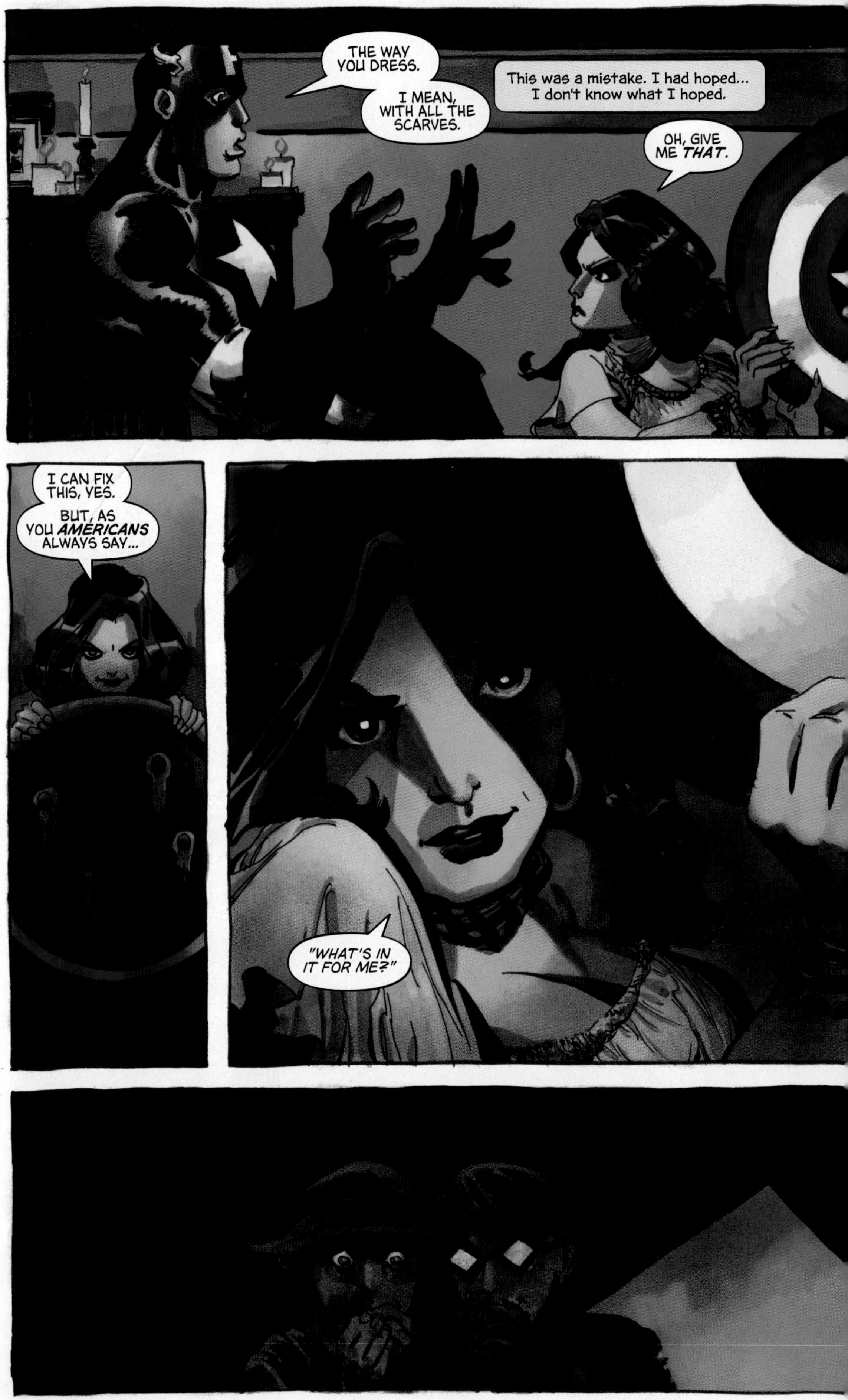
THE WAY YOU DRESS.
I MEAN, WITH ALL THE SCARVES.
This was a mistake. I had hoped... I don't know what I hoped.
OH, GIVE ME *THAT*.
I CAN FIX THIS, YES.
BUT, AS YOU *AMÉRICANS* ALWAYS SAY...
"WHAT'S IN IT FOR ME?"

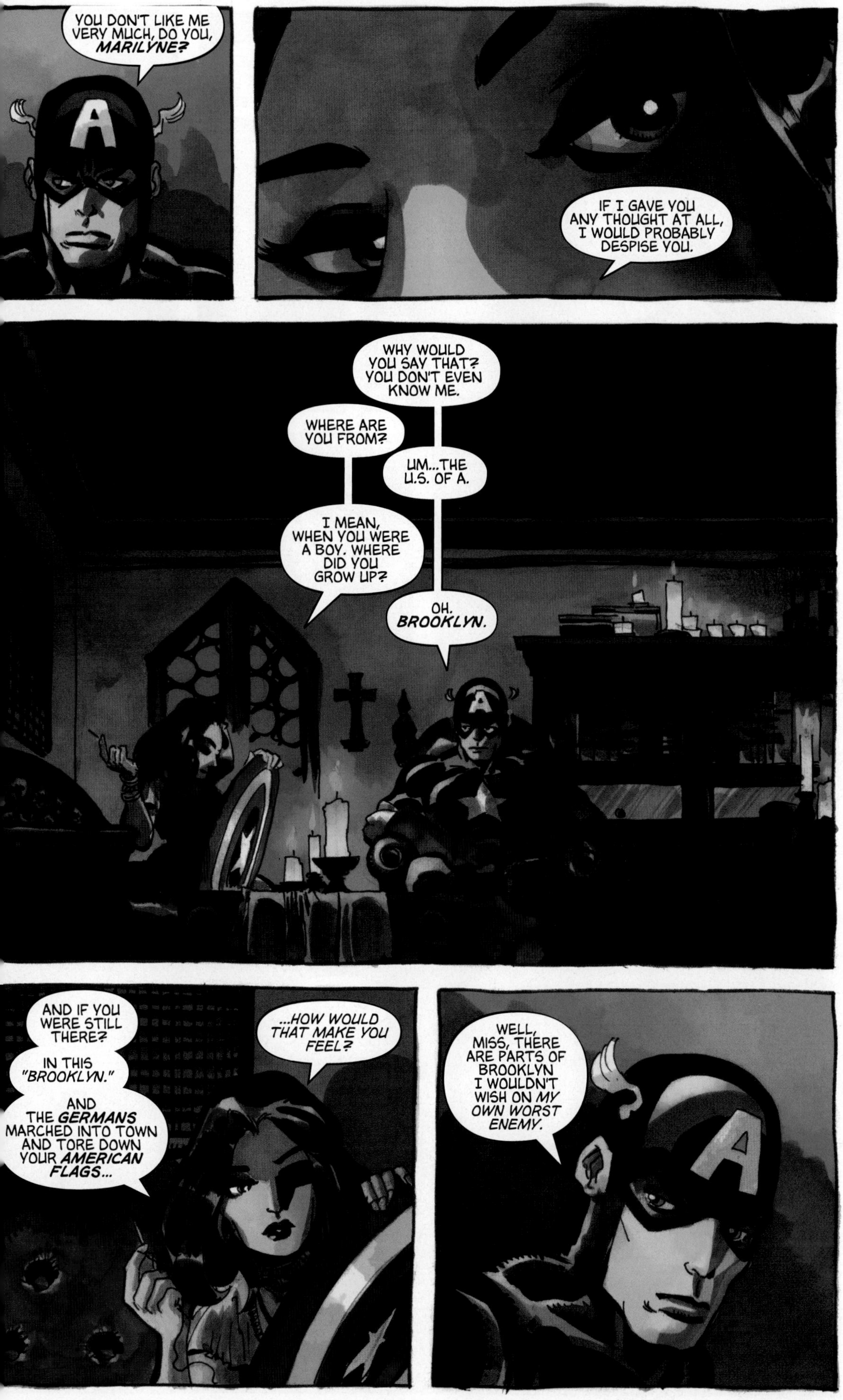
YOU DON'T LIKE ME VERY MUCH, DO YOU, MARILYNE?
IF I GAVE YOU ANY THOUGHT AT ALL, I WOULD PROBABLY DESPISE YOU.
WHY WOULD YOU SAY THAT? YOU DON'T EVEN KNOW ME.
WHERE ARE YOU FROM?
UM...THE U.S. OF A.
I MEAN, WHEN YOU WERE A BOY. WHERE DID YOU GROW UP?
OH. BROOKLYN.
AND IF YOU WERE STILL THERE?
IN THIS "BROOKLYN."
AND THE GERMANS MARCHED INTO TOWN AND TORE DOWN YOUR AMERICAN FLAGS...
...HOW WOULD THAT MAKE YOU FEEL?
WELL, MISS, THERE ARE PARTS OF BROOKLYN I WOULDN'T WISH ON MY OWN WORST ENEMY.

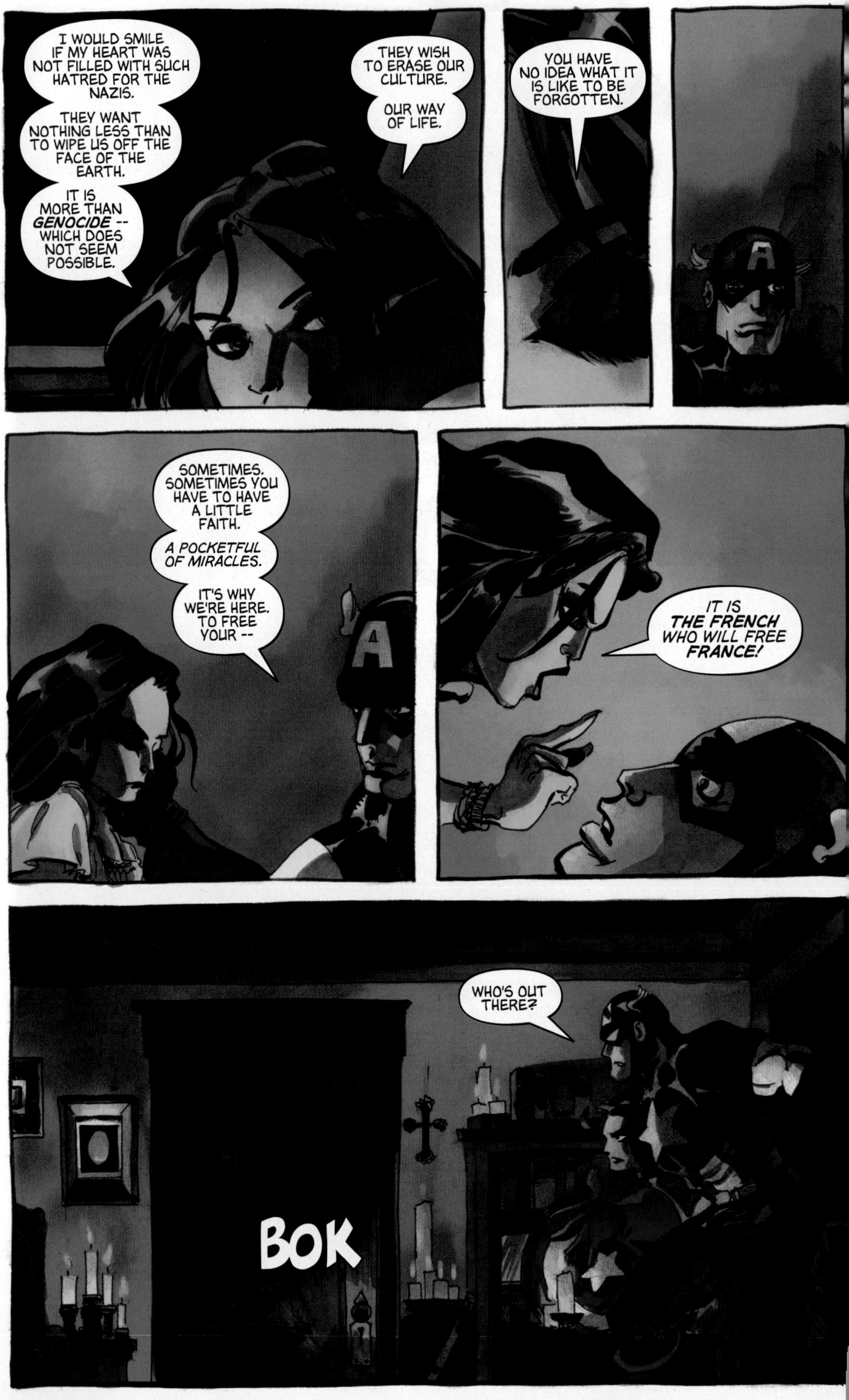

I WOULD SMILE IF MY HEART WAS NOT FILLED WITH SUCH HATRED FOR THE NAZIS.
THEY WANT NOTHING LESS THAN TO WIPE US OFF THE FACE OF THE EARTH.
IT IS MORE THAN *GENOCIDE* -- WHICH DOES NOT SEEM POSSIBLE.
THEY WISH TO ERASE OUR CULTURE.
OUR WAY OF LIFE.
YOU HAVE NO IDEA WHAT IT IS LIKE TO BE FORGOTTEN.
SOMETIMES. SOMETIMES YOU HAVE TO HAVE A LITTLE FAITH.
A POCKETFUL OF MIRACLES.
IT'S WHY WE'RE HERE. TO FREE YOUR --
IT IS ***THE FRENCH*** WHO WILL FREE ***FRANCE!***
WHO'S OUT THERE?
BOK

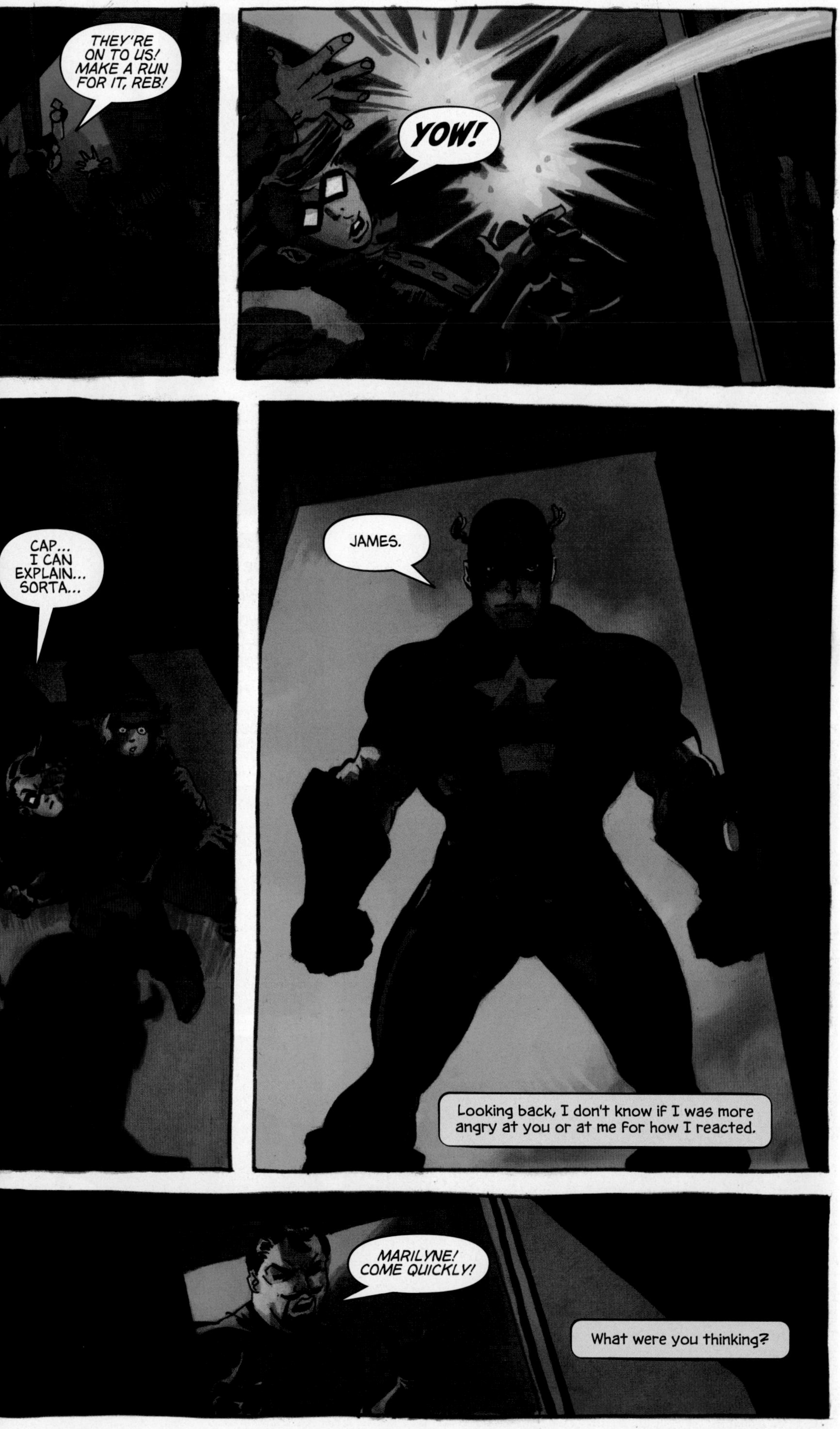
THEY'RE ON TO US! MAKE A RUN FOR IT, REB!
YOW!
CAP... I CAN EXPLAIN... SORTA...
JAMES.
Looking back, I don't know if I was more angry at you or at me for how I reacted.
MARILYNE! COME QUICKLY!
What were you thinking?

WE HAVE A -- HOW YOU SAY -- A "SOURCE" INSIDE THE GESTAPO.

THEY WILL LOOT *THE LOUVRE.*

HITLER HAS BOASTED HE WILL HAVE *THE MONA LISA* HANGING IN HIS KITCHEN.

AND THEN THEY WILL BURN THE MUSEUM AND ITS TREASURES TO A PILE OF ASH.

I AIN'T BUYING IT.

THAT LITTLE WALLPAPER HANGER SENDS HIS TWO BEST DOBERMANS TO PICK UP SOME FINGER PAINTINGS?

MAYBE *VON STRUCKER* IS AN ERRAND BOY. MAYBE.

BUT *THE SKULL?* HE'S GOT BIGGER FISH TO FRY.

THE SKULL'S SET UP BASE CAMP AT *THE EIFFEL TOWER.* I SAY WE MAKE A MOVE ON HIM THERE.

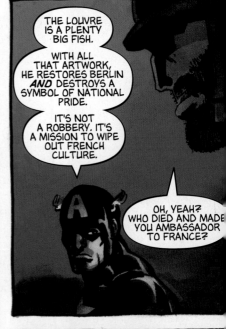

THE LOUVRE IS A PLENTY BIG FISH.

WITH ALL THAT ARTWORK, HE RESTORES BERLIN *AND* DESTROYS A SYMBOL OF NATIONAL PRIDE.

IT'S NOT A ROBBERY. IT'S A MISSION TO WIPE OUT FRENCH CULTURE.

OH, YEAH? WHO DIED AND MADE YOU AMBASSADOR TO FRANCE?

THE LOUVRE IS NOT SUCH A SMALL PLACE.

IT WILL TAKE ALL OF US.

TOGETHER.

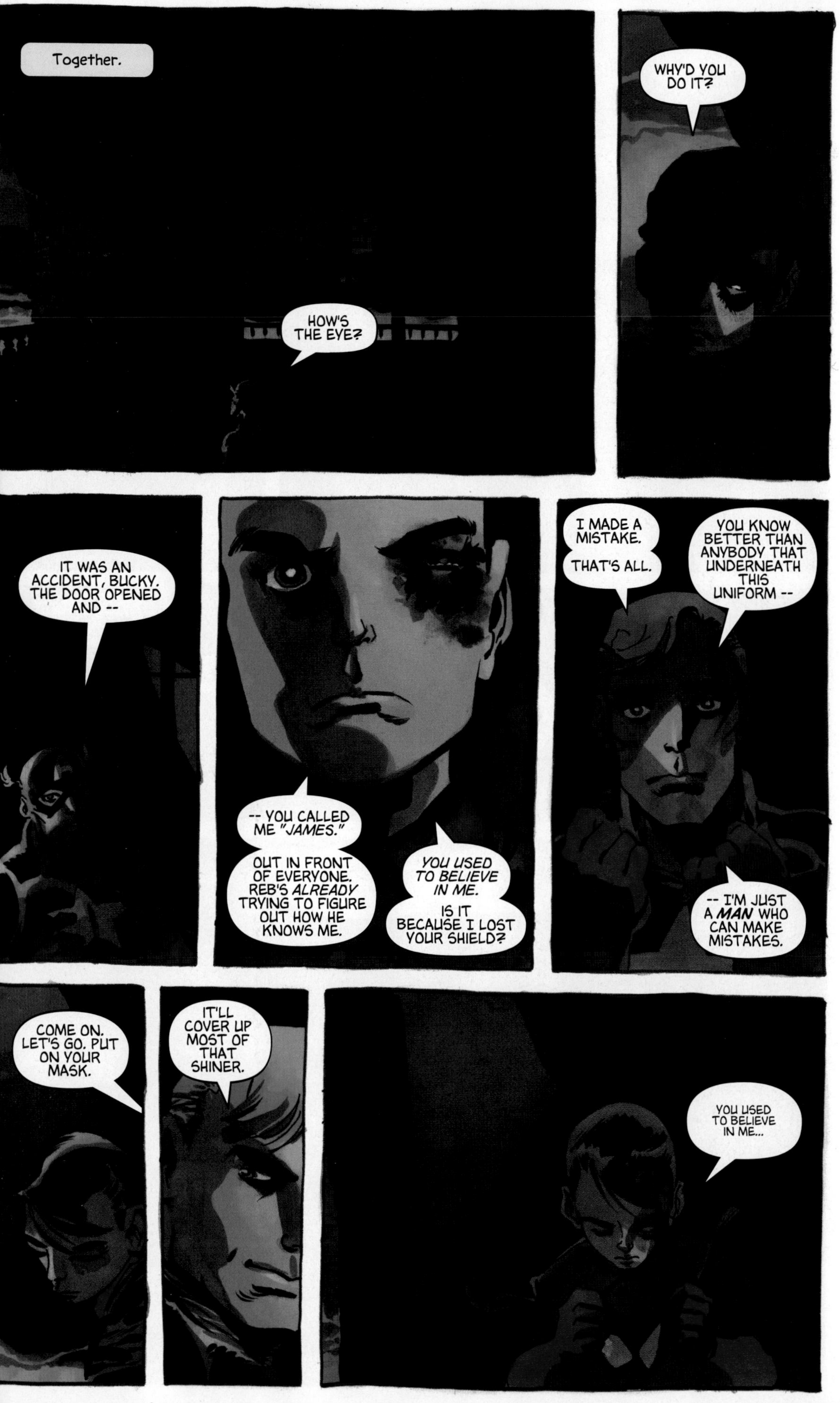
Together.
HOW'S THE EYE?
WHY'D YOU DO IT?
IT WAS AN ACCIDENT, BUCKY. THE DOOR OPENED AND --
-- YOU CALLED ME "JAMES."
OUT IN FRONT OF EVERYONE. REB'S ALREADY TRYING TO FIGURE OUT HOW HE KNOWS ME.
YOU USED TO BELIEVE IN ME.
IS IT BECAUSE I LOST YOUR SHIELD?
I MADE A MISTAKE.
THAT'S ALL.
YOU KNOW BETTER THAN ANYBODY THAT UNDERNEATH THIS UNIFORM --
-- I'M JUST A MAN WHO CAN MAKE MISTAKES.
COME ON. LET'S GO. PUT ON YOUR MASK.
IT'LL COVER UP MOST OF THAT SHINER.
YOU USED TO BELIEVE IN ME...

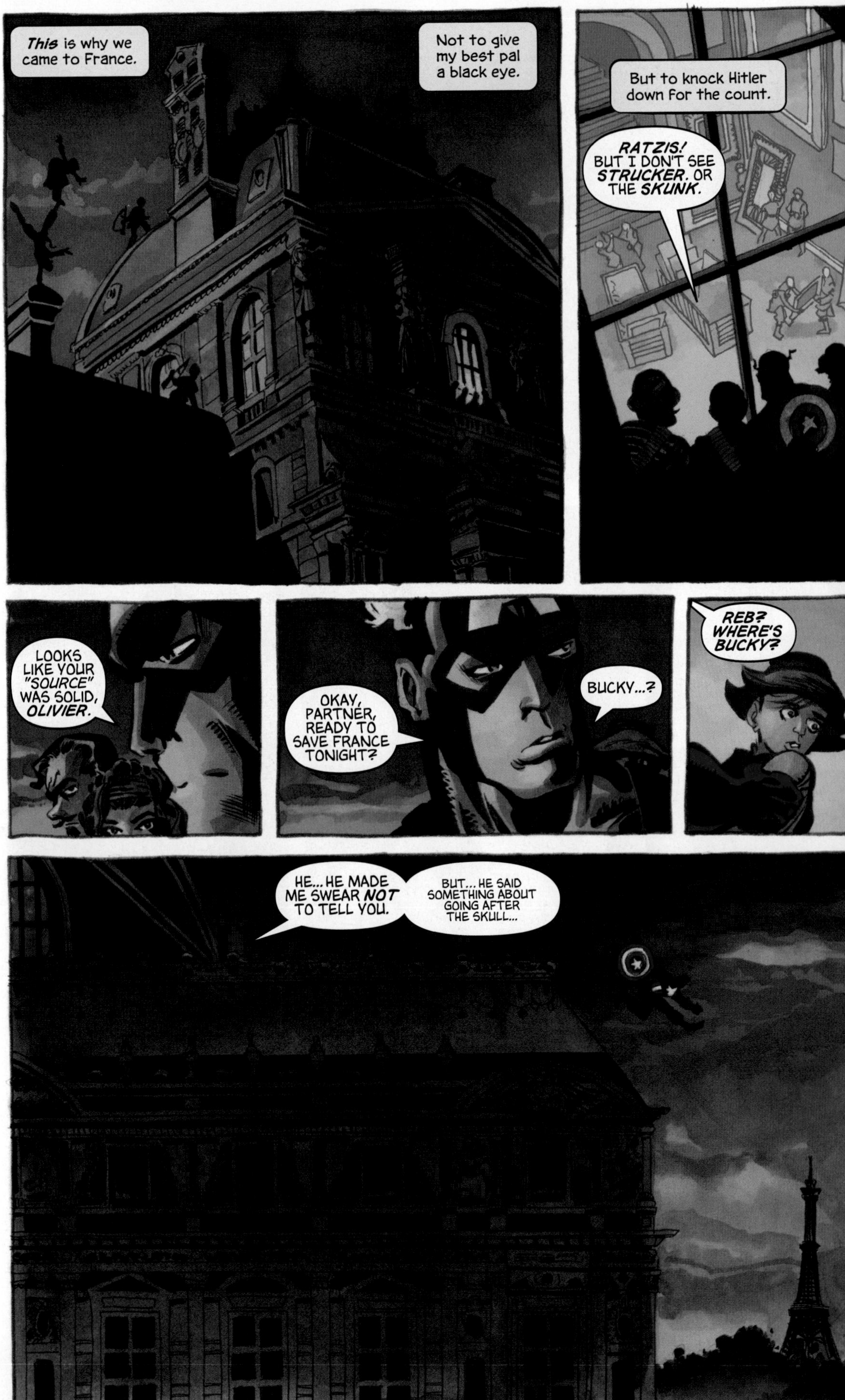
This is why we came to France.
Not to give my best pal a black eye.
But to knock Hitler down for the count.
RATZIS! BUT I DON'T SEE STRUCKER. OR THE SKUNK.
LOOKS LIKE YOUR "SOURCE" WAS SOLID, OLIVIER.
OKAY, PARTNER, READY TO SAVE FRANCE TONIGHT?
BUCKY...?
REB? WHERE'S BUCKY?
HE... HE MADE ME SWEAR NOT TO TELL YOU.
BUT... HE SAID SOMETHING ABOUT GOING AFTER THE SKULL...

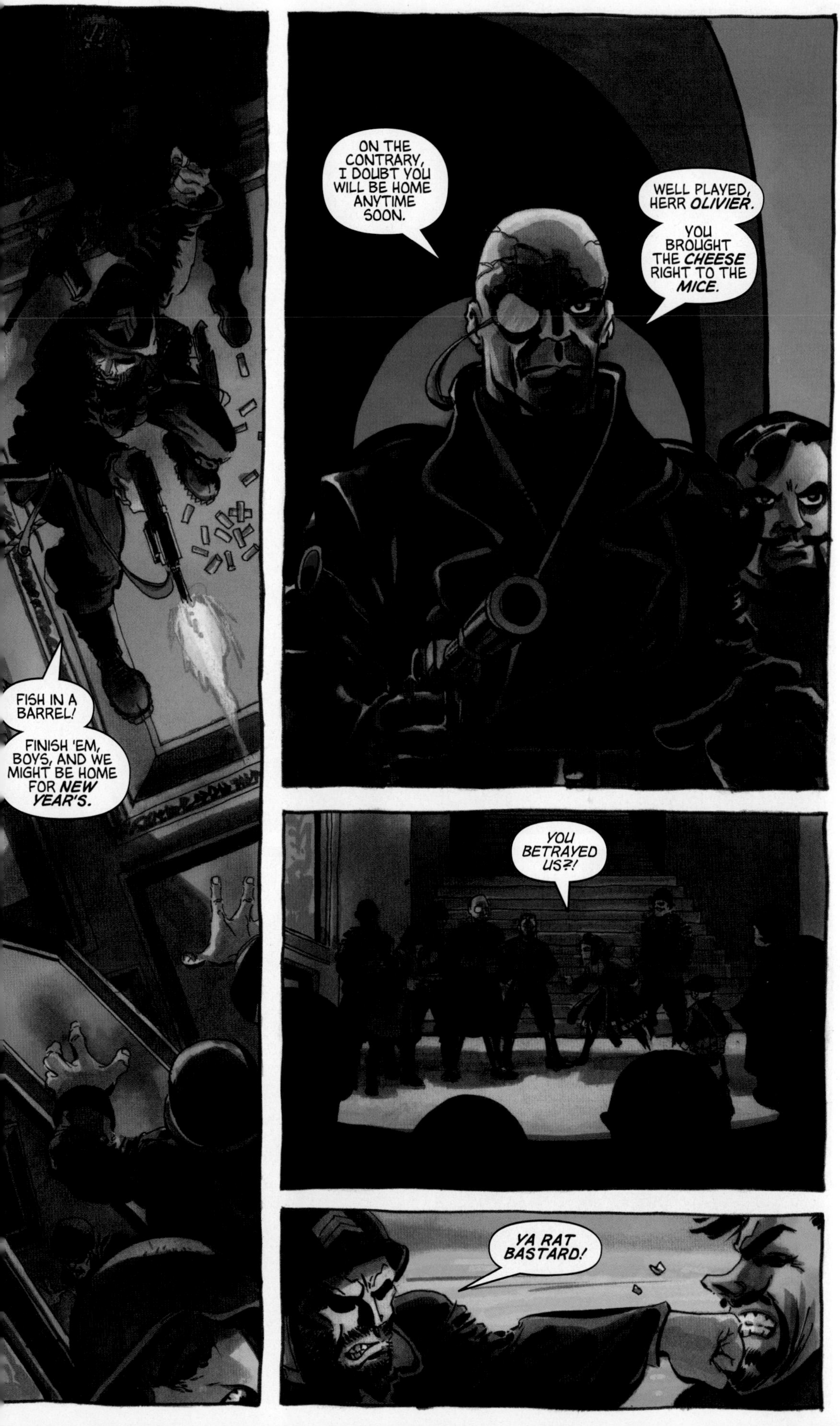

FISH IN A BARREL!
FINISH 'EM, BOYS, AND WE MIGHT BE HOME FOR *NEW YEAR'S.*
ON THE CONTRARY, I DOUBT YOU WILL BE HOME ANYTIME SOON.
WELL PLAYED, HERR *OLIVIER.*
YOU BROUGHT THE *CHEESE* RIGHT TO THE *MICE.*
YOU BETRAYED US?!
YA RAT BASTARD!

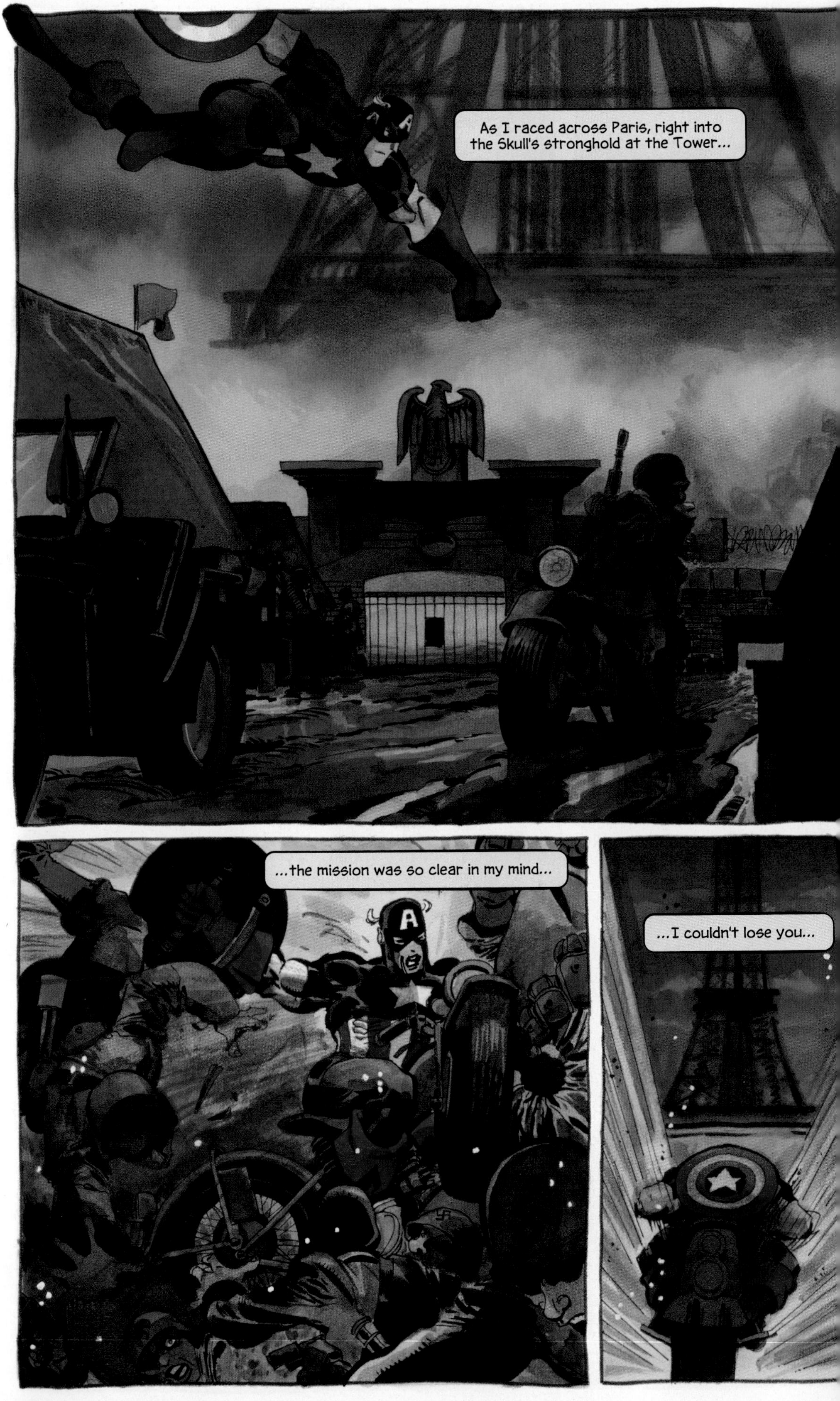
As I raced across Paris, right into the Skull's stronghold at the Tower...
...the mission was so clear in my mind...
...I couldn't lose you...

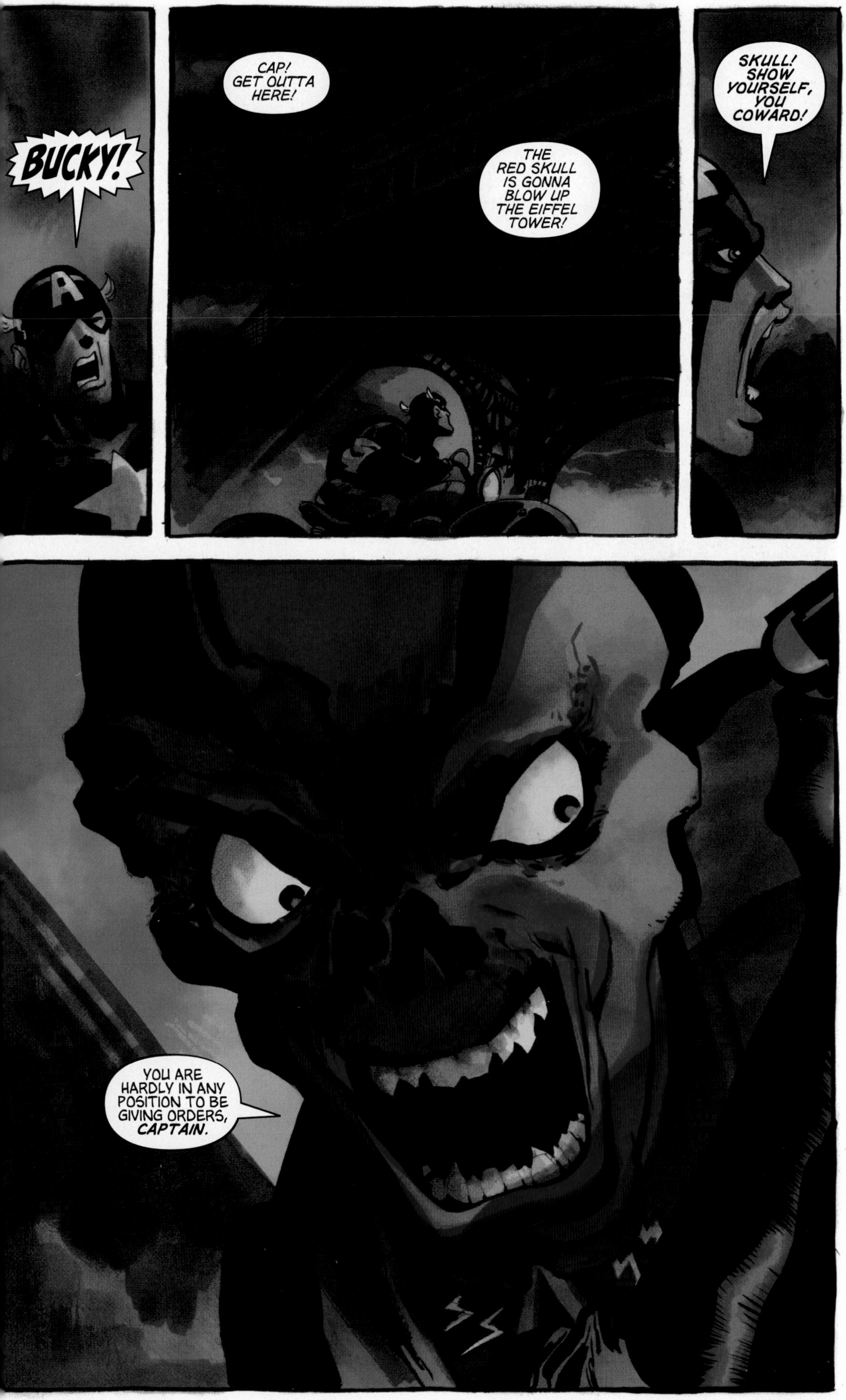
BUCKY!
CAP! GET OUTTA HERE!
THE RED SKULL IS GONNA BLOW UP THE EIFFEL TOWER!
SKULL! SHOW YOURSELF, YOU COWARD!
YOU ARE HARDLY IN ANY POSITION TO BE GIVING ORDERS, CAPTAIN.

YOU MUST DECIDE WHICH IS MORE IMPORTANT.
SOME COUNTRY HALFWAY AROUND THE GLOBE THAT HAS ALREADY FALLEN UNDER MY BOOT.
OR THE LIFE OF SOMEONE WHO MEANS THE WORLD TO YOU?
DON'T LISTEN TO HIM, CAP! YOU GOTTA STOP HIM!
EVEN IF I GOTTA DIE!
It was never about black or white or good or evil. The mission. The orders.
...I couldn't lose you...
LOEB SALE

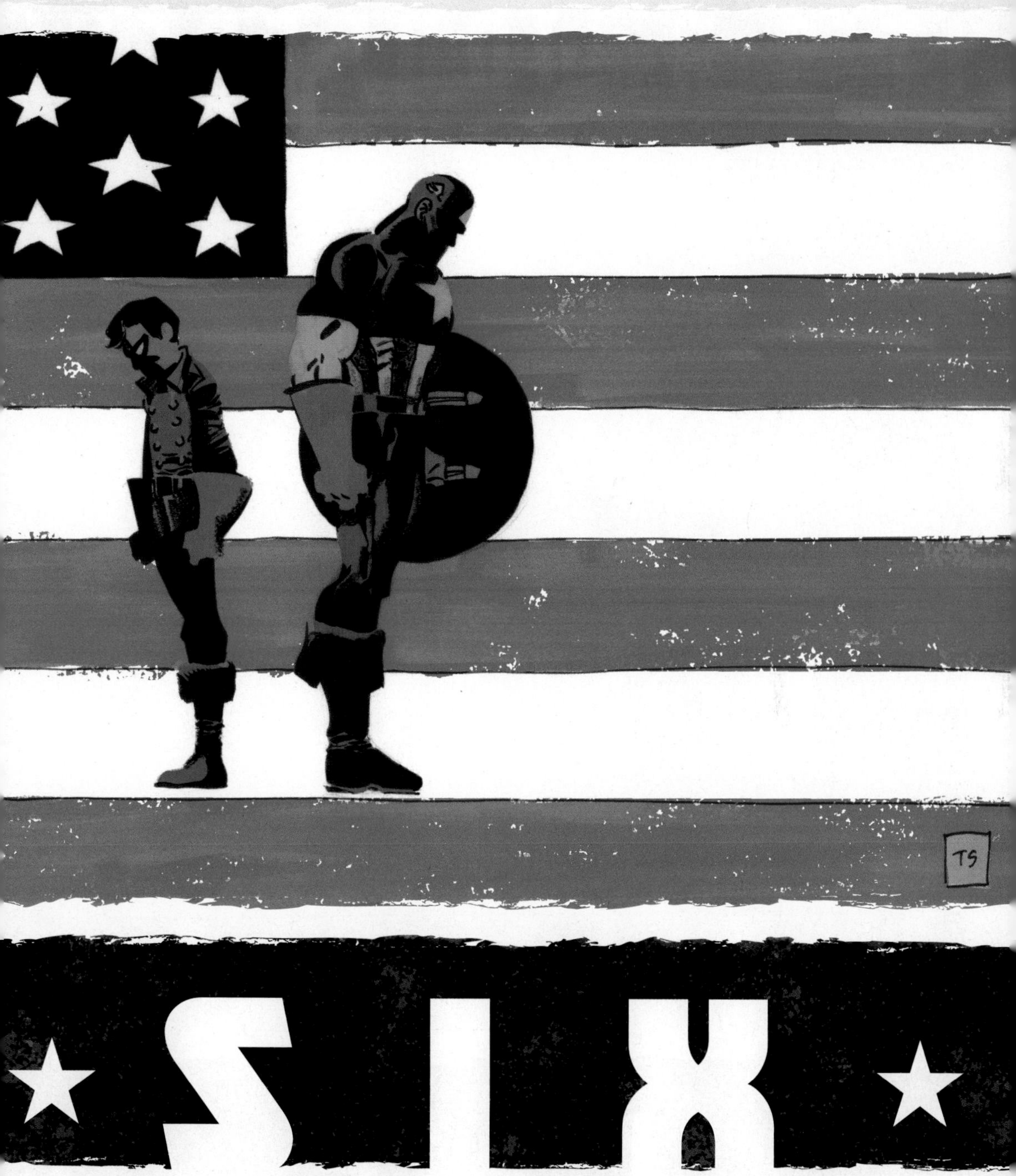
TS
SIX

IT'S A WONDERFUL LIFE

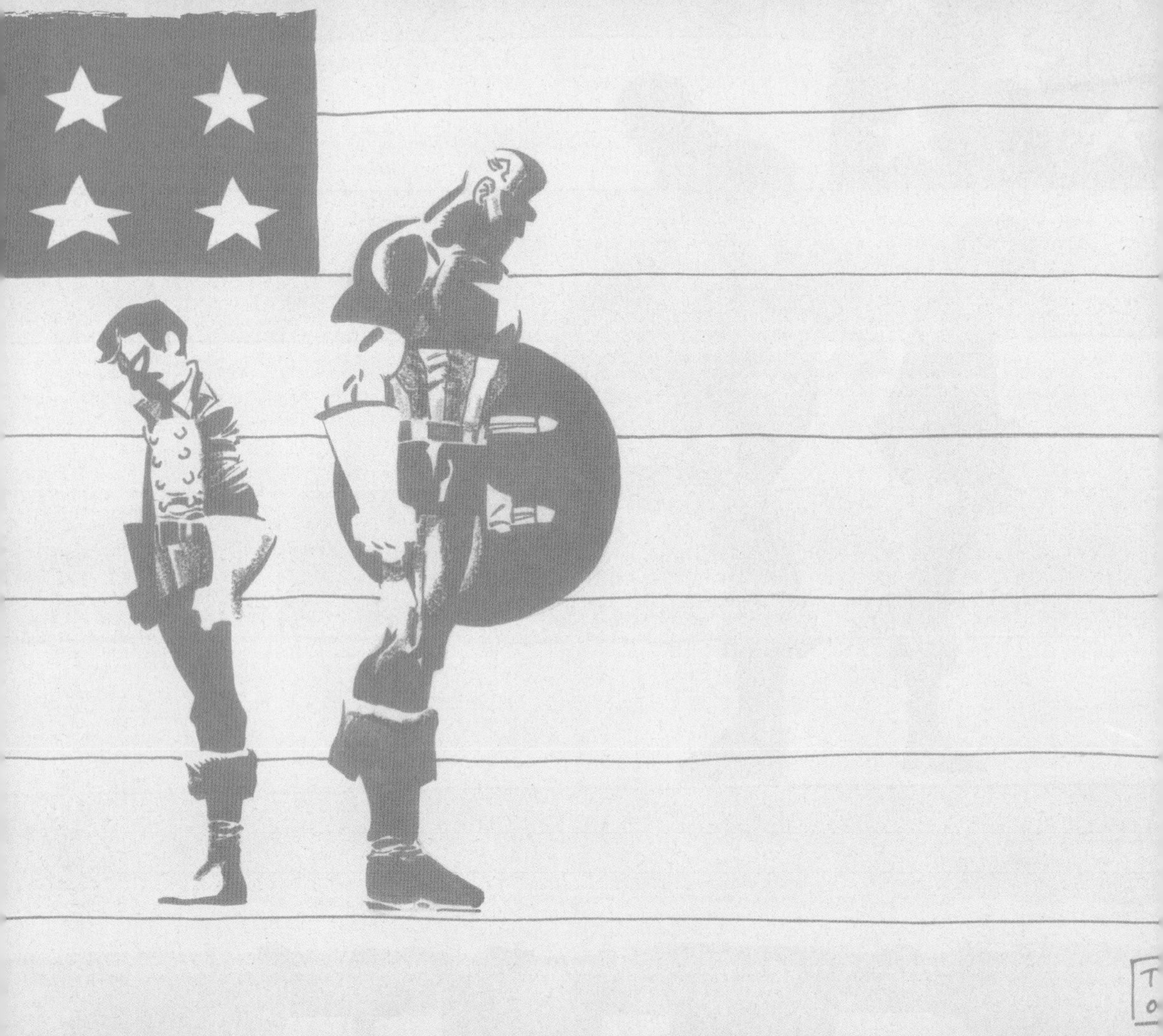

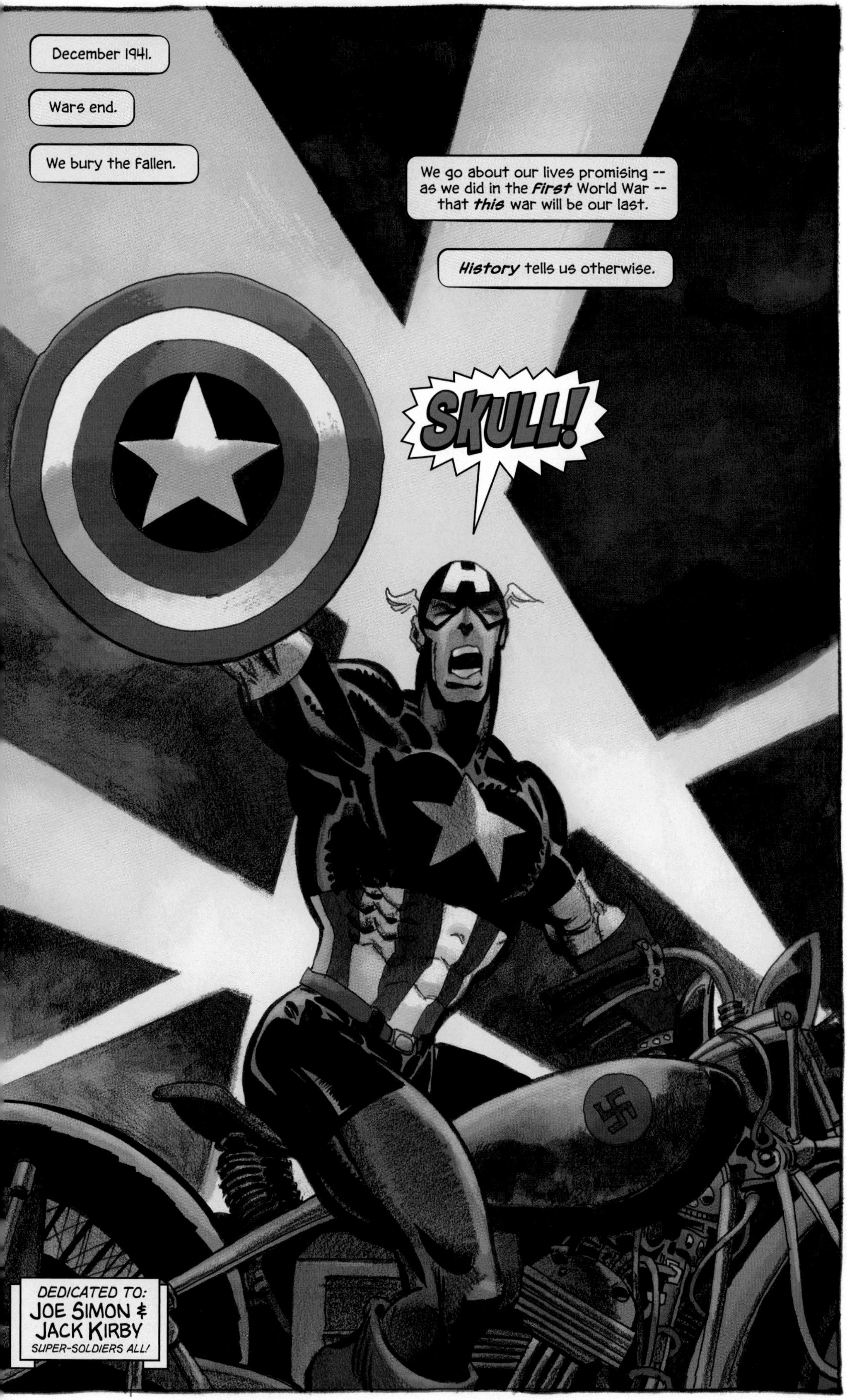

December 1941.
Wars end.
We bury the fallen.
We go about our lives promising -- as we did in the *First* World War -- that *this* war will be our last.
History tells us otherwise.
SKULL!
DEDICATED TO: JOE SIMON & JACK KIRBY SUPER-SOLDIERS ALL!

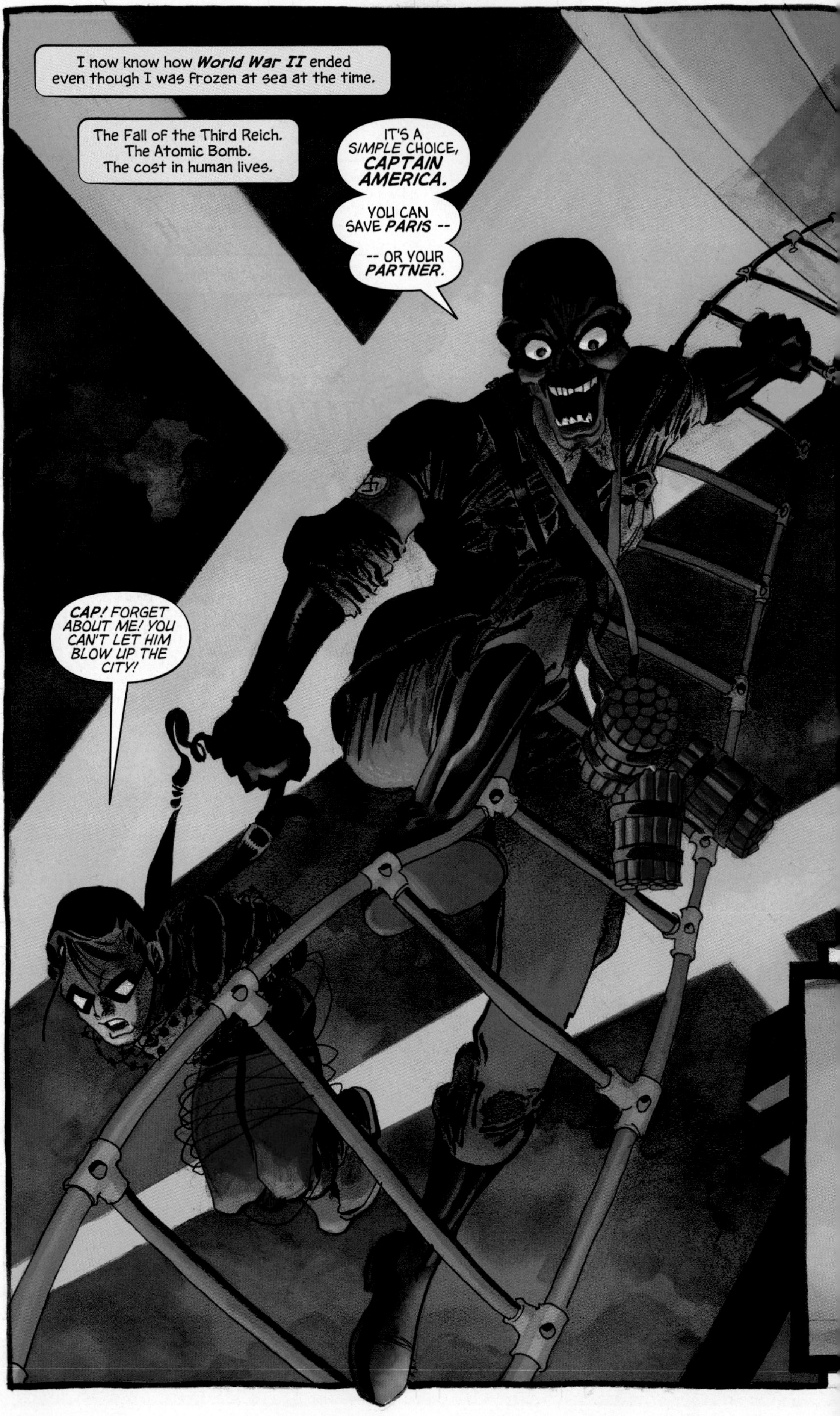

I now know how *World War II* ended even though I was frozen at sea at the time.
The Fall of the Third Reich. The Atomic Bomb. The cost in human lives.
IT'S A SIMPLE CHOICE, CAPTAIN AMERICA.
YOU CAN SAVE PARIS --
-- OR YOUR PARTNER.
CAP! FORGET ABOUT ME! YOU CAN'T LET HIM BLOW UP THE CITY!

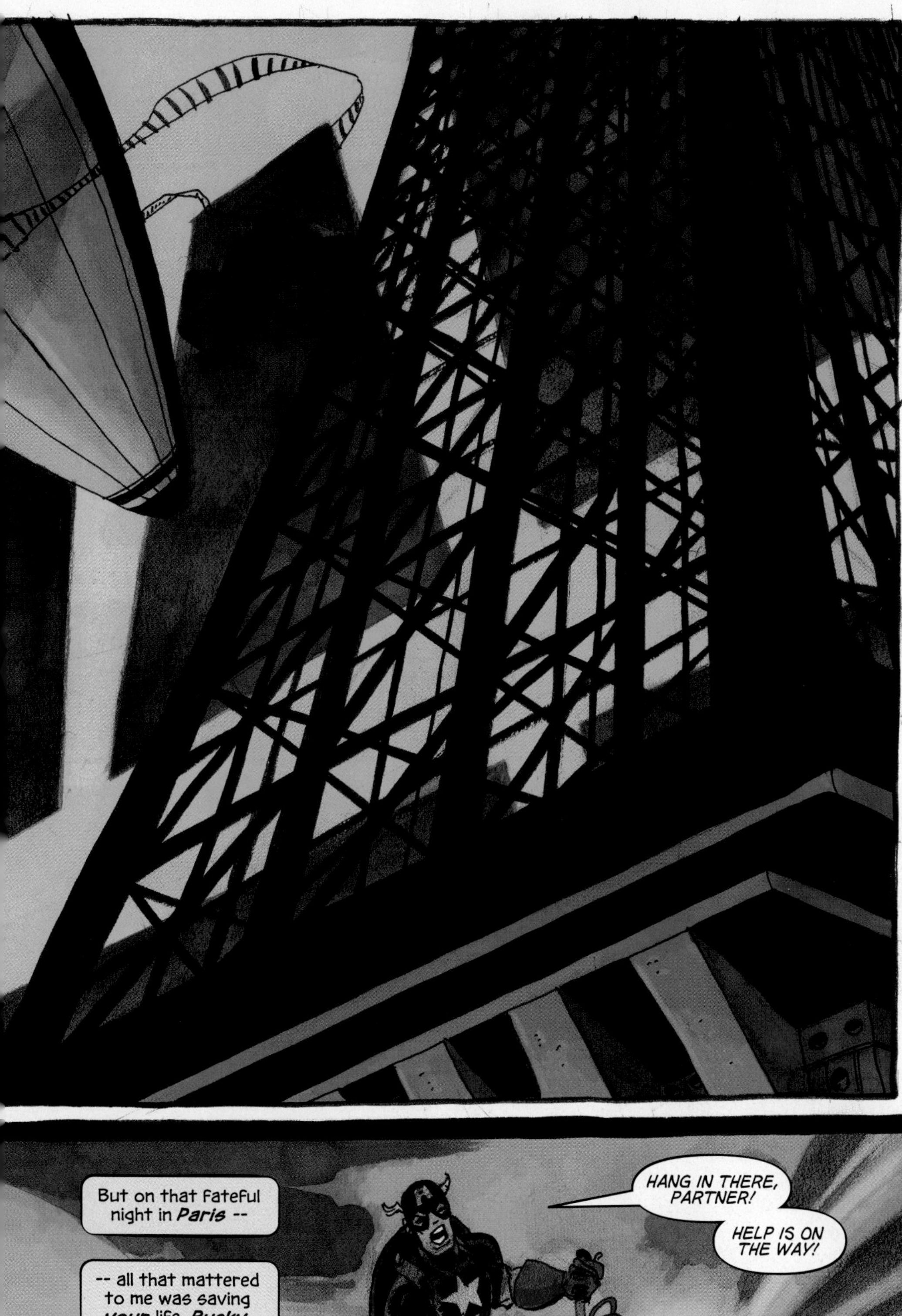

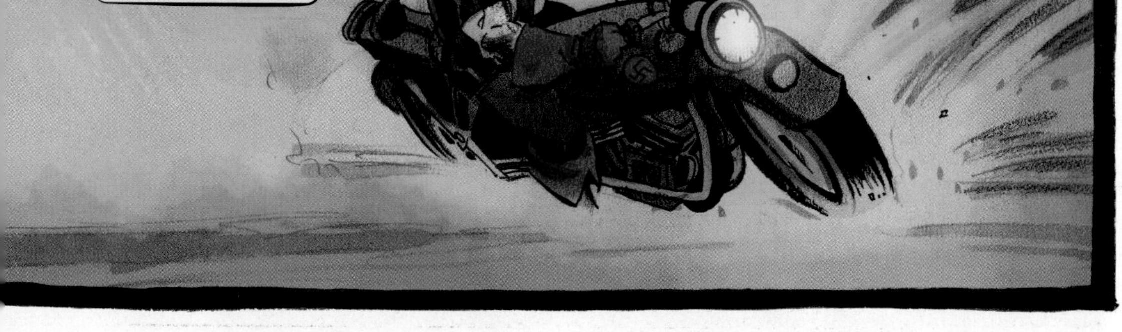

But on that fateful night in *Paris* --
-- all that mattered to me was saving *your* life, *Bucky*.
HANG IN THERE, PARTNER!
HELP IS ON THE WAY!

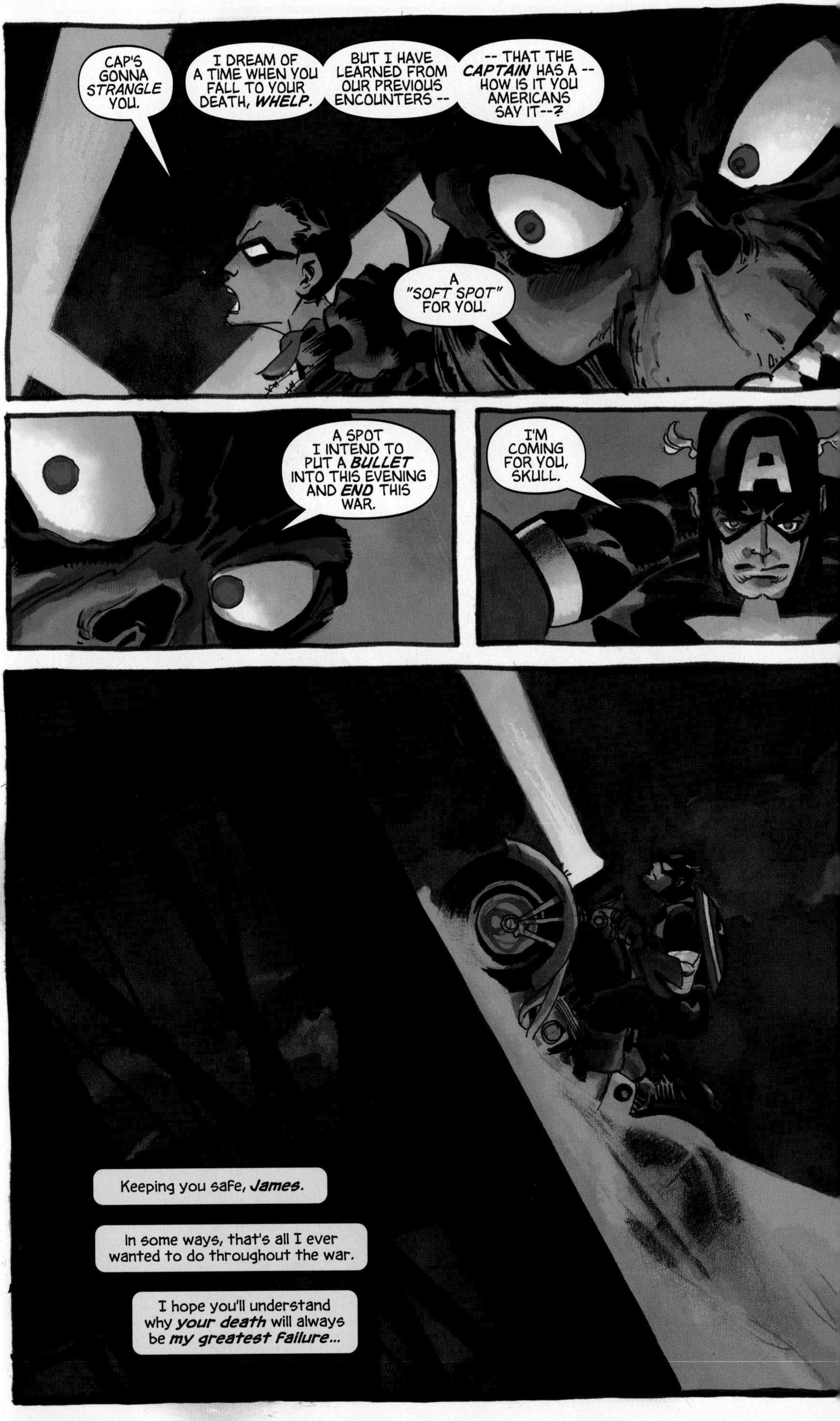
CAP'S GONNA STRANGLE YOU.
I DREAM OF A TIME WHEN YOU FALL TO YOUR DEATH, WHELP.
BUT I HAVE LEARNED FROM OUR PREVIOUS ENCOUNTERS --
-- THAT THE CAPTAIN HAS A -- HOW IS IT YOU AMERICANS SAY IT--?
A "SOFT SPOT" FOR YOU.
A SPOT I INTEND TO PUT A BULLET INTO THIS EVENING AND END THIS WAR.
I'M COMING FOR YOU, SKULL.
Keeping you safe, James.
In some ways, that's all I ever wanted to do throughout the war.
I hope you'll understand why your death will always be my greatest failure...

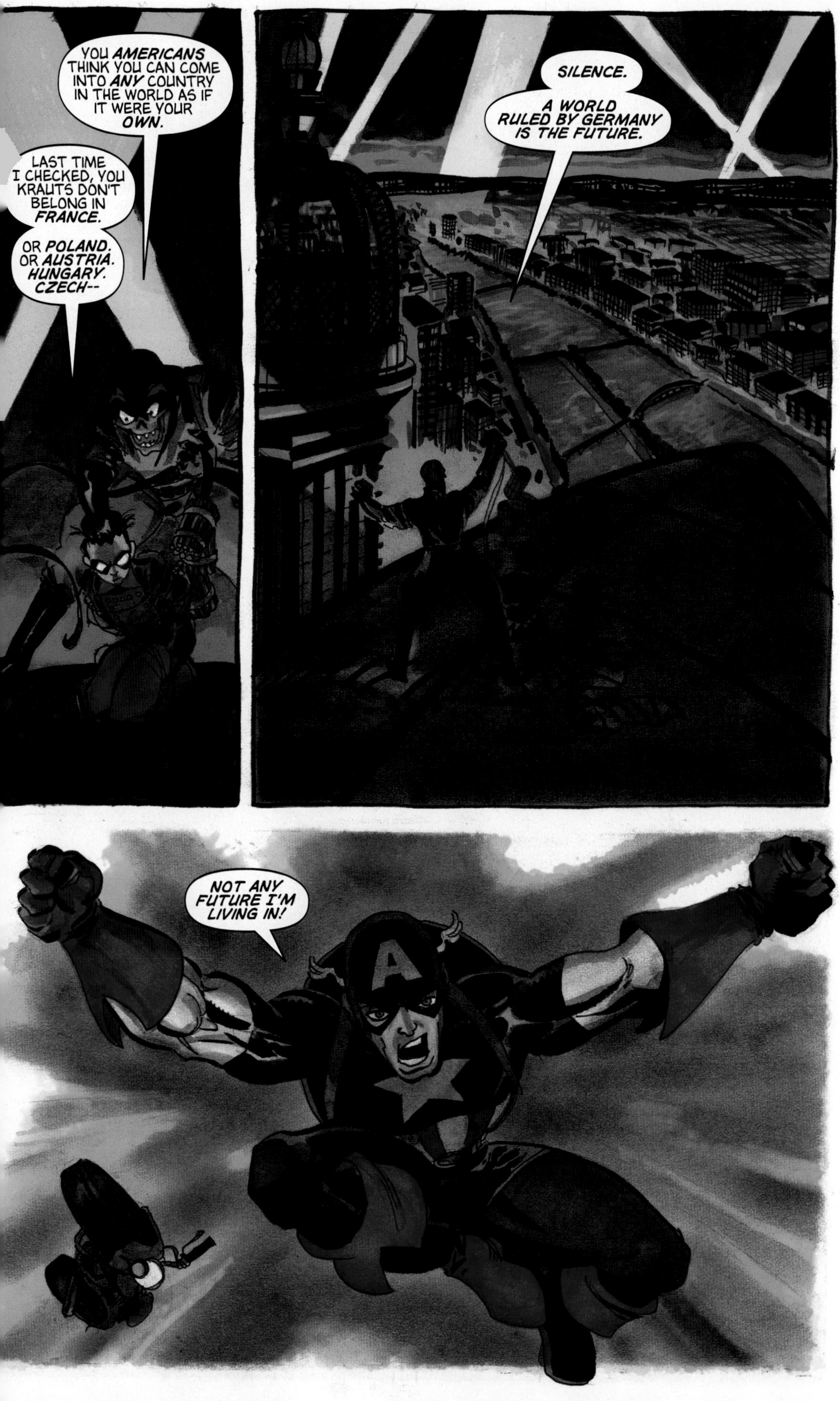
YOU AMERICANS THINK YOU CAN COME INTO ANY COUNTRY IN THE WORLD AS IF IT WERE YOUR OWN.
LAST TIME I CHECKED, YOU KRAUTS DON'T BELONG IN FRANCE.
OR POLAND. OR AUSTRIA. HUNGARY. CZECH--
SILENCE.
A WORLD RULED BY GERMANY IS THE FUTURE.
NOT ANY FUTURE I'M LIVING IN!

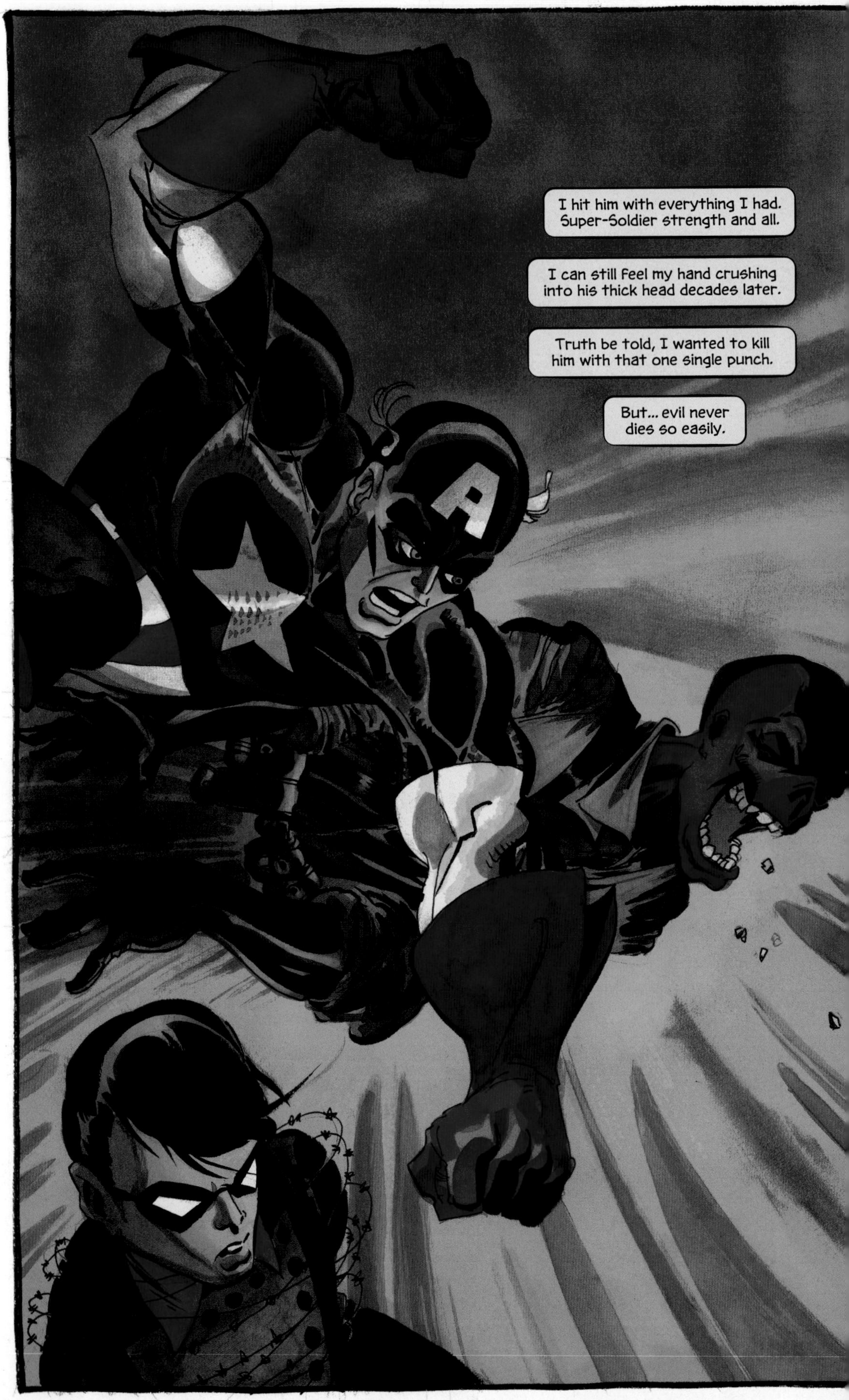
I hit him with everything I had. Super-Soldier strength and all.
I can still feel my hand crushing into his thick head decades later.
Truth be told, I wanted to kill him with that one single punch.
But... evil never dies so easily.

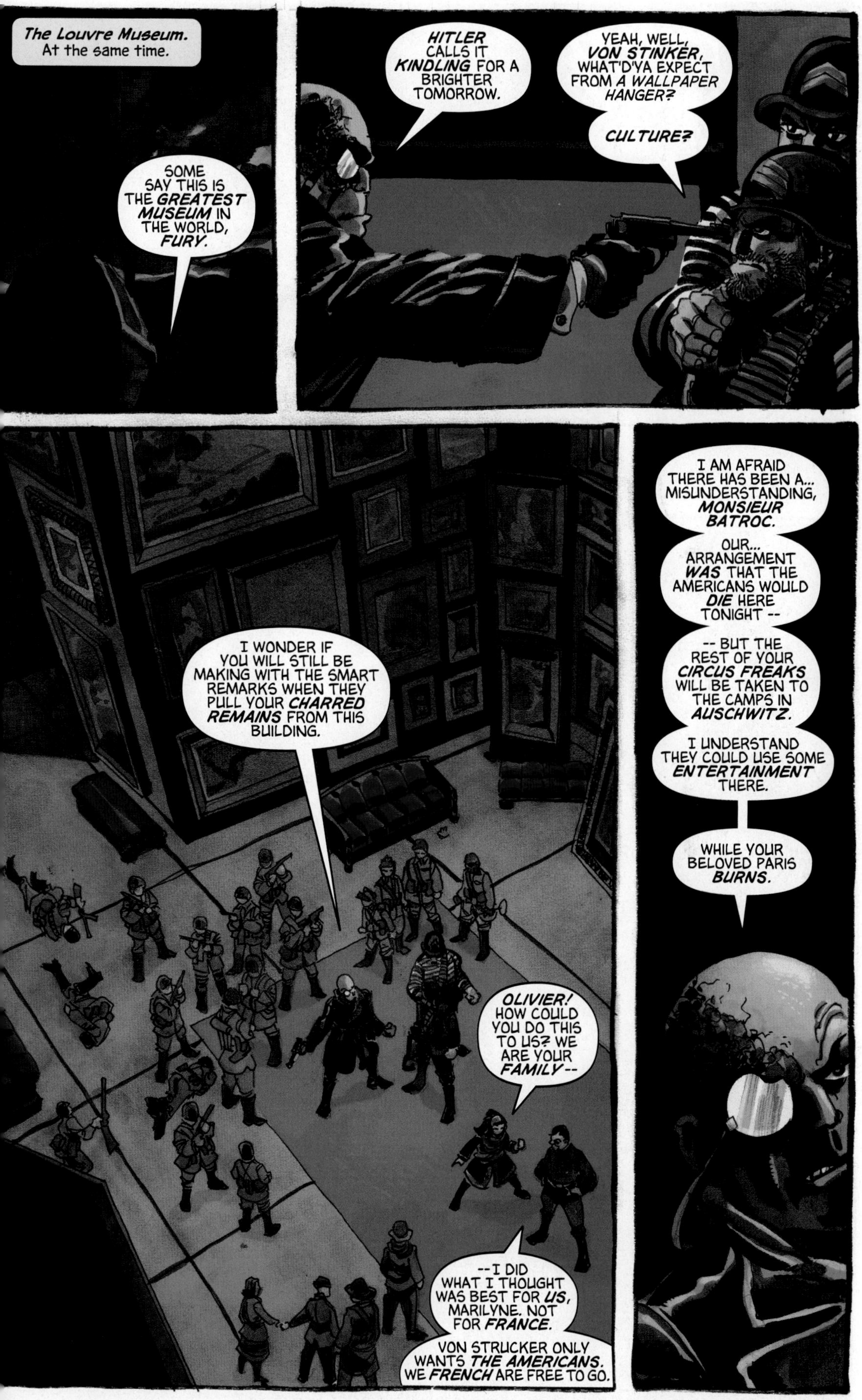
The Louvre Museum. At the same time.
SOME SAY THIS IS THE GREATEST MUSEUM IN THE WORLD, FURY.
HITLER CALLS IT KINDLING FOR A BRIGHTER TOMORROW.
YEAH, WELL, VON STINKER, WHAT'D'YA EXPECT FROM A WALLPAPER HANGER?
CULTURE?
I WONDER IF YOU WILL STILL BE MAKING WITH THE SMART REMARKS WHEN THEY PULL YOUR CHARRED REMAINS FROM THIS BUILDING.
OLIVIER! HOW COULD YOU DO THIS TO US? WE ARE YOUR FAMILY--
--I DID WHAT I THOUGHT WAS BEST FOR US, MARILYNE. NOT FOR FRANCE.
VON STRUCKER ONLY WANTS THE AMERICANS. WE FRENCH ARE FREE TO GO.
I AM AFRAID THERE HAS BEEN A... MISUNDERSTANDING, MONSIEUR BATROC.
OUR... ARRANGEMENT WAS THAT THE AMERICANS WOULD DIE HERE TONIGHT --
-- BUT THE REST OF YOUR CIRCUS FREAKS WILL BE TAKEN TO THE CAMPS IN AUSCHWITZ.
I UNDERSTAND THEY COULD USE SOME ENTERTAINMENT THERE.
WHILE YOUR BELOVED PARIS BURNS.

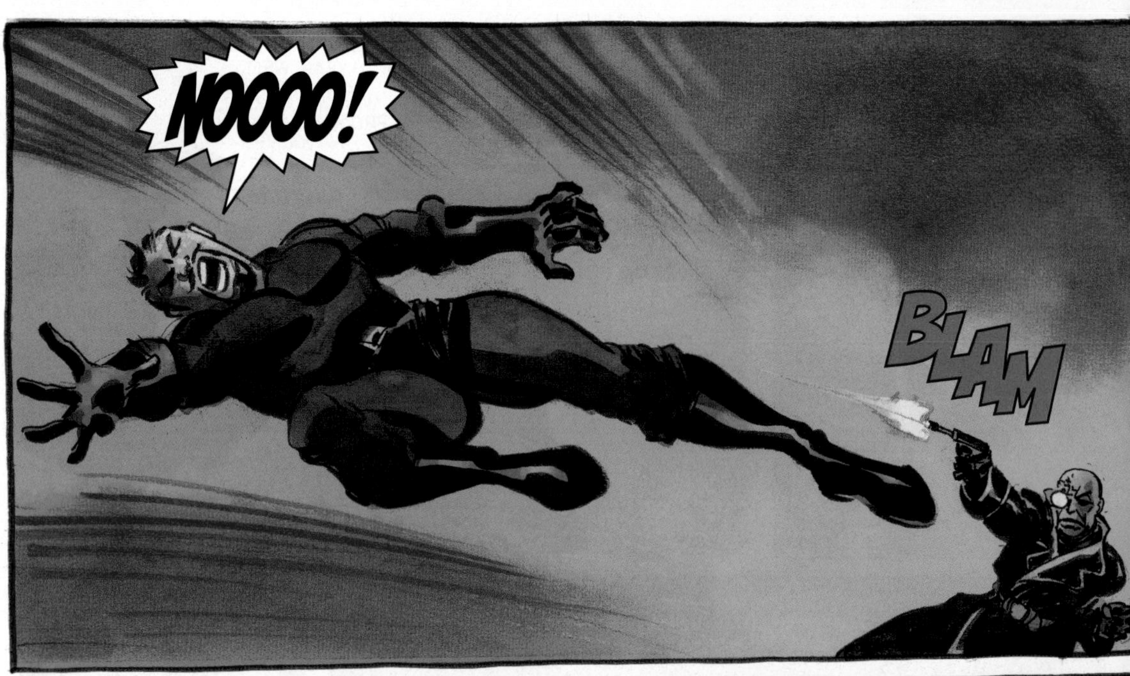
NOOOO!
BLAM

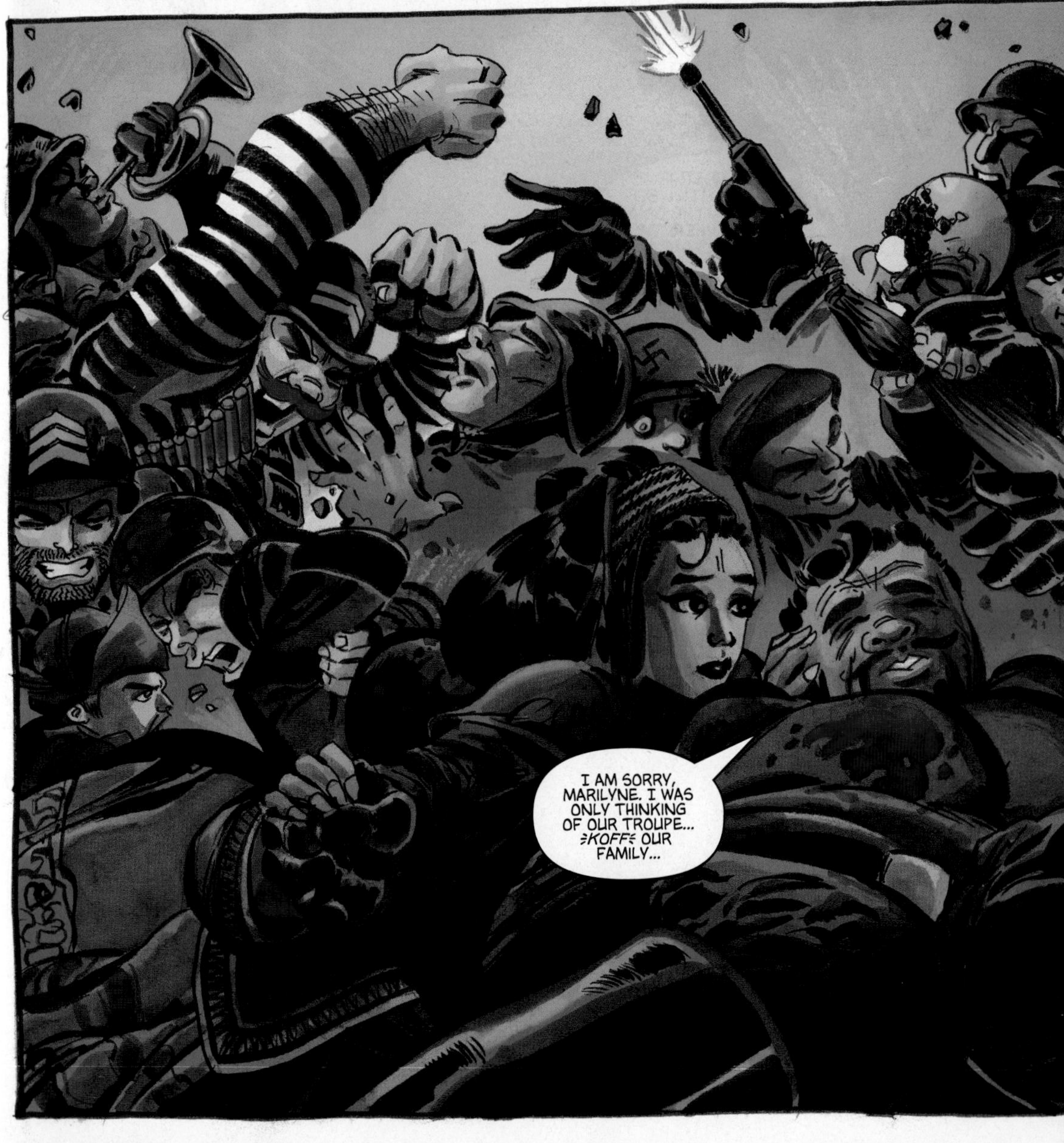
I AM SORRY, MARILYNE. I WAS ONLY THINKING OF OUR TROUPE... =KOFF= OUR FAMILY...

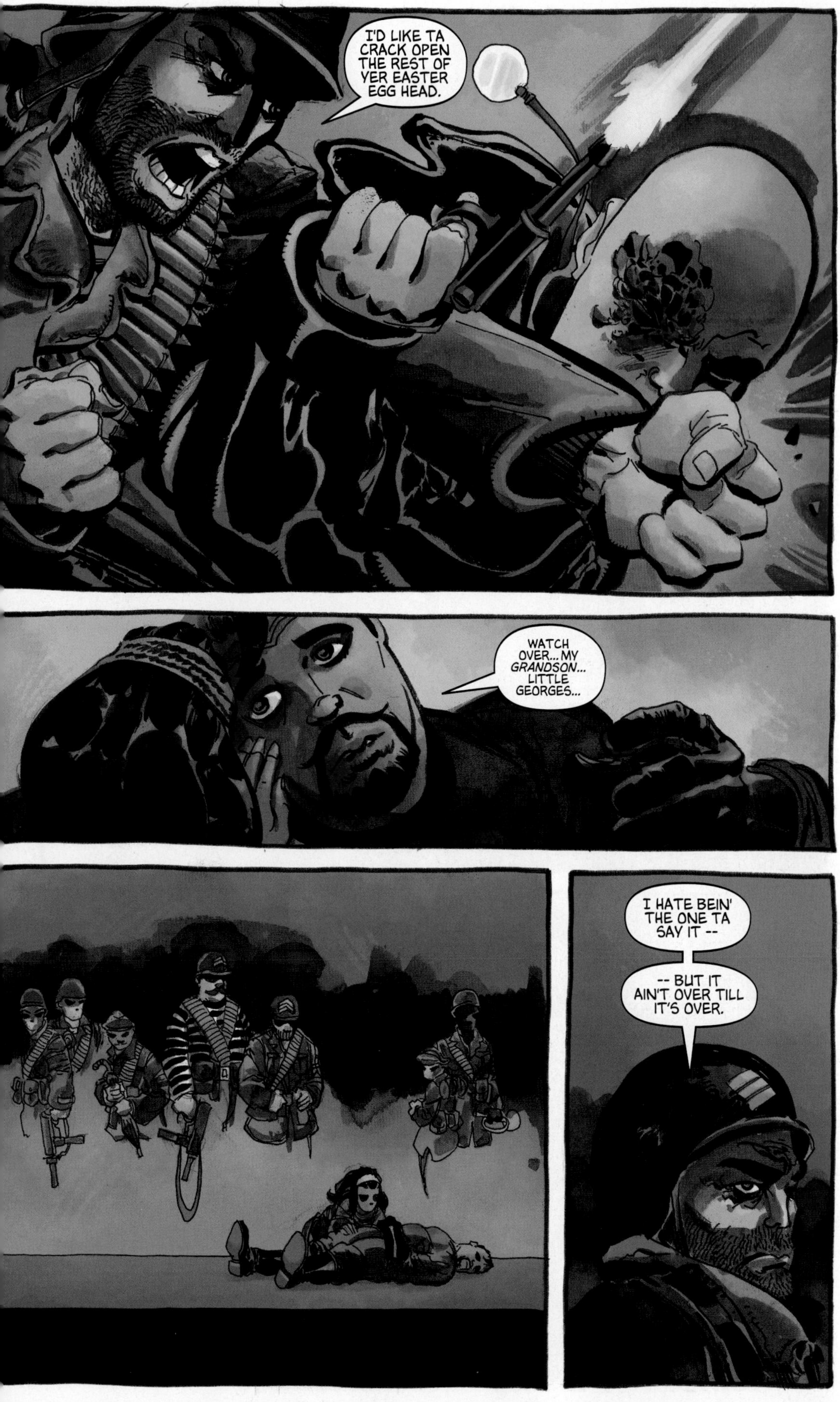
I'D LIKE TA CRACK OPEN THE REST OF YER EASTER EGG HEAD.
WATCH OVER... MY *GRANDSON*... LITTLE GEORGES...
I HATE BEIN' THE ONE TA SAY IT --
-- BUT IT AIN'T OVER TILL IT'S OVER.

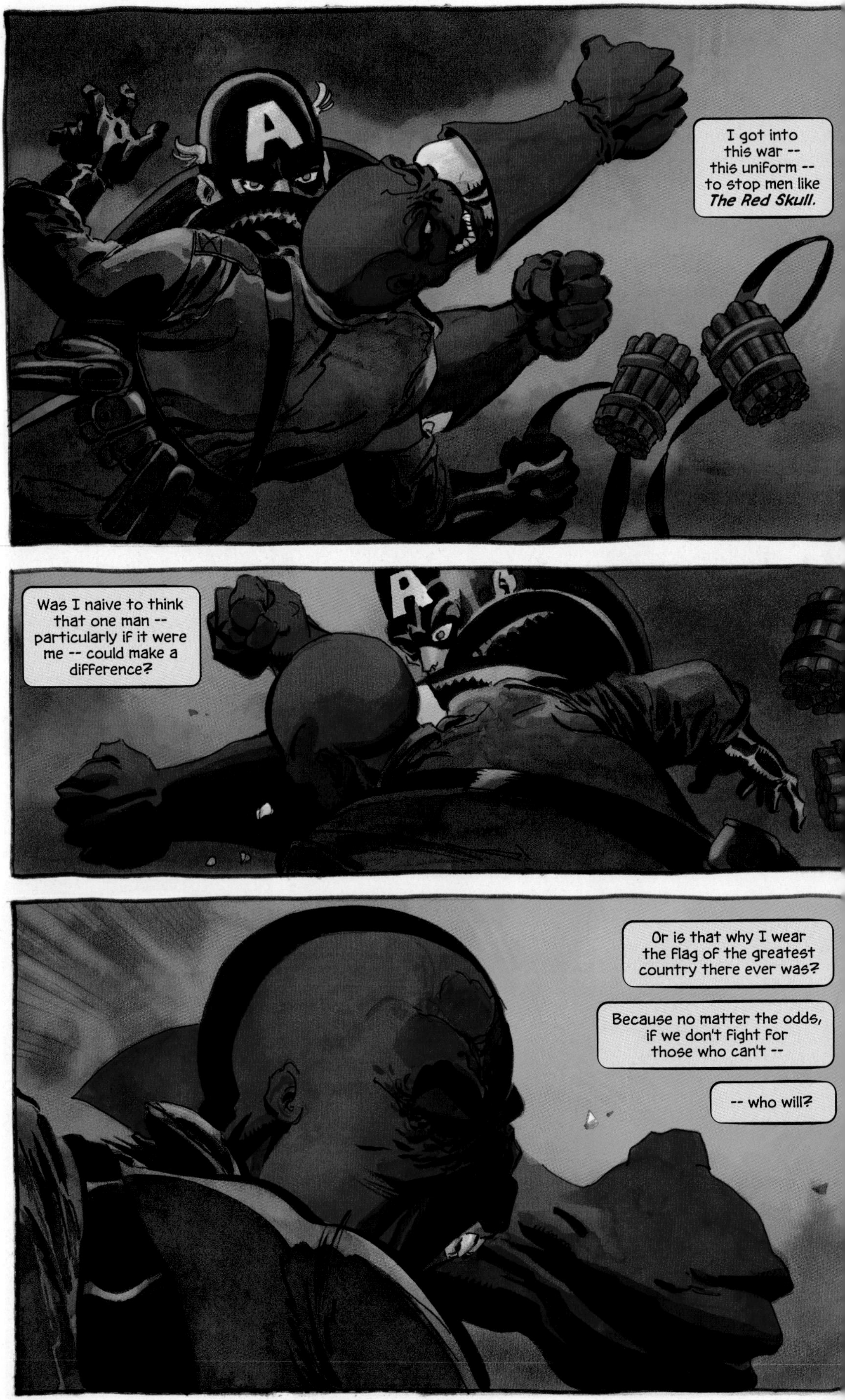
I got into this war -- this uniform -- to stop men like *The Red Skull.*
Was I naive to think that one man -- particularly if it were me -- could make a difference?
Or is that why I wear the flag of the greatest country there ever was?
Because no matter the odds, if we don't fight for those who can't --
-- who will?

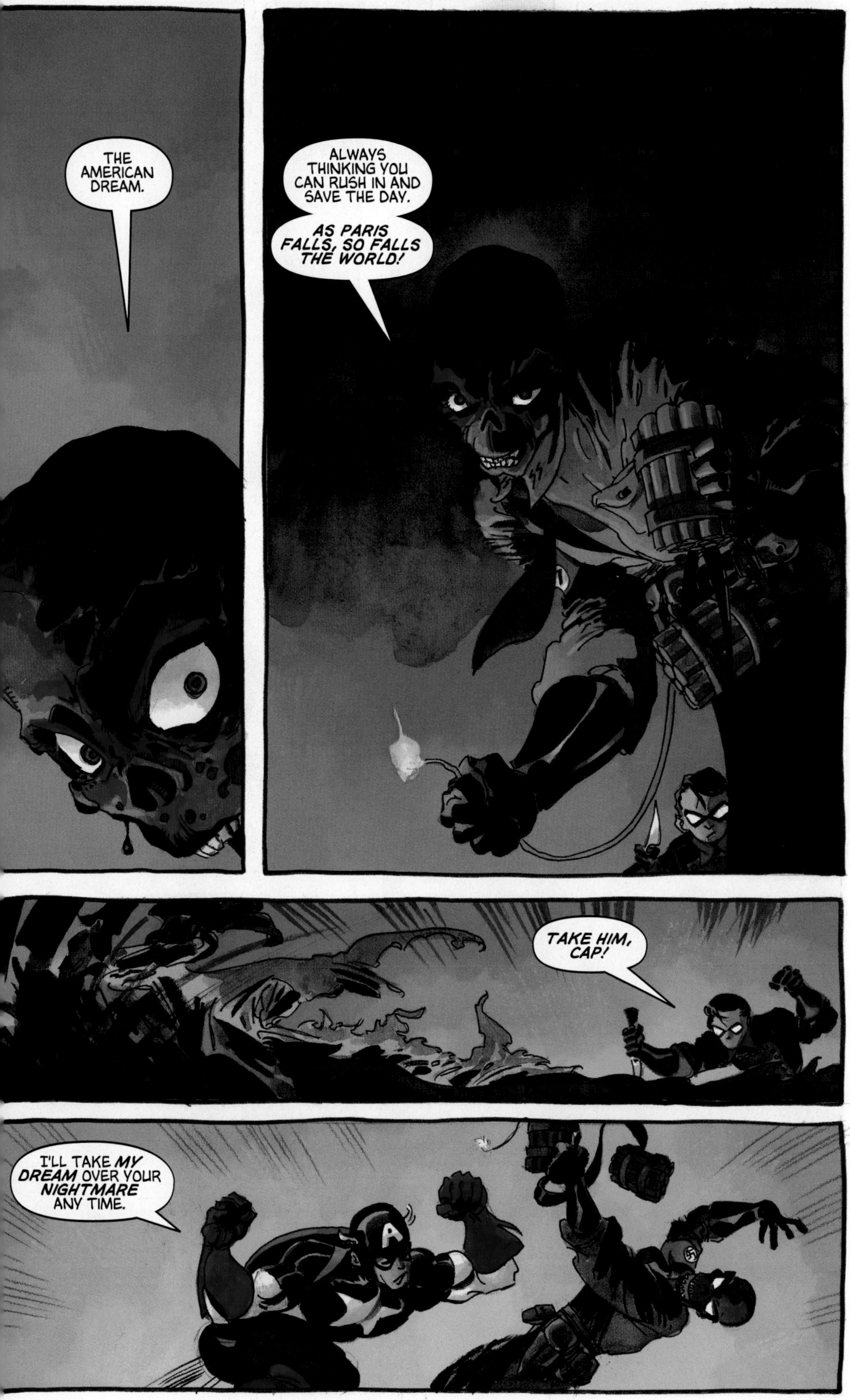
THE AMERICAN DREAM.
ALWAYS THINKING YOU CAN RUSH IN AND SAVE THE DAY.
AS PARIS FALLS, SO FALLS THE WORLD!
TAKE HIM, CAP!
I'LL TAKE MY DREAM OVER YOUR NIGHTMARE ANY TIME.

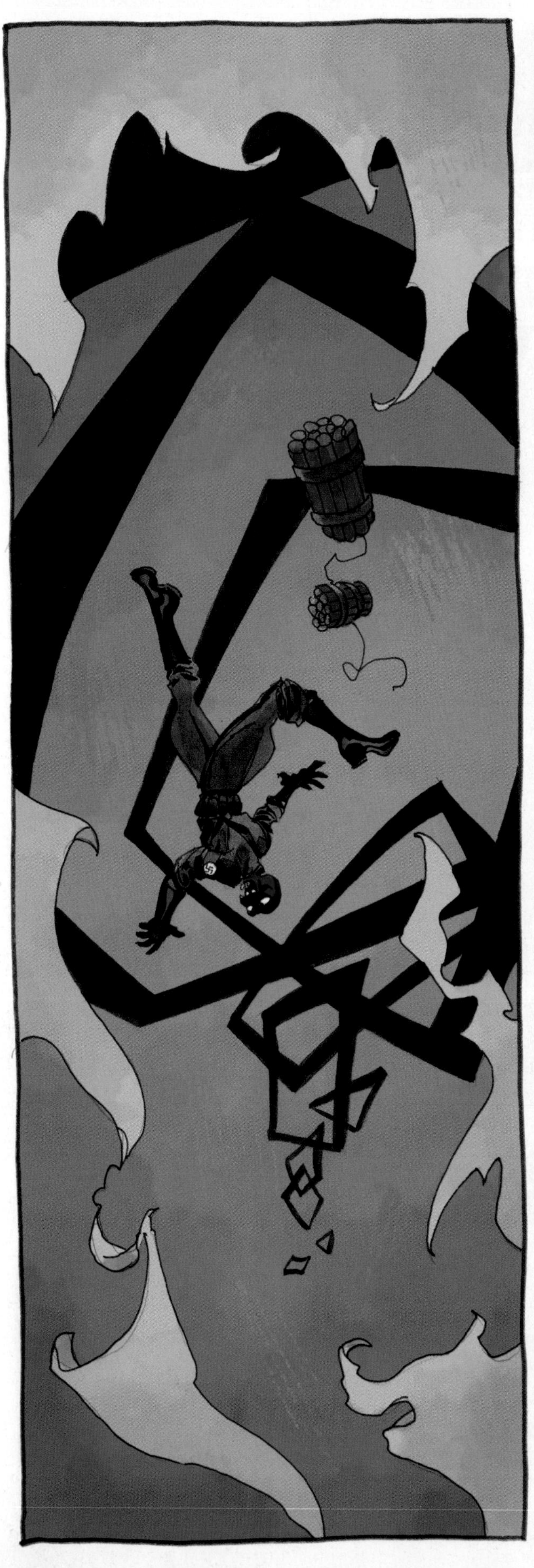

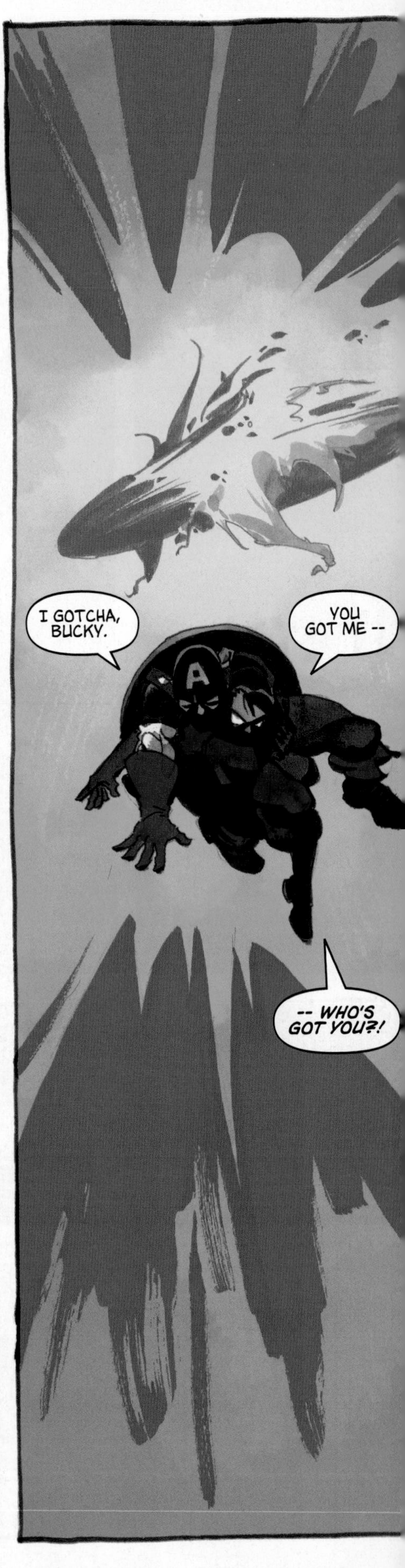
I GOTCHA, BUCKY.
YOU GOT ME --
-- WHO'S GOT YOU?!

WHAT WERE YOU THINKING?
GOING UP AGAINST THE SKULL ALL BY YOURSELF?!
REALLY?! WE'RE GONNA DO THIS NOW?
THE LAST WORDS I'M GONNA HEAR BEFORE I GET TO HEAVEN IS YOU YELLIN' AT ME?!
YOU'RE NOT GOING TO DIE.
NOT ON MY WATCH.

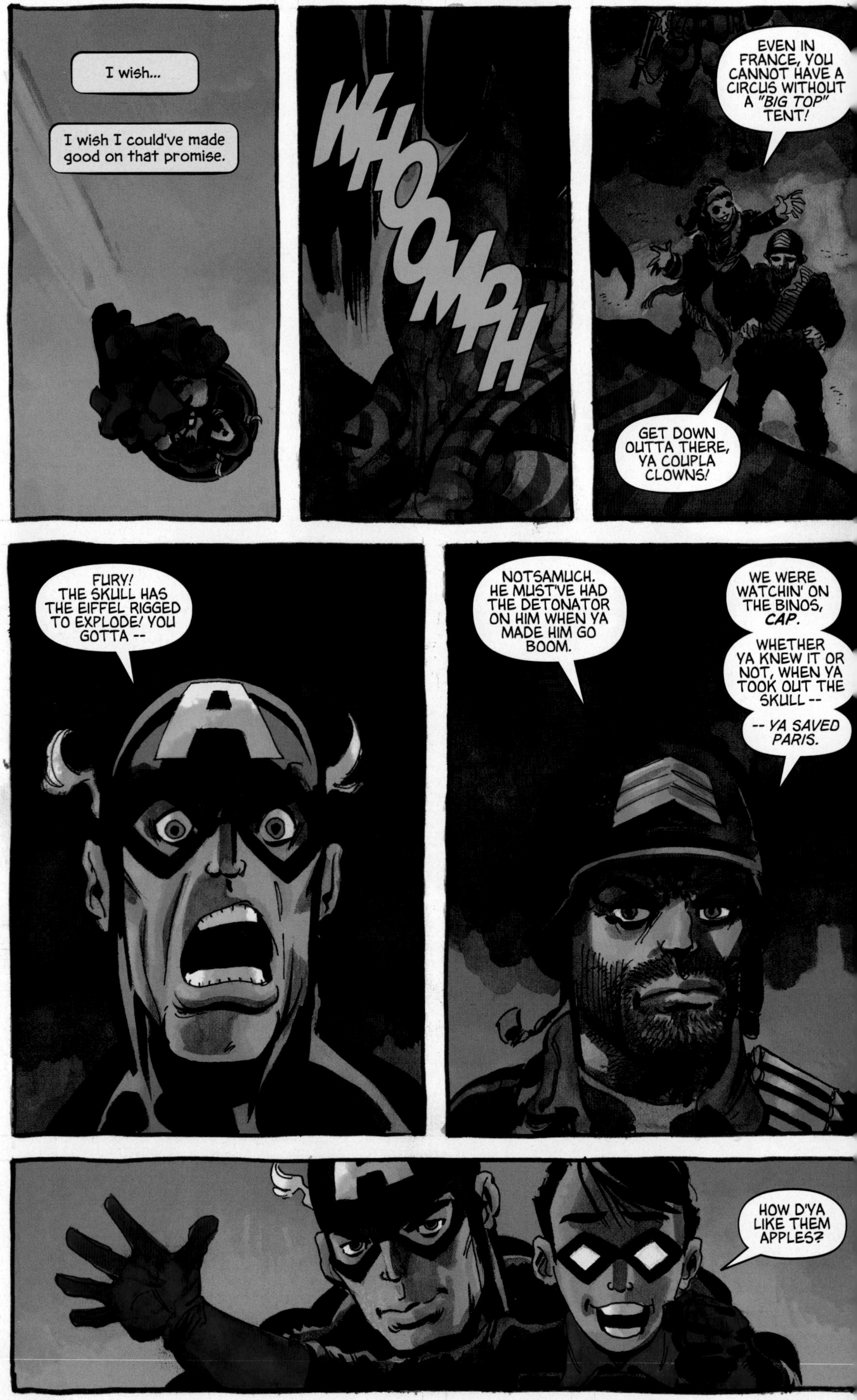
I wish...
I wish I could've made good on that promise.
WHOOMPH
EVEN IN FRANCE, YOU CANNOT HAVE A CIRCUS WITHOUT A "BIG TOP" TENT!
GET DOWN OUTTA THERE, YA COUPLA CLOWNS!
FURY! THE SKULL HAS THE EIFFEL RIGGED TO EXPLODE! YOU GOTTA --
NOTSAMUCH. HE MUST'VE HAD THE DETONATOR ON HIM WHEN YA MADE HIM GO BOOM.
WE WERE WATCHIN' ON THE BINOS, CAP.
WHETHER YA KNEW IT OR NOT, WHEN YA TOOK OUT THE SKULL --
-- YA SAVED PARIS.
HOW D'YA LIKE THEM APPLES?

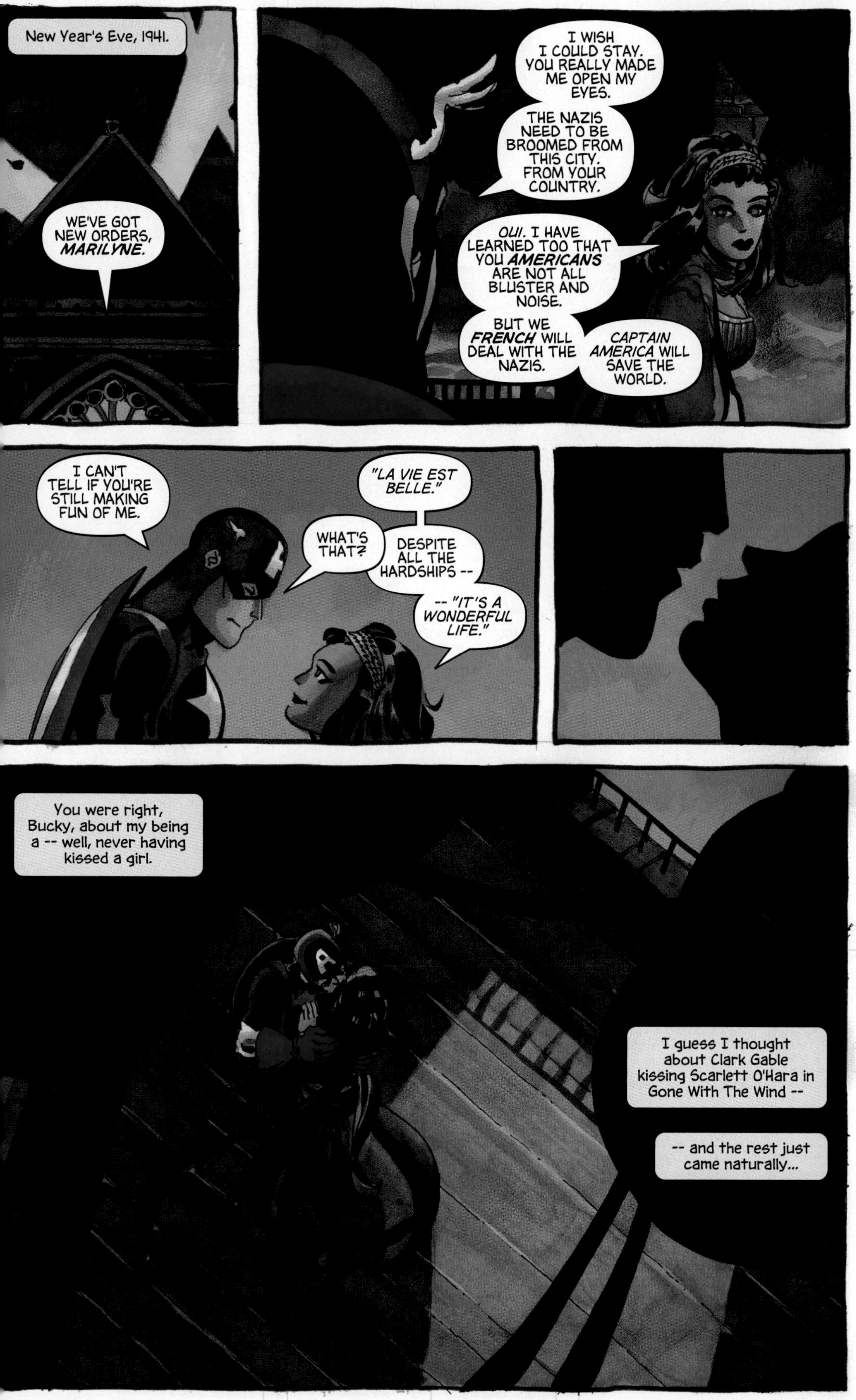
New Year's Eve, 1941.
WE'VE GOT NEW ORDERS, *MARILYNE.*
I WISH I COULD STAY. YOU REALLY MADE ME OPEN MY EYES.
THE NAZIS NEED TO BE BROOMED FROM THIS CITY. FROM YOUR COUNTRY.
OUI. I HAVE LEARNED TOO THAT YOU ***AMERICANS*** ARE NOT ALL BLUSTER AND NOISE.
BUT WE ***FRENCH*** WILL DEAL WITH THE NAZIS.
CAPTAIN AMERICA WILL SAVE THE WORLD.
I CAN'T TELL IF YOU'RE STILL MAKING FUN OF ME.
"LA VIE EST BELLE."
WHAT'S THAT?
DESPITE ALL THE HARDSHIPS --
-- *"IT'S A WONDERFUL LIFE."*
You were right, Bucky, about my being a -- well, never having kissed a girl.
I guess I thought about Clark Gable kissing Scarlett O'Hara in Gone With The Wind --
-- and the rest just came naturally...

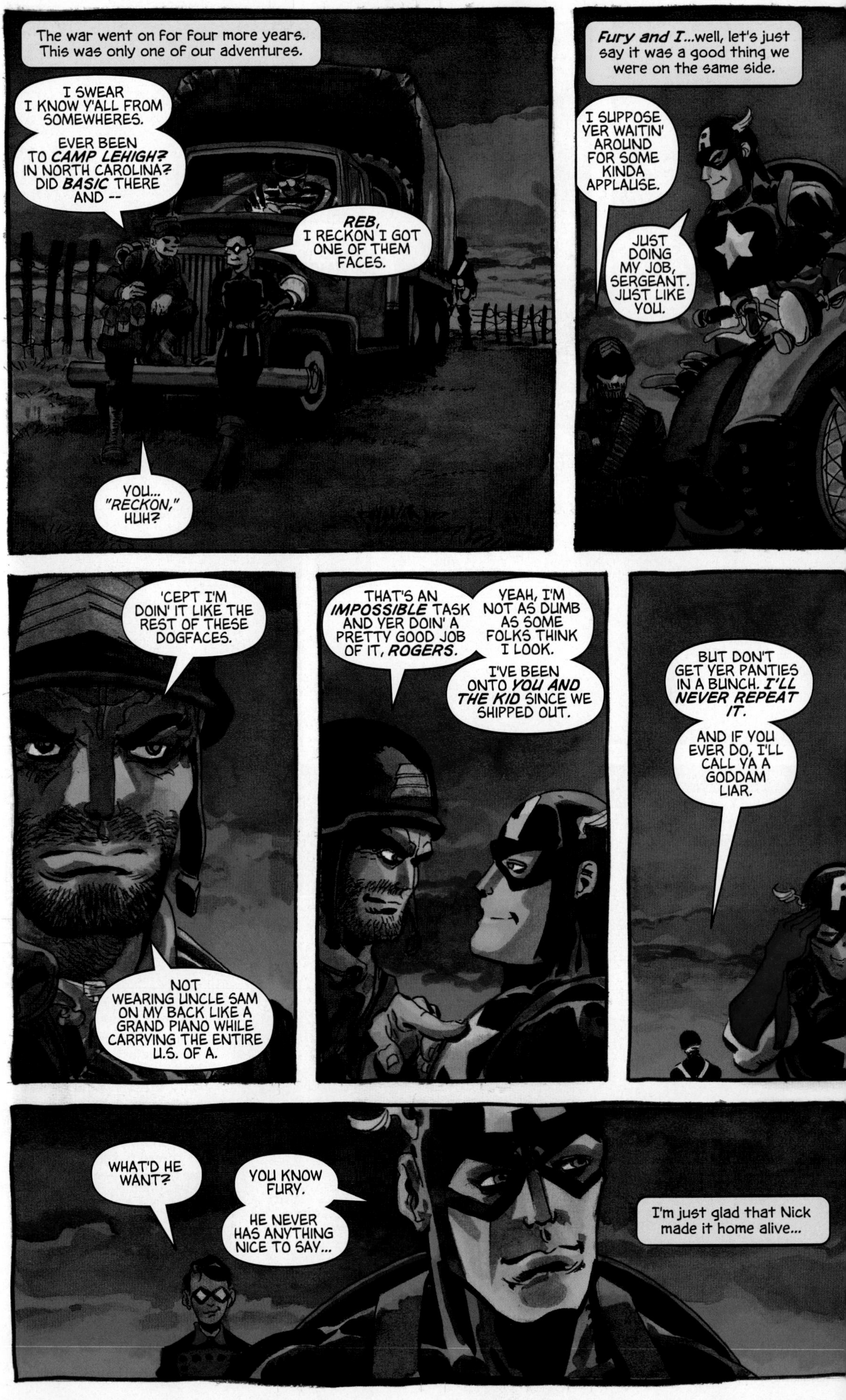
The war went on for four more years. This was only one of our adventures.
I SWEAR I KNOW Y'ALL FROM SOMEWHERES.
EVER BEEN TO CAMP LEHIGH? IN NORTH CAROLINA? DID BASIC THERE AND --
REB, I RECKON I GOT ONE OF THEM FACES.
YOU... "RECKON," HUH?
Fury and I...well, let's just say it was a good thing we were on the same side.
I SUPPOSE YER WAITIN' AROUND FOR SOME KINDA APPLAUSE.
JUST DOING MY JOB, SERGEANT. JUST LIKE YOU.
'CEPT I'M DOIN' IT LIKE THE REST OF THESE DOGFACES.
NOT WEARING UNCLE SAM ON MY BACK LIKE A GRAND PIANO WHILE CARRYING THE ENTIRE U.S. OF A.
THAT'S AN IMPOSSIBLE TASK AND YER DOIN' A PRETTY GOOD JOB OF IT, ROGERS.
YEAH, I'M NOT AS DUMB AS SOME FOLKS THINK I LOOK.
I'VE BEEN ONTO YOU AND THE KID SINCE WE SHIPPED OUT.
BUT DON'T GET YER PANTIES IN A BUNCH. I'LL NEVER REPEAT IT.
AND IF YOU EVER DO, I'LL CALL YA A GODDAM LIAR.
WHAT'D HE WANT?
YOU KNOW FURY.
HE NEVER HAS ANYTHING NICE TO SAY...
I'm just glad that Nick made it home alive...

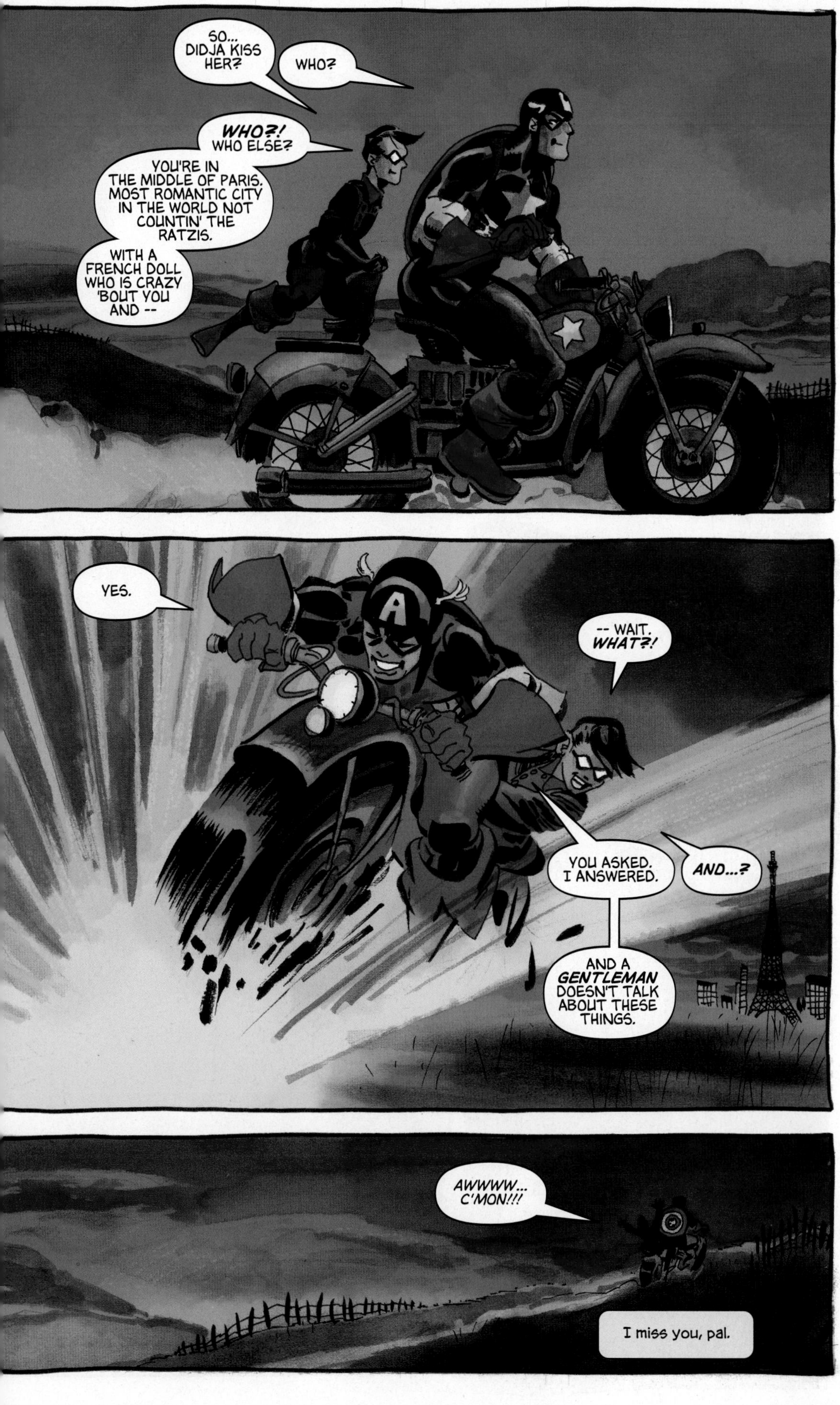

SO... DIDJA KISS HER?
WHO?
WHO?! WHO ELSE?
YOU'RE IN THE MIDDLE OF PARIS. MOST ROMANTIC CITY IN THE WORLD NOT COUNTIN' THE RATZIS.
WITH A FRENCH DOLL WHO IS CRAZY 'BOUT YOU AND --
YES.
-- WAIT. WHAT?!
YOU ASKED. I ANSWERED.
AND...?
AND A GENTLEMAN DOESN'T TALK ABOUT THESE THINGS.
AWWWW... C'MON!!!
I miss you, pal.

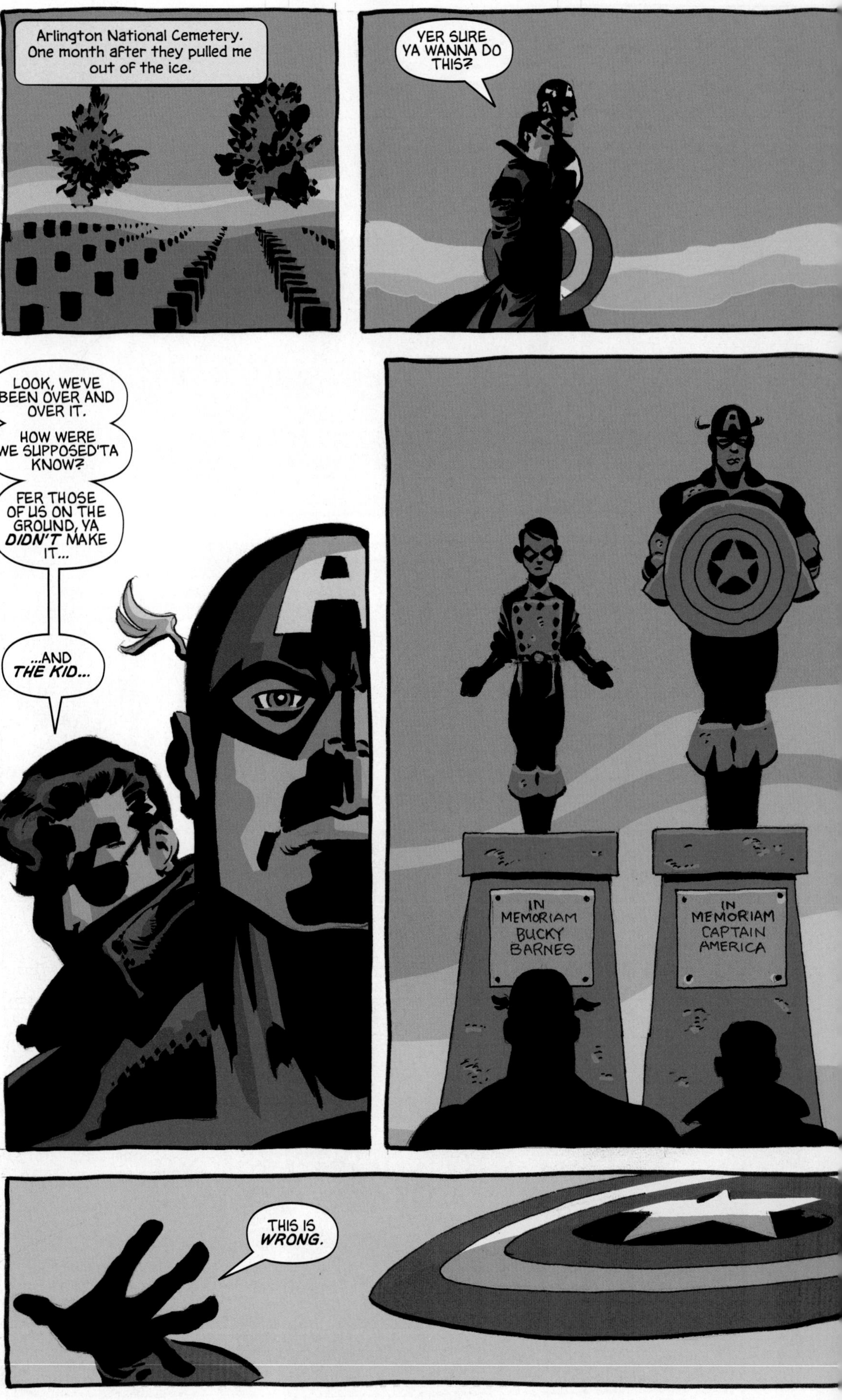
Arlington National Cemetery. One month after they pulled me out of the ice.
YER SURE YA WANNA DO THIS?
LOOK, WE'VE BEEN OVER AND OVER IT.
HOW WERE WE SUPPOSED'TA KNOW?
FER THOSE OF US ON THE GROUND, YA *DIDN'T* MAKE IT...
...AND *THE KID*...
IN MEMORIAM BUCKY BARNES
IN MEMORIAM CAPTAIN AMERICA
THIS IS *WRONG.*

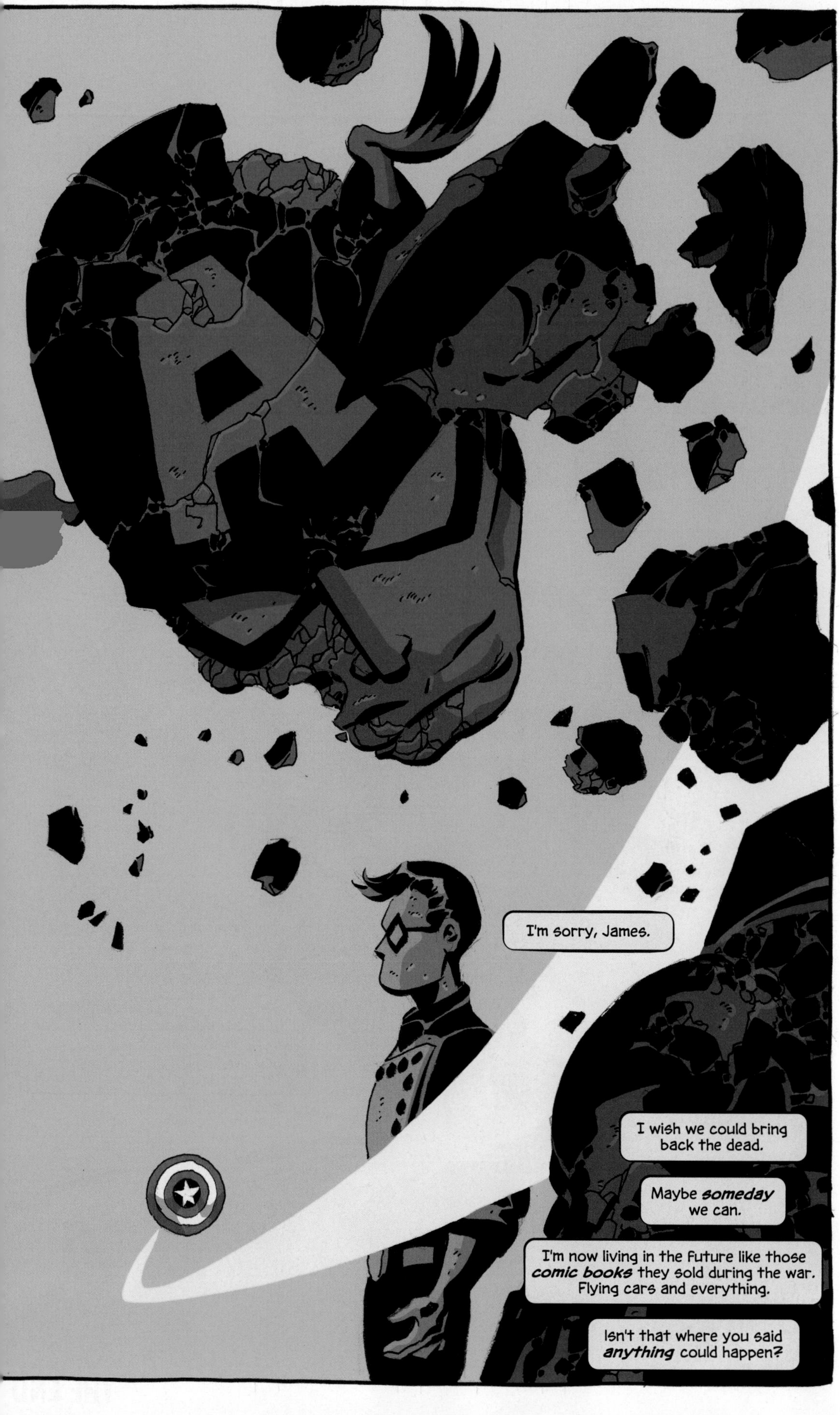
I'm sorry, James.
I wish we could bring back the dead.
Maybe *someday* we can.
I'm now living in the future like those *comic books* they sold during the war. Flying cars and everything.
Isn't that where you said *anything* could happen?

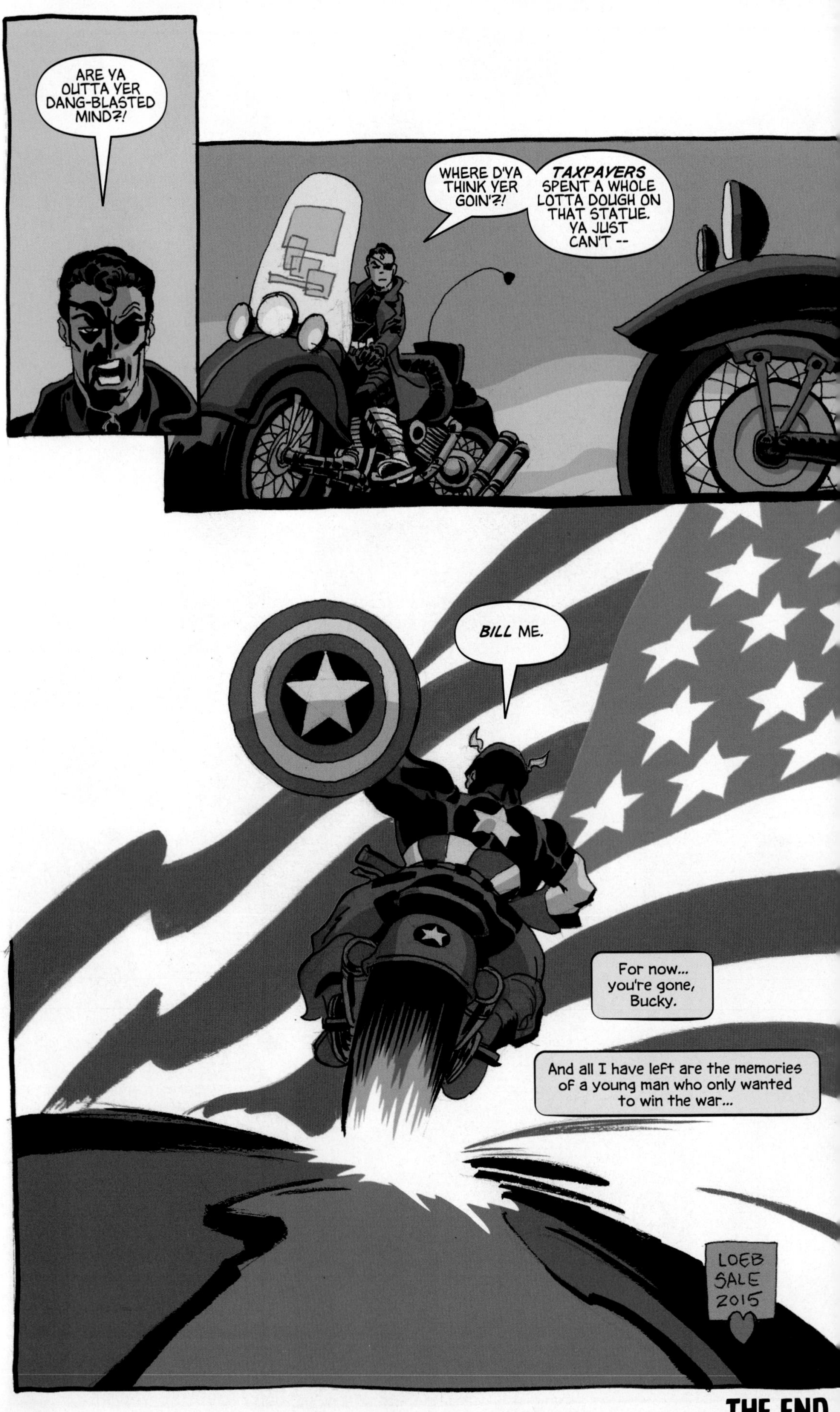

ARE YA OUTTA YER DANG-BLASTED MIND?!
WHERE D'YA THINK YER GOIN'?!
TAXPAYERS SPENT A WHOLE LOTTA DOUGH ON THAT STATUE. YA JUST CAN'T --
BILL ME.
For now... you're gone, Bucky.
And all I have left are the memories of a young man who only wanted to win the war...
LOEB SALE 2015

THE END

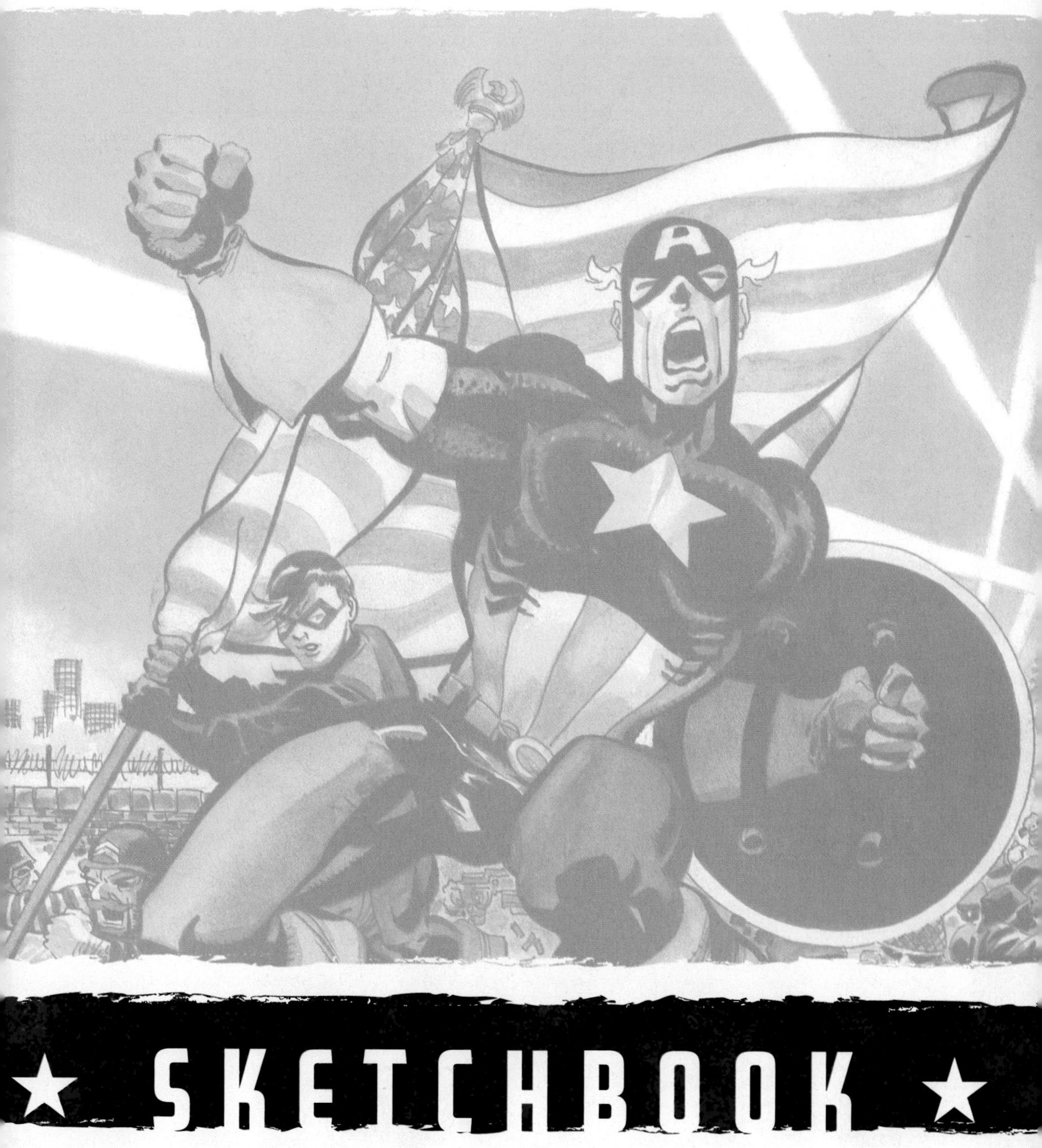

★ SKETCHBOOK ★

Everything Used to Be Black & White

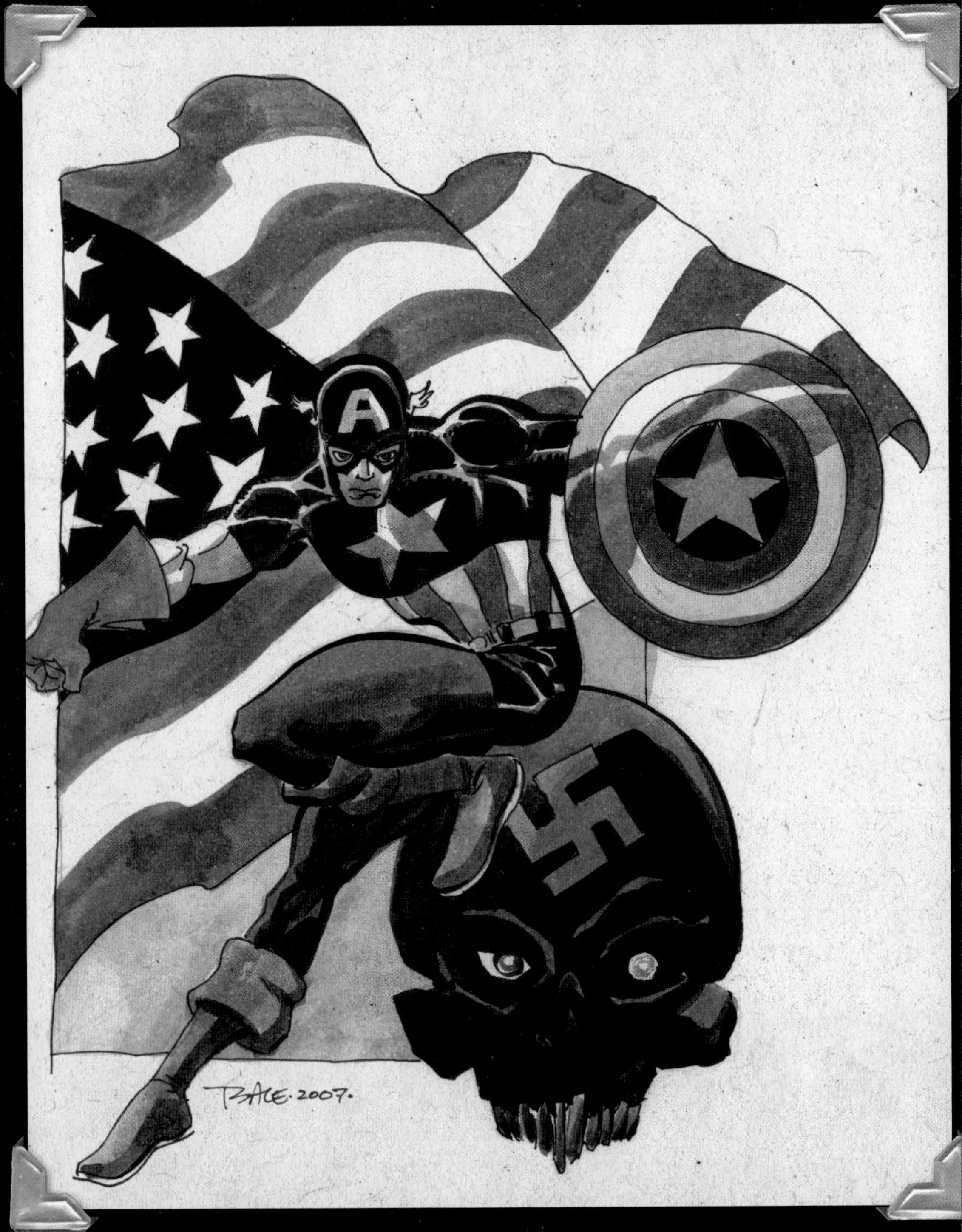

A
TSALE. 2007.

an Interview with the Storytellers

MATT AND KAREN, FROM
DAREDEVIL: YELLOW

PETE AND GWEN, FROM
SPIDER-MAN: BLUE

UNITED STATES ARMY
OFFICIAL DOCUMENT

DECLASSIFIED

CONFIDENTIAL
AMERICAN CONSULATE GENERAL
APO 054   US. FORCES

Date: JUNE 1, 2008

From: RICHARD STARKINGS

Subject: INTERVIEW WITH JEPH LOEB AND TIM SALE

RICH: Guys, it's been five years since HULK: GRAY...and since you were gray, too, Jeph, what happened to your hair? And while you sidestep that question, remind readers about the concept behind the Loeb/Sale coloring books...sorry, COLOR books.

JEPH: The color books were/are a place where Tim and I can tell stories about the beginnings of characters we both grew up loving. There is this unifying theme of the colors in that there are in all of the lives of these characters a very practical reason why we picked that particular color -- i.e. Daredevil's costume was yellow for a short period of time. But there had to be another meaning that gave the story some weight. Again, using DD: YELLOW as an example, yellow is often used to describe cowardice, and since Matt's father was a boxer whose life was tied to being a man without fear, it felt relevant to that character. Spidey felt blue that Gwen was not in his life. In a black and white world (at least in General Ross' mind) The Hulk actually fell into a patch of grey. As to why CAP: WHITE is "white" -- that has yet to be revealed. And it doesn't have to do with skin color -- which technically would be pink.

TIM: The conceptual aspect of the COLOR books just follows in a tradition that I am proud of sharing with Jeph. We come at what we do, the stories we tell, with great joy, but also a sense that we always want a feeling of something special. That's why the concepts, that's why the miniseries.

RICH: Tim, you worked your way through the top DC icons -- both of them -- and have been slowly checking off the major Marvel characters -- what do you find interesting about CAPTAIN AMERICA and what makes him iconic?

TIM: Well, "Working with Jeph" is the flippant and easy answer, and there is a lot of truth to it, but there also is the powerful tug of the fact that these were the characters I read as a teenager, these Marvel characters. Never read DC growing up, only Marvel. There was a freshness to them that I had no historical context for, just a strong feeling that things were being done with them that were more exciting and unlike anything else I'd ever seen.

I suppose I'm trying to catch some of that lightning-in-a-bottle feeling I experienced as a 13-year-old boy when Jack Kirby and Steranko were frying my brain.

RICH: Why do you think, as you have put it in the splendid IMAGE book TIM SALE: BLACK AND WHITE, that Marvel has the best characters?

TIM: Did I say that? The interviewer must have plied me with drink. I know that for me personally, I related very strongly with what Stan Lee concocted, the heroes-with-problems soap operas, and that aspect added a layer of interest towards the characters for me.

Plus, did I mention that the art was just so damn cool?

RICH: Jeph, why set this story so far in Cap's past? WWII is what, a hundred years ago now?

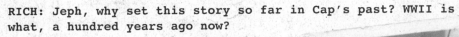

DECLASSIFIED   -2-

THE HULK AND BETTY,
FROM HULK: GRAY

LOEB, AGE 7, HARD AT WORK
ON HIS NEXT SCRIPT...

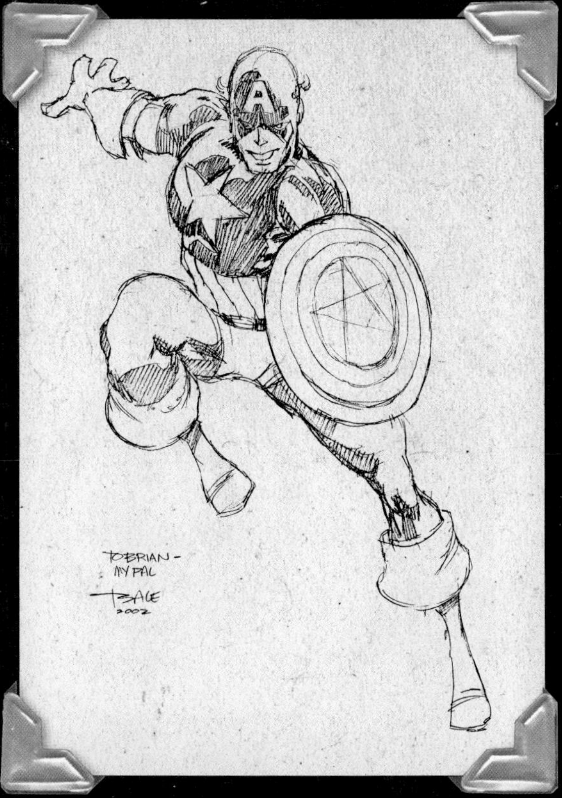
TO BRIAN - MY PAL
T SALE
2002

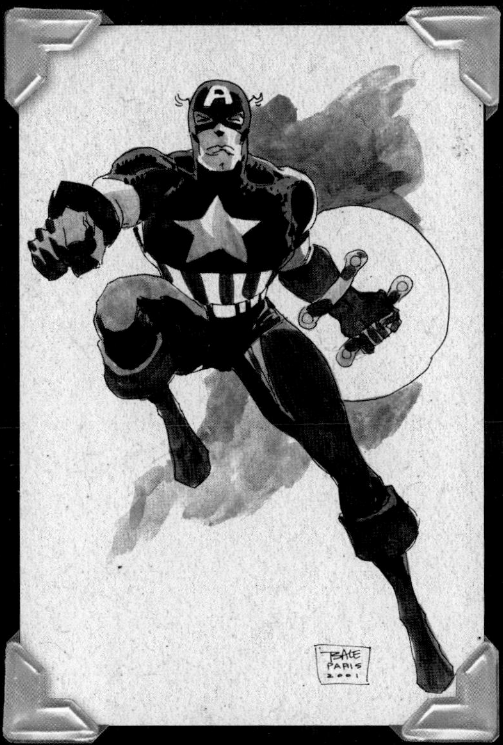
T SALE
PARIS
2001

STRIKE A POSE: SALE'S ONLY PREVIOUS PROFESSIONAL DRAWINGS OF CAP WERE FOR FANS AT COMIC CONVENTIONS.

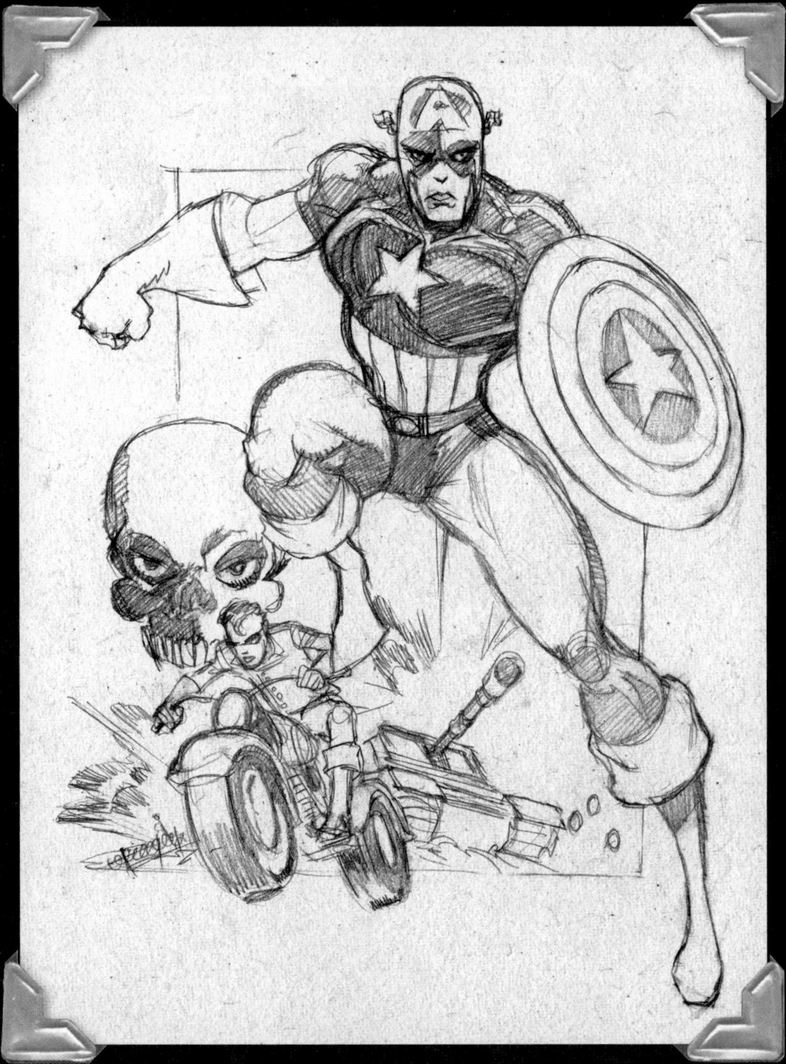

SPECIAL THANKS TO KEN MARTIN, GEORGE MOORER, JASON PALMER, JUSTIN PORTER, MARK SCHWIEKERT, AND THE REST OF THE FINE FOLKS AT THE TIMSALE1.COM FORUM.

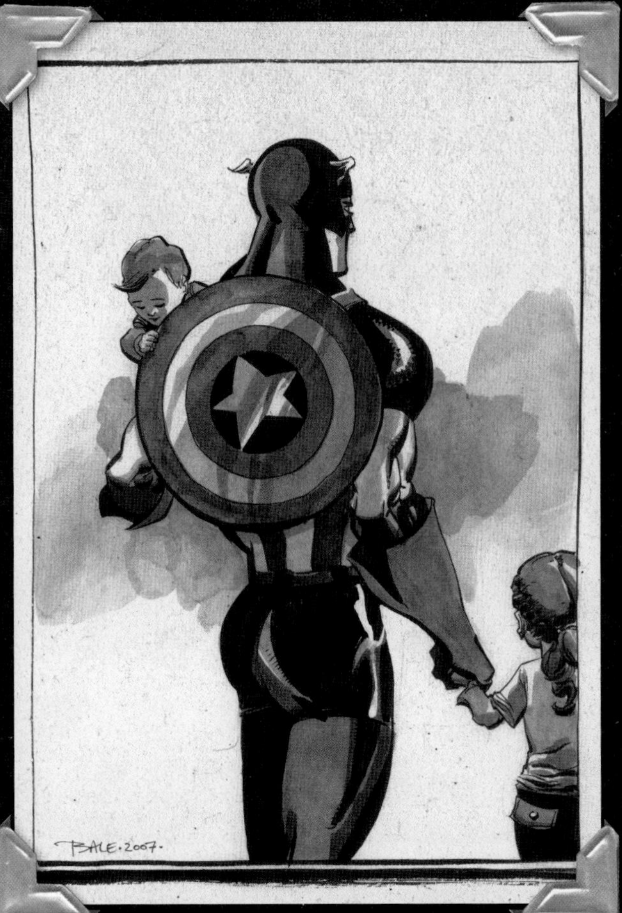
BALE·2007·

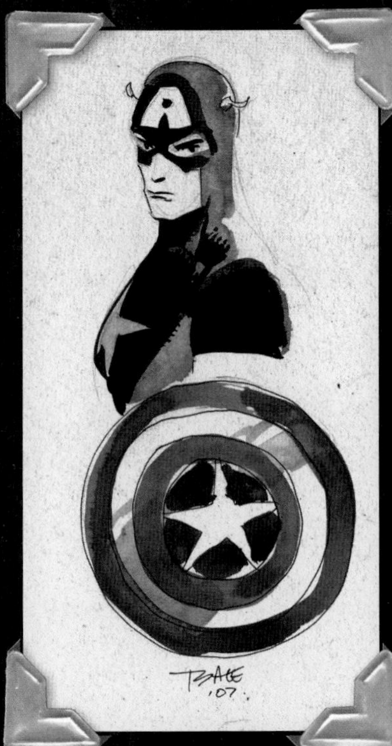
BALE
'07

MORE COMMISSIONS AND CONVENTION SKETCHES

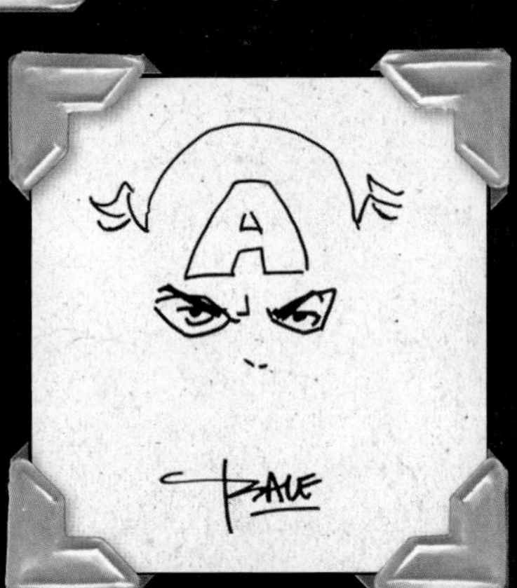
BALE

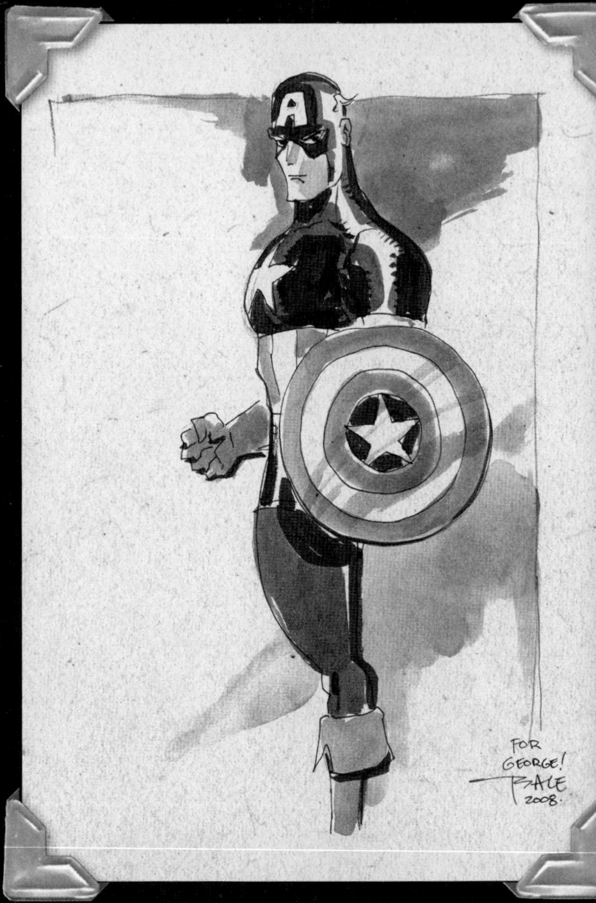
FOR
GEORGE!
BALE
2008.

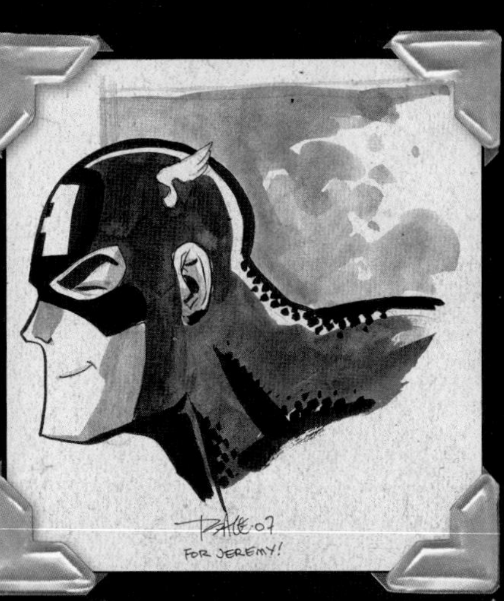
BALE·07
FOR JEREMY!

SERIAL NUMBER   1. NAME (Print)
2605   STEVEN ROGERS   533
                (First)   (Middle)   (Last)

2. ADDRESS (Print)
417 FIFTH AVENUE   NEW YORK CITY   N.Y.
(Number and street or R. F. D. number)   (Town)   (County)   (State)

                                    6. COUNTRY OF
                                       CITIZENSHIP
        4. AGE IN YEARS   5. PLACE OF BIRTH
                               NEW YORK

UNITED STATES ARMY DECLASSIFIED
OFFICIAL DOCUMENT

JEPH: Well, for some of us it was just yesterday. This seems like a
good spot to point out that despite his dashing good looks, Tim is
actually OLDER than I am -- by quite a few years.

TIM: Eh? What'd ya say, sonny?

JEPH: Anyway, I think it's more difficult to tell a Captain America
story in present day when the idea of a man running around in an
American flag might not be the best idea. The themes work just as well
in WWII where the sides were more clear-cut, so being Cap doesn't have
to be a problem in the storytelling. He has nothing to prove back then
because he's already the hero of the piece. Nobody can argue "Nazis
bad."

**RICH: Jeph, you've forced Tim to draw pictures of young boys against
his will once before, when you introduced Robin into DARK VICTORY. Is
Cap's relationship with Bucky similar to Batman's relationship with
Robin?**

JEPH: Not really. Batman is a grown man who is something of a
surrogate father to Robin. Certainly in the case of Bruce Wayne and
Dick Grayson. Bruce is perpetually 29 years old and Dick was -- at the
time of his parents' death -- only 10 years old. Quite a difference.
Now, with Bucky, this is a teenager who lived on an Army base. Steve
couldn't have been much older, having wanted to enlist, so he's in his
early 20s. They were probably five years apart, so they were more like
the youngest brother in a large family with an oldest brother. In Cap
#0 we tackle why Steve would take a young man into battle (which was
also a big question in Dark Victory -- How does Batman justify taking
a boy into the war against the freaks?). When you think of Bucky
as closer to Rick Jones' age -- the teenager in the Hulk -- (and I
suspect that was on somebody's mind when Rick was created) the dynamic
changes hugely. When Steranko made Rick the "new" Bucky, you saw
how true that rang. Those stories in Cap #110, 111 and 113 are huge
influences on both Tim and me.

TIM: I was struck with something as I read Jeph's scripts for CAP
WHITE. And that is the fact that I was bored to death with Stan Lee's
'60s take on Cap's anguish over Bucky's death, and how one-note it was
when Rick Jones became the surrogate Bucky...and how Jeph can make the
same basic facts so much more fun and fresh and sad at the same time.
Not at all boring.

And let me hasten to add, if it is not clear even though I have said
it repeatedly, that I am a ginormous Stan fan.

RICH: DD: YELLOW, SPIDEY: BLUE and HULK: GRAY were all about the girls

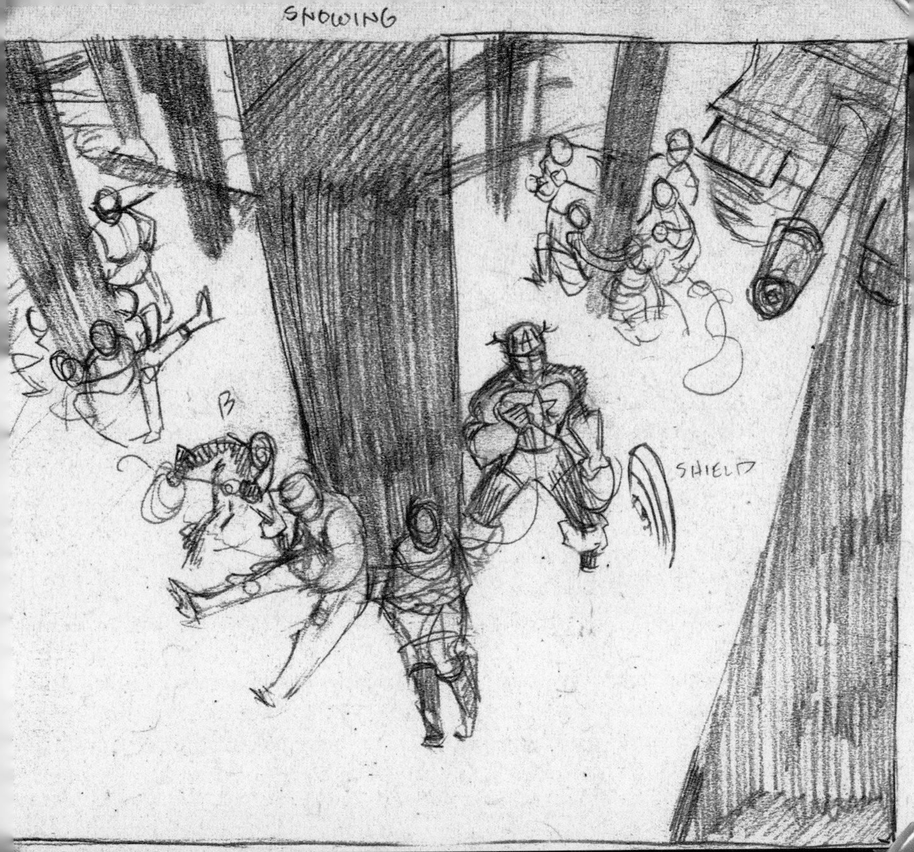
SNOWING
B
SHIELD

PENCILS TO INKS TO WASH FOR ISSUE #3

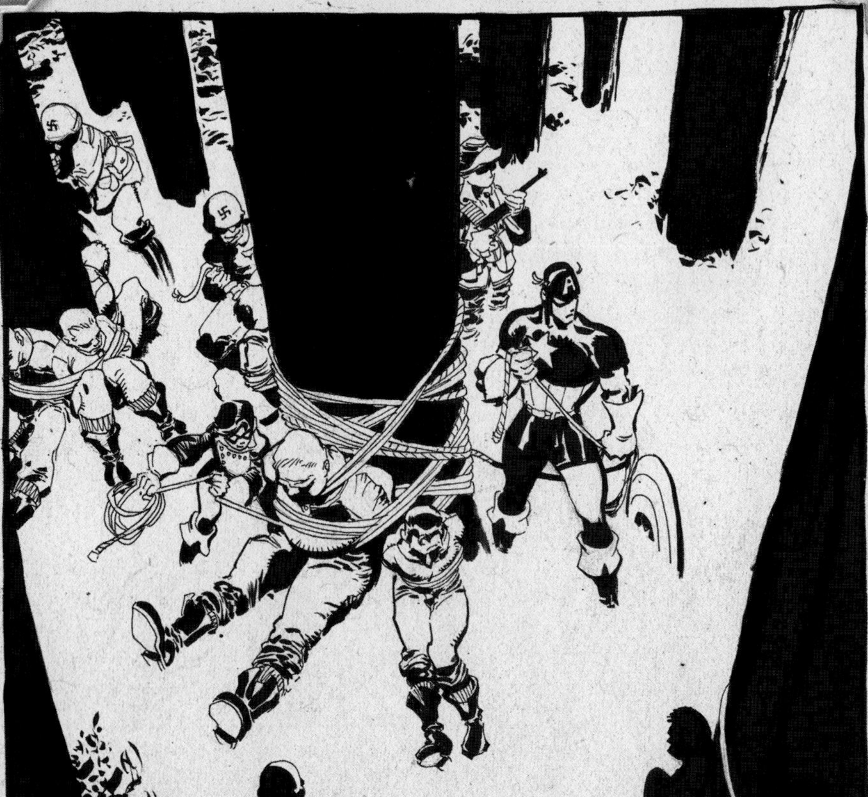

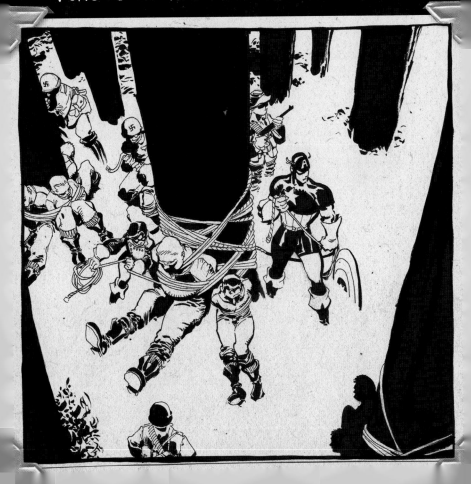

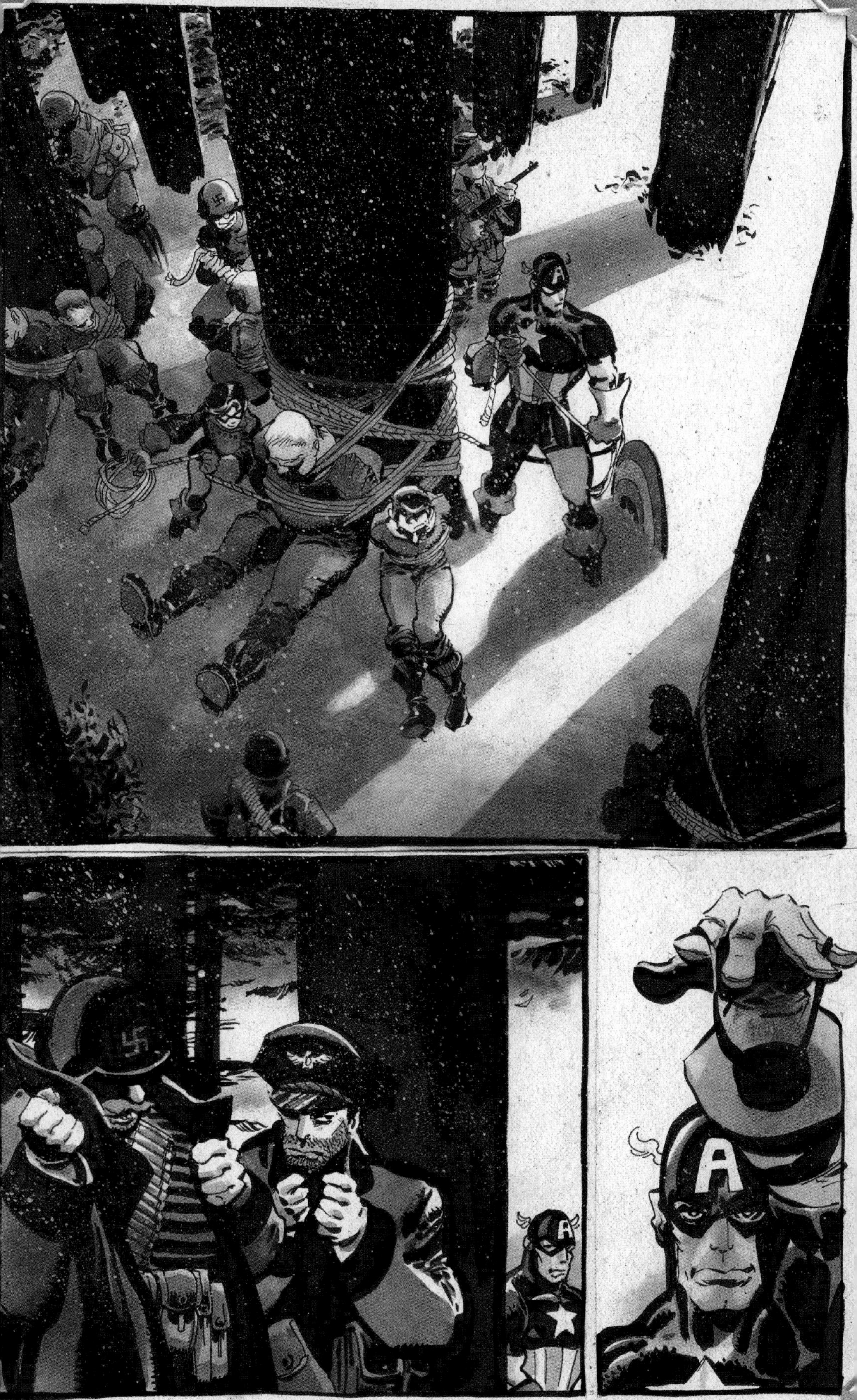

each of the characters loved. CAP has never been especially connected to one romance in particular. Do you think that he is too much of a father figure and is that the most important aspect of Bucky's appearance in the strip? The young GI alongside the seasoned vet?

JEPH: Well, as I discussed above, while it is often portrayed as Cap was "a seasoned vet," he really wasn't. All you have to do is look at the dates. Steve was a 98 lb. weakling AFTER the draft had started. By late 1941, he's Captain America and took Bucky with him from Fort Lehigh, so they came out of basic training together. What was different is they both wanted desperately to get into battle -- a concept that is hard to understand (at least for me) in the present. Having said that, by the time Bucky died, which was in 1945, they'd been together for four years. Four years in battle will change anyone. I know a man who landed on the beach on the third day of D-Day in Normandy. Every single man in his company was killed on the beach. He became an alcoholic and never returned to being the man he was before the war. So there's a bond that's coupled with Cap's own guilt about what happened to Bucky in the end.

TIM: Jeph speaks very well about war, and the concept that us two fellas, who have never had to experience it, are telling a story about it, is not lost. But in many ways, I feel strongly that it adds a different perspective, a worthy perspective. In the same way that, for instance, foreign-born artists can make profound movies about tortured gay cowboys or 1970s troubled suburban families or Elizabethan societal fiction. Being an artist is about looking, and having something to say.

RICH: Is it important that Cap is aloof romantically? Aloof and somewhat innocent, as one might imagine a parent?

JEPH: Well, not in my mind. I think it had more to do with -- and I'm not sure it's been played this way -- that being rated 4F in the draft was about the worst thing that could happen to a young man. I sort of remember -- and I might be making this up (as Tim will tell you I often do) -- that in one retelling of the origin, Steve comes out of the recruiting hall having been classified 4F. Now, as if that's not bad enough, there are two girls on the street who point and giggle at him as if he were wearing a jacket that says "4F" on the breast pocket and "Kick Me" stuck on his back. So for me, it's more about inexperience. Once he becomes Cap, Steve is a chick magnet, no doubt about it. But, my guess is that Bucky's had more experience with women that Steve has -- and we'll be playing with that in CAP: WHITE.

TIM: I'm not sure what Jeph has in mind regarding women, and Steve's relationships, but in my head Steve Rogers is romantic-neutral. He's a fightin' man. But that's what I love about Jeph's writing, that he may just want to explore what it would be like if you woke up no longer a 98 lb. weakling, and were suddenly attractive to women.

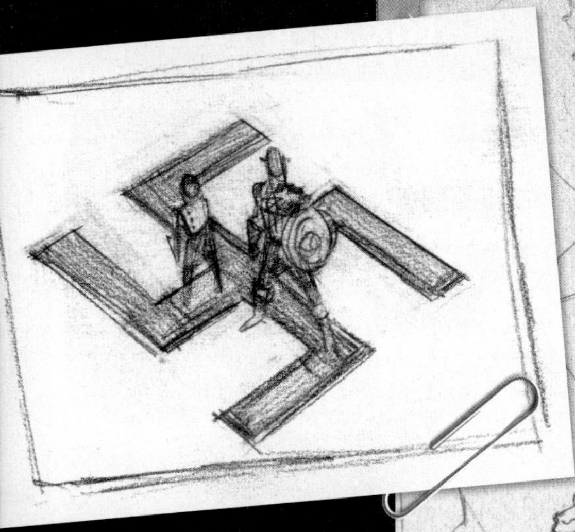

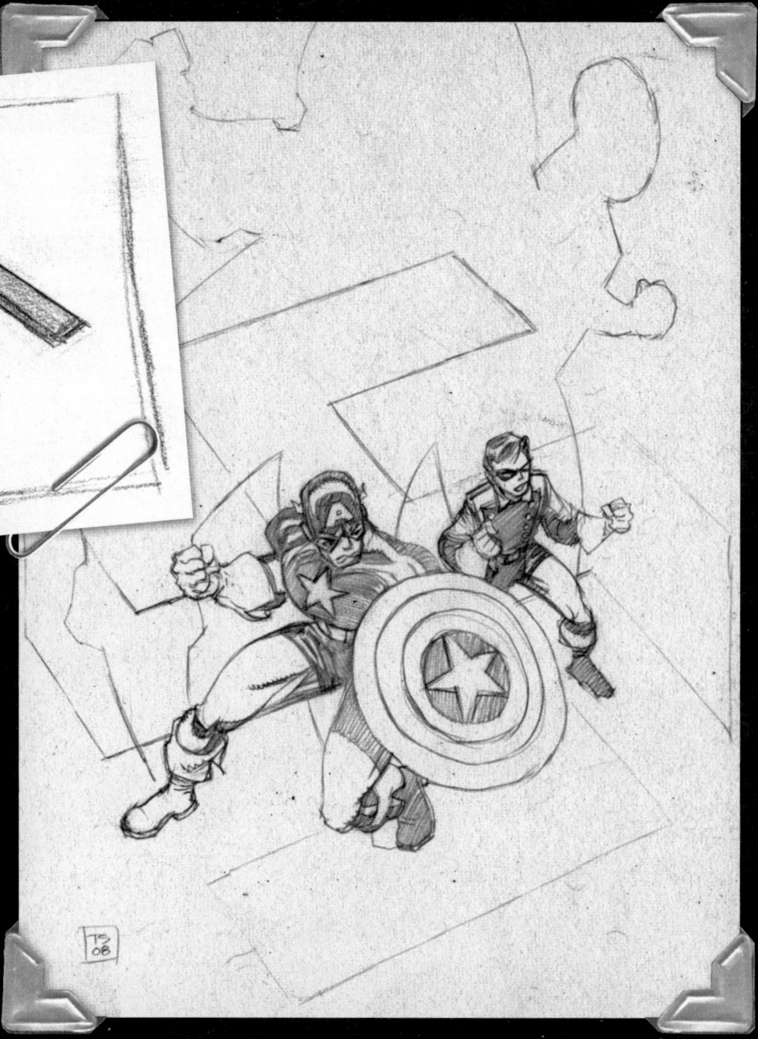

SKETCH AND PENCILS FOR THE COVER TO ISSUE #0.

A GIFT FOR DAVE STEWART.

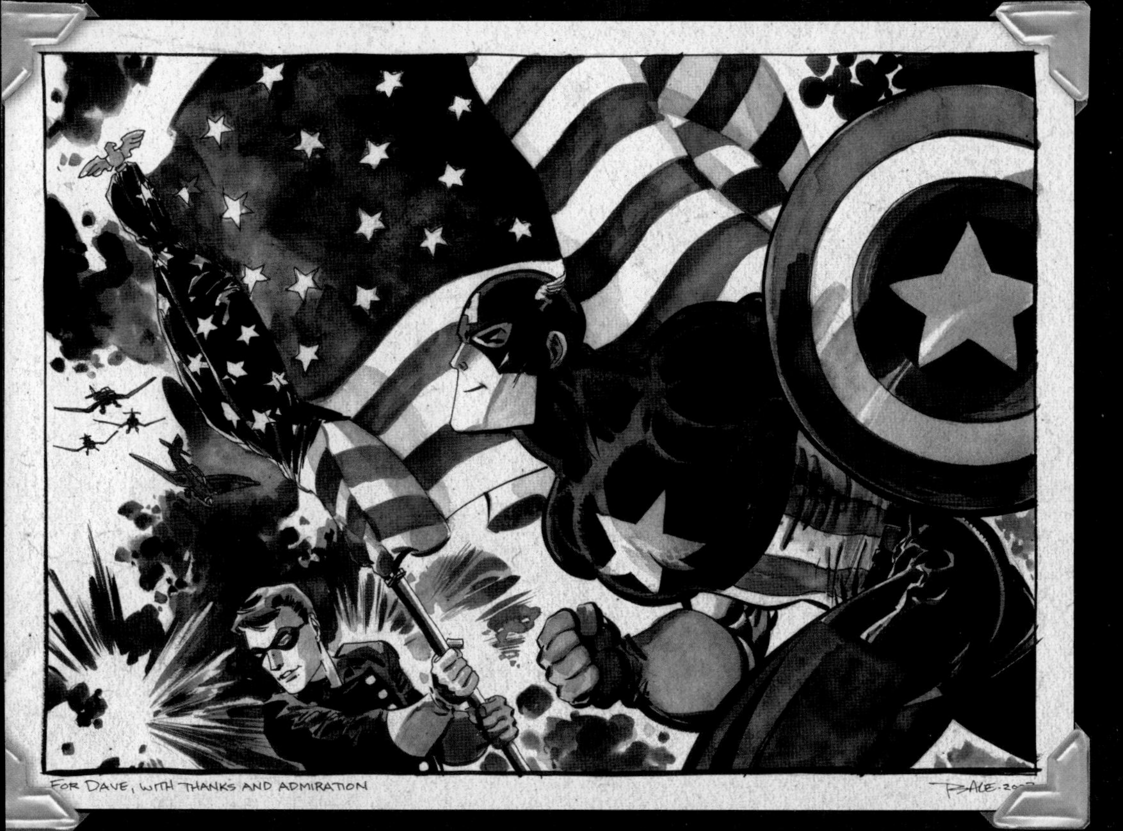
FOR DAVE, WITH THANKS AND ADMIRATION

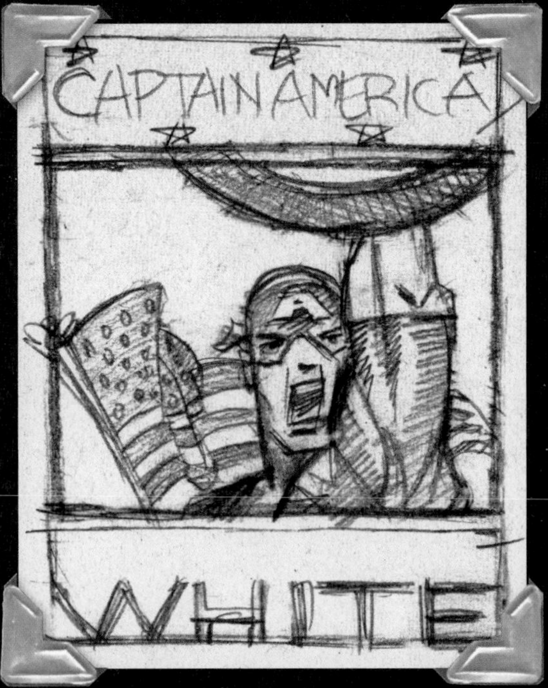
CAPTAIN AMERICA
WHITE

BIRTHDAY CARD
FOR JEPH, 2008

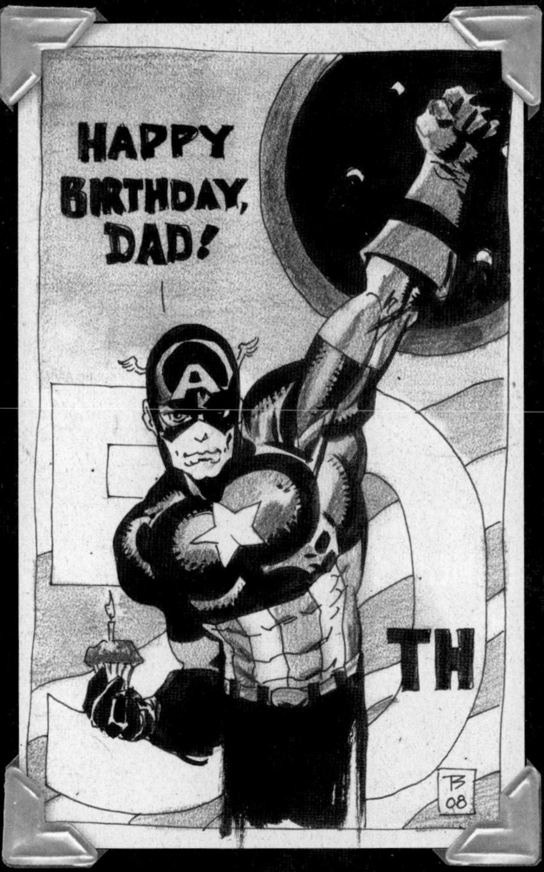
HAPPY BIRTHDAY, DAD!
TH
TB 08

ABOVE: SKETCH FOR
THE COVER TO ISSUE #1

BELOW: UNUSED COVER

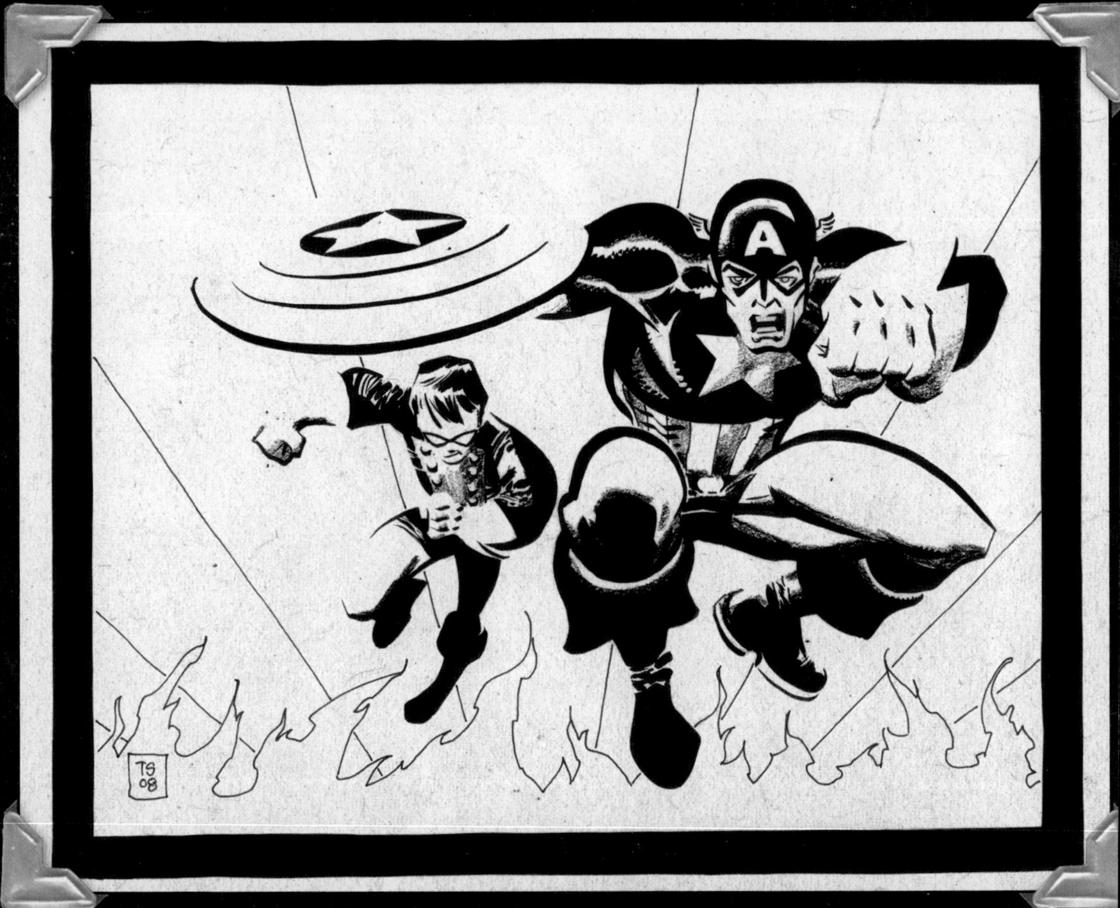
TS 08

I love your idea, Jeph, that Bucky is more women-savvy than Steve.

RICH: Jeph, how much of your own experience of being a father comes into your work when you write about this kind of relationship?

JEPH: The line between father and son and brothers are all blurred in my life. As you and Tim both know about Sam (Jeph's son who died of cancer at 17 years old), he was far older than his years. He was not only my son, he was my best friend too. I think I understand how Steve felt about the responsibility he had toward Bucky in that way.

RICH: Tim, you've complained bitterly about Jeph insisting that you draw cars and other vehicles before -- how do you feel about having to reference motorbikes, Army Jeeps and German tanks for this series?

TIM: You trying to start a fight there, you Limey dogface? Having to draw jeeps and tanks and stuff is all part of taking on the challenge of drawing the best Captain America story I can possibly draw. I am an enormous fan of Harvey Kurtzman's TWO-FISTED TALES and FRONTLINE COMBAT, and the level of care towards authenticity he asked, and what Archie Goodwin promoted in his writing and editing of the done-too-soon BLAZING COMBAT. All involved did their best to honor the men and women that fought, by telling stories as respectfully researched as they could. I'm, uh, struggling to get there. I now have the start of a scary library of WWII books, I'll tell you that.

I suppose I gather strength from seeing how the great Jack Kirby, a WWII vet of the Battle of the Bulge and Cap's co-creator, bent reality to make his stories more exciting, and don't drive myself crazy with making every nut and bolt historically accurate, but I want it to FEEL that way.

RICH: America is at war again, does CAP: WHITE have a message about the human cost of war? Should it? Shouldn't it?

TIM: Of course, in my view. "Human cost of war" should be at the core of any war story. It's only reality that gets it muddled up.

JEPH: I don't know if we'll touch on it directly, but as I've mentioned elsewhere in this startling interview, the idea of signing up to go to battle is completely foreign to me. I look at a movie like THREE KINGS and I don't know how anybody could go over to Iraq, and

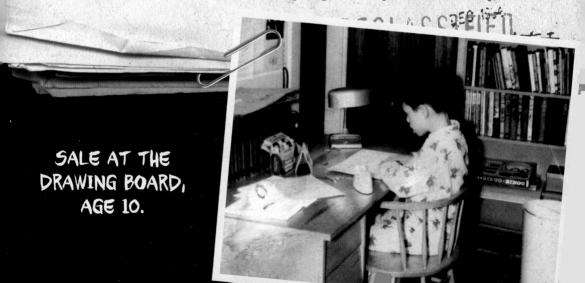

SALE AT THE
DRAWING BOARD,
AGE 10.

that movie had George Clooney! Cap's adventures were thrilling and over the top and meant as propaganda to get young men to join up. The message comes through Bucky's death -- that even the strongest soldier can still feel the reality of what they are doing. I just want it to play very quietly. I don't want to be preachy and I'm not a fan of "war comics" that hit you over the head with "the human cost of war."

TIM: Well, I am a fan of many of them, from Kubert's ENEMY ACE, to Kanigher and Toth's "White Devil...Yellow Devil!" from STAR-SPANGLED WAR STORIES #164, but I know what Jeph means, and I do not think CAP: WHITE should be that. Captain America at some point maybe, but not CAP: WHITE, not at all.

RICH: Ed Brubaker recently revived interest in Cap with his recent run on the title, which ended in Cap's death. Does Cap have to die to be relevant today?

JEPH: Do I think it's difficult to tell a story with a guy wearing the American flag in the present? Yes. When I wrote FALLEN SON: THE DEATH OF CAPTAIN AMERICA, which looked at the aftereffects and grief of Cap as fallen hero, I purposely avoided the "relevant" issue. Cap was/is cool. He's as close as Marvel has to Superman. The right guy to inspire us. And Cap's version of America is close to Superman's in that "Norman Rockwellian kind of world" that drove Tim in SUPERMAN FOR ALL SEASONS.

RICH: Would he carry a gun?

JEPH: He did in some of those Golden Age comics. Present day? It's a useful thing to get people to talk about the book. Should he? Meh. He's got the coolest weapon in the world -- the shield. NOBODY has

DECLASSIFIED DEC 15 RELEASED

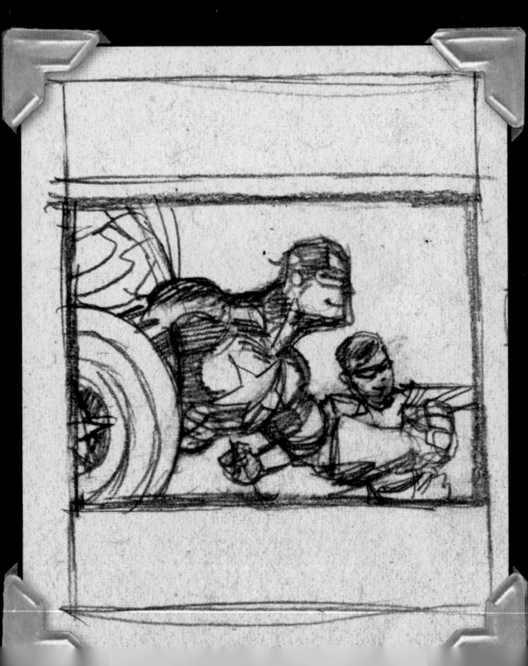

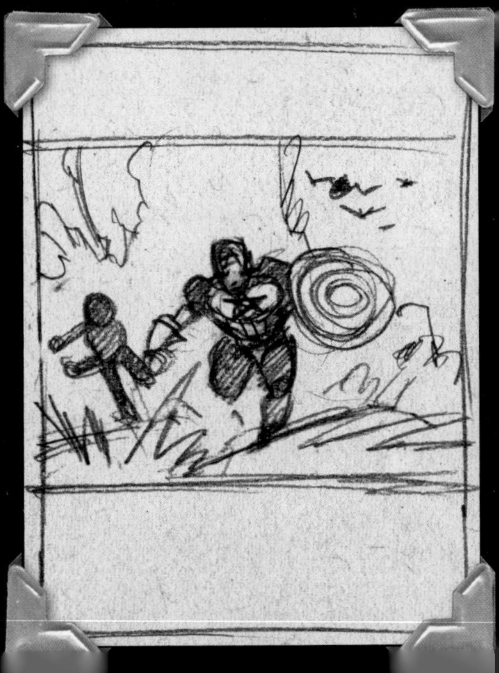

COVER SKETCHES

DECLASSIFIED

UNITED STATES ARMY
OFFICIAL DOCUMENT

that. Not one you can throw like a boomerang! Not even The Fighting American, Joe Simon's OTHER patriotic hero -- who you both know I had a great deal of experience with.

TIM: Not in any stories I will ever tell. I personally have no interest at all in comic heroes who shoot people.

JEPH: Not even Nick Fury and the Howling Commandos? HA!

TIM: You shut up! Okay, how about this: I will never draw a story where a costumed super hero who has a history of fighting for higher ideals (debate the possibility of "fighting" and "higher ideals," all you college students) takes out a gun and shoots somebody. I loves me some noir, some Howlers, but I like my Captain Americas and Supermans to be of different stuff.

Plus, Jeph is right. How cool is that shield? That and super strength and super reflexes? How did the Nazis stand a chance?

RICH: Is it more attractive to both of you as creators to sentimentalize the characters and to look back on them through rose-tinted spectacles rather than drag them kicking and screaming into the 21st century?

TIM: Well I think there is a big area in between, don't you? Just because it is set in the past doesn't mean it has to be seen through rose-tinted spectacles (isn't the language of our English friend cute, Jeph?), just as modernizing them should not have to mean the boringly familiar refrain that tragedy and violence equals seriousness.

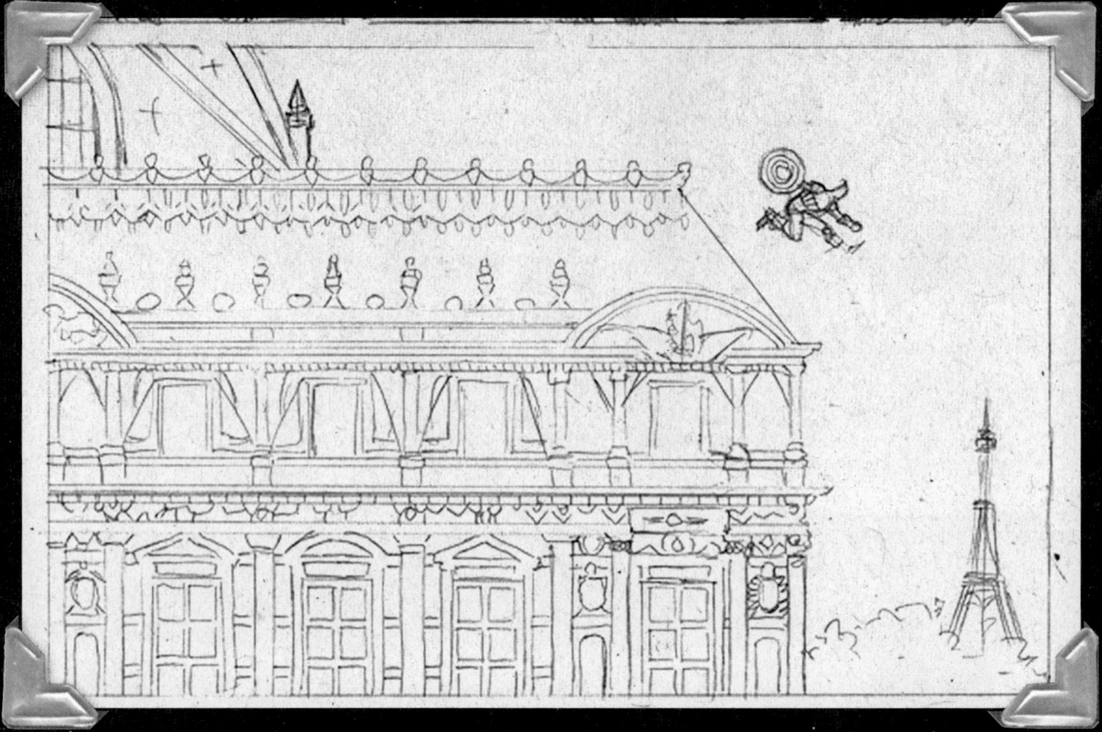

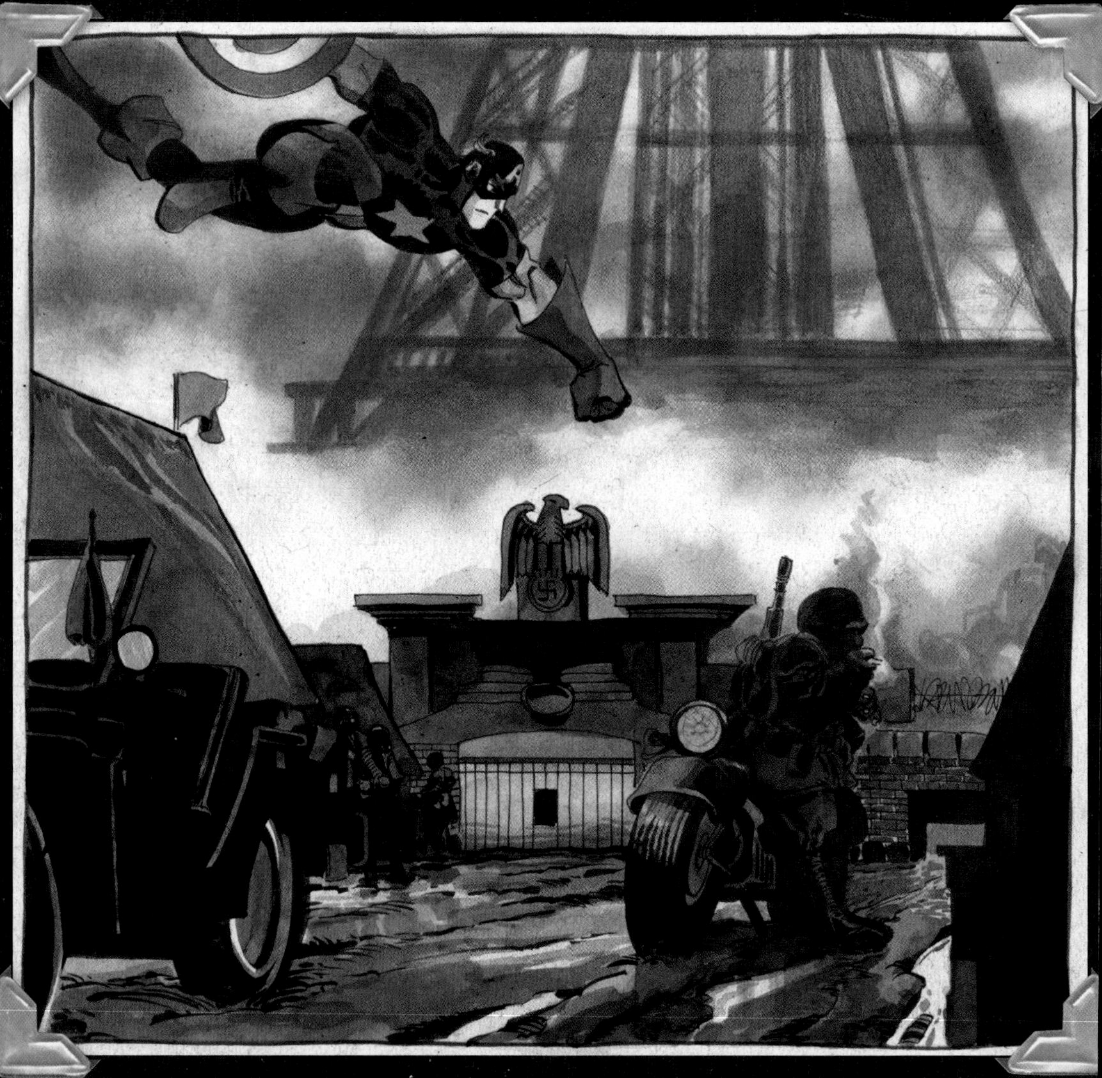

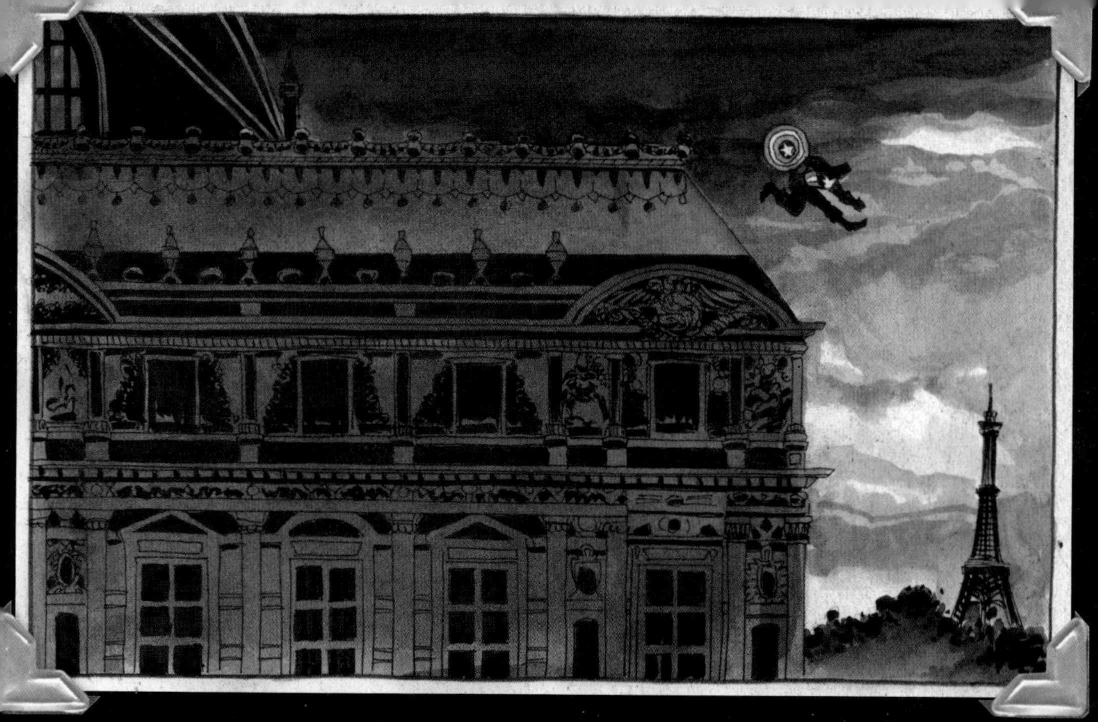

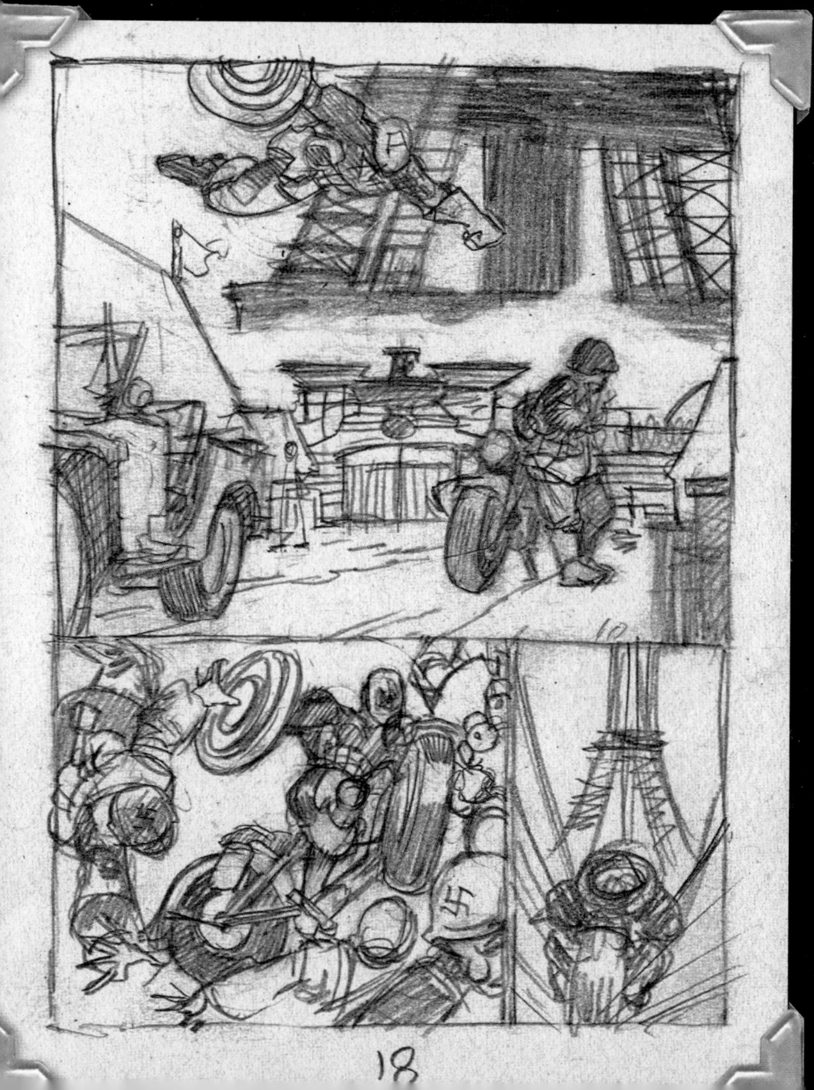
18

PENCILS AND
INK WASH FOR
ISSUE #4

One of the reasons I adore working with Jeph so much is that he walks that line so well; better than anyone else in comics, in my opinion. And those are the stories that touch and move me.

JEPH: C'mon. Do you think I'm gonna top that? =gush!=

RICH: So, what next? Loeb/Sale on ULTIMATES vol 5? VENOM: NOIR? DAZZLER: RAINBOW?

TIM: Not with a ten-foot pole, will I answer that.

JEPH: We get asked this a lot. The color books, as a brand, were meant to look at the characters who defined the Marvel universe. As cool as Venom and Dazzler might be to folks, they aren't DD, Spidey, Hulk or Cap by any means. There are, however, members of the Avengers and maybe the Fantastic Four who could be worth looking under the hood at. It's all about the best story we can tell. Tim has a pretty great handle on what he wants to draw. My guess is something will stick.

TIM: I have some ideas. Never you mind, dogface. Loose lips sink ships!

REGRADED CONFIDENTIAL
ON
BY CDR USAINSCOM FOIP
Para 1-603 DoD5200. 1 R

~~CONFIDENTIAL~~

037

DECLASSIFIED

SKETCH AND INKS FOR ISSUE 6 COVER

TS
08

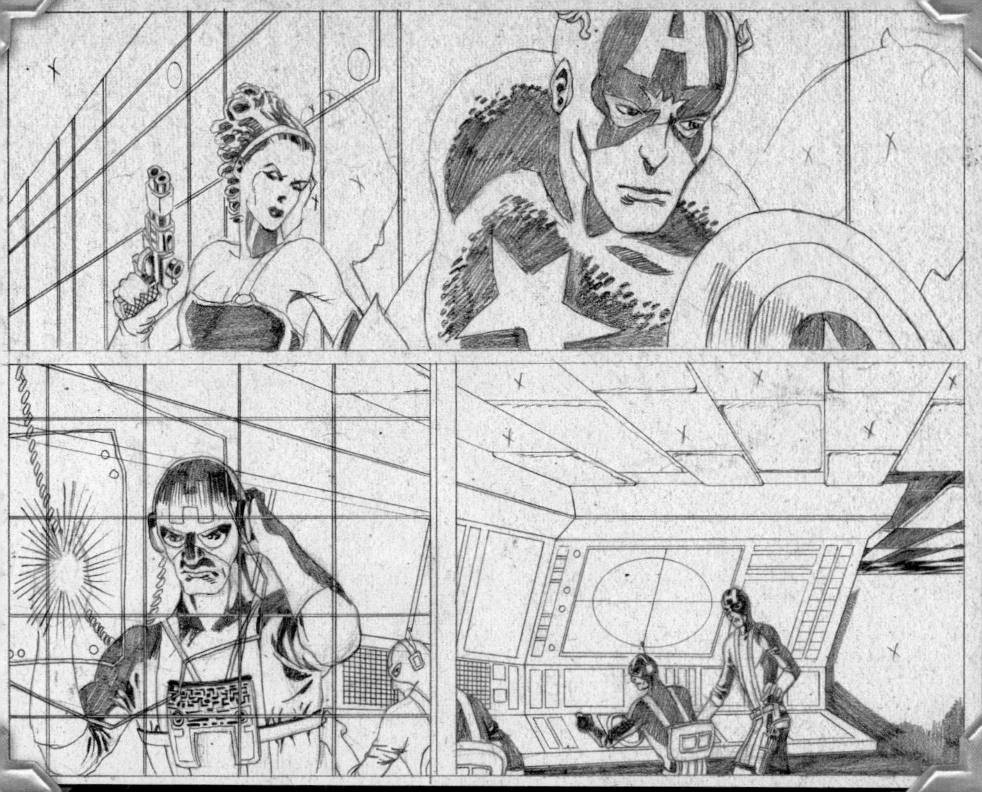

CAP PAGES DRAWN ON SPEC AND SUBMITTED TO MARVEL, 1980

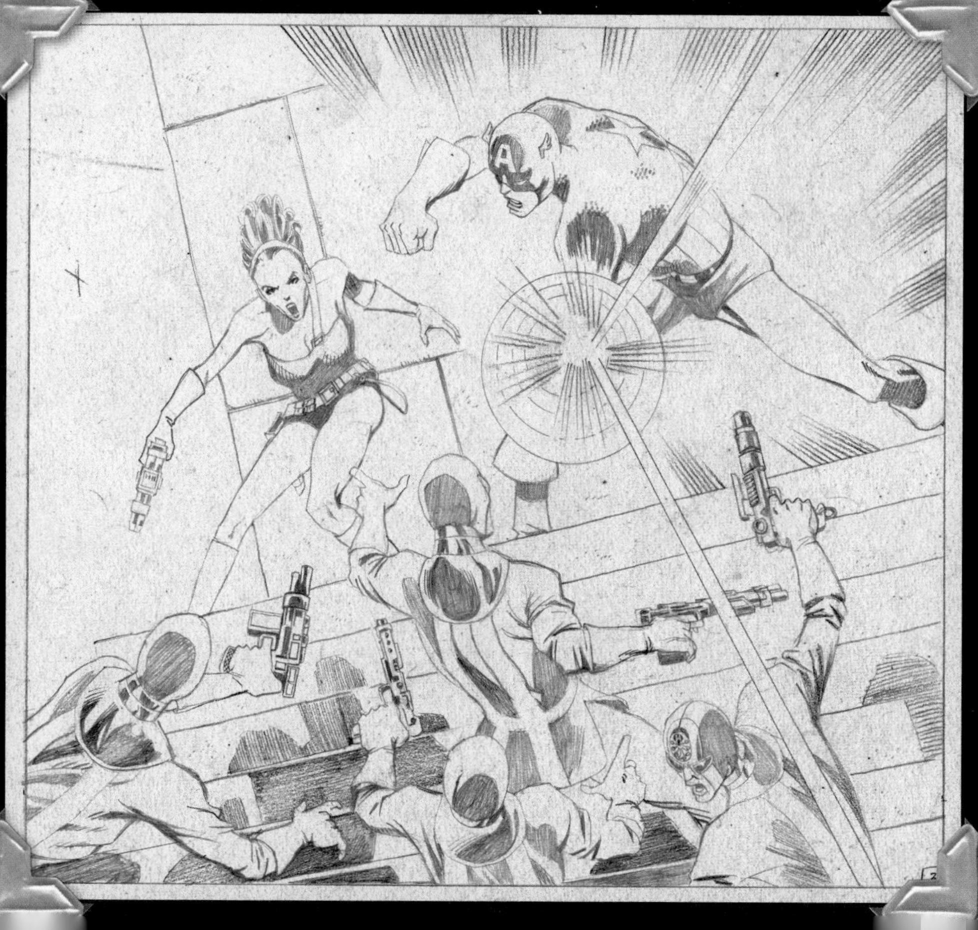

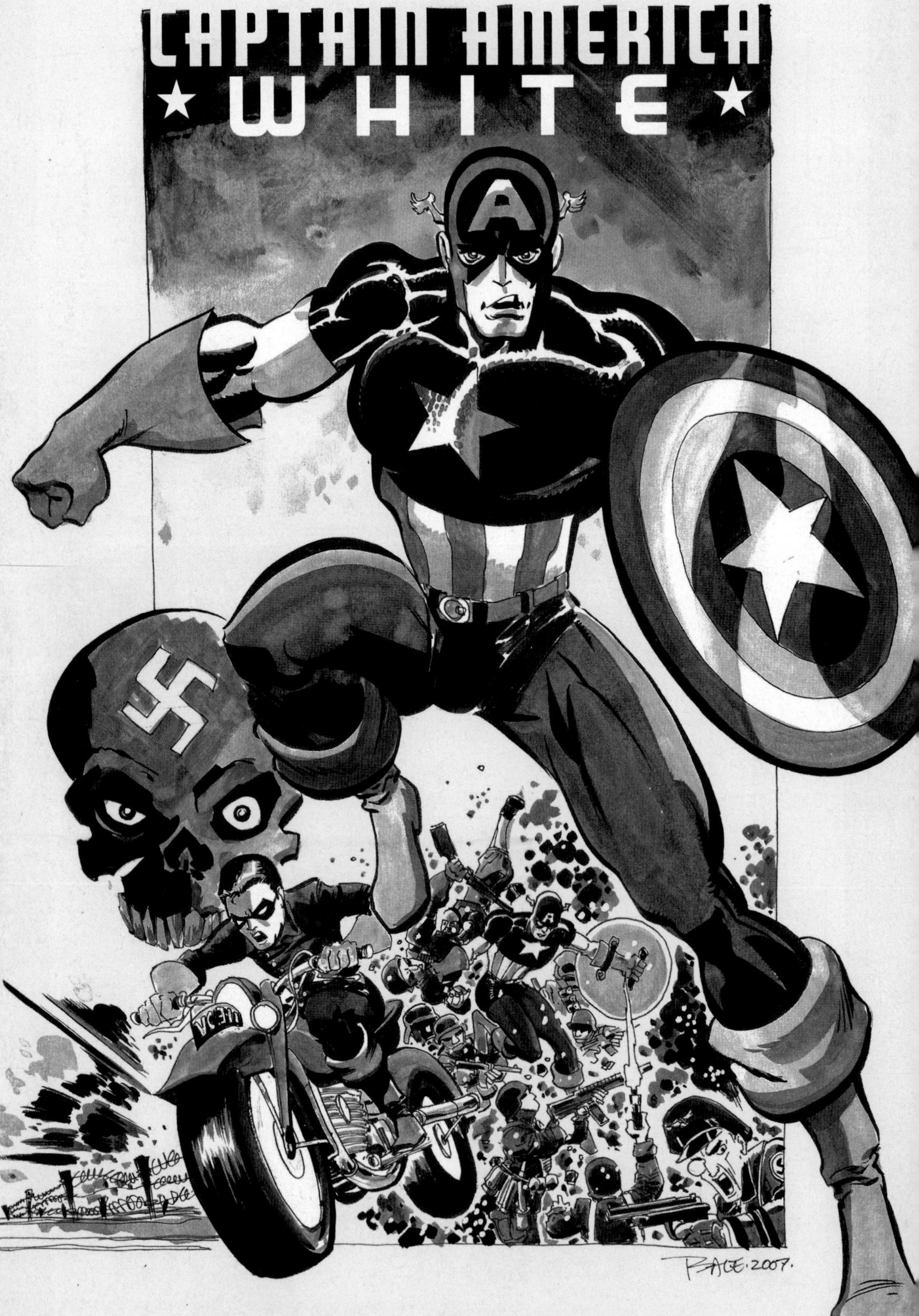
CAPTAIN AMERICA
WHITE
BAGE.2007.